# A Union of multiple identities

MANCHESTER
UNIVERSITY PRESS

In memory of
Angus Donald Macintyre (1935–94)
Friend, tutor and historian

# A Union of multiple identities

## The British Isles, c. 1750–c. 1850

EDITED BY
LAURENCE BROCKLISS
AND DAVID EASTWOOD

Manchester University Press

MANCHESTER AND NEW YORK

*distributed exclusively in the USA by St. Martin's Press*

*Published by* Manchester University Press
Oxford Road, Manchester M13 9NR, UK
*and* Room 400, 175 Fifth Avenue, New York, NY10010, USA

*Distributed exclusively in the USA by*
St. Martin's Press, Inc., 175 Fifth Avenue, New York, NY10010, USA

*Distributed exclusively in Canada by*
UBC Press, University of British Columbia, 6344 Memorial Road, Vancouver, BC, Canada V6T 1Z2

*British Library Cataloguing-in-Publication Data*
A catalogue record for this book is available from the British Library

*Library of Congress Cataloging-in-Publication Data*
A union of multiple identities: the British Isles, c1750–c1850 / edited by Laurence Brockliss and David Eastwood.
    p.  cm.
    Includes bibliographical references and index.
    ISBN 0–7190–5046–4 (cl)
      1. Great Britain—Civilization—19th century.  2. Nationalism—Great Britain—History—19th century.  3. Nationalism—Great Britain—History—18th century.  4. Great Britain—Civilization—18th century.  5. Group identity—Great Britain—History.  6. National characteristics, Scottish.  7. National characteristics, British.  8. National characteristics, English.  9. National characteristics, Irish.  10. National characteristics, Welsh.  11. Nationalism—Ireland—History.  I. Brockliss, L. W. B..  II. Eastwood, David.
    DA533.U55    1997
    941.07—dc21                                                              97-10563

ISBN 0–7190–5046–4 *hardback*

First published 1997

01  00  99  98  97      10  9  8  7  6  5  4  3  2  1

Typeset by Carnegie Publishing, Preston
Printed in Great Britain by Biddles Ltd, Guildford and King's Lynn

# Contents

# Illustrations

# Notes on the contributors

*Toby Barnard* is Fellow and Tutor in Modern History, Hertford College, Oxford.

*Laurence Brockliss* is Fellow and Tutor in Modern History, Magdalen College, Oxford.

*Robin Eagles* teaches history at Ampleforth College.

*David Eastwood* is Professor of Social History, University of Wales, Swansea.

*Roy Foster* is Professor in Irish History, University of Oxford.

*Boyd Hilton* is Fellow of Trinity College and University Lecturer in History, Cambridge.

*K. Theodore Hoppen* is Reader in History at the University of Hull.

*Michael John* is Professor in History, University of East Anglia.

*Colin Kidd* is Lecturer in Scottish History, University of Glasgow.

*Oliver MacDonagh* is Emeritus Professor in History, Australian Catholic University.

*Peter Mandler* is Reader in Politics and Modern History, London Guildhall University.

*Prys Morgan* is Reader in History, University of Wales, Swansea.

# Preface

This collection of essays began as a series of papers delivered to a colloquium held at Magdalen College, Oxford, in July 1996. It is intended as a contribution to one of the most important and contentious contemporary historiographical debates in the field of modern British history – the development and nature of Britishness as a lived identity in the eighteenth and nineteenth centuries. The essays are also intended as a tribute to the memory of Angus Macintyre, President-elect of Hertford College and Fellow and Tutor in Modern History at Magdalen from 1965 until his tragic death in a road accident in December 1994. Angus Macintyre was one of the country's most respected authorities on the history of the British Isles in the first half of the nineteenth century, who contributed greatly in particular to a more sensitive understanding of Anglo-Irish relations in the age of Peel and O'Connell. He was also, as Roy Foster's commemorative essay in this volume makes clear, a British historian whose identity and approach to his subject was fashioned by the complex and often contradictory cultural roots from which he sprang. A volume dedicated to exploring the multiple, especially the different spatial, identities of the subjects of the British crown in the late Hanoverian and early Victorian age seemed the perfect tribute to both the man and the historian. The essays are the work of historians who were Angus Macintyre's friends, colleagues or former pupils. This reflected his broad historical interests, which embraced the continent of Europe as well as the British Isles and social and cultural history as well as parliamentary politics. The editors and the contributors would like to thank the President and Fellows of Magdalen College for hosting the initial colloquium in honour of Angus Macintyre, and Manchester University Press for agreeing to publish the papers presented there in amended form. They would especially like to thank Vanessa Graham of Manchester University Press for her encouragement and assistance in seeing the book through from its commission to publication. The warmth and tolerance she displayed throughout in dealing with the editors and contributors perfectly embodied the spirit of the historian to whom the book is dedicated.

L.B.
D.E.

# Foreword

## Angus Macintyre:
## Historian of multiple identities

### ROY FOSTER

No better way to celebrate Angus Macintyre's life and work than by addressing multiple identities: the concept elegantly reflects his intellectual interests, his background, and indeed his subtle and many-sided personality. It is that complexity which his kept him so alive in the minds of those who knew and loved him. His own background and inheritance were emblematic. On his father's side, the Macintyres were originally Argyll Scots from the country around Loch Etive. By the early nineteenth century Angus's forebears were living in Perthshire but they were attracted to Australia by the prospect of purchasing land in 1827 (not forcibly emigrated, as he was always quick to point out). His father was Australian-born, but when he died in 1939 his Irish wife brought her small children, Angus and his brother, back to the family house, Furness, in County Kildare. Thus from the beginning of his life Angus moved between worlds, and came from a family which had crossed and recrossed borders.

And even the separate cultural identities which his family represented were themselves complex entities. Through his mother, Evelyn Synott, Angus was closely connected with the world of the old Catholic gentry of the Irish Pale: those families derived from Norman settlers who kept their religion, and sometimes their lands, and are called 'Old English' to distinguish them from the newer settlers of the seventeenth century (whom Toby Barnard deals with later in Chapter 8). The Synott-Netterville clan stand for an important Irish tradition looking both ways. The identity – indeed, the political culture – is Catholic but gentry; nationally-minded, but closely connected with English values and, often, with an English education; sometimes prominent in the British army; called by the 'new' nationalism of the late nineteenth and early twentieth century 'Castle Catholic'. Angus's grandfather Nicholas Synott is an emblematic figure – Governor of the Bank of Ireland, JP, Kildare Street Club member, landowner, restorer of the Victorianised Furness to something like its architect's Palladian intentions. Much as Angus's Scots ancestors would look across the narrow straits to Ulster, his Irish forebears were highly conscious of the differing identities to which they owed allegiance in Ireland. He knew this too; brought up as a Protestant, he nonetheless attended mass and was tutored at Furness by the local Catholic priest, who usefully taught him Latin to a level of sophistication far beyond his prep. school peers. In spending his entire student and teaching life in Oxford he added another dimension. Coexistent with a trinity of quintessentially *echt* English passions – the Press Complaints Commission, the MCC and P. G. Wodehouse – and his long and devoted service to teaching *British* history and editing the *English Historical Review*, there remained his Scots perspective (often invoking the Auld Alliance with France) and his commitment to Irish history.

This last often meant ploughing a lonely furrow. Still – always a man who knew how to handle a tractor – he worked away, and scattered seeds where he could. His historical imagination lives on, not only in the writings and editions under his name and in the scrupulously produced *EHR*, which he transformed between 1978 and 1986, and the Oxford Historical Monographs, which he oversaw between 1971 and 1979, but in the minds of his pupils and colleagues. This is in part due to the breadth and imagination of his approach. In an unpublished talk given to an audience at the University of North Carolina in April 1991[1] he commented on the need for historians to broaden out their definitions of what might be called as literary evidence: not only the 'figures of universal stature', like Joyce, Yeats, Shaw and Beckett, but also those whom Angus with his discriminating eye called the 'first-rate second-raters', His own teaching followed this through – invoking his knowledge and love of French literary culture as well as political history, and his suggestive use of sources in ballad and poetry as well as fine literature. Angus's foothold in three kingdoms meant a vantage on Europe too. (He stoutly maintained that the lecture which impressed him most in all his Oxford career was not anything to do with British or Irish politics but Isaiah Berlin's dazzling demonstration of how Rousseau invented guilt: not guilt towards God, which we apparently knew about already, but guilt towards our fellow creatures.)

Another unpublished article, on the British in Paris during the Peace of Amiens, characteristically starts and ends with an inspired local reference: the plane tree planted in Magdalen to celebrate the peace in 1801. But it is anything but insular in its perspective. Interestingly, too, he focuses on Charles James Fox (one of the more distinguished as well as one of the more colourful products of Angus's old college, Hertford, where he would eventually be elected Principal). Fox was perhaps an obvious figure of sympathy – Francophile, Radical, sympathetic to claims for Irish autonomy, but at the same time deeply rooted in English political culture and indeed helping to define it. (Robin Eagles addresses such issues later in Chapter 4.) Reading Angus on those eager English visitors to Paris, it is hard not to sense his sympathy with this perspective – as with that of Joseph Farington, whose diary he edited, and through whose painter's eye he makes us see French society in general, and Napoleon in particular.[2]

Just as illuminating, however, is the theme of multiple identities which emerged in a work of Angus's which long antedates the phrase, and the fashionability of the concept. This is his magnum opus, *The Liberator: Daniel O'Connell and the Irish Party, 1830–1847*, published in 1965. On the very first page the old problem of Anglo-Irish relations is stated with a force and subtlety which were at the time unusual among both English and Irish historians; even the aside that the West-minster representation enjoyed by Ireland under the Union was 'not ungenerous' is a use of the double negative worthy of Gibbon. And there were other subtleties too. On the face of it (and to go by its title) *The Liberator* was a study of O'Connell's political tactics in the 1830s. The research – rich, diverse, and scrupu-lously referenced – was grounded in the Peel papers, the reflections of Greville and his contemporaries, the analysis of Nassau Senior and others, parliamentary papers, and – always dear to Angus – the press. But from the outset he was determined to challenge, with a characteristic modest decisiveness, previous dis-missals of O'Connell. We may agree with the judgement of the historian Sir Llewellyn Woodward (and of Charles Greville) that the Liberator's 'best work was done for Ireland before 1830', remarked Angus; but 'if this record is not necessarily to be reversed, it will at least be valuable to understand the grounds for it'.[3]

Much in his work did reverse that verdict, as well as confirming his own belief, unfashionable at the time, that O'Connell was indeed the greatest leader Catholic Ireland had produced. And in order to do this, he had to move back and forth in time, and travel easily from Ireland to England, in re-establishing the contexts, constraints and limitations within which O'Connell operated. The authority with which he did this was new: because Angus knew this ground. He knew, specifically, the Catholic gentry background; on his very first page he delicately (but with a certain quiet pleasure) corrects the assumption of Eric Hobsbawm that O'Connell was a peasant leading peasants. The world from which O'Connell came, and in which he remained half-immersed, is analysed with flair – emerging as something nearer a European-style *petit noblesse* than anything like a English squire-archy.[4] Two-thirds of the Repeal party, we are shown, come from the class of landowners, JPs, Deputy Lieutenants – both Catholic and Protestant. The vital importance of landholding is stressed.[5] He similarly illuminates the situation of the Irish peasantry by a European comparison.[6] And the O'Connell party, denig-rated by contemporaries as his 'tail', make sudden sense when seen as an eighteenth-century 'connexion' rather than a nineteenth-century party – with all the bonds, freedoms and traditional loyalties which this implies. Here he used that alluring sense of time warp which in some Irish contexts puts things through a different prism. From the beginning, too, he emphasises the European aspect of O'Connell's style, appeal and reputation[7] – though one suspects this is something he might have returned to later, in greater detail.

There are many ways in which *The Liberator* was an innovative book, more than is often realised, perhaps because of its deceptively concentrated title. The two long chapter on issues of the Poor Law and tithe reform, for instance, are far removed from political history as it was conceived in the early 1960s; indeed, the treatment of the Irish Poor Law legislation turns into one of the most intelligent and widely informed discussions of reactions to early nineteenth-century Irish poverty that has yet appeared. Looking at the issue from an Irish and an English vantage, we see how British legislative modes were inapplicable to Irish conditions;

the range of sources and perceptions enables an interactive history of British and Irish politics, grounded on contemporary economic analysis and political imperatives, which would not be equalled until the very recent work of Cormac Ó Gráda.[8] The analysis of the relations between O'Connell and the Anti-Corn Law League presented a conjunction not previously addressed by scholars, however apparent to contemporaries. The relish in local *causes célèbres* takes us behind the political appearance to the reality as it appeared to contemporaries. (And there was no one better at delightedly decoding the story behind the story.) The concept of Saxon misunderstanding was peculiarly shaped to his purposes; so was the political use of anti-Englishness.[9] His discussion of Irish stereotyping was ahead of its time,[10] while the description of O'Connell in society is perfectly judged ('his politeness to Englishmen [was] tinged with a mixture of humility and pride'[11]).

The story also looked forward. The political geography of O'Connellite Ireland foretold the effective partition of Ireland between Unionist and nationalist.[12] And, most of all, *The Liberator* pointed the way for others to follow. At the time of publication its reception in Ireland was respectful but muted – possibly because it achieved something no historian in Ireland had attempted. But its influence is clearly seen in subsequent publications. The work on county politics foreshadows the area which – as is demonstrated in chapter 10 – Theo Hoppen was to make his own. Suggestions about the implicitly pro-Catholic policy of Peel, in Irish terms, pointed to a line of enquiry which has since been prospected by Donal Kerr. Some selective remarks on the political nature and importance of Dublin Corporation find echoes in recent work by Jacqueline Hill. Discussing the importance of the press, Angus touched on a subject just beginning to be excavated as exhaustively as it deserves.[13] In other areas still, such as the personality and record of William Smith O'Brien, he deftly sketched out ideas which remain unexplored. But a recent issue of *Irish Historical Studies* contains an article on O'Connell's liberal rivals which invokes *The Liberator* in its first footnotes, revisits the territory and quotes it approvingly in the conclusion.[14]

Angus's private reflections on O'Connell also predict the historiographical consensus which has developed thirty years later – as is shown in a absorbing letter to his old friend John Grigg, written shortly after publication.

> It is impossible to deny O'Connell's greatness before and up to Emancipation. He not only created a 'modern' political movement, almost from nothing and with pretty unpromising material, and used it successfully to gain certain, well-defined, ends. He also re-created the Irish as a nation, uniting them as perhaps they had never before been united, or since. Hence, in my view, I had to deal with the second half of the career of an indisputably great man and yet (and this became more clear as I got more deeply into the subject) in some way, the career went bad on him. (Cf L[loyd] G[eorge]?) There *were* achievements, the most important and far-reaching being the creation of a political system which, in many essentials, subsisted down to, say, 1914; and of an instrument, the Irish parliamentary party, which was to play a central role in nineteenth-century and early twentieth-century politics. There were also, as you say, terrible blunders. I would even say that O'Connell, having built his party, did not really know what to do with it – hence the meagre returns for Ireland despite O'Connell's

parliamentary power, hence the disastrous entanglement in patronage. Above all, the failure to repeal the Union. And here one is up against the fact that O'Connell, though a nationalist to the core, had no clear plan for Ireland's future, except in the broadest sense of a middle-class, gentry 'Home Rule' legislature. At least Parnell and Co. had a clear idea of what they wanted, and a movement more broadly based than O'Connell's. Yet, the whole political position was so different in O'Connell's time; and given his instincts together with the virtual *unanimity* of the English governing classes against Repeal, he was certain to fail. And after all, even Parnell and Redmond, with a great English party *on their side*, failed, basically perhaps because they were using O'Connell's constitutional and democratic methods and so could be (and were) outflanked by the physical force men of 1916 ... Ireland's misfortune is that her whole historical formation [?] has meant that her best men have been, in the strictest sense, failures. On this delphic note, I had better stop or this letter will become a pamphlet.[15]

His reflections on O'Connell's long-term reputation and Anglo-Irish relations cast forward intriguingly to a consideration of Gladstone. It is worth reminding ourselves that in 1965 books like Patrick O'Farrell's *England and Ireland*, Oliver MacDonagh's *States of Mind* and Leland Lyons's *Culture and Anarchy* were still unwritten; so indeed were Maurice O'Connell's great edition of O'Connell's correspondence and Oliver MacDonagh's magisterial two-volume biography, which uses those letters to such good effect.[16] Here, again, Angus was ploughing a lonely and original furrow; and here, too, he scattered seed to be reaped by others.

If he had been spared to us, where would his work have gone on to? Certainly he would have travelled further into his Anglo-French project, of which we have tantalising foretastes in that article about travellers to France in 1801–3 and in the Farington diary. His teaching as well as his writing bore this out, and generations of undergraduates profited from it. But he would also have returned to Ireland. His interest in O'Connell and Young Ireland had persisted; subsequent historiography confirmed his analysis of the necessity for both elements to keep a foot in the English and the Irish camps. O'Connell needed to do this for reasons of political strategy (and the radical, modernising, utilitarian bent which Angus was perhaps the first to pinpoint); Young Ireland found themselves necessarily using the English language, and the tropes of English romanticism, to communicate the message of Irish nationalism (and secularist and pluralist values whose pedigree owes much to the English radical tradition).

This was the kind of complexity which appealed to him, as did the process of tracing a cultural formation back to more distant and paradoxical roots than normally assumed. Thus he early on advocated putting the Irish cultural revival of the *fin-de-siècle* in the context of a long revolution in consciousness, stretching back to the antiquarians and historians of the later eighteenth century. This was how he liked to explore the interaction between Ireland and Britain: so often exploitative and disastrous, but also – if intermittently – productive and fulfilling.

And these are the themes which he addressed in that lecture at the University of North Carolina in April 1991 (which survives handwritten, with characteristic economy and practicality, on the reverse of forty-odd postcards printed for the purpose of acknowledging contributions to the *EHR*). It reflects his recent reading of Marianne Elliott's *Wolfe Tone*, Joseph Lee's *Ireland 1912–85* and the later writings of Leland Lyons and Oliver MacDonagh, but it is very much his own. Under the general title of 'History, literature and the Irish Question', Angus dealt with the historical importance of Irish writing in English: beginning, and eventually ending, with the way literature was (and is) used to convey suppressed signals. This was demonstrated, he maintained, not only in the way that history-writing was conceived of as a political act in Ireland, or poetry as a call to arms; it also played its part in the process whereby the concept of class had long been evaded by Irish historians, and by analysts of Irish nationalism. (Not for him the still repeated shibboleth about nineteenth-century Ireland having 'no middle class'.) But his principal intention was to draw a parallel between three eras when cultural politics, as he put it, 'ran side by side with political movements and conflicts' in Ireland, and interpenetrated them: the 1790s, the 1840s and the turn of this century. He looked at the United Irishman poetry of William Drennan, the stirring Young Ireland ballads of Thomas Davis, and eventually the poetry of Yeats. Above all, he was interested in what this meant for a sense of national identity.

> Irish nationalism was developed as a series of sets of changing ideas about what it meant to be Irish. The history of Ireland is the history of ideas about Ireland, ideas held and shaped by the Irish (and the English). These ideas can of course be related to specific objective social and economic contexts but it is a mistake to see ideas as mere epiphenomena. This is particularly true of Ireland.

Thus he explored definitions of Irishness that transcend nativism and strict religious identification – demonstrated (with a characteristic flourish) by Oscar Wilde's middle names, Fingal and O'Flahertie. Wilde was relevant, too, as a writer who (like Shaw, like Yeats) spanned the Irish Sea in his life and arguably in his work. Angus also thoughtfully reconsidered the nationalism of Tom Moore (despised in Ireland as the favourite of English drawing rooms), focusing on his political writings rather than his ballads and lyrics, and identifying him as founding father of the death trope so popular in nationalist literature. He brought in eighteenth-century theories about the Carthaginian origins of the Irish – stylishly illustrated by means of Joyce's puns in *Finnegan's Wake*. But the connections are anything but random. Moore, for instance, is firmly linked with competing notions of nineteenth-century nationalism by his connection with the rhetoric of O'Connell, who – as Angus spotted – quoted him constantly, and he analysed the Irish use of confrontational rhetoric, expressed in a literary form. 'Accusations and insults are a perfectly valid form of communication, far preferable to silent ignorance, and the Irish became experts at decoding the signals behind the rhetoric of apparent opponents, to the bafflement of English and foreigners.'

Above all – and this is not always popular with American audiences – Angus was unafraid to confront the seamier and less noble side of the Irish nationalist enterprise; and he pinpointed the necessary degree of invention which is inseparable from creating a nationalist historiography ('a people dissatisfied with the present will grasp at any version of the past'). Thus he illustrated how the politicisation of history-writing in Ireland has made interpretation of Irish history a political football since the eighteenth century and earlier. This conferred a special potency on Irish literature, which so often became grist to the mill – and which could have a more direct power still, in inspiring action through an evocation of the past.

In his conclusion he addressed the issue of the political responsibilities and effects of literature, focusing on Yeats as a nationalist intellectual with notably multiple identities – a Protestant, a pluralist, a professional writer with an English base and a preternatural sensitivity towards the ambiguities of Irishness. All this Angus was brilliantly equipped to observe. In the end, he contradicted Auden's celebrated line that 'Poetry makes nothing happen':

> Words do not by themselves send men out to shoot and be shot. Ideas behind the words do ... Yeats had some responsibility for the deaths of the men executed in 1916, but so in their time had Moore, Drennan, Davis. The Provisional IRA is not distinguished intellectually, but I wouldn't mind betting that some of the terrorists draw on this rich tradition of rhetorical protest and celebration of violence. But this is only one tradition. Irish people today, on both sides of the border, draw on a *richer* cultural tradition which is distinctively Irish but draws on English, indeed Anglo-American sources. They still speak to each other, still shout, and are still good at decoding hidden messages.

This connects back with *The Liberator*, published more than a quarter of a century before, which similarly presented elements in the movement towards Irish autonomy as more tangled and ambiguous than is sometimes accepted but all the more deserving of their rightful place in history for that. While celebrating much in the Irish nationalist tradition, it also stresses the inevitable connections between these islands and their histories. An earlier, favourite, quotation which Angus used in that North Carolina lecture was invoked by Gladstone as he wrestled with Home Rule. 'The Channel forbids union, the Ocean forbids separation.' That remark, which illuminates much to do with triple kingdoms and multiple identities, comes from the eighteenth-century Irish patriot Henry Grattan. If it had a special resonance for Angus, if it articulated a hidden message which his Irish–Scottish–English historian's ear decoded, it may be partly because Grattan was a family connection of Angus's through his mother, and his library had ended up in Furness, where Angus spent his youth. Multiple though he was, Angus was an utterly integrated man. His historical work – both in his writing and in his teaching – lives because he brought a vivid personal engagement to it. His personality was such that the effect, for his colleagues, students, readers, was unforgettable. And to remember him – intellectually and socially – is, and always will be, pure pleasure.

### Notes

1 It was given there partly because he was visiting his daughter Kate, another historian who in the family tradition had crossed borders; I should like to thank her, Ben, Magnus and Joanna for giving me access to this and other unpublished writing of Angus's.

2 'Temperament, social position and interests all influenced the reactions of British visitors to their Parisian experiences ... Nearly all revelled in the vibrant social and cultural life of the capital,

yet their comments show a perception of its hectic quality, the vitality and ostentation masking divisions and tensions. There are many descriptions of the central figure in this brilliant world. Many were favourable or critically admiring. Expecting to see the soldier, his visitors were impressed by his civilian, almost modest image – a tribute to Napoleon's capacity as an actor since this was exactly the impression he was now aiming to convey. Farington, who as a painter studied him carefully, thought Napoleon's countenance "of a higher style than any picture or bust" he had seen; he noted his confidence, his "intent and searching look" (though he thought he detected "something rather feverish than piercing in the expression of his eyes"); was impressed by his dress – "much more plain than his officers" – by his unstudied and natural actions, above all by his "freedom from *Assumption of a look of Character*" ...'.

3  *The Liberator: Daniel O'Connell and the Irish Party, 1830–47* (London, Hamish Hamilton, 1965), p. xvi.

4  *Ibid.*, p. 75.

5  *Ibid.*, p. 104.

6  *Ibid.*, p. 44–5.

7  *Ibid.*, p. 13, n. 2.

8  See especially *Ireland: a New Economic History, 1780–1939* (Oxford, Clarendon Press, 1994), and chs 5 and 6 in W. E. Vaughan (ed.), *A New History of Ireland*, v, *Ireland under the Union* i, *1801–70* (Oxford, Clarendon Press, 1989).

9  *The Liberator*, pp. 13, 21, 25, 168.

10  *Ibid.*, pp. 148–9.

11  *Ibid.*, p. 158.

12  *Ibid.*, p. 71.

13  See K. T. Hoppen, *Elections, Politics and Society in Ireland, 1832–85* (Oxford, Clarendon Press, 1984); Donal Kerr, *Peel, Priests and Politics; Sir Robert Peel's Administration and the Roman Catholic Church in Ireland, 1841–46* (Oxford, Clarendon Press, 1983); Jacqueline Hill, 'The Protestant response to Repeal: the case of the Dublin working class' in R. A. J. Hawkins and F. S. L. Lyons (eds), *Ireland under the Union: Varieties of Tension. Essays in Honour of T. W. Moody* (Oxford, Clarendon Press, 1980); Marie-Louise Legg, 'Newspapers and nationalism: the Social and Political Influence of the Irish Provincial Press, 1850–92', Ph.D. thesis (London, 1992).

14  Robert Sloan, 'O'Connell's liberal rivals in 1843', *Irish Historical Studies* 30: 117 (May 1996), 47–65.

15  31 August 1965; my thanks to John Grigg for lending me this letter.

16  Patrick O'Farrell, *England and Ireland since 1800* (Oxford, Oxford University Press, 1975); Oliver MacDonagh, *States of Mind: a Study of Anglo-Irish conflict, 1780–1980* (London, Allen and Unwin, 1983); F. S. L. Lyons, *Culture and Anarchy in Ireland, 1890–1939* (Oxford, Clarendon Press, 1979); M. R. O'Connell (ed.), *The Correspondence of Daniel O'Connell*, 8 vols (Shannon and Dublin, Irish Manuscripts Commission and Blackwater Press, 1972–80); Oliver MacDonagh, *The Hereditary Bondsman: Daniel O'Connell, 1775–1829* (London, Weidenfeld and Nicolson, 1988) and *The Emancipist: Daniel O'Connell, 1830–47* (London, Weidenfeld and Nicolson, 1989).

# Introduction

# A Union of multiple identities

## LAURENCE BROCKLISS
## AND DAVID EASTWOOD

Twice within less than a century the British State was formally transformed. In 1707 the dynastic union which had united England, Wales and Scotland since 1603 was transformed into a parliamentary union. In 1800 this new British State reached across the Irish Sea, dissolved Ireland's autonomous parliamentary institutions, and established a new State, the United Kingdom.[1] Terminology mattered here. The State created by the Act of Union with Ireland was united only in very particular senses. The unifying institutions were Crown and Parliament. Beneath, or beyond, these central institutions of the British State, diversity continued to flourish. The Act of Union with Scotland had left Scotland with a Presbyterian religious establishment, a distinct legal culture and a quite different educational system. In a similar way, Ireland lost its Parliament but retained a quite separate administrative system, and the formal mechanisms of the Union did nothing to diminish its economic and religious distinctiveness.

Thus the people who formed the new British State constituted by the Act of Union of 1800 embodied many different and conflicting identities. The religious culture of the new State was already diverse and became still more heterogeneous. Although Anglicanism was formally Established in England, Wales and Ireland, and Presbyterianism in Scotland, Catholicism was the religion of the majority of Irishmen and Presbyterianism the confession of the majority in its most prosperous province, Ulster. Catholicism, too, remained profoundly influential in the Scottish Highlands. Nonconformity in general, and Methodism in particular, were making considerable headway, and Methodism would do much to help rearticulate popular Welsh identities in the nineteenth century. Language, too, divided the new State, although perhaps less powerfully than religion. English was, of course, the official language of the new Britain, but the Celtic peoples in 1800 retained a good deal of their linguistic and cultural identity. Bilingualism had yet to penetrate large areas of Wales and Ireland, and again differences between Highland and Lowland Scotland were important. Growing economic integration and the educational reforms of the mid-nineteenth century would diminish linguistic and cultural diversity within the United Kingdom, but, as Chapter 10 shows, these kinds of process were slow and complex, and the displacement of older identities could create new and equally potent differences.

Perhaps the most striking characteristic of the United Kingdom, as established in 1800, was the space it allowed to different identities. Every Briton in 1800 possessed a composite identity. Certainly the British State embodied something approaching the political and cultural primacy of the English, but here primacy should not be equated with hegemony. Other identities persisted, and were even rediscovered, in the nineteenth century. There was nothing peculiar about the fact that the British people at the turn of the nineteenth century were an amalgam of identities. This was equally true of the inhabitants of other European States. However, what was more extraordinary in the British case was the extent to which a particularly pervasive spatial identity was seen in national terms.

In the eyes not only of Britons but also of most Europeans, the new State of the United Kingdom consisted of three or perhaps four distinct nations. An English identity was the most fully developed: born of 900 years of political and administrative unity; honed by centuries of struggle with the Celtic periphery, France and Spain; and imbued with a distinctive cultural gloss by the Reformation, Englishness in 1800 was a highly charged proto-nationalist affinity. A sense of Scottishness was almost as strongly rooted: here too political, if not administrative, unity went back to the tenth century, and a powerful sense of nationhood, developed through wars with southern English neighbours, was cemented by the Reformation. Jacobitism hinted at the ambiguities in this sense of nationhood but underscored its continued imaginative appeal. Similarly, if the architects of union with England embodied or elaborated a new identity, an Anglo-Scottish identity, this was a composite which acknowledged Scotland's distinctness if not now its autonomy. By contrast, one may argue, it was the frictions between visions of Irishness which made Irish identity. A still ascendant Anglo-Irish elite found refuge in land, literature and the Church of Ireland. The distinctions between the culture of the Ascendancy and the Catholic majority and the Presbyterian minority were, if anything, becoming still more sharply articulated. Only perhaps in Wales was nationality relatively weakly felt. This was in part a function of Wales's long integration into the English State which, in 1536 and 1543, had robbed Wales of real institutional distinctiveness, and in part a function of Wales's geography. But those factors which had hitherto conspired to dilute perceptions of Welsh nationhood in the nineteenth century helped to revive it. Highland Wales ceased to be perceived as dismal and unyielding and became a symbol of beauty and distinction. Language, religion and new industry offered the rudiments from which a new confident sense of Welshness might be fabricated.

Specifically nineteenth-century developments created new and complex identities within the United Kingdom. Economic change created new communities, new patterns of internal migration, new cities and new cultural identities. By 1850 industrialisation had not only created new industrial zones in South Wales, Ulster and the Clyde-Forth corridor of Scotland, it had also given a new sharpness to English regional identities. The cultural and political influence of Manchester swiftly came to mirror its economic importance, and, where Manchester led, Birmingham, Leeds, Sheffield and Newcastle swiftly followed. Within the new United Kingdom the space for regional, ethnic, national, linguistic and religious identities was constantly contested, and something of these contests emerges from the essays in this collection.

Above all, the new United Kingdom was a multi-national state, not just an amalgam of many identities. In this regard it was very different from most other nineteenth-century European States, especially its near neighbour, France: no one in 1800 saw the Burgundians or Bretons as a nation. The only obvious point of comparison was the Habsburg empire, where again the State was the dynastic creation of three historically separate entities – the Habsburgs' Austrian lands (a series of duchies and counties within the Holy Roman Empire) and the kingdoms of Bohemia and Hungary. In Austria's case, though, the union was much older – it went back to the early sixteenth century – but also much less complete, for apart from the 1780s and 1850s there was no attempt to turn a dynastic union into a political and administrative reality.

The significance of a deeply rooted sense of Englishness, Scottishness and Irishness in 1800 was all the greater in that feelings of Britishness were as yet thinly developed. Although the three nations (or sections of them) had come into conflict with one another much more forcibly in the middle of the seventeenth century than ever before, recent research suggests that this did not encourage greater unity. Rather the reverse: even the English and Scottish aristocracies in the second half of the century kept themselves to themselves. It was only in the course of the eighteenth century, as Linda Colley has shown, that a genuine British identity began to grow in the course of the century-long war with France. In the era of the Napoleonic wars this identity almost certainly grew stronger as large sections of the adult male population were mobilised in the militia to repel the expected invasion and the press whipped up anti-French feeling. However, *pace* Colley, it is difficult to see how a sense of Britishness fashioned merely by overseas conflict could be sustained in the century-long peace with the western European powers which followed Napoleon's fall. To the extent, too, that anti-French feeling was interwoven with a visceral anti-Catholicism, the British identity of the eighteenth century was hardly likely to unite the people of these islands in any real sense. Indeed, it seems more plausible to assume that at the end of the Napoleonic wars, the only Britons for whom Britishness was a primary and permanent identity comprised the small proportion of the educated and well-to-do who operated in an all-British context. Socially, this was a group confined to the aristocracy and the upper reaches of the gentry, who met together, if not annually, at least periodically, in their London houses, intermarried and sent their sons increasingly to the top English public schools. Occupationally the group was limited to the officer corps of the army and navy, the expatriate officials of the East India Company and the retinues of the embassies abroad – careers that brought together, often in a confined space at an early age and for a long time, people from all over the United Kingdom whose sense of a common identity was reinforced by their frequent and often perilous contacts with the 'other'.

The aim of the present book is to explore the way in which a viable British State was created out of a myriad of ethnic, religious, economic and spatial loyalties. While appreciating the importance of other identities, the essays in this volume are particularly concerned with the key problem of nationality. Ranging broadly over the eighteenth and nineteenth centuries, their emphasis falls on the period between the battle of Waterloo and the Crimean War. This, in our view, was the period in which the fundamental characteristics of the Union State were evolved. Although the later commitment to an ever expanding empire would give a harder, ideological edge and purpose to the United Kingdom, imperialism did not radically alter its structure.

The book begins with four chapters exploring the development of Britishness as a lived identity. Arguably a relatively skeletal identity at the time of the Act of Union of 1800, what is most intriguing about its history after Waterloo is its failure to put on significant flesh in an age of nationalism. True, there were several factors helping to cement the Union in the first half of the nineteenth century. The very existence of a common political and administrative system based, however narrowly, on a system of representation was guaranteed to fashion some sort of identification with the new State in time. So, too, would the pervasive experience of industrialisation, at least within Great Britain. On the one hand the industrial revolution helped to mix up the population of these islands more than had been the case for many centuries; on the other hand, to the extent that British industrialisation was precocious, it helped give the United Kingdom a specific material identity. Industrialisation, moreover, promoted and made possible better communications, which in turn encouraged the elite to travel more freely, be it for reasons of health or leisure in a period that saw a growing Romantic interest in wild, mountainous landscapes and a more positive evaluation of the Celtic periphery. And industrialisation begat Anglicisation as the ever more vibrant commercial society extended the frontiers of the English language into the farthest corners of the realm.

However, unification was by stealth, not design. There was no consistent attempt by different governments to strengthen Britishness in the first half of the nineteenth century. As Chapter 1, by Laurence Brockliss on professionalisation, reminds us, the institutionalisation of the Union remained weak. The Union was always essentially a political and administrative construct. Britons were never dragooned into living their lives in an all-British context. In the important case of the professions not only was there little Establishment interest in formalising recruitment procedures or institutionalising their administration, but the limited professionalisation which did take place was allowed to occur in a traditional national context.

Given the centrifugal pressures within the United Kingdom, there were moments in the nineteenth century when the Union might have been subverted. Perhaps the two most potent threats in the first half of the century were the formal challenge to the Union embodied in Daniel O'Connell's Irish party and the recurrent challenges posed by domestic radicalism in general and Chartism in particular. Chapter 2, by David Eastwood, attempts to relocate Peelite Conservatism in its British context, showing how Peel sought to develop a liberal

Conservatism purporting to confront the politics of interest by framing or presenting policy in a language which privileged (the British) nation over party. Crucial to Peelism was the political dividend which he believed would flow from prosperity, and an equally clear perception of the convulsive consequences of industrial stagnation and popular unrest. Viewed in a British context, Peel's ultimately flexible defence of the Union, his willingness to seek accommodations between the interests of land, labour and industry, and his clear sense of Britain's imperial authority take on new meanings, not least as carefully calibrated responses to the challenges facing the United Kingdom internally in the 1830s and 1840s.

Peel's was not the only Conservative strategy for attempting to reconcile British poitical institutions with the cultural and ideological realities of industrialisation; nor was it the most enduring. As Chapter 3, by Boyd Hilton, shows, 'a large, anonymous, mass society required a more corporate style of paternalism, and Disraeli was perceptive enough to see that this was possible'. Whereas Peel sought to unite the nation around a very particular accommodation between land and *haut-bourgeois* public values, Disraeli was prepared to mobilise at least some of the masses against certain sentiments of the classes. Disraeli's willingness to move towards a broader franchise in 1867 was, in part at least, a move towards constructing an electorate which might be 'more national'. The failure of a provincial, Dissenting, industrial culture to dominate later nineteenth-century Britain was, on this reading, an intended consequence of Disraelian Conservatism. In so far as Disraeli had a nationalist vision, it was strikingly English. Despite the Unionist sympathies of the Disraelian Conservative party, the consequence of Disraeli's English nationalism was that the Conservative party became an increasingly English party.

If many leading politicians were content to operate within the framework of the Union without seeking to develop strong or prescriptive national identities, neither did the Establishment attempt to foster Britishness negatively in the decades after 1815. If the xenophobia of the media had played an important part in fashioning a British identity in the eighteenth century, the establishment of a friendly French State largely brought an end to their jingoistic rhetoric. This happened all the more quickly in that the depth of anti-French feeling generated by the second Hundred Years War can be greatly exaggerated. As Chapter 4, by Robin Eagles, shows, there was always an important section of the elite, especially Whigs, enamoured of things French in the eighteenth century. Even the events of the Revolutionary and the Napoleonic era did not kill off Francophilia. French fashions continued to set the tone in the first half of the nineteenth century and Britons flooded to the Continent in growing numbers. Britons were taught to take pride in the defeat of the French – the United Kingdom was soon awash with civic memorials to the victories of British arms – but they were not taught to be bigots. The new United Kingdom seems to have been culturally very open, hence the ease with which Continental exiles of all political hues could settle here. This is not to say that Protestant Britons in particular welcomed foreigners with open arms, merely that their identity as *Britons* was not constructed from a hatred of or contempt for the Continental 'other'.

The State therefore let a British identity grow of its own accord. It did not systematically try to subordinate or destroy existing national identities. As the next three chapters make clear, the fortunes of these identities within the island of Great Britain were themselves in a state of flux. Chapter 5, by Peter Mandler, shows how a distinct, novel and subversive form of Englishness was promoted by the popular media in the 1820s and 1830s, which encouraged the literate working man to pine for a Tudor past of peace and social harmony. Different from the medievalism popular in elite circles, it was a form of Englishness implicitly critical of military might and overseas expansion. It was an identity, too, very different from the aggressive popular Protestantism which had defined English nationhood in the seventeenth and eighteenth centuries. Even if its influence was socially limited and its audience never completely free from the grip of the *Book of Martyrs*, its promotion reminds us how protean and unstable a construct national identity is.

Prys Morgan's Chapter 6, on Welshness, teaches a similar lesson. In 1750 a Welsh identity seems to have existed only in the eyes of the English, who saw their Cambrian neigbours as wild, peculiar relatives. In the course of the second half of the eighteenth century a much more positive Welsh identity was fashioned by members of the burgeoning Welsh middle class who took a novel pride in the Welsh language, literature and landscape. After 1800, however, this Romantic vision of Welshness began to look increasingly absurd in a country undergoing rapid heavy industrialisation and fast deserting its Anglican inheritance in the Church of Wales. By the mid-nineteenth century a much more utilitarian and urban image of Welshness had been developed. The Welsh were taught to see themselves as God's chosen people in succession to the English and to equate Welshness with Nonconformity. At the same time, they were encouraged to think of themselves as peculiarly virtuous and law-abiding, a nation of teachers in the making.

Some Scots, too, were busy constructing a new Scottish identity in the first part of the nineteenth century. According to Colin Kidd, in Chapter 7, the lead here was taken by Scottish Tories fearful lest creeping Anglicisation since 1707 should swallow up a separate Scottish identity altogether. Not only, then, was Scotland's independent legal system defended to the hilt, but Scots were encouraged to venerate their independent medieval past and embrace the formerly derided Highland dress as their 'authentic' national costume. Other Scots, however, believed the real threat to Scottish identity lay in industrialisation, not Anglicisation. Convinced that Scottish city dwellers had lost touch with the values and virtues of their Presbyterian ancestors, they preached an exclusive, not inclusive, vision of Scottishness, which emphasised the resurrection of the Kirk through disestablishment and defined the true Scot as a Protestant Saxon.

None of these new conceptions of nationality was a threat to the Union, for none of their protagonists ever advocated dismemberment of the United Kingdom or believed that the English, Welsh and Scots could not live comfortably together. The handful of Welsh men and women who did come to feel that participation in the United Kingdom was no longer possible did not stay to proselytise but departed to found a colony in Patagonia. Irish Catholic national consciousness, on the other hand, was to prove a much more problematic identity to subsume permanently within the United Kingdom. Although there is no reason to suppose that the Union with Ireland was damned from the beginning – for Irishness was really only a landed and mercantile identity in 1800 and certainly not yet associated indelibly with Catholicism – the arranged marriage was destined not to last in the long term, despite much goodwill on either side. Subsequent chapters in the volume offer some insights into when and why breakdown irredeemably occurred.

Toby Barnard's Chapter 8 on the eighteenth-century Irish gentry confirms that the prospects of the Union were initially good. While the Protestant landowners who traditionally ran the administrative and political system had partly copied their *mores* from their dispossessed Catholic forebears and lived in a manner frequently out of kilter with polite society in Great Britain, the new Catholic middle class was hard-working and sober, like its Dissenting counterpart on the other side of the Irish Sea. There was nothing inevitable, therefore, in the alienation of the most dynamic sector of Irish life. Oliver MacDonagh's account of the political philosophy of O'Connell further bears out this impression. MacDonagh's O'Connell was not an Irish racial nationalist, just as he was never a man of blood. He never argued that the Irish were a historically distinct ethnic or religious people whose purity must not be sullied by incorporation in a political and administrative union with Great Britain. Rather, his argument for Home Rule was based on the utilitarian case that only through self-government could Irish interests be properly addressed. In other words, he refused to accept that the Peelite position was possible. Equally, though, had Peel or any other Unionist statesman successfully called his bluff, then the justification for Home Rule on O'Connellite terms would have disappeared.

Obviously, the disaster of the Irish famine, if it hastened the disintegration of the first Home Rule movement, demonstrated that O'Connell's analysis was highly plausible. As Theo Hoppen's Chapter 10 argues, however, in the second half of the nineteenth century other forces were undermining the shaky foundation of the Union besides the shadow of starvation. Paradoxically, the very success of the Union in the pre-famine decades made a nationalist movement based on the dying culture of the Gaelic west a possibility. Before 1850 Connacht was an isolated backwater that had played little part in O'Connell's Home Rule campaign. By 1870, thanks to the development of an integrated economy and better communications, Connacht had become tamed. Like the Scottish Highlands fifty years before, it could be now be safely identified as the guardian of the nation's historic soul. At the same time, weight was given to the nationalist claims about Irish distinctiveness by the Union government. While Whig and Tory administrations from 1820 to 1860 had gone out of their way to treat Ireland in the same way as the rest of Great Britain, later administrations saw the country as a special case: Ireland remained in the Union until 1922 but had the status of a colony.

The last chapter, by Michael John, takes up this point with relation to the monarchy's patrimonial territory of Hanover. Unlike Ireland, of course, Hanover was never a part of the United Kingdom, but that was not simply a result of geography or geopolitical reality: after all, the province was no farther away from England than Ireland, and the European powers could not have stopped its inclusion in the Union in 1815. Rather, the British government never had any wish to join Hanover to the British State. As in the eighteenth century, its possession continued to be seen as a nuisance, and the dynastic accident which led to the severance of ties in 1837 was seen as a godsend. Hanover, then, in the early nineteenth century, like Ireland after 1870, was treated differently. Hanover's importance in the context of this volume, however, lies primarily in what its history has to tell us about the relative success of the nineteenth-century multi-national British state. Hanover was an absolute monarchy which proved unable to establish a working and permanent liberal constitution after 1830 because of the intransigence of its landed elite. Both conservatives and liberals used an historico-legal political language inherited from British political philosophy, but a shared discourse did not encourage accommodation. In consequence liberals were forced to adopt the radical language of natural rights and German nationalism and ended welcoming Bismarck. In Hanover's case Germanness became destabilising because of a very un-British failure of political dialogue.

The history of the Hanoverians' other kingdom, therefore, helps us to understand why the United Kingdom could flourish as a multi-national state in an era when the large-scale absence of fit between the boundaries of nations and States was causing growing problems everywhere else in Europe. The Conclusion explores this point in more detail. The United Kingdom's success as a union rather than a nation State is shown to lie in its peculiarly precocious social and economic development but also in the equally peculiar role of Parliament, an institution whose sovereignty was accepted by most Britons: change could come only through winning the case in the Commons, not on the streets. This is contrasted with the situation in France, a quintessential one-nation State, where sovereignty lay with the people and stability could be obtained only by making Frenchness and loyalty to France a primary identity. It is contrasted, too, with a united Germany, which suffered from the obverse problem to the British one, being largely a one-nation State, but a State cobbled together from numerous long-standing, if often unstable, independent polities. In the German case the American federal solution made perfect sense. Britons wanted to hold on to their pristine but evolving national identities; Germans to their decentralised political traditions.

## Note

1 The literature on the emergence of Britishness and the British State is growing in volume and sophistication. The most influential works, including those on which this Introduction is based, are listed in the section on Further Reading at the end of the volume.

# 1

# The professions
# and national identity

## LAURENCE BROCKLISS

The new British State of the first half of the nineteenth century remained a patrician polity. Although the Reform Acts of 1832 brought a larger cross-section of the population into the political nation, the State still remained predominantly the property of the educated and well-to-do. As a result, the new British nation which had begun to form in the eighteenth century was certain to be, to use Anthony Smith's phrase, a laterally constructed *ethnie* where the conception of Britishness was born out of the lives and actions of the elite. At the same time, given the elite's deep-rooted attachment to traditional national loyalties centred on the three component parts of the United Kingdom, and given too the extent of religious pluralism in the new State, it was equally certain that this British *ethnie* would be, to use Smith's term again, a civic rather than an ethnic creation.[1] In the eighteenth and early nineteenth centuries a definite sense of Britishness had been forged through the constant wars with France.[2] With the return of peace in 1815, the extent to which this loyalty would be retained and cemented depended on a series of interlinking factors: the level of institutional homogeneity, the pace of economic integration, and the degree to which traditional loyalties were subsumed under a common pattern of acculturation.

An important factor in determining the intensity of this emerging British identity would be how quickly and completely the elite came to live and work in an all-British environment. Arguably, there would only be a powerful, hegemonic constituency for the new State established in 1800 once a significant part of the elite thought of the United Kingdom as its natural frame of reference, not as an occasional administrative presence or as a distant relative whose fortunes were followed in moments of leisure. The present chapter examines the degree to which one section of the elite – members of the professions – began to broaden its horizons in a more British direction in the first half of the nineteenth century.

The professions are an obvious starting point for studying the formation of a truly British elite in the Age of Reform. In the first place, at the time of the Union with Ireland, the only members of this group who uniformly operated in an all-British context were officers in the army and navy. Secondly, as the United Kingdom became a wealthier, more populous, somewhat freer and more complex society membership of the professions increased far faster than other sections of the elite. On the one hand, the traditional professions of Church, law and medicine benefited from the opportunities brought by religious pluralism and an ever more litigious and health-conscious people. On the other, the process of State-building, agricultural improvement, industrialisation and urbanisation spawned completely new professions, such as engineering and architecture, and lent new dignity and attraction to others, notably journalism, teaching and the civil service. By 1851 members of the professions numbered 300,000 and in England comprised nearly 4 per cent of the male working population.[3] Thirdly, in an age when the cultural and political influence of the aristocracy began to be questioned, it was from the professions that the country's opinion-formers, political activists and its tribe of authors were largely drawn.[4] Consequently, the stronger and more positive the British identity of this expanding and dynamic section of the elite, the wider and more deeply a sense of Britishness would be disseminated through the population at large, since its British prejudices would inevitably inform its public utterances and published writings.[5]

It might be expected that the most likely group within the professional classes to develop an all-British character in the first half of the nineteenth century and take on the historic mantle of promoting a deeper British identity would have been the members of the new professions whose livelihood was closely tied up with the burgeoning economic and political power of the new British State. This, though, was not to be. The new professions may have gained a semantic existence and thus possessed distinct identities in the public mind, but they remained largely structureless. None evolved into a genuinely all-British organisation through the imposition of a uniform system of formal training and licensing and the establishment of a single, respected policing authority.

This was particularly true of the new service professions, such as teaching, accountancy, journalism and the civil service, for which there were generally no entry qualifications or administrative organisation whatsoever. Only the insignificant actuarial profession had its own London institute, founded in 1848, and had made admission to its ranks (from 1850) conditional on passing an examination. The new practical professions that grew up in the wake of the industrial revolution were only a little more formalised. Engineers, surveyors and architects had no uniform educational background and learnt their skills as designers and draughtsmen in their employer's office. Originating from a wide variety of artisan careers, they remained wedded to the concept of apprenticeship. So, too, did veterinary surgeons, auctioneers and land and estate agents. By the mid-century, admittedly, the engineers, architects and veterinaries had established quasi-governing bodies that gave the careers an institutional identity but these bodies had as yet no real licensing or teaching role, membership was not compulsory, and only a small proportion of those registered as practising these professions in the 1851 census belonged. Most practitioners were raised, trained and worked locally.[6]

As the most visible, best developed and one of the largest of these new careers, the structural development of the engineering profession up to 1850 can be considered as illustrative of them all. The leading figures in the profession – Telford, the Stephensons, the Brunels – certainly operated in an all-British environment.

*> transport : professions*

Thomas Telford, son of a Dumfriesshire shepherd, probably did more to make the new United Kingdom a living reality than any other Briton in the first three decades of the century, building bridges, roads and canals the length and breadth of Great Britain for a mixture of private, county and State patrons.[7] Moreover, he saw his improvements to the country's communications network as part of a strategy of unification which would draw Ireland economically into the Union. As early as 1803 he was backing the digging of the Caledonian canal as *inter alia* a way of improving commercial exchange between the eastern coast of Great Britain and Ireland and between Ireland and the Continent.[8] It is scarcely surprising, then, that Telford, the communications impresario of the new British State, should have established his business headquarters in London, symbolically outside the Union Parliament in Abingdon Street.

Telford and the other engineering geniuses of the industrial era, however, were exceptional. Often operating on an international, not a national, stage, they lived the life of the modern film star, that would earn them innumerable, usually foreign, decorations and ensure them a resting place in Westminister Abbey. The lives of the large majority of the State's 5,000-plus engineers in the mid-nineteenth century were much more mundane and local. Apprenticed after a brief education and at an early age to the machine man in the local factory or colliery, they practised their craft in their native region, moving from one local workplace to the next in the manner of George Stephenson in his younger days. Only the fortunate and skilful might experience a wider world, if called to another part of the country by an entrepreneur who had come to hear of his talent on the industrial grape vine.

The leading engineers of the first generation, furthermore, did nothing to promote the organisation of their profession. Telford, an autodidact who had learnt the principles of bridge-building by constructing dry-stone walls and studied architecture by walking the streets of Edinburgh, was highly suspicious of all formal education.[9] An apprenticeship was everything, he declared in a letter to a friend in 1830. 'This is the true way of acquiring practical skill, a thorough knowledge of the materials employed in construction, and last, but not least, a perfect knowledge of the habits and disposition of the workmen who carry out our designs.'[10] George Stephenson, another autodidact, had the much the same prejudices. Although his son, Robert, was given an education, first in the village school at Long Benton and then at Mr Bruce's school in Newcastle, he was removed at the age of fifteen (in 1818) and apprenticed to the 'head viewer' at Killingworth colliery to learn pit engineering. Thereafter his formal education was finished, apart from a six months' visit to Edinburgh in 1820, where he attended lectures on the natural sciences and natural history and, through his father's growing reputation, made some useful contacts.[11] George Stephenson, too, was unethusiastic about attempts to institutionalise the profession. The Institution of Civil Engineers, the heir of a London club founded by John Smeaton in 1771, was established in 1818 and was granted a royal charter in 1828. Thereafter British engineers had a public, corporative existence and the profession could conceivably have begun to develop a tight structure.[12] The elderly Telford accepted nomination as president in 1820 but George Stephenson never joined, purportedly because the doyen of railway engineering had too much self-esteem to stoop to providing the Institution with the required *curriculum vitae*.[13] Without his support, however, the Institution was scarcely likely to flourish in its early years.

Admittedly, the second generation of engineering stars were less coy about institutional organisation and formal education. Robert Stephenson joined the Institution in 1830, along with I. K. Brunel, who had been trained in France, and by the 1840s it was recognised by a number of leading figures in the profession, notably the precocious Scot William Rankine, himself an Edinburgh student, that the future engineer required theoretical as well as practical training.[14] As a result it soon became possible to study civil engineering as an academic subject.[15] The London College of Civil Engineers opened in 1834 and the new university colleges of Durham and King's (London) established courses in engineering from 1838. Other courses were introduced at Glasgow University in 1840 and University College London and Trinity College Dublin in 1841.[16]

Nevertheless, no attempt was ever made in the first half of the nineteenth century to make the academic study of engineering compulsory for admission to the Institution: Telford's prejudice in favour of practical learning still ran deep. Nor did the Institution make much effort to gain organisational control over the profession. Admission was by nomination, and members were struck off only if they failed to pay their dues. Although the Institution intermittently published its proceedings from 1838, it never sponsored a professional journal. In many ways it was little more than a London club with provincial associates that met weekly to listen to papers submitted by its members. Not surprisingly, its membership in 1850 comprised only a small proportion of practising engineers in the United Kingdom – under 20 per cent.[17]

Moreover, from the mid-nineteenth century the Institution (though it tried) could not even legitimately represent itself as the sole mouthpiece of the British engineering profession. The Institution seems to have been perceived as a London, not even as an English, corporation, and within the first few decades of its existence residual provincial and regional loyalties asserted themselves against metropolitan (albeit unstructured) dominance. As early as 1835 the Civil Engineers' Society (from 1844 Institute) of Ireland was established and ten years later began to produce its own *Transactions*. Worse was to follow. In 1848 the Midland engineers met at Birmingham and founded a rival Institute of Mechanical Engineers, inveigling George Stephenson into being its president. Nine years later the South Wales Institute of Engineers was created at Merthyr Tydfil and a separate Institution of Engineers in Scotland was set up in Glasgow. In the second case the moving spirit was William Rankine, erstwhile member of the London Institution and recently appointed professor of engineering (1855) at the Scottish university. In his opening address to the new body Rankine went out of his way to rouse the Scottish identity of his audience, reminding them that Glasgow, not London, was the metropolis of engineers. In the following decades the London Institution insisted that these rival bodies (and other, later English regional foundations) were its subordinates and objected strongly to their incorporation. The damage, however, was done. In the second half of the nineteenth century the engineering profession came to be organised nationally and regionally rather than on a Union-wide basis.[18]

The failure of the flagship profession of the industrial age to evolve in an all-British context after the Act of Union was mimicked even more strongly in the history of the dominant profession of the *ancien régime* – the Church. Of course, the successful encasement of the British clergy in an all-British framework in the first half of the nineteenth century was a much more difficult task. Engineering was a new structureless profession; it would bifurcate into a series of specialist careers by 1900, but before 1850 it was a seamless web. The Church, in contrast, was an ancient profession, long since divided into discrete denominations, whose relative strength varied greatly across the British Isles from country to country. However, too much emphasis can be laid on the geographical distribution of religious allegiance in these islands in determining the structure of the British Churches after 1800. There may have been a clear majority religion in each of the three historic kingdoms on the eve of the Union but none had a monopoly. Futhermore, with the expansion of various forms of Nonconformity in England and Wales, the advent of official religious pluralism, Irish immigration to England and Scotland, and the split in the Church of Scotland in 1843, the ground was laid for a more evenly coloured religious map. The religious development of the United Kingdom in the first half of the nineteenth century ought therefore to have encouraged a more British-orientated organisation of the competing Churches. In fact, just as the new profession of engineering began to divide into national factions, so the organisation of the Churches remained confined in their traditional national straitjacket. Admittedly, there was a degree of transnational movement within the different denominations, as areas with surplus clergy exported them to those with a deficit. Yet the amount of movement was surprisingly small within a supposedly integrated State, where the majority of inhabitants spoke the same language.[19] By and large, the United Kingdom's 36,288 clergymen in 1851 were educated, ordained and employed within their home country, thus again cementing traditional loyalties rather than fostering a more deeply felt British identity.

Again the example of the largest and most visible denomination – the ministry of the Anglican communion, 14,000 strong – will suffice to demonstrate the lack of movement and integration. In 1800 the Anglican Church under various titles was the established Church in England, Wales and Ireland, and had a limited following in the north-east of Scotland. In the following half-century, although establishment, even in England, came under attack, there was no attempt to meet the threat by creating a powerful all-British ecclesiastical organisation. In contrast to earlier centuries, the large majority of entrants to the Anglican clergy in this period possessed a university arts degree. However, this did not mean that they had shared a common educational experience. For the most part, clergy in the Church of England and Wales were trained in the humanities and philosophy at

Oxford or Cambridge (whichever was closer to home),[20] Irish clerics at Trinity College Dublin, and the handful of Scottish episcopalians at their local Scottish university, where there was no religious test. Nor did aspirant graduate clerics come together for their theological studies. Although several theological colleges were founded for non-graduate entrants to the ministry, beginning with St Bee's in 1817, the idea that the graduate clergy might require specialist institutionalised theological training was still largely frowned on in 1850. What institutional provision there was by the mid-century was the result of *ad hoc*, often short-lived, diocesan initiatives. Graduate entrants to the ministry usually prepared for ordination privately in their undergraduate college, even Cambridge ordinands, who, from 1840, were first required to sit a theology examination, the misnamed Cambridge Voluntary.[21]

This traditional pattern of clerical formation was consolidated by the dominant patronage system of appointments where Anglicanism was the established Church. Ordination tended to be delayed until there was a prospect of a cure-of-souls, and benefices were largely in the gift of lay and institutional patrons, who distributed their largesse to relatives or local clients. The more gifted might become college fellows and receive in time a college living in a town or village with which they had no association, but the average Anglican clergyman would tend to find a resting place near his native hearth.[22] Given the patronage system, then, there was no point in taking an arts degree in any university but the nearest, where the aspirant cleric who had not already successfully ingratiated himself with a local patron might hope to make the acquaintance of his son.

Transnational mobility in the Anglican Church before the second half of the nineteenth century was confined to two groups. In the first place, a continual stream of anonymous Irish graduates found a benefice in England: between 1844 and 1853, 8·1 per cent of ordinands in the Church of England and Wales were graduates of Trinity College Dublin, while in some dioceses the figure was much higher, 20 per cent in the new diocese of Ripon in 1841–43.[23] This reflected the fact that Trinity produced too many aspirant clerics for the Church of Ireland and that large swathes of the industrialising north of England and of Wales, which were areas of Church rather than lay patronage, had difficulty attracting Oxbridge clerics.[24] Secondly, a much smaller trickle of high-flyers in the Church of England gained plum jobs in other national branches of the Anglican Church, notably the Oriel tutor, Copleston, who became Bishop of Llandaff, and his Oxford pupil, Richard Whately, appointed Archbishop of Dublin in 1831. Anglicans from other parts of the British Isles, however, did not gain reciprocal promotion in the Church of England before 1850. The Balliol-educated Scot and future Archbishop of Canterbury, Archibald Campbell Tait, was already a rising star in the 1840s, when he replaced Arnold as headmaster of Rugby, but it was 1856 before he gained his first episcopal preferment. Irish Anglicans waited even longer. It was to be 1868 before William Connor Magee became the first Irishman to receive a bishop's mitre in the Church of England since the Reformation.[25]

The second learned profession, the law, whose members (including clerks) numbered some 43,000 by 1851, remained just as entrenched in its traditional national ways. Admittedly, in this case there was no possibility of creating a single British legal profession, for by the terms of the 1707 Act of Union between England and Scotland the Scots had been guaranteed the continuation of their separate legal system. The Scottish legal profession, therefore, would always have a separate identity centred on the courts of Edinburgh, not London. That said, though, England, Ireland and Wales operated under the same common-law system and there was nothing preventing the appropriately qualified from setting up in legal practice in any part of the United Kingdom, whatever their place of origin. What is striking is once more the absence of significant transnational mobility in what would have been considered, at its upper reaches, a highly lucrative profession.

This is not to say there was no mobility. A number of Irish and Scots did leave their native lands to join the English bar, and some gained fame and fortune, notably the Scots, Lord Chancellors Erskine, Brougham and Campbell and the reformer, Francis Horner. Equally, a handful of Englishmen became Scottish advocates in the footsteps of the Christ Church-educated Sir John Stoddart. Nonetheless, the numbers should never be exaggerated. Most Scots who became common-law barristers registered at Lincoln's Inn: in the years 1800–09 only twenty-three did so; in the decade 1840–49 the number was even less.[26] Those who established themselves in England, too, often did so by chance. Erskine, for instance, a younger son of the indigent tenth Earl of Buchan, initially entered the navy in 1764 as a midshipman. On shore leave in England in 1773 he apparently attended an assize court presided over by Lord Mansfield, caught the legal bug, and registered at an Inn in 1775.[27] Campbell's progress to the English bar was less bizarre but equally unconventional. A son of the manse, he was destined to join the Church of Scotland, but after attending St Andrews had the opportunity in 1797 to spend time in London acting as tutor to a West India merchant family and quickly found the lure of the capital too strong to leave.[28]

It would seem, therefore, that only the well-born and ambitious or those with, albeit sometimes fortuitous, English contacts risked a legal career outside their native land. This was quite understandable in the case of the United Kingdom's 15,000 solicitors (in Scotland called 'writers', 'procurators' or 'law agents') and bevy of legal clerks who made up the lion's share of the legal profession in 1850, for it reflected the extremely inchoate structure of their legal training. Whereas entrance to the Church (especially the three dominant confessions) required a long period of university or university-style study and included some form of theological training, if never necessarily a theological degree, there was no common pattern of entry to the lower and middle reaches of the legal profession. In many respects, despite the profession's antiquity, recruitment patterns at this level more closely resembled those of the new professions. No common educational background was demanded – indeed, institutionalised learning of any kind was no prerequisite – and recruits generally learnt on the job, often as formal apprentices. As a result, many if not most solicitors and their clerks were raised, trained and worked in the same locality. Just like members of the new professions their horizons were unextended by their career and most remained locked in a narrow regional, not even national, world.

Solicitors everywhere usually left school in their early teens and were apprenticed locally. Their apprenticeship complete, English and Irish entrants to the profession had to travel to their national capital to be examined and registered on a high court roll before returning home to begin their careers. However, the actual examination was conducted orally and often perfunctory, and only the Irish were expected to spend any time in attendance at the high courts as part of their training. In England an important development occurred in 1836, from which date solicitors were required to take a written examination organised by the fledgling, London-based Law Institution (later Law Society), incorporated in 1831. Even in England, though, this was the limit of the attempt to professionalise that branch of the law. The Law Society itself remained largely a metropolitan body – in 1848 it still only had 288 regional members – and it suffered the competition of a number of provincial societies. The Law Society did attempt to provide courses in different aspects of the law from 1833 but attendance was never made compulsory and the young solicitor who wished to supplement his apprenticeship training was forced in the main to rely on the growing number of legal textbooks and journals.[29] In Scotland, in contrast, there was no central register of law agents before 1873. Would-be practitioners usually applied for admission by examination (of some kind) to their local faculty of procurators (based in the county town), but membership was never compulsory and many rural law agents acted as writers without a professional attachment. In Scotland, although an increasing number of procurators from 1800 had followed a course of Scots law at a Scottish university, a compulsory and initially decentralised examination of prospective law agents was instituted only in 1865 and there was to be no equivalent of the Law Society before the 1940s.[30]

On the other hand, the relative absence of transnational mobility in the case of the Union's barristers, 4,000 in number by 1851, requires deeper examination. Although training for the bar in the United Kingdom was also relatively unformalised, applicants in the majority of cases would have spent years away from home in the course of their education and preparation for their career, and Irish candidates in particular would have gained more than a passing acquaintance with the habits of their English cousins.[31] In the first place, unlike most solicitors, the great majority of barristers would have had a university education or its equivalent, for a good knowledge of classical literature and history and a solid acquaintance with rhetoric and logic were considered essential for successful advocacy. The London-born legal reformer and MP Samuel Romilly, who had had little formal education when called to the bar in 1783 and gained proficiency in the Latin language through personal study, was an anomalous figure even at the beginning of the period.[32] Most barristers, too, would have had to have spent long periods of time in Edinburgh or London. Courses in civil and Scottish customary law were provided at Edinburgh University from the eighteenth century, and Scottish barristers were expected to attend before applying to join the

Edinburgh Faculty of Advocates, although they were under no obligation to take a degree.[33] Usually candidates mixed attending lectures with private reading, like the founder of the *Edinburgh Review*, Francis Jeffrey, who joined the Scottish bar in 1794.[34] English and Irish barristers, in contrast, were never provided with or required to attend formal instruction in the law before the middle of the century. The three Anglo-Irish universities were supposed to teach civil law, and common-law lectures were provided at Oxford from the mid-eighteenth century, but no formal instruction was available in London before the foundation of University and King's Colleges, and then the lectures seem to have been overly theoretical and beyond the students' ken.[35] Rather, admission to both the English bar and the Irish bar required students to register as a member of one of the four London Inns of Court for three to five years (dependent theoretically on whether they had a university degree).[36] Even though little was demanded of matriculands beyond keeping terms by eating a few dinners, it was customary to spend some time in London attending the courts, making contacts and gaining practical experience through contracting to work for a period of time for an established barrister or special pleader.[37]

Barristers, then, were mobile by background, just as they were to be mobile in their career, most spending months every year away from London, Dublin and Edinburgh on their chosen circuit.[38] That a far greater number, especially natives of Ireland, did not end up based in the metropolis seems surprising. It is hard not to feel, as in the case of the Church, that deeply held national loyalties retained all but the ambitious in their native land even when opportunities for movement were there. In an important respect, too, the relatively informal structure of training for the English bar must have discouraged many, especially the Irish. Entry to the English bar may not have required candidates to study in a law faculty and gain a degree but the emphasis on practical learning could be costly. Staying in London, studying as an apprentice, and becoming a qualified barrister could be prohibitive for all but the rich. Campbell paid £20 per annum for his chambers in Lincoln's Inn, 100 guineas to spend the year 1803 attached to the offices of an eminent special pleader, and £120 to be called to the bar in 1806. Inevitably, his minister father could not support his expensive change of career and he survived the six years moonlighting as a reporter on the *Morning Chronicle*, working as a salaried clerk, and sponging off his physician brother.[39] Serving a legal apprenticeship, moreover, was seen as a rite of passage and hard to avoid. Those who literally read for the bar in a garret room were deemed to be lowering the tone.

The English bar, therefore, was for the well-heeled Englishman. Irishmen like Daniel O'Connell, studying in London but unable to afford the cost of devilling for a practising counsel, were virtually guaranteed to have to join the Irish bar, irrespective of their religious allegiance.[40] Moreover, parental costs did not come to an end once a barrister was admitted. While it was recognised that the English bar was a very open profession, where the talented really could rise to the top, it was equally understood that the initial years would be lean – Romilly attended the Midland circuit six or seven times in the 1780s without making progress.[41] Parents, then, entered into an open-ended financial commitment when they decided to train their sons for the English bar, and many Scots and Irish fathers must have blanched at the prospect. Jeffrey's father, a deputy clerk to the Edinburgh Court of Session, was one who definitely turned his back on an initial ambition to make his son an English lawyer, going no further than sending him to Oxford for a year to polish his accent.[42]

Of the three traditional professions, only medicine could be said to have developed an all-British structure in the first half of the nineteenth century. In 1750 the medical profession was even more informally organised than the law. There was the same distinction between the university-educated elite and the apprentice-trained majority but there were no clear-cut functional divisions of the kind that separated barristers and solicitors, and the boundaries of the profession were blurred by the existence of an ever-growing coterie of quacks who practised medicine without any professional training. In theory the medical profession was a tripartite structure comprising faculty-trained, often graduate, physicians with a consultancy role and surgeons and apothecaries who carried out their orders. The small number of physicians in the British Isles, however, had always meant that this hierarchical structure remained largely an ideal, only ever realised before 1700 in London, Edinburgh, Glasgow and Dublin, where the medical profession had its own corporative identity. Even in these towns, though, any pretence that each part of the profession had its own distinct sphere had broken down by the mid-eighteenth century and most medical men, like their colleagues in the rest of the British Isles, were general practitioners combining consultancy with performing operations and dispensing medicines.[43]

In the course of the century 1750 to 1850 the structutre of the medical profession changed dramatically. The boundaries were never tightened so as to exclude legally the untrained, so that many of the 41,000 Britons who defined themselves as medical men in 1851 were part-time or rogue healers plying other occupations, often grocers or distillers. Nor was there any attempt to establish or extend the model hierarchical structure: the typical trained doctor in the mid-nineteenth century was still a general practitioner.[44] Nor, too, was the profession opened up to new groups, for its informal organisation had always ensured that its recruitment was confessionally mixed, even if entry to the medical corporations was historically closed to Catholics. Nevertheless, there were substantial developments in patterns of medical training and the organisation of the profession.

This was most noticeable at its upper echelons. In the first place, the number of graduate physicians expanded exponentially. In 1750 only about twenty-five Britons gained a degree in medicine per year and there can have been no more than 750 graduate physicians in the British Isles.[45] A century later it was not unknown for 300 medical degrees to be awarded a year,[46] and in 1851 the United Kingdom boasted 3,551 graduate physicians. More important, there had been significant changes in their educational *cursus*. Before 1750 most British physicians, regardless of confessional background, were trained abroad, either at Leiden or at Paris, and their medical degree was frequently obtained with little effort on the way home at the University of Rheims.[47] This reflected the fact that none of the British universities at this date boasted a medical faculty of any importance. After 1750, with the establishment of the highly reputed Edinburgh faculty, the rush to the Continent in search of a medical education was quickly checked, if not totally stemmed on the part of Irish medical students until the outbreak of the French revolution.[48] In the first half of the nineteenth century Edinburgh was the medical school *par excellence* of the British graduate physician, drawing students from all over the British Isles to the Scottish capital. In the ten years 1830–39, for instance, the faculty graduated 1,102 physicians: 389 were Scots, 301 English, 292 Irish and four Welsh.[49] Not all British physicians after 1800, admittedly, graduated at Edinburgh, for many took their degrees at other Scottish or British universities, especially Glasgow, whose medical faculty became a second important Scottish centre of medical education in the first half of the nineteenth century.[50] But even if a British physician graduated elsewhere, he had nearly always spent some time at Edinburgh. By the mid-nineteenth century, then, members of the fast expanding elite of the medical profession, whatever their confessional, social or geographical background, had shared a common educational experience in the Scottish capital.[51]

Their Edinburgh sojourn, however, was not the physicians' only common point of reference. The century after 1750 also witnessed a Europe-wide revolution in the conception of what constituted a good medical training for the elite of the profession. No longer was it deemed sufficient to have a deep theoretical knowledge of health and disease imparted in the faculties: more important, the young physician was expected to begin his career with a good practical knowledge of anatomy, dissection and bedside care.[52] Edinburgh certainly provided opportunities for clinical instruction, and the Edinburgh infirmary was one of the first hospitals in Europe to open its doors officially to medical students.[53] It was not a large enough town, though, to satisfy the practical needs of the large number of medical students who flocked to its faculty. By the end of the eighteenth century there was only one plausible centre for practical medical studies: London, with its 1 million inhabitants, many hospitals and newly established private medical schools. The British physician in 1850, then, had rubbed shoulders with his colleagues while studying in the metropolis as well as at Edinburgh.[54] Indeed, he might even have been to Dublin, for the Irish capital also served as a second significant centre of practical medical training in the first half of the nineteenth century, as its hospitals, faculty and private medical schools offered quality clinical and anatomical instruction more cheaply and in less crowded conditions.[55]

Admittedly, these developments did not mean that British physicians in the early Victorian era experienced an identical educational *cursus*, for as yet no specific training was demanded of a medical graduate beyond three years of study at a medical faculty. Although most graduate physicians would have had a good classical and scientific education, they were under no compulsion to attend a university arts course. Nor were they expected to pursue their medical studies in any order. The individal *cursus* depended on geographical and confessional background and the extent of the parental purse, for practical training was in the hands of hospital physicians and surgeons, who behaved like medical entrepreneurs. Thus the English Quaker and philanthropist Thomas Hodgkin, born at Tottenham, outside London, was initially educated at home and studied at Guy's and other London hospitals before taking a degree at Edinburgh in 1823. His Edinburgh-born contemporary, in contrast, Robert (later Sir Robert) Christison attended Edinburgh High School, then studied arts and medicine at his home university, before going south to London in 1820.[56] Nor did the graduate physician of the first half of the nineteenth century necessarily have an exclusively British medical education. As in previous centuries many, if now probably only a minority, had spent some time on the Continent. The Paris faculty in particular, acknowledged as the leading medical school in Europe at least until 1830, remained a popular destination once the Napoleonic wars were over.[57]

However, the uniqueness of the individual physician's *cursus* does not detract from the overall uniformity in the pattern of professional education. Physicians in the first half of the nineteenth century were largely trained in a common and all-British context that must have gone a long way to mitigating the power of ingrained national loyalties. Furthermore, many made their living in an all-British environment. Admittedly, there is little evidence of English physicians setting themselves up in practice in Ireland or Scotland, but Irish and Scots physicians moved to England in droves. Some idea of the scale of the Scottish emigration is revealed by the fact that there were only 511 physicians resident in Scotland in 1851, when Edinburgh alone graduated forty Scots per annum in the 1830s. Had they all stayed in Scotland the number would have been double.[58] Significantly, the Scots and the Irish did not just occupy the empty spaces their English brethren did not deign to fill. From the mid-eighteenth century they took advantage of the fact that it was possible to become a licentiate of the London College of Physicians without holding an Oxbridge degree or being an Anglican, and when the college partially relaxed its entry rules in the first half of the nineteenth century a handful became actual Fellows. Of the thirty-nine licentiates created in the 1760s and 1770s, eleven were Scots and five Irish; of the ninety-one created in the ten years 1801–10, the numbers were twenty-one and fourteen; while of the seventy-six fellows elected between 1826 and 1850, if the large majority were still born in England and Wales, seven came from the other parts of the British Isles.[59]

The upper reaches of the medical profession in 1850 can thus be justly described as a British elite. Moreover, a significant proportion of non-graduate medical practitioners also began to operate in an all-British context, at least during their years of training. General practitioners still usually began their careers as apprentices, but it increasingly became the convention after 1800 that they should set up in practice only after they had submitted themselves to a licensing examination before one of the medical corporations. In England from 1815 this became obligatory. Anyone thereafter who wished to dispense medicine had by law to be examined by the London Society of Apothecaries, and in the period 1820 to 1844 the number who did so annually ranged from 300 to 400.[60] This requirement meant not only that henceforth all English general practitioners had to come up to London to be examined but also that they had to gain a degree of formal instruction in order to pass. As a result, the Apothecaries Act confirmed a trend already visible before 1815, whereby the future English general practitioner as well as the future physician sought practical instruction in the London medical schools.[61] Many tyro general practitioners, too, from all over the United Kingdom aped their betters by seeking theoretical instruction at Edinburgh, with the result that many, perhaps the majority, of the students in its lecture halls had no intention of taking a degree. The faculty seldom awarded more than 100 doctorates a year but in its heyday in the 1820s Edinburgh welcomed 400 new students per annum.[62] Admittedly, most presumably eventually returned to their local hearth, but before they did so a large proportion, especially in the early nineteenth century, were even more deeply immersed in an all-British environment by serving as doctors in the armed forces or to the East India Company.[63]

Consequently, when the British State finally took the plunge in 1858 and legislated to define the medical profession more closely by requiring the newly formed General Medical Council to keep a register of all licensed practitioners, it can be assumed that the large majority of the 15,000 medical men who were found to have the requisite pieces of paper (four to five times the number of physicians) had undergone some form of training outside their immediate locality.[64] Inevitably, then, the newly defined profession came to organise itself in an all-British context. In the course of the first half of the nineteenth century a number of practitioner societies were founded in different parts of the United Kingdom, following in the footsteps of the London Association of Apothecaries and Surgeons set up in 1812 to lobby for the Apothecaries Act. Ominously, these included the Irish Medical Association, established in 1839 as an Irish medical pressure group. In the end, however, the wider Union context triumphed over the provincial and the regional, and it was the British Medical Association, founded in 1855, and its organ, the *British Medical Journal*, that came to speak for the profession. Significantly, the BMA was careful to appear a British and imperial organisation, not just a metropolitan one, by holding its annual conferences in different cities, meeting for the first time in Ireland in 1867.[65]

The explanation for the failure of all but the medical profession to develop a a genuinely British structure in the period lies partly in the less than adequate  steps that were taken towards their professionalisation.[66] The new professions remained chiefly organised as crafts: if there was training at all, it was by a system of apprenticeship, and though a number of the new professions had developed an institutional voice, they had not developed governing bodies with policing powers. The older profession of the law also remained a career where apprentice-based or on-the-job training was considered the best form of professional education. Lord Campbell was as enthusiastic and dogmatic about the virtues of practical learning as Telford.[67] Medicine, on the other hand, was the one profession where steps were taken to introduce a more formally structured pattern of training, albeit one that was still incomplete. Ironically, this was a consequence not of the theoretical being elevated at the expense of the practical but of the novel conviction that practical training in dissection and patient care could be successfully pursued only in the big London hospitals and dispensaries.

However, it should not be inferred that had the British professions been more fully professionalised in the first half of the nineteenth century in the manner of their French and other Continental counterparts they would automatically have evolved an all-British structure.[68] The example of the Church gives pause for thought. The Church, irrespective of denomination, was the one profession, old or new, at the end of the eighteenth century, which already demanded of its recruits a lengthy immersion in institutional learning. Yet in no sense is it possible to talk of the clergy forming an all-British profession in the first fifty years of the new British State. The clergy, on the contrary, formed a series of nationally organised professions, as they had always done. In other words, had there been a more active drive towards professionalisation in the British Isles before 1850, it seems likely that the powerful pull of traditional national identities would have skewed the process in a national rather than an all-British direction. This was already happening in the case of engineering and would become a definite feature of the subsequent era of professionalisation. Accountancy, for instance, would be just one of many professions where distinct governing bodies would be formed for Scotland and for England and Wales.[69] Medicine, arguably, escaped such 'nationalisation' only by chance. Had London had a university with a flourishing medical faculty in the first half of the nineteenth century, had Dublin developed as a medical centre as quickly as Edinburgh, or had Edinburgh been a larger town, it is possible to imagine a scenario where the elite of the profession, the graduate physicians, would have encountered a satisfactory theoretical and clinical training in their home country and there would have been little or no ethnic intermingling. The all-British educational *cursus* was never an official prescription.

Even in the long term, then, professionalisation could have acted universally as a solvent of traditional national identities only if the process had been State-directed, as it was in France, where Napoleon restructured the professions into an expanding set of State and private careers entered after a period of uniform, formal training not just in a French but often in a Parisian context. This, however, was not to be. The British government showed little interest in reorganising the professions throughout the nineteenth century. Admittedly, it established numerous Royal Commissions and parliamentary select committees to look into particular professions but only following lobbying by interested groups of reformers and their parliamentary spokesmen. Moreover, when the government did intervene, it did little to hasten the process or encourage restructuring along all-British lines. Too often reports were simply buried or the most anodyne changes introduced which gave due weight to influential interest groups, such as the Inns of Court or the medical corporations. Thus in 1858, rather than consolidating the fortuitous drift towards an all-British framework for the medical profession by establishing a single certificated path of entry based on examinations taken in or organised from London, the Medical Act of that year ordered the General Medical Council to recognise as licences to practise the diplomas of *eighteen* different medical bodies, based in eight cities (four in Scotland).

It is hard not to feel that the government was as committed to 'learning on the job' and as uninterested in cementing British ties as most members of the professions. Its attitude towards professionalisation was as gradualist as its approach to reform of the *ancien régime* State generally. It was not even interested before 1850 in creating a uniform system of secondary education, along the lines of French *lycées* or Prussian *Gymnasia*, so as to ensure that members of the wider elite, whatever their background or future career, would have had a common and distinctly British schooling. Britons continued to receive a general education in many and varied ways. According to parental means and taste, they attended long-established municipal day schools, boarded in private academies or were placed in the charge of a private tutor. If an increasing section of the future elite was passing through the growing number of so-called public schools in the mid-nineteenth century, thanks to the successful dissemination of Arnoldian values, it was not owing to government support.[70]

However, the government's reluctance to force the pace of professionalisation must also reflect unwillingness on the part of a body of men beholden ultimately to a narrow electorate to move ahead of general professional opinion. Most members of the professions were happy with their unstructured organisation and all were deeply conscious of their traditional national roots. Even a cursory study of the letters and memoirs of professional men reveals that the English, Scots and Irish (though never the Welsh) were always treated as distinct peoples with their own national characteristics, like the Germans or French. There is little evidence that professional people in the first half of the nineteenth century ever saw themselves primarily as Britons. Englishmen might use the terms 'England' and 'English' indiscriminately to mean either their home country and its inhabitants or the British Isles as a whole – something Scots would never do. But neither group used the terms 'Britain' or 'Britons' as anything other than a geographical marker. Scots who came to London either remained consciously Scots or, like Lord Campbell, went native, despised all things Caledonian (especially a Scots accent) and began to talk of themselves as English.[71]

Britishness for most professional people in the first half of the nineteenth century was never their primary spatial identity. It was not even an identity that would be thrust upon the professional man when travelling abroad, for Europeans and Americans as eminent as Napoleon and President Monroe insisted on treating the new British State as England.[72] Travellers from north of the border, like the physician Christison in Paris, had not only to bear the indignity of being called English but also, on revealing that they were in fact Scots, being forced to explain why they were not wearing a skirt.[73] Such incidents could only help to enforce traditional national identities. Indeed, given the stubborn loyalty of even the most mobile of professional people, such as Christison himself, who studied in London and visited England on several occasions during his career as an Edinburgh professor, it would be interesting to know how deeply British even those Britons who permanently moved in an all-British environment actually felt in this period. Certainly at the turn of the nineteenth century Britishness was not the primary identity of two of the country's leading naval officers, Collingwood and Nelson.[74] Afloat for months, sometimes years, in their wooden walls, they spoke of England, the English navy and English sailors in their letters home and to each other. Only when they communicated with the Admiralty did they deploy British officialese. It is not suprising, then, that in the heat of the moment of going into his final battle Nelson should have ordered a politically incorrect signal to be sent to the British fleet; nor that his signals officer, another Englishman, should have queried the verb 'confide' but not the noun subject of the message.[75]

This is not to say that Britishness was only an official identity for professional people of the early Victorian era. If it was not usually their primary spatial identity, it was still a lived reality. Just as much as other Britons, members of the professions came under the influence of a host of integrative institutional, economic and cultural forces that were slowly forming a common British identity in the first half of the nineteenth century. Thus, for all his Scottishness, Christison was also a conscious Briton, whose Britishness was territorial, racial and cultural. Immediately on crossing to France in 1820 he was struck by the dress and stunted stature of the natives. In Paris he lived with a group of Anglo-Scottish medical students who continually flaunted their common Protestantism, poked fun at French 'falsification' of recent history, and on New Year's Day 1821 sang *Rule, Britannia* in the streets.[76] Nonetheless, the significance of the fact that the professions in the first half of the nineteenth century, to the extent that they were organised at all, were organised for the most part along traditional national lines should not be underestimated. Not only did the history of professionalisation in the United Kingdom before 1850 set down a marker that would determine the direction of professional organisation when it was more intensively pursued in the second half of the century and beyond. More important, the predominantly traditionalist national character of British professionalisation ensured that it would be much easier to dismantle the Union in 1921 than would otherwise have been the case. A strongly bonded British professional community in the early twentieth century might well have seriously weakened the threat of Irish nationalism.

## Notes

1 A. D. Smith, *National Identity* (Harmondsworth, Penguin, 1992), esp. chs 1 and 3.
2 L. Colley, *Britons: Forging the Nation* (London, Yale University Press, 1992).
3 Absolute figures are impossible before the 1841 census and even then problems arise from inaccurate or inadequate occupational registration. The latest study of the professions for this period is P. Corfield, *Power and the Professions in Britain, 1700–1850* (London, Routledge, 1995), esp. p. 32 (breakdown of the size of the professions according to the census of 1851).
4 Contemporaries recognised the importance of the professions: see H. Byerley Thomson, *The Choice of a Profession: a Concise Account and Comparative Review of the English Professions* (London, Chapman and Hall, 1857).
5 A further factor for studying the British professions in a national context is their neglect in the

seminal K. Robbins, *Nineteenth-Century Britain: Integration and Diversity* (Oxford, Oxford University Press, 1988).

6 The best histories of individual new professions are: F. M. L. Thompson, *Chartered Surveyors: the Growth of a Profession* (London, Routledge, 1968), chs 3–6; B. Kaye, *The Development of the Architectural Profession in Britain* (London, Allen and Unwin, 1968); R. A. Buchanan, *The Engineers: a History of the Engineering Profession in Britain, 1750–1914* (London, Jessica Kingley, 1989).

7 S. Smiles, *Lives of the Engineers, with an Account of their Principal Works: Comprising also a History of Inland Communications in Britain*, 3 vols (London, John Murray, 1861–62), ii. 292–494.

8 *Life of Thomas Telford written by Himself*, ed. J. Rickman (London, Hansard, 1838), appendix C, p. 302: Telford backed the canal in his government-sponsored 'Survey of the Highlands'.

9 Telford, *Life*, pp. 15–17, on his Edinburgh visit in 1780.

10 Smiles, *Lives of the Engineers*, ii. 482–3. See also Telford, *Life*, pp. 2–3.

11 Smiles, *Lives of the Engineers*, iii. 60–3, 142, 145–8.

12 Buchanan, *The Engineers*, chs 2–4.

13 *Ibid.*, pp. 479–80.

14 H. B. Sutherland, *Rankine: his Life and Times* (London, Institution of Civil Engineers, 1973).

15 The army had run courses in military engineering at Woolwich since the eighteenth century: see W. Porter, *History of the Corps of Royal Engineers*, 2 vols (London, Longmans, 1889), i. 154–5 and ii. 169–74.

16 Buchanan, *Engineers*, pp. 165–70; R. B. McDowell and D. Webb, *Trinity College, Dublin, 1592–1952* (Cambridge, Cambridge University Press, 1982), pp. 180–4.

17 Buchanan, *Engineers*, p. 233: 664 out of 3,000 in Great Britain.

18 Buchanan, *Engineers*, pp. 75–6 and ch. 7; William J. M. Rankine, *The Institution of Engineers in Scotland ... On the Nature and Objects of the Institution. An Introductory Address* (Glasgow, Mackenzie, 1857).

19 Obviously, the predominance of Welsh and Gaelic in large parts of Wales, Ireland and the Scottish Highlands prevented the transference of monoglot English-speaking clergy to the Celtic fringe, but this did not preclude transference in the other direction.

20 Hardly any had attended the new Anglican colleges of Durham or King's London by 1850.

21 F. W. B. Bullock, *A History of the Training for the Ministry of the Church of England in England and Wales from 1800 to 1874* (St Leonard's, Budd and Gillatt, 1955); A. Haig, *The Victorian Clergy* (Beckenham, Croom Helm, 1984), pp. 72–82.

22 Pre-1850 Oxford had 542 fellowships, Cambridge 426: see Haig, *Victorian Clergy*, p. 29.

23 Haig, *Victorian Clergy*, pp. 32, 194–5. Some of these may have been English students who had gone to Trinity to gain a cheaper education.

24 McDowell and Webb, *Trinty College*, pp. 137–8. In attractive rural dioceses there were few Trinity graduates: see J. Obelkovich, *Religion and Rural Society: South Lindsay, 1825–1875* (Oxford, Oxford University Press, 1976), pp. 120–1

25 *The Life and Correspondence of William Connor Magee, 1821–91*, ed. J. C. MacDonell (London, Isbister, 1896), i., esp. pp. 198–203.

26 *The Records of the Honourable Society of Lincoln's Inn*, II, *Admission from AD 1800 to AD 1893* (London, Lincoln's Inn, 1896), *sub annis*.

27 John, Lord Campbell, *Lives of the Lord Chancellors and Keepers of the Great Seal of England*, 8 vols (London, John Murray, 1845–47), vi. 368–85.

28 *Life of John Lord Campbell*, ed. Hon. Mrs Hardcastle, 2 vols (London, John Murray, 1881), i. 3–191.

29 H. Kirk, *Portrait of a Profession: a History of the Solicitors' Profession, 1100 to the Present Day* (London, Oyez, 1976), esp. chs 1–3, 6; W. N. Osborough, 'The regulation of the admission of attorneys and solicitors in Ireland, 1600–1866', in D. Hogan and W. N. Osborough (eds), *Brehons, Serjeants and Attorneys: Studies in the History of the Irish Legal Profession* (Dublin, Irish Academic Press, 1990), pp. 101–51.

30 There is no study of the history of Scottish solicitors. I am indebted to information supplied by

Dr John Cairns of the Department of Private Law, University of Edinburgh. Some information can be garnered from P. S. Lachs, 'Scottish legal education in the nineteenth century,' in E. W. Ives and A. H. Manchester (eds), *Law Litigants and the Legal Profession* (London, Royal Historical Society, 1983), and S. D. Girvin, 'Nineteenth-century reforms in Scottish legal education', *Journal of Legal History*, 14 (1993), 127–41. Only three faculties of procurators were corporate bodies before 1865.

31 The best account of the history of the English bar in this period is R. Cocks, *Foundations of the Modern Bar* (London, Sweet and Maxwell, 1983), esp. chs 1–3; also D. Duman, 'Pathway to professionalism: the English bar in the eighteenth and nineteenth centuries', *Journal of Social History*, 13 (1979–80), 615–28; and *id.*, 'The English bar in the Georgian era', in W. Prest (ed.), *Lawyers in Early Modern Europe and America* (London, Holmes and Meier, 1981). For the Scots bar see A. Murdoch, 'The advocates, the law and the nation in early modern Scotland', *ibid.*; N. Wilson, 'The Scottish bar: the evolution of the Faculty of Advocates in its historical setting', *Louisiana Law Review*, 2: 28 (1968), 235–58; and J. Cairns, 'History of the Faculty of Advocates to 1900', in *The Laws of Scotland. Stair Memorial Encyclopaedia*, xiii (Edinburgh, Law Society of Scotland and Butterworth, 1992), 499–536.

32 *Memoirs of the Life of Sir Samuel Romilly*, ed. by his sons, 3 vols (London, John Murray, 1840), i. 1–67.

33 Sir A. Grant, *The Story of the University of Edinburgh During its First Three Hundred Years*, 2 vols (London, Longman, 1884), i. 284–92.

34 Henry, Lord Cockburn, *Life of Lord Jeffrey*, 2 vols (Edinburgh, Black, 1852), i. 21, 51–73.

35 Cocks, *Modern Bar*, pp. 41–51. In Ireland an attempt was first made in 1850 to offer a complete course in civil and common law in Dublin that all Irish barristers would have to follow in part: see McDowell and Webb, *Trinity College*, p. 193. Dublin was ahead of London, where readerships in constitutional history and Roman law were established in the Inns of Court only in 1852 with the creation of the Council for Legal Education.

36 Hence the number of Irish names in the Inns' registers. Fifty-five out of 239 matriculands at Gray's Inn were from Ireland in the period 1800–09, 106 out of 179 in 1840–44. See *The Register of Admissions to Gray's Inn, 1521–1889*, ed. J. Foster (London, Hansard, 1889), *sub annis*. Would-be members of the Irish bar had often to recross the Irish Sea because they also had to keep terms as a member of Dublin's King's Inns.

37 A special pleader was an expert in legal procedure who had generally not been called to the bar; quite a large proportion of matriculands at the Inns were never called.

38 Only with the establishment of county courts after 1847 did barristers begin to be based in regional towns.

39 *Life of Lord Campbell*, i. 50–191, esp. pp. 60, 70, 133–7, 191.

40 O. MacDonagh, *The Life of Daniel O'Connell, 1775–1847* (London, Weidenfeld and Nicolson, 1991), pp. 29–49. Catholics could join the Irish bar from 1792; applicants to the English bar still had to take an oath against popery in the 1800s: see *Life of Lord Campbell*, i. 189, account of his induction, 1806.

41 Romilly, *Memoirs*, i. 72–94: he eventually succeeded by breaking with tradition and attending quarter sessions as well as the assize court and thereby got known by local solicitors. On the relative openness of the Scottish and English bars see *Life of Campbell*, i. 48, 52–3.

42 Cockburn, *Life*, p. 50.

43 The best introduction to the structure of medical practice in the eighteenth century is D. Porter and R. S. Porter, *Patient's Progress: Doctors and Doctoring in Eighteenth-Century England* (Oxford, Polity Press, 1989), esp. ch. 2.

44 For this group see I. Loudun, *Medical Care and the General Practitioner, 1750–1850* (Oxford, Oxford University Press, 1986).

45 L. W. B. Brockliss, 'Before Edinburgh: the production of graduate physicians in the British Isles, 1500–1800' (unpublished paper), table 3 (degrees home and abroad). The estimated total number of physicians is based on the assumption of a thirty-year working life.

46 Loudun, *Medical Care*, p. 271; McDowell and Webb, *Trinity College*, p. 502; M. Moss (Glasgow

Archives), unpublished graphs of medical degrees bestowed at Edinburgh, Glasgow, Aberdeen and St Andrews.

47 Brockliss, 'Before Edinburgh', table 2 (foreign degrees): in the 1740s 111 out of 198 degrees gained by British students were bestowed abroad.

48 *Ibid.*, table 6 (Irish graduates of Rheims).

49 *Nomina eorum qui gradum medicinae doctoris in academia Jacobi Sexti Scotorum regis, quae Edinburgi est, adepti sunt* (Edinburgh, Neill, 1846), pp. 89–121. Students registered according to their kingdom of origin: presumably a number of Welsh students registered as English.

50 D. Dow and M. Moss, 'The medical curriculum at Glasgow in the early nineteenth century', *History of Universities*, 7 (1988), 243 (fig. 1).

51 For the life of an Edinburgh medical student in this period see L. Rosner, *Medical Education in the Age of Improvement. Edinburgh Students and Apprentices, 1760–1826* (Edinburgh, Edinburgh University Press, 1991), esp. chs 2, 3 and 7.

52 The latest study of this development is T. N. Bonner, *Becoming a Physician: Medical Education in Britain, France, Germany and the United States, 1750–1945* (New York and Oxford, Oxford University Press, 1995).

53 G. B. Risse, *Hospital Life in Enlightenment Scotland: Care and Teaching at the Royal Infirmary of Edinburgh* (Cambridge, Cambridge University Press, 1986).

54 On the growth of practical medical training in London see esp. S. Lawrence, 'Science and medicine at the London hospitals: the development of teaching and research, 1750–1815', Ph.D. dissertation, University of Toronto, 1985.

55 McDowell and Webb, *Trinity College*, pp. 87–9; T. P. C. Kirkpatrick, *History of the Medical Teaching in Trinity College Dublin and of the School of Physic in Ireland* (Dublin, Hanna and Neale, 1912), pp. 188 ff.

56 The Wellcome Institute for the History of Medicine, MS PP/HO, Box 8, files 1–6, Hodgkin's letters 1809–24; *The Life of Sir Robert Christison, Bart.*, ed. by his sons, 2 vols (Edinburgh, Blackwood, 1885–86), i. chs 1–9.

57 Visited by both Hodgkin and Christison. For the Paris School see esp. E. Ackerknecht, *Medicine at the Paris Hospital* (Baltimore, Md, Johns Hopkins University Press, 1967).

58 Assuming a thirty-year working life.

59 W. Munk, *The Roll of the Royal College of Physicians of London*, 3 vols (London, Royal College of Physicians, 1828), ii. 228–324 and iii. 1–96; G. H. Brown, *Lives of the Fellows of the Royal College of Physicians of London, 1826–1925* (London, Royal College of Physicians, 1955), pp. 1–61. For changes governing the election of Fellows see Sir G. Clark, *A History of the Royal College of Physicians of London*, 2 vols (Oxford, Oxford University Press, 1964–66), ii. 564–71, 682–91.

60 Loudun, *Medical Care*, ch. 12, esp. p. 187.

61 *Ibid.*, pp. 48–52.

62 Rosner, *Edinburgh*, p. 162 and chs 5–6. Some of these students would graduate in other faculties.

63 Three hundred each year were recruited into the army and navy pre-1815: see Loudun, *Medical Care*, pp. 208–9.

64 For the Medical Act of 1858 and earlier attempts at registration see *ibid.*, ch. 14. The number who initially registered is given in Corfield, *Professions*, p. 147.

65 Loudun, *Medical Care*, ch. 13; J. F. Fleetwood, *A History of Medicine in Ireland* (Dublin, Skelling Press, 1983), pp. 296–301; P. Vaughan, *Doctors' Commons: a Short History of the British Medical Association* (London, Heinmann, 1959), esp. chs 1–3; P. W. Bartrip, *Mirror of Medicine: a History of the British Medical Journal* (Oxford, Oxford University Press, 1990), chs 1–2.

66 The only other profession to organise itself along all-British lines was science, whose tutelary body for the whole of the United Kingdom was the British Association for the Advancement of Science, founded in 1831. But science was not yet a full-time occupation and its practitioners were few in number; the Association had only 800 members in 1850.

67 Cocks, *Modern Bar*, pp. 56–64.

68 For developments in France see below, Conclusion, pp. 200–1.

69 Scottish accountancy was regionalised with incorporated bodies being established at Edinburgh,

Aberdeen and Glasgow in 1854, 1855 and 1867. The London-based Institute of Chartered Accountants in England and Wales was formed in 1870.

70 T. W. Bamford, *Rise of the Public Schools* (London, Nelson, 1967); J. Roche, *A History of Secondary Education in England, 1800–70* (London, Longman, 1986).

71 E.g. *Life of Lord Campbell*, i. 113, 202, 220, 233, 236.

72 *Letters of Napoleon*, selected, trans. and ed. J. M. Thompson (Oxford, Oxford University Press, 1934), *passim*; Cockburn, *Life of Jeffrey*, i. 218–19: journal account of Jeffrey's interview with Monroe during his 1813 American trip.

73 *The Life of Sir Robert Christison*, i. 274: Paris visit, 1820–21.

74 *A Selection from the Public and Private Correspondence of Vice-Admiral Lord Collingwod, interspersed with Memoirs of his Life*, ed. G. L. N. Collingwood, 2 vols (London, Ridgway, 1828), *passim*, but see esp. i. 161–7, Collingwood's official report on Trafalgar.

75 C. Hibbert, *Nelson: a Personal History* (Harmondsworth, Viking,1994), pp. 366–7.

76 *The Life of Sir Robert Christison*, esp. i. 261.

# 2

# 'Recasting Our Lot':
# Peel, the nation, and the
# politics of interest

## DAVID EASTWOOD

When Sir Robert Peel returned to office on 20 December 1845 *The Times* celebrated in revealing terms: 'The wonderful anomalies that are centred in his person give him the key of many classes and influences, which no other man can command. Sir Robert Peel is Minister again, and the nation is reassured.'[1] If Peel had a single objective in his mature career, it consisted largely in 'reassuring the nation'. In late 1845, of course, the nation was much in need of reassurance. The position of people and places within the constitution was again being contested. The Maynooth crisis had reopened the question of Roman Catholic rights, and for many heralded a challenge to the very basis of the still fragile Anglo-Irish Union. The Irish potato famine cruelly exposed the extent to which Ireland was socially and economically, as well as religiously and culturally, distinct from England and indeed from lowland Scotland and Wales. The Corn Law crisis, and the strident extraparliamentary politics of the Anti-Corn Law League and the Anti-League which accompanied it, underscored Britain's unease with a destiny as a manufacturing nation. Against this background *The Times* welcomed Peel's resumption of the premiership as the return of a politician and a political style which would enable the nation to transcend sectarianism.

Significantly Richard Cobden advanced a precisely similar view six months later, when he urged Peel to remain in office at the head of a new administration committed to free trade and political liberalisation. Peel's resignation would, Cobden insisted, be nothing less than 'a national misfortune'.[2] The exchange of letters between Cobden and Peel on 23 and 24 June 1846 is profoundly revealing of the transformation at the heart of the British State which Peel's mature career seemed to epitomise. The melodrama of Peel's and Cobden's public relationship was well known, and symbolised something of the political and cultural torsions between the politics of land, still thought to be embedded in the Conservative party, and the culture of industrial Britain, at once emboldened and embittered by the limited reconfiguration of power wrought by the Reform Act of 1832. In 1842, when industrial Britain faced perhaps the most devastating depression of the nineteenth century, Peel believed that the Anti-Corn Law League was, intentionally or inadvertently, fomenting a national crisis of potentially revolutionary dimensions. Chartism was at its most pervasive and potent, unemployment and hunger gripped most of the principal manufacturing centres, and the League and its allies seemed willing, at least momentarily, to abet a general strike whose principal object would have been to overwhelm Parliament and the political settlement of 1832.[3] In the summer months of 1842 the British ruling class was imperilled personally as well as politically. By late August 1842 Peel was himself laying down a considerable store of arms to defend Drayton Manor, and assuring his wife that 'Our security must lie in being prepared for it [the danger of attack] and determined to repel it'.[4] Peel's relations with his opponents, notably with the leaders of the League, focused class and political frictions. On 17 February 1843 Cobden accused Peel of being 'individually responsible for the present state of the country'. With the memory of the assassination of Edward Drummond, Peel's private secretary, in January still painfully fresh, Peel sprang to his feet, construed Cobden's comments as legitimising attempts on the Premier's own life, and insisted that he would not be 'influenced by menaces either in the House or out of it'.[5] The distance, both personal and political, between the bitter exchanges of February 1843 and Peel's notorious resignation speech, in which he lavished praise on Cobden's 'pure and disinterested motives' in campaigning for repeal, was immense. Peel's great peroration played badly in the House, being quite uncharacteristically populist in tone and almost aggressively demagogic in idiom. The Cobden eulogy was followed by a long closing sentence in which Peel seemed to celebrate not only the severing of party ties but also the weakening of party as an instrument of government. He feigned indifference to his being 'execrated by every monopolist who ... clamours for protection because it conduces to his own individual benefit'. In Peel's new political vision these monopolists were, to say the least of it, uncomfortably close to the heart of the agricultural interest. And finally Peel chose to entrust his reputation and memory to 'those whose lot is to labour, and earn their daily bread by the sweat of their brow'.[6]

This wilful wounding of friends, savaging of party, and calculated *rapprochement* with those who had been construed as political, personal and class enemies, may have bewildered Aberdeen and Gladstone, alienated Wellington and struck the diarist Greville as 'claptrap', but it cemented Peel's popular reputation. The Liberal provincial press embraced Peel, acclaiming him as a national rather than partisan figure. There can be little doubt that Peel sought this apotheosis, and cherished a public status which owed nothing to party and everything to national acclamation. As Donald Read has demonstrated, by his death Peel had achieved a transcendent status as a national symbol which was rare, if not unique, amongst mere politicians. The powerful synergy of mourning and acclamation which accompanied Peel's death is more closely paralleled by the public response to the death of military heroes such as Nelson, or military men-cum-politicians such as Wellington, than in the mourning of other mere politicians, the younger Pitt included.[7] Most striking, perhaps, was the obituary carried in the Chartist *Northern Star*, which insisted that Peel's death was regretted

by men of all classes and all parties. We believe that the great mass of the people, whose political predilections are of a moderate description, and who do not take any active part in political struggles, looked upon the deceased Statesman as the right hand of the country.[8]

Viewed in this way, Peel's final political achievement was to identify himself, and his mature liberal Conservative ideology, not with party, class or interests, but with nation, State and empire. If his politics consisted in balancing interests, his reputation and his presumed political vantage point were beyond mere interests.[9] Certainly Cobden took this to be Peel's position when he wrote to him, confidentially, on 23 June 1846 seeking to dissuade him from resignation and encouraging him to form a new, non-party, coalition administration: a national government in all but name. 'Are you aware,' Cobden asked Peel, 'of the strength of your position in the country? If so, why bow to a chance medley of factions in the Legislature, with a nation ready and waiting to be called to your rescue?' This stark juxtaposition of party and nation doubtless struck Cobden as wholly consonant with Peel's own presentation of his position since he resumed office on 20 December 1845. Cobden went on to insist that intelligent public opinion was both vocally and substantially supportive of Peel. 'I will not speak of the populace, which to a man is with you; but of the active and intelligent middle classes, with whom you have engrossed a sympathy and interest greater than was ever before possessed by a minister.'[10] Cobden's reading of Peel's position and political intentions was, as we shall see, misconceived, but his misconception was understandable and indeed widely shared by contemporaries and subsequent commentators alike. Peelite Conservatism, as defined in the Tamworth Manifesto of 1834 and practised in the Ministries of 1841–46, appeared to be a sustained exercise in engrossing the active sympathy of the middle class. Was not the Tamworth Manifesto an address to the middle classes; an occasion manufactured by Peel, Croker, Barnes and other advisers when Peel might avail himself of

> a legitimate opportunity, of making a more public appeal – of addressing, through you, to that great and intelligent class of society, of which you are a portion, and a fair and unexceptionable representative – to that class which is much less interested in the contentions of party than in the maintenance of good government?[11]

Eric Evans assures us that 'This, rightly, has been interpreted as a bid for middle-class votes.'[12] Yet this is to misconceive both what Peel said and what he intended. Peel's referent was not a social but a political class, an imagined political community which would embrace electors from divergent social backgrounds, and with widely differing economic experiences. For Peel there was no distinctive, still less no antagonistic, middle class interest. This was clarified, in typically Peelite language, in his speech at Merchant Tailors' Hall in May 1835, soon after his minority administration had fallen, where, in a remarkable passage, Peel simultaneously universalised middle-class virtue, embedded the middle-class idea in the great social web of the empire, and suggested that any difference of rank or status arose organically from the exercise of middle-class virtues – 'industry, patient perseverance, and strict integrity' – within 'this great community'. Thus Peel den[ied] that we are separated by any fancied line of interest, or of pride, or of privileges, from the middle classes of the country ... If we ourselves do not belong to the middling classes of society, I want to know how wide the interval may be that is presumed to separate us? ... I say we disclaim any separation from the middling classes of society in this country ... we are bound to them by a thousand ramifications of direct personal connexion, and common interests, and common feelings.[13]

Whatever their substance, in form Peel's politics were not the politics of class. Class, after all, might legitimise party just as party might invest class with a divisive and partisan political meaning. Hence Peel's preference for a symbolic language of empire, community, nation, and his simultaneous rejection of discourses of class, party and sectional advantage.

What Peel did admit, albeit in a highly particular form, was a language of interests. This was clear in Peel's synoptic statement of his government's principles of action in the Tamworth address.

Our object will be the maintenance of peace, the scrupulous and honourable fulfilment, without reference to their original policy, of all existing engagements with Foreign Powers, the support of public credit, the enforcement of strict economy, and the just and impartial consideration of what is due to all interests, agricultural, manufacturing, and commercial.[14]

In admitting the reality of interests within the polity, Peel did not concede that such interests were in any sense necessarily antagonistic. Indeed he was careful to construct interests in material terms, and his typology of interests was essentially economic. Thus simultaneously Peel's political language limited the domain of friction between interests and invested the State with the responsibility for harmonising, or balancing, interests within the nation. When it suited him, as it did at Merchant Tailors' Hall, Peel could universalise commercial virtue whilst always reserving to government the right to determine 'what is due to all interests'. If Peelite Conservatism was anything it was conceived as a grand exercise in distributive justice.

Nowhere was this clearer than in Peel's fiscal strategy. In preparing the 1842 budget Peel spoke constantly of discovering a sound policy which was consonant 'with the permanent interests of the country'.[15] He embraced the reintroduction of the income tax precisely because its incidence and benefits were widely distributed. Thus, in this search for fiscal rectitude and revived prosperity 'the wisest course for the country, for the capitalists, for all classes, would be to raise four or five millions for the next five years by a property tax ... and diminish the pressure of taxation on the great articles of consumption'.[16] Peel's reading of the position of Britain in 1842 was stark. He saw as clearly as anyone the magnitude of the economic depression which was crippling all sectors of the economy, and attributed this deepest of nineteenth-century recessions to a general failure of consumption.[17] There can be no doubting Peel's commitment to dynamic, sectorally balanced economic growth. As he told Croker in August 1842, 'We must make this a cheap country for living, and thus induce parties to remain and settle here – enable them to consume more, by having more to spend. It is a fallacy to urge that the loss falls on the agriculturalists. They too are consumers.'[18]

Peelite policy was determined by a very particular understanding of Britain's recent development and future state. Peel, of course, was no Malthusian but, like so many of his generation, he recognised sheer force of numbers. Britain's high-pressure demographic regime, its large urban populations and its high level of public indebtedness were sustainable only if manufacturing and commercial prosperity continued to increase. This acceptance of the centrality of manufacturing to Britain's present and future lay at the heart of what came to be celebrated as Peel's 'practical statesmanship'.[19] He put the case most eloquently in a letter to Croker in late July 1842, at precisely the moment when economic depression looked set to spark social revolution.

> Look at the congregation of manufacturing masses, the amount of our debt, the rapid increase of poor rates within the last four years, which will soon, by means of rates in aid, extend from the ruined manufacturing districts to the rural ones, and then judge whether we can safely retrograde in manufacturers. If you had to constitute new societies, you might on moral and social grounds prefer cornfields to cotton factories, an agricultural to a manufacturing population. But out lot is cast, and we cannot recede.[20]

Peel's private rhetoric was paralleled by his public commitment both to reviving manufacturing prosperity and to insisting that the benefits of manufacturing were national rather than sectional. He told the House in March 1842 that he was introducing an income tax

> not only for supplying the deficiency in the revenue, but of enabling me with confidence and satisfaction to propose great commercial reforms, which will afford a hope of reviving commerce, and such an improvement in the manufacturing interests as will react on every other interest in this country.[21]

To this extent, accepting that 'our lot is cast' represented not the end of policy but its beginning: it represented a vision of Britain on which all else was premissed. Peelism was a heroic attempt to reconcile the constitutional instincts of Toryism with the realities of having become a manufacturing nation. In this context it is striking that Peel shared, or came to share High Tories' sense of the importance of conciliating economically, whilst excluding politically, the interests of labour. Peel may have supported the New Poor Law, and been at best lukewarm in his support for serious factory legislation, but he undoubtedly conceived of the income tax as an instrument for redistributing some of the fiscal burden away from labour. His rhetoric indicated the broad thrust of policy.

> No man can feel a more intimate conviction than I do, that whatever be your financial difficulties and necessities, you must so adopt and adjust your measures as not to bear on the comforts of the labouring classes of society. My conviction is, that it would not be expedient, with reference to the narrow interests of property, that that should be done.[22]

In practice policy went still further, transferring around £3·7 million worth of tax from duties which fell predominantly on articles of mass consumption to a direct tax on incomes of over £150 per annum.[23]

At one level Peelite fiscal policy represented a continuation of the kind of liberal Toryism forged in the 1820s by Lord Liverpool, F. J. Robinson, William Huskisson, Thomas Wallace and Peel himself.[24] At its core was a desire to reconcile the unenfranchised majority to parliamentary government based on a highly restricted franchise. Yet Peel's liberal Conservatism of the 1840s operated in a still more volatile environment and was bolder in conception and presentation than anything essayed under Liverpool.[25] The unspoken intention of the income tax, and the redistributionist rhetoric which accompanied it, was a determination to deprive the Chartists of a central plank in their platform. Chartists had inveighed passionately against 'unconstitutional taxation', by which they meant indirect taxation which was regressive in its incidence.[26] Their case had gained still more force from Baring's 1840 budget, which had further squeezed mass consumption by a 5 per cent hike in duties.[27] If Chartism weakened after 1842, the fiscal and political stance of the 1842 budget played a crucial part in that weakening. As the threat of Chartism receded, Peel started to revise the language of interests so as formally to accord labour a central role in policy, although not, of course, in policy making. By 15 May 1846 the interests of labour had become the 'greatest object' of policy. Peel told the House that

> My earnest wish has been, during my tenure of power, to impress the people of this country with a belief that the legislature was animated by a sincere desire to frame its legislation upon the principles of equity and justice. I have a strong belief that the greatest object which we or any other government can contemplate should be to elevate the social condition of that class of people with whom we are brought into no immediate relationship by the exercise of the elective franchise. I wish to convince them that our object has been so to apportion taxation, that we shall relieve industry and labour from any undue burden, and transfer it, so far as is consistent with the public good, to those who are better enabled to bear it ... [28]

Constituting the material condition of the labouring classes as 'the greatest object' of policy seemed to repudiate, if silently, the constitutional imperatives of traditional Toryism. From here to Peel's resignation speech, with its eulogies to Cobden, cheap bread and the working man, was a short, apparently even ineluctable, step.

Peel's balancing of interests was carefully calibrated. The labouring classes were to be reconciled to party and empire by the promise of prosperity but not of political power. Manufacturing and commerce were assured of their central role in the economy, but the commercial classes were to pay as individual income tax payers for the tariff reductions they sought as an economic interest. In this Peelite audit of interests, agriculture was initially accorded limited protection, but the nature and extent of protection were determined by national rather than sectional interests. When considering a revision of the sliding scale for the corn tariff, Peel told Ripon in October 1841 that

> The principle on which we ought to proceed in reviewing the Corn Laws is, to disregard the consideration of future clamour, or extravagant expectations on either side, and

to bear in mind as far as we can the permanent and comprehensive interests of the country; among which encouragement to domestic [corn] production occupies a promi-nent place.[29]

By 1842 Peel was persuaded that these 'permanent and comprehensive' national interests required an abatement of agricultural protection and the institution of a more technically efficient sliding scale. That Peel carried his 1842 Corn Law was testimony to his reputation as a financier and his authority in the wake of the 1841 election rather than to his willingness to conciliate the landed interest. When Charles Arbuthnot told Peel that 'many of our Ultra friends are dissatisfied with the measures of the last session' Peel was unflinching in his insistence that they misconceived their own and the nation's interests. 'I would most earnestly advise them to look beyond the present, and seriously to ponder upon some other matters that ... are in truth more important to them and to their property than the fall in the price of stock, or of pigs, or of wheat.' For Peel the future of property and protection was intimately connected with the future of places such as Paisley.

> For upwards of a year eight or nine thousand persons on average have been supported in that one town not by work – for there is no demand for labour – but by voluntary charity ... I, who have no sort of connection with Paisley, have subscribed twice, being satisfied that if nothing were done we might take the choice of hundreds dying, or of a frightful outbreak, and attack upon property. The first question we shall have to consider in the Cabinet is, What is to be done with these people at Paisley during next winter.

Peel concluded that it was 'his firm belief' that if prices and unemployment continued at current levels the security of property would be imperilled.[30]

It may be argued that Peel's response to the Irish famine in 1845 paralleled his response to manufacturing distress in 1842. In both cases policy towards the agricultural interest was determined by wider considerations of social distress and the security of property. There are, however, two crucial differences. The first is that Corn Law repeal, if anything, worsened Ireland's economic position, and, whatever Peel's motivation in moving to free trade in grain, immediate or medium term relief for Ireland cannot have been a part of it.[31] Secondly, in 1841–42 Peel remained a committed protectionist. The object in 1842 was not to pave the way towards free trade but to reconstruct the tariff and develop new fiscal instruments. The priority and, as Angus Macintyre always maintained, the achievement of 1842 was efficient protection. The strategy, in short, was tariff reform, predicated on a conviction that an efficiently ordered and economically sensitive system of taxes and tariffs gave government the most appropriate instruments for balancing interests within the nation, and indeed beyond. In this context Peel's policy towards Ireland in the 1842 budget was revealing. Pitt's wartime income tax had, of course, antedated the Act of Union, and as a result the income tax had never been levied in Ireland. Not only was there no history of income tax in Ireland, the infrastruc-ture for its assessment and collection was absent. Moreover the imposition of an income tax on Ireland would have been something of a propaganda gift for

O'Connell. Peel put all this most delphicly, remarking that 'in the state of society in Ireland there is something peculiar, which makes the devising of machinery for its [income tax's] collection [a] matter of grave consideration'.[32] Nevertheless Peel was convinced that 'no part of the empire will be more benefited' by tariff reductions than Ireland, and that Ireland ought to bear its fair proportion of public charges. He thus proposed to equalise the duties on spirits, which stood at 2s 8d per gallon in Ireland but 7s 10d in England, insisting that equalisation of duties within the empire was, in itself, a sound and integrative policy. More strikingly still, Peel went on to impose the income tax on absentee Irish landlords. To this extent income tax would be used as a lever to encourage both the repatriation of the Irish landowning class and the repatriation of capital to Ireland.[33] Nothing better illustrates Peel's mature belief that strengthening the Union entailed legislative sensitivity to local circumstances, especially in Ireland, or his willingness to use fiscal instruments to achieve broader political ends.

By this stage it ought to be clear that if Peel had succeeded, as Cobden claimed, in engrossing an unprecedented sympathy with the intelligent middle classes, such popularity was not the aim but an unintended consequence of his policy. In so far as Peel aimed at engrossing sympathy – and the evidence of his political rhetoric suggests that by 1846 he would go far to court popularity – it was not the sympathy of a class but the sympathy of the nation he wished to engross. Thus Cobden's construction of the political logic of 1846 was virtually diametrically opposed to Peel's. The crux of his June 1846 letter culminated in a plea for Peel to exchange the politics of party for a new politics of class.

> Do you shrink from the post of governing through the *bona fide* representatives of the middle class? Look at the facts, can the country be otherwise ruled at all? There must be an end of the juggle of parties, they are mere representatives of traditions, and some man must of necessity rule the State through its governing class. The Reform Bill decreed it; the passing of the Corn Bill has realized it. Are you afraid of the middle class? You must know better than to suppose that they are given to extreme or violent measures. They are not democratic.[34]

Peel probably did not believe that the middle class was democratic, although he did believe that in campaigning for electoral reform and Corn Law repeal they forged social and political alliances whose tendencies were dangerously democratic. By 1846 did not shrink so much from ruling through the representatives of the middle class as from ruling through the representatives of any class. If the language and structures of party systematised sectional interests within Parliament and the electoral process, the language of class, especially the hegemonic language of the middle class employed by Cobden, systematised sectional interests within public opinion and sought to collapse the interests of the nation into the interests of the middle class. Peel thus dismissed Cobden's call to dissolve and go to the country on a free trade platform. Policy and political alliances were, Peel insisted, to be built 'not on temporary personal sympathies, not on concurrence of sentiment on one branch of policy, however important that may be, but on general approval of [a Minister's] whole policy'.[35] Hence, despite the public *rapprochement*, Peel regarded Cobden's proposals as a Mephistophelean temptation, giving him power but transforming Corn Law repeal into a triumph for the middle class. It was politically crucial for Peel to project Corn Law repeal not only as a personal triumph over party but as a triumph of national over sectional interests.

> Dissolution after the repeal of the Corn Laws might have given me a majority. But that majority would have consisted in great measure of men of democratic principles, approving of my conduct as to the Corn Laws, sympathising with me on account of the calumnies and shameful injustice of my opponents – but with no other bond of political sentiment between us. I am a Conservative – the most Conservative act of my life was that which has caused the sacrifice of power.[36]

There could be no victory beyond repeal because, in the manner of its execution, the repeal of the Corn Laws became nothing less than the apotheosis of Peelism. As Peel told the House on 29 June, when resigning,

> I have now executed the task which public duty imposed on me … I can say with truth that Her Majesty's government, in proposing those measures of commercial policy which disentitle them to the confidence of many who heretofore gave them their support, were influenced by no other motive than the desire to consult the interests of this country. Our object was to avert dangers which we thought were immanent, and to terminate a conflict which, according to our belief, would soon place in hostile collision great and powerful classes in this country'.[37]

Social peace, a heroic gesture to establish a new equilibrium between interests, was presented by Peel as his crowning achievement.

Peel's resignation speech has passed into legend as a truly heroic parliamentary moment, its great peroration sealing Peel's reputation. The preceding sections of Peel's resignation speech are equally revealing, and in some ways more quint-essentially Peelite. A substantial portion of the speech was given over to informing the House of the Oregon settlement as a result of which the United States abated its territorial claims, enabling Britain to retain Vancouver Island whilst securing equal access to the Columbia river to both countries. In form and substance Peel's resignation speech brought together two central concerns of his premiership: trade and empire. There has been a fashion for underplaying Peel's imperial vision. Whilst it would be mistaken to cast Peel as an enthusiastic proponent of further imperial expansion, he was a passionate and persuasive defender of the commercial utility and moral tendency of the British empire. Peel's reputation as a 'practical' statesman – whatever that may mean – should not be allowed to occlude the extent to which he believed policy was shaped by the imperatives of a highly specific national history. Just as recent history had determined that Britain's lot was cast as a commercial and manufacturing nation, so precisely the same period had confirmed Britain's status as an imperial power.

Peel thought it 'impossible to deny that the period in which our lot, and the lot of our fathers, has been cast – the period which has elapsed since the first outbreak of the first French revolution – has been one of the most memorable periods which the history of the world will afford'.[38] Victory in the French revolutionary and Napoleonic wars simultaneously helped stem the democratic tide, secure foreign markets and confirm Britain's imperial status. Peel celebrated the years of peace following 1815 – the period during which 'our lot has been cast' – as years of imperial achievement, which sanctified the struggle of the revolutionary and Napoleonic wars in terms of cultural and commercial imperialism.

> There will be a time [Peel assured the House in 1842] when the countless millions that are sprung from our loins, occupying many parts of the globe, living under institutions derived from ours, speaking the same language in which we convey our thoughts and feelings – for such will be the ultimate results of our wide-spread colonisation – the time will come when those countless millions will view with pride and admiration the example of fortitude and consistency which our fathers set during the years of war.[39]

This emphasis on the language, culture, and expansiveness of Britishness took Peel close to the kind of constructed 'official nationalism' which Benedict Anderson regards as characteristic of mid-nineteenth-century nationalism.[40] Three years later, when justifying the continuation of the income tax, Peel again insisted on the moral and commercial advantages of empire. He did not doubt the cost of imperial defence and imperial administration; nevertheless he passionately opposed a retreat from an imperial policy 'which laid the foundation in different parts of the globe of dependencies animated by the spirit of Englishmen, speaking the English language, and laying the foundation, perhaps, in future times, of free, populous and commercial states'. Peel went on to link empire, potential overpopulation and enterprise, insisting that it would be wise 'to provide an outlet for that population, and a wide field for that enterprise'.[41] Throughout there was impressive consistency in Peel's imperial vision, which was simultaneously expansive, loose and quintessentially English.

If in 1845 Peel's fiscal policy was shaped in significant measure by the need to provide for stronger imperial defence through substantially augmented defence estimates, in 1842 he had justified the introduction of income tax not simply as a domestic but as an imperial imperative. The great evil of Britain's current and accumulated budget deficit had an important imperial dimension. The war with China, unrest in Australia and the Canada loan constituted significant burdens on the Treasury. Moreover, in India revenue in 1840 appeared to be running some £2·4 million below expenditure. Indian and British finances were, Peel insisted, mutually interdependent 'and the collateral and indirect effect of disorders in Indian finances would be felt extensively in this country'. More fundamentally still, Indian security was non-negotiable, and Peel committed the House to making 'every effort which may be necessary for the purpose of repairing partial or occasional disasters, and vindicating the authority of her Majesty's name in India'.[42] In characteristically Peelite langauge an extensive imperial commitment was here being guaranteed.

By the mid-1840s Peel was increasingly disposed towards the language not so much of liberalism but of liberality. The hard-edged certainties which had buttressed his Toryism in the 1820s had begun to abate. The liberal Toryism of the

1820s gave way to liberal Conservatism in the 1830s. Peel's insistence by the mid-1830s on describing himself, almost habitually, as a liberal Conservative certainly represented a formal attempt to distance himself from what he now regarded as the factional fundamentalism of the Ultra Tories. It enabled him to describe his political stance without immediately annexing that position to the catechism of party. Aspects of this political evolution are familiar, and have been aptly described by Boyd Hilton as the 'ripening' of Sir Robert. Thus Peel retained his firm commitment to the Anglican establishment but increasingly distanced himself from the fierce anti-Catholicism which he had espoused until the later 1820s.[43] The transition between Peel's firm intention to resign if Catholic Emancipation passed in the Lords in 1826 to his augmentation and establishment of the Maynooth grant in 1845 represented not abandonment of his Anglicanism but the rejection of anti-Catholicism as a necessary corollary of that Anglicanism.[44] In the same way Peel's insistence on keeping Dissenters at the margins of the constitution in the 1820s gave way in the 1830s to a desire to integrate them fully into British society. Thus in the Tamworth Manifesto, whilst upholding the continued exclusion of Nonconformists from the ancient universities, Peel went on to

> expressly declare that, if regulations, enforced by public authorities superintending the professions of law and medicine and the studies connected with them, had the effect of conferring advantages of the nature of civil privileges on one class of the King's subjects from which another class are excluded, those regulations ought to undergo modification, with the view of placing all the King's subjects, whatever their religious creeds, upon a footing of perfect equality with respect to any civil privilege.[45]

Three months later, in the House, Peel actually proposed a substantial measure which would have established civil marriage, on the grounds that since the 'scruples of the Dissenters are really sincere, no one can deny, not only the justice, but also the policy, of affording them the relief which they require'.[46] In 1844 Peel happily brought forward the Dissenters' Chapels Act on grounds of 'individual justice' which guaranteed the rights of Unitarians to continue to enjoy the proceeds of bequests initially made to endow trinitarian worship.[47] This willingness to reach an ever more generous accommodation of Dissent and recusancy within the Peelite polity had its counterpoint in Peel's political and personal support for the established Church. Establishing the Ecclesiastical Commission in 1835 was a clear token of Peel's Broad Church reformism, seeking to enhance the effectiveness of the Church through vigorous internal reform. The 1843 New Parishes Act, which empowered the Ecclesiastical Commission to spend up to £600,000 creating new parochial districts where the population exceeded 2,000 helped substantiate this ecclesiastical reformism. Peel's personal commitment was clearly signalled by his assigning £4,000 of his ministerial salary to church building in 1843.[48] By the 1840s Peel was seeking not so much to promote free trade in religion as liberality in the State's attitude towards the religious plurality of British society. His objection in his 1844 memorandum on policy towards Maynooth seminary was that the present system of niggardly and ungracious State support represented the worst of all worlds. Most notably it resulted in a situation where 'The State gets no credit for indulgence or liberality'.[49] Viewed in this way, Peel's mature religious policy was an analogue of his fiscal policy, embodying willingness to use the State to mediate between diverse religious interests within Britain. The intention was to accommodate diverse religious and economic interests to a still conservative Parliament, a limited monarchy, and an enduring legislative union.

In Ireland Peel came to press this liberalising tendency furthest. If his years as Chief Secretary for Ireland (1812–18) left him with an enduring Sense of the importance of British State power in Ireland, his mature political position saw him moving towards a more creative vision of ways in which that state power might be employed. The Maynooth proposals of 1845 were the most celebrated and constitutionally significant of Peel's Irish measures, but his proposal the same year to establish non-denominational colleges at Cork and Galway, and in Ulster (probably at Belfast or Armagh) was in its way an equally bold if similarly conceived initiative.[50] Both proposals were, in part at least, a response to O'Connellism, or rather attempts to diminish what had become O'Connell's natural constituencies. Peel's vision of a moderate Catholic clergy, appeased by modest State support, and an expanded, more culturally cosmopolitan Irish middle class, was a reforming vision of considerable social ambition. At the heart of Peel's mature Irish policy was a social and cultural programme which amounted to a remaking of the Irish middle class. It would be easy to construe this as a grand attempt to Anglicise Ireland, yet there was a growing appreciation on Peel's part of the legitimacy of Irish difference within the Union. In the wake of the 1845–46 crisis Peel's prescriptions for Ireland combined advocacy of an activist, amelioratory role for the State through Poor Law reform, drainage, fisheries, public works and assisted emigration with willingness to embrace such symbolically and substantively significant measures as State endowment for the Catholic clergy in Ireland.[51] There was no reconciliation with O'Connell to parallel the reconciliation with Cobden but there was a sense in which Peel, belatedly perhaps, came to see what a capacious liberal-conservative policy might do for Ireland. In a limited sense Peel came to recognise that he might uphold the Union by working with rather than against the grain of Irishness.[52]

If there was something which was ambiguous in Peel's mature and posthumous reputation, even that ambiguity was momentarily creative. Even if the movement from protection to free trade may be explained in terms of Peel's deep commitment to a tariff reforming agenda, this was a transition which seemed to entail the political repudiation of pledges given and policies formerly espoused. Similarly the distance from Peel's aggressive Protestantism in the 1820s to his accommodation with moderate Catholicism and rational Dissent in the 1840s was so great that many could see nothing but calculated betrayal. The political destabilisation which 1846 wrought, the political friendships which Peel tested, former opponents with whom he latterly flirted as political allies all testified to 'the wonderful anomalies' which *The Times* believed were now 'centred in his person'. At a moment when the centrifugal tendencies wrought by massive economic upheaval, structural tensions within the Union and the spectre of mass politics might have conspired to overwhelm the existing political order, Conservative newspapers were wise to celebrate the wonderful anomalies of Peel's public reputation.

There was, then, more to Peel's national politics than carefully calibrated economic managerialism. He had equally strong faith in the efficacy of the defining institutions of the British State – Crown, Church, Parliament, even empire. What profoundly concerned Peel was that special interests would subvert general interests. For these reasons Peel not only distrusted but wished to destroy such overtly sectarian movements as Cobdenism, Chartism and O'Connellism. If Chartism was defeated by prosperity and the League by reform, Peel's attempt to overcome O'Connellism and strengthen the Union rested on a carefully improvised combination of economic management and reformism. But to understand Peelism in terms of narrowly political strategies is to misunderstand both its range and subtlety. The politics of sectarianism were sustained by languages of sectarianism towards which Peel was profoundly hostile. Habitually Peel preferred the language of status to the language of class, a latitudinarian Establishment to religious enthusiasm, and the idea of good government to the language of party. In his attempts to transcend party, faction and sectarian interest Peel was increasingly thrown back on to the idea of the British nation. This weak nationalism was a defining theme not only in Peelite policy in the 1830s and 1840s but also in Peel's huge popular appeal. It is woven through Peel's parliamentary set-pieces, and it momentarily redefined Britain in the 1840s. In this, as in so many other ways, Peel had no successor, but, that notwithstanding, the Peelite moment was a crucial moment for the meaning of Britain in the nineteenth century.

## Notes

1 *The Times*, 23 December 1845.

2 Richard Cobden to Robert Peel, 23 June 1846, pr. John Morley, *The Life of Richard Cobden*, one-vol. edn (London, Fisher Unwin, 1903), pp. 390–7, here at p. 391.

3 G. Kitson Clark, 'Hunger and politics in 1842', *Journal of Modern History*, 25 (1953), 355–74; Norman Gash, *Sir Robert Peel*, new edn (London: Longman, 1986), pp. 330–62. Peel's belief that the League was fomenting general unrest in 1842 was shared, albeit from a quite different *a priori* by the Chartist leader Feargus O'Connor; see *The Trial of Feargus O'Connor and Fifty-eight others at Lancaster* ... (Manchester: Abel Heywood, 1843), pp. v–x.

4 Peel to Julia Peel, 20 August 1842, pr. George Peel (ed.), *The Private Letters of Sir Robert Peel* (London, John Murray, 1920), p. 203.

5 Nicholas C. Edsall, *Richard Cobden, Independent Radical* (Cambridge Mass., Harvard University Press, 1986), pp. 102–26; Donald Read, *Peel and the Victorians* (Oxford, Blackwell, 1987), p. 122.

6 Gash, *Sir Robert Peel*, p. 604.

7 Read, *Peel and the Victorians*, pp. 158–286; Gerald Jordan and Nicholas Rogers, 'Admirals as heroes: patriotism and liberty in Hanoverian England', *Journal of British Studies*, 28 (1989), 211–24.

8 *Northern Star*, 6 July 1850, cited in Read, *Peel and the Victorians*, p. 277.

9 Philip Harling offers a similar reading of Peelism by provocatively restyling Peelite Conservatism 'Conservative Disinterestedness', *The Waning of 'Old Corruption': the Politics of Economical Reform in Britain, 1779–1846* (Oxford, Clarendon Press, 1996), pp. 228–54.

10 Cobden to Peel, 23 July 1846, pr. in Morley, *Cobden*, pp. 392–3.

11 Sir Robert Peel, *Address to the Electors of the Borough of Tamworth*, pr. *Speeches of the Right Honourable Sir Robert Peel, Bart. during his Administration, 1834–1835, etc.*, 2nd edn (London, Roake and Varty, 1835), p. 2.

12 Eric J. Evans, *Sir Robert Peel. Statesmanship, Power and Party* (London, Routledge, 1991), p. 37; Ian Newbould, 'Sir Robert Peel and the Conservative party 1832–41: a study in failure?' *English Historical Review*, xcviii (1983), 529–57.

13 *Speeches of Sir Robert Peel during his Administration 1834–35*, pp. 293–4. See also Dror Wahrman, *Imagining the Middle Class: the Political Representation of Class in Britain, c. 1780–1840* (Cambridge, Cambridge University Press, 1995), pp. 341–3.

14 *Speeches of Sir Robert Peel during his Administration 1834–35*, p. 8.

15 Peel to Lord Ashburton, 18 October 1841, pr. in Charles Stuart Parker (ed.), *Sir Robert Peel from his Private Papers*, 2nd edn, 3 vols (London, John Murray, 1899), ii 500.

16 *Ibid.*, p. 499.

17 Sir Stafford H. Northcote, *Twenty Years of Financial Policy* (London, Saunders Otley, 1862), pp. 1–47; Sydney Buxton, *Finance and Politics; a Historical Study. 1783–1885*, 2 vols (London, John Murray, 1888), i. 43–58.

18 Peel to Croker, 3 August 1842, pr. Parker, *Peel*, ii. 530.

19 Read, *Peel and the Victorians*, pp. 25–6, 65, 95, 247–8, 313.

20 Peel to Croker, 27 July 1842, pr. Parker, *Peel*, ii. 529.

21 *Hansard*, 3rd Ser., lxi (1842), col. 439.

22 *Ibid.*, col. 434.

23 The politics of Peel's 1842 budget were carefully calibrated, repudiating 'old corruption', Whig fiscal incoherence and consumptionist critiques of indirect taxation. Harling, *Waning of 'Old Corruption'*, pp. 240–8.

24 Boyd Hilton *Corn, Cash, Commerce: the Economic Policies of Tory Governments, 1815–30* (Oxford, Oxford University Press, 1977), pp. 171–302; Alexander Brady, *William Huskisson and Liberal Reform* (Oxford, Oxford University Press, 1928).

25 In these and other ways the development of Peel's economic and fiscal thinking between the 1820s and the 1840s was more profound than Boyd Hilton implies in his important 'Peel: a reappraisal', *Historical Journal*, 22 (1979), 585–614.

26 For the crucial section of the Chartist petition see R. C. Gammage, *History of the Chartist Movement, 1837–54*, new edn (London, Merlin Press, 1969), pp. 87–9.

27 Buxton, *Finance and Politics*, i. 40–2.

28 Cited in Read, *Peel and the Victorians*, p. 172.

29 Peel to Ripon, 19 October 1841, pr. Parker, *Peel*, ii. 497.

30 Peel to Arbuthnot, pr. Parker, *Peel*, ii, 532.

31 Brian Jenkins, *Henry Goulburn, 1784–1856: a Political Biography* (Liverpool, Liverpool University Press, 1996), pp. 320–4; Cormac Ó'Gráda, *Ireland before and after the Famine. Explorations in Economic History, 1800–1925*, new edn (Manchester and New York, Manchester University Press, 1993).

32 *Hansard*, lxi (1842), col. 445.

33 *Ibid.*, cols 445–7.

34 Cobden to Peel, 23 June 1846, pr. Morley, *Cobden*, p. 395.

35 Peel to Cobden, 24 June 1846, pr. Morley, *Cobden*, p. 400.

36 Peel to John Hope, 3 August 1846, pr. Peel, *Private Letters of Peel*, p. 282.

37 Printed in M. Guizot, *Memoirs of Sir Robert Peel* (London, Bentley, 1857), pp. 295–6.

38 *Hansard*, lxi (1842), cols 464–5.

39 *Ibid.*, col. 465.

40 Benedict Anderson, *Imagined Communities: Reflections on the Origin and Spread of Nationalism*, rev. edn (London and New York, Verso, 1991), pp. 90–5.

41 *Hansard*, 3rd Ser., lxxvii (1845), cols 464–5.

42 *Hansard*, 3rd Ser., lxi (1842), cols 428–9.

43 Boyd Hilton, 'The ripening of Robert Peel', in M. Bentley (ed.), *Public and Private Doctrine:*

*Essays in British History presented to Maurice Cowling* (Cambridge, Cambridge University Press, 1993), pp. 63–84.

44 Donal A. Kerr, *Peel, Priests and Politics: Sir Robert Peel's Administration and the Roman Catholic Church in Ireland, 1841–46* (Oxford, Clarendon Press, 1982).

45 *Speeches of Sir Robert Peel during his Administration, 1834–35*, p. 6.

46 *Ibid.*, p. 150; Jenkins, *Henry Goulburn*, pp. 257–62.

47 G. I. T. Machin, *Politics and the Churches in Great Britain, 1832–68* (Oxford, Oxford University Press, 1977), pp. 165–6, 188.

48 Norman Gash, *Reaction and Reconstruction in English Politics, 1832–52* (Oxford, Clarendon Press, 1965), pp. 90–1; Gash, *Sir Robert Peel*, pp. 383–4.

49 Cited in Read, *Peel and the Victorians*, p. 138.

50 Kerr, *Peel, Priests and Politics*, pp. 290–351.

51 Gearoid Ó Tuathaigh, *Ireland before the Famine, 1798–1848* (Dublin, Gill and Macmillan, 1972), pp. 208–13.

52 Angus Macintyre, *The Liberator: Daniel O'Connell and the Irish Party, 1830–47* (London, Hamish Hamilton, 1965), pp. 262–80; Oliver MacDonagh, *O'Connell: the Life of Daniel O'Connell, 1775–1847* (London, Weidenfeld and Nicolson, 1991), pp. 138–42, 570–1, 599.

## Acknowledgement

My conceptions of Peel were shaped by Angus Macintyre, who taught me the Peel special subject at Oxford. Later we taught that special subject together in seminars which were an unalloyed pleasure. This chapter would have gained immeasurably from Angus's advice, and his not having been able to read it is an ineffable sadness. I hope he would have enjoyed it.

# 3

# Disraeli, English culture, and the decline of the industrial spirit

## BOYD HILTON

There is a familiar version of nineteenth-century British political history which runs something like this. The Great Reform Act of 1832 created a discontinuity and brought the *ancien régime* or 'long eighteenth century' to a close. Peel was the first politician to pick up the new pieces. His 'Register! Register!' speech was a recognition of the electoral opportunities open to parties which organised, while the Tamworth Manifesto (1834) signalled his attempt to turn old Toryism into a new Conservatism which would be pragmatic, adaptable and capable of assimilating the 'professional, mercantile and industrial middle classes'[1] into the party of the landed interest. His policy triumphed in the 1841 election, which was followed by a second administration in which Peel did more to stabilise and encourage the business community than any of his predecessors. The Conservative party seemed set to re-establish itself as the natural party of government, and would probably have done so had not a spitefully ambitious Disraeli fomented division over the increased grant to Maynooth College in 1845, and then – abetted by the honourable but stupid Bentinck – forced a split over the repeal of the Corn Laws in 1846.[2] The Peelite free traders and free marketeers left the Conservative party – many of them permanently – while the mainly back-bench rump of protectionists and paternalists retained the title but went into almost perpetual opposition for more than twenty years. The party revived from the 1870s onwards, first under Disraeli and then under Salisbury, but it did so – according to this interpretation – only by ditching the old Disraelian policies and by following a 'neo-Peelite' policy based on individualism, classical political economy and appeal to the middle classes. 'It was Peel's Liberal-Conservatism, drawing in the bourgeoisie, not Disraeli's faded popular Toryism, looking to the masses, that was to be the basis of its adaptation to social change.'[3] It follows from all this that Peel's 'place as the founder of modern Conservatism is unchallengeable',[4] even though there was a hiatus of about forty years between the culmination of his own career in 1846 and the fulfilment of his aspirations for the party.

Against this interpretation it may be argued that neither the Great Reform Act nor Tamworth marked much of a discontinuity, and that the bones of political contention remained broadly the same after 1832 as they had been before – the same, indeed, as they had been since the 1780s, when Pitt first established a governing alliance between executive-minded politicians like himself and a majority of the mainly landed back-bench MPs. It is certainly true that after 1832 Peel sought to distance himself from the more rabidly Ultra Tory of these MPs, but then so had his predecessors Wellington, Canning, Liverpool and Perceval. The suggestion that Peel reorientated his party towards the middle classes in the 1830s fails to take account of the fact that a large portion of what might be called the *upper* middle class – bankers, rich merchants, fee-earners and the salariat – had always tended to support the Pittites or Conservatives rather than the opposition Whig party. As for what might be called the *lesser* and frequently Dissenting middle class – industrialists, retailers, the shopocracy – these were the £10 occupiers who gained the borough vote in 1832 and whom Peel had dismissed as a 'vulgar, privileged pedlary'.[5] No party leader actively discourages support from any quarter, but it is most unlikely that Peel went out of his way to rebuild the Conservatives on the support of these lesser middle classes, and even if he did it can be said categorically that he failed, since it is now established that the 1841 election was won in the counties and small boroughs on an Ultra programme of defending agriculture and the Church of England.[6] Such being the case, the schism which resulted from the Maynooth grant and then Corn Law repeal cannot simply be blamed on Disraelian high politics, but was normative in the sense that it sliced along the lines of an internal party tension which had existed since the 1820s. As Ian Newbould has written, 'Peel's parliamentary defeat in 1846 was only the final signal that what he represented had been similarly defeated in 1841.'[7]

Then again, while the Conservative party was certainly on the back foot from 1846 to 1874, it is not so clear that Disraeli manoeuvred it back towards a Peelite position or that its subsequent revival was based on 'neo-Peelite' policies. The case for seeing the later Disraeli as a 'neo-Peelite' rests on his acceptance of free trade and the gold standard, and it is certainly true that, having given up protection as a lost cause, he never challenged these tenets of Peel's and Gladstone's political economy. However, since free trade and the gold standard were uncontentious issues during the great mid-Victorian boom of 1850–73, Disraeli's acquiescence was not all that significant. Much more controversial now were issues of public spending (especially on social welfare) and the level and incidence of taxation, and here it could be argued that Disraeli continued to oppose Peelite–Gladstonian orthodoxy. Peter Ghosh has conducted a carefully balanced investigation of the similarities and differences between the strategies forged by Disraeli and Gladstone in response to the post-Crimean War financial crisis of 1857–62, and it seems clear from this that the two strategies were fundamentally antithetical. Of course Disraeli did not approve of taxing and spending for their own sake, and of course he appreciated the need for financial equilibrium, but unlike Gladstone in this period he had no wish to make a transfer from indirect to direct taxation, and unlike Gladstone he believed in the doctrine (Ghosh even calls it his 'leading idea') that 'expenditure depends on policy'.[8] Not only should Treasury considerations not be allowed to hamper the conduct of military operations, not only should wartime spending not be compensated for by a squeeze on social spending ('an expenditure arising out of the natural development of the country'),[9] but also, as

Ghosh puts it, 'economy need not be sought for its own sake in peacetime'. No wonder Gladstone exploded! Finally it should be pointed out that in raising money privately for the purchase of Suez Canal shares, instead of negotiating openly through Parliament or a parliamentary commission, Disraeli signalled a defiant throwback to the 'closet and backstairs' methods of Castlereagh and Vansittart, in reaction against which the 'liberal' financial tradition of Huskisson, Peel and Gladstone had been forged in the first place. It was particularly fitting that this secret deal should have been negotiated through Lionel Rothschild, eldest son of N. M. Rothschild, Huskisson's old *bête noire*.

As for the Conservative revival after 1870 being based on Peelite principles, it seems far more likely that the shift of middle-class business and industrial opinion towards the Tories in the later nineteenth century was due to the growth of distinctly un-Peelite sentiments in favour of imperialism, 'fair trade' and bimetallism. Ewan Green, for example, has argued that these policies created a 'producers' alliance' between agriculturists and manufacturers,[10] so, although tariff reform split the party for a decade after 1903, it probably benefited the Conservatives in the longer term.

In reality Peel's policies were adopted not by Disraeli but by the Gladstonian Liberal party, so much so that it would have struck Salisbury or Balfour as eccentric to describe Peel, the two-time turncoat, as a founding father of Conservatism. It was only with the decline of the Liberal party following the First World War, and the migration of economic liberalism into the Conservative party, that moral and economic individualism became core Conservative values. After Thatcher it *can* plausibly be claimed that Peel was indeed the 'founder of modern Conservatism', but the hiatus has been more like 140 years than forty.

This second version of nineteenth-century politics puts Peel in his place, but does it also entail a more positive view of Disraeli's contribution? There is no point in trying to revive the old myth of 'Tory democracy'[11] or to subscribe to the recent myth of 'one-nation Toryism'. Indeed, there seems little to dispute in the account of Disraelian politics developed by Paul Smith and Lord Blake some thirty years ago. One would have to be incurably romantic to suppose that, in pressing the Reform Bill of 1867, Disraeli did not have party political considerations mainly in mind. Whereas Russell's and Gladstone's Bill of the previous year would have given the Liberals 'control of the boroughs for half-a-dozen years to come',[12] Disraeli's Bill sought to consolidate Conservative strength in the counties by a favourable redistribution of seats and by sucking the urban 40s freeholders out from the county electorate and into the boroughs.[13] The Ministry of 1874–80 brought in a creditable sheaf of social reforms, but they were cautious, consensual, permissive rather than compulsory, and framed with an eye to middle-class sensitivities regarding taxes and rates. Except for the trade union legislation, moreover, Disraeli did not take a great deal of personal interest in them. He did put his back into defending the Establishment, claiming in 1861 that 'the maintenance of the Church is the great question of the age'.[14] He was prominent in the Church Defence Associations from 1857 onwards and took a serious interest in such policies as concurrent endowment and public worship regulation.[15] Finally, and most famously, he 'donned the Palmerstonian mantle' and successfully identified the Conservatives rather than the Liberals as the patriotic and nationalist party. None of this was negligible, but it can hardly be said to amount to a Disraelian philosophy or social vision. As Paul Smith puts it, Disraeli was 'a detached and deeply sceptical man, who did not believe in much . . . The Disraelian version of Toryism was a strange mixture of insight and *opéra bouffe*'.[16]

Indeed, for many historians Disraeli's only really mammoth achievement was purely political – to have kept his party alive following the crisis of 1846. At the time there seemed every likelihood that the old Conservative party would disappear, not because of any elemental historical force but simply because the flow of Macaulayan rhetoric, together with Peel- and Russell-inspired executive expectations, seemed likely to prove self-fulfilling. It represented a narrow sectional interest, and with protection gone it had little *raison d'être*. Despite some recent attempts by historians to winkle out spots of intellect on the Conservative benches, it remains true to describe the party as a collection of booby squires, who valued Westminster simply because it was 'the best club in the land', and who for much of the time found very little fault with Palmerston's Low Church, patriotic policies.[17] It was still a large party (227 MPs in 1847, 299 in 1852, 260 in 1857, 306 in 1859 and 288 in 1865) but it contained hardly any members of front-bench calibre (justifying Wellington's 'Who? Who?' jibe of 1852) and few who took a serious interest in the sort of governmental concerns discussed at the Social Science Association, for example. It cannot even be seen as hungry for office, since, as Lord Blake has pointed out, its leader, Derby, lost five general elections in a row without any attempt being made to unseat him. Disraeli alone, it has been argued, kept these rags, tags and bobtails going,[18] not because he had any clear vision of what he thought the party stood for, not even because he was all that ambitious for office himself (if ambition means being single-minded in the pursuit of it), but simply because he saw the party as an extension of his own personality and needed it as much as it needed him. Lord Blake has shown how he saw politics as warfare, in which oppositions should constantly 'oppose' whatever governments did, right or wrong. A. J. P. Taylor has suggested that he saw politics as a great game, a succession of cabals, intrigues and betrayals. 'The field always prefers a huntsman who halloos them on,' said Taylor,[19] and Disraeli – though never completely trusted and not always liked by his followers – kept their expectation of a kill constantly alive, all through the years of Palmerston's ascendancy and Gladstone's prime, when a more realistic party leader might well have given up. It was a heroic personal effort, but it was also purposeless in that, when he finally achieved something like real power in 1874, he quickly lost interest and took himself off to the Lords.

So was Disraeli merely a supreme party tactitian? The few attempts which have been made to turn him into something more have naturally focused on the politics of 'Young England', which Disraeli had indulged in during his anti-Peel days. It is probable that Disraeli did not take 'Young England' very seriously. Historians should do so, however, since the ideals which it espoused – including decentralisation, welfare for the poor, feudalism, 'back to the land', back to guilds and apprenticeships, hatred of industrialisation and all other forms of modernity – such ideals were very widely shared in the years after 1832, and intensified during the terrible depression and social unrest of 1837–43, as David Roberts and Alice Chandler have shown.[20] The Oxford Movement's *Tracts for the Times* (1834–41), Oastler's northern philippics (1830–39), Dansey's *Horae Decanicae Rurales* (1835), Pugin's *Contrasts* (1836), Gladstone's *The State in its Relations with the Church* (1838), Carlyle's *Chartism* (1839) – for all these authors the implicit or explicit enemies were liberalism, individualism, utilitarianism, political economy and bureaucratic centralism. Pugin's call for a return to the middle English pointed style as the template for urban regeneration matched Dansey's 900 page investigation of medieval ecclesiastical lore in 'heavy, archaic, gothic typeface'.[21] Indeed, so much social criticism took this form that one could easily suppose that High Tory romanticism was in the mainstream, except of course that it is those who feel they are swimming against the tide of opinion who tend to publish most furiously. Assuredly it was a minority position, but it was in deadly earnest for all that.

At first sight this early Victorian paternalism seems to have found an echo in the subsequent 'merrie England' yearnings of Ruskin, Morris, the Pre-Raphaelite Brotherhood and Headlam's Guild Socialists. Two differences, however, are crucial. Not only were these later Victorian medievalists arguing from a left-wing perspective but their approach was essentially nostalgic. They appealed to the Middle Ages as symbolising an ideal with which to reproach the materialism of the present, but unlike the earlier medievalists they were not truly *political* because they did not seriously suppose that it might actually be possible to go backwards into the past. And they did not suppose it to be possible because something had happened between the 1840s and the later Victorian period to change the way in which the British nation felt about itself. Although towns and cities had been developing at a frightening pace for the previous half-century, it was only during the 1850s that Britain became mentally urbanised in the sense that economic growth – and therefore, by implication, the growth of towns – came to seem natural, normative and therefore irreversible. There are many reasons for this development and they can be sketched only lightly here. First, the sudden easing of social tensions after 1848 made the need to reverse the industrial revolution seem less imperative. At the same time various constraints which had operated to make economic growth seem hazardous (at best) were suddenly removed. In particular the widespread Malthusian fears over food supply and famine were dissipated during the 1850s, and it came to be supposed once again, as it had been in the eighteenth century, that large families and a youthful population were conducive to the happiness of States. Moreover, the fact that other countries were now perceived to be catching Britain up made growth itself seem not only natural but even essential if the acknowledged 'workshop of the world' were not to fall behind in the race. The 1851 census, showing that for the first time a majority of British people lived in towns, had a considerable psychological impact, as did the Great Exhibition in the same year, and the fact that the 1850s were the greatest decade of railway building. It was then also that the great industrial cities began to aspire to civic grandeur in Greek, Gothic and Italian Renaissance dress. Then that novels invariably adopted an urban setting as the natural habitat for the development of human personality and relationships.[22] Then that a linear sense of time passing replaced a previous assumption that time moves in cycles, a subconscious intellectual shift which made it impossible to conceive of a regression to some pre-industrial past. Finally there was the repeal of the Corn Laws. They had given a practical cast to the policies of 'Young England' because they were instruments for keeping capital in agriculture against the dictates of the market, but once the Corn Laws had been truly 'dead and damned' there was a fatalistic sense of inevitability about the onward progress of industrialisation.

Because Disraeli lived through this change in the national psyche he left behind him that aspect of 'Young England' which envisaged a reversion to the Middle Ages. But it would be wrong to think that he also abandoned what might be called its communitarian and paternalist aspects, or that he succumbed to a Peelite or market-based political economy. Since it has too often been assumed that any links between Disraeli the 'Young Englander' and Disraeli the Prime Minister must lie in the area of social reform, his timidity in legislating on education, public health and housing during the second administration has been taken as evidence that such links could not have been very strong. This is misleading, however, since (as Angus Macintyre argued) 'Young England's' paternalism was never about legislative social reform in a positive sense (as distinct from negative legislation to control the maximum number of hours worked by factory women and children), and it was certainly not about *dirigiste* centralisation.[23] Indeed, from the moment he entered the Commons Disraeli attacked the Whigs' 'cheap and centralised government' – over the New Poor Law, for example – and proclaimed instead the true Tory 'principle of opposing everything like central government' and favouring 'in every possible degree the distribution of power'.[24] The essence of 'Young England's' paternalism was not intervention but a belief in vertical personal relations, in mutual obligation and loyalty, in control and dependence – in short, 'the regeneration of aristocratic leadership'[25] – and Disraeli's instincts remained paternalist in that sense to the end. What did change was that after the 1850s he could no longer conceive of Britain as a collection of landed estates, where the rich walked around patting the poor on the head and giving them the price of a cup of tea. A large, anonymous, mass society required a more corporate style of paternalism, and Disraeli was perceptive enough to see that this was possible – indeed, that the trappings of public life could be exploited to create a sense of communal uplift and social cohesion.

As a result of the Thatcher years historians have become more sensitive to the importance of image in fashioning political appeal, and they have therefore become more appreciative of Disraeli, who was probably the first Prime Minister to strive for what is now called a 'feel-good factor'. And although he did not (as nowadays) define the latter in economic or material terms, he would probably not have succeeded as well as he did during his brief moment of *sursum* in the early 1870s if the fruits of the mid-Victorian boom were not still being widely diffused.[26] The enlargement of the electorate in 1867 had placed a greater psychological distance between the voters and Westminster, which began as a result to enjoy the glamour and fame now accorded to the worlds of media and entertainment. Instinctively Disraeli saw that this opened up opportunities for a politics of slogan and gesture. By purchasing shares in the Suez Canal he traded on the mystique of the City. By proclaiming the Queen Empress of India he glorified monarchy. By cutting a dash at the Congress of Berlin he pandered to residual anti-Europeanism. And by developing a rhetoric of patriotism, Protestantism and social welfare he touched chords with an enlarged and less discriminating electorate.

It was on these lines that in 1867 Disraeli explained his decision to admit a 'larger number' of working men to the borough franchise than merely the £7 householders favoured by Russell and Gladstone in their Bill of 1866.

> I think that the danger would be less, that the feeling of the larger number would be more national, than by only admitting what I call the Praetorian guard, a sort of class set aside, invested with peculiar privileges, looking with suspicion on their superiors, and with disdain on those beneath them, and with no friendly feelings towards the institutions of their country and with great confidence in themselves. I think you would have a better chance of touching the popular heart, of evoking the national sentiment, by embracing the great body of those men who occupy houses and who fulfil the duties of citizenship by the payment of rates, than by the more limited and in our opinion, more dangerous proposal.[27]

Obviously Disraeli hoped to exploit the resentment of the manual (and, as it were, 'rough') workers against the £7 householders – those typically skilled, upwardly striving, teetotal, sabbatarian, Nonconformist 'Little England' artisans, all of whom were expected to support the Liberal party in the 1860s. In describing the English working class as 'brave, good-natured, and true' he was not merely teasing Gladstone (who would have preferred words like 'frugal', 'hard-working' and 'respectable') but tapping in to the tradition of John Bull,[28] Jolly Jack Tar, 'roast beef and plum pudding'. It was a bucolic vision of the people, owing something to Cobbett but adapted to urban conditions, and prefigured in *Sybil* (1845). Disraeli had no time for Gladstone's description of the franchise as a 'lever of elevation'. In proposing to fix it at £7 Gladstone envisaged it as dangling just above the heads of most artisans, and encouraging them to save that little bit extra in order to occupy the superior dwelling which would bring with it the rewards of full citizenship. Then, as their neighbours were witness to the event, so they would strive likewise for the same reward. Now this was exactly the type of mechanistic, individualistic, competitive and ultra-respectable society which Disraeli loathed. Far better to trust to the 'larger number' who – while far from being the itinerant residuum – could be mobilised against the go-getting do-gooders. Paradoxically, both Gladstone and Disraeli might have taken opposite sides in 1867 if they could have foreseen the gradual movement of the middle classes – and therefore of those superior artisans aspiring to be middle-class – towards the Conservative party. When Salisbury made his famous statement about the potentialities for 'villa Toryism' in 1882 he was referring precisely to that 'Praetorian guard' whom Disraeli had sniffed at fifteen years earlier.

A similar mixture of principle and tactical adroitness applies to his government's decision to legalise peaceful picketing in 1875. The passage of the Second Reform Act had set up a competition for the votes of craft workers, and this political fact probably counted for more than any ideological presuppositions about trade unions. Recent research has established that, contrary to myth, the intentions behind Disraeli's legislation were not greatly different from those which lay behind the Liberal government's labour legislation of 1871.[29] Nevertheless, and most important, Disraeli was able to accommodate the policy rhetorically far more easily than Gladstone. When he said in 1867 that 'the rights of labour have been to me always as sacred as the rights of property' he may (or may not) have been talking humbug, but if it was humbug it was precisely the same humbug that he had spoken in response to the Chartist petition in July 1839.[30] Trade unions posed a theoretical dilemma for Gladstonian Liberals by showing up the contradictions between their notions of political and economic freedom. They believed that workers should be free to associate *individually* in whatever way they wished, while at the same time opposing the right to act *collectively* in restraint of trade. Disraeli, on the other hand, genuinely preferred that craft workers should improve their pay and conditions in association rather than that each should bargain with his boss to find his own personal rung on the wage ladder. Disraeli was a *collectivist* in the nineteenth-century sense of the word – that is, before it acquired its connotations of State authority – and used the consciously Burkean rhetoric of 'little platoons' to counteract the liberal notion that individuals should plug into the market, itself protected by a minimal but *centralised* State. In that sense it is not improper that so many historians should have given him and not Gladstone the 'credit' for the labour legislation of the 1870s.

Parliamentary reform and labour legislation were important because later Victorian Conservatism undoubtedly appealed to significant sections of the working class. Martin Pugh has shown how the Primrose League (founded 1883, 1 million members by 1891) consciously updated eighteenth-century 'roast beef and plum pudding' rhetoric into 'football, beer, and skittles'. Patrick Joyce has analysed the practical operation of urban paternalism in industrial Lancashire. Jon Lawrence's investigation of the Conservative appeal to women has demonstrated how the party was able to exploit the current and conventional notion of 'separate spheres' to turn both masculine and feminine discourses to its advantage (the empire reinforcing house and home, and vice versa).[31] All this recent research modifies the interpretation established by Paul Smith and Robert Blake, but it does not overturn their central contention, which was that the Conservatives' conquest of urban England (the party owed half its strength in the Commons to urban constituencies in 1885)[32] was based mainly on its growing support among the *middle* rather than the *working* class.

So did Disraeli welcome the assimilation of the middle classes into the Conservative party? It is not easy to answer this question because his rhetoric was honed in a period when the 'middle class' was split up into many different sub-groups. For example, when he said that 'the rights of labour' were 'as sacred as the rights of property', he may seem to have been disparaging employers, and undoubtedly he did oppose those – usually thought to be the small ones – who ground the faces of the poor. However, he did not take the Marxist view that workers were generically pitted against their employers, but held to an older radical tradition which saw the threat to both working men and their employers as coming from finance capitalism – in other words, from those *upper* middle classes whom Peel had pandered to. Disraeli was the opposite of Peel, praising the entrepreneurial and industrial middle class but disliking the upper bourgeoisie. Entrepreneurs, like landowners and labourers, had a stake in the country as well as the opportunity to be model employers, whereas merchants, financiers and *rentiers* were citizens of the world, caring not which country they enriched so long as they enriched themselves. Angus Macintyre pointed out with his typical acuteness that the idea of the '*moral economy* of manufactures', a phrase used by the French observer Léon Faucher to describe Greg and Co.'s kindly management of their factory at Quarry Bank, 'was in the same order of things as the Duke of Richmond's active autocracy and the Earl of Chichester's search for "God's moral economy" on his estates in Sussex'.[33] Masters *and* men were stakeholders in a way that the liberal plutocracy and the radical shopocracy were not. So when Disraeli said that 'the Conservative Party is a national party or it is nothing' he did not so much mean that it should embrace *all* parts of the community in some overarching way as that it should exclude *un*national types like Cobdenites, cosmopolitans and liberal intellectuals. As Avner Offer has shown, he would have liked to have introduced a system of central grants in aid of rates, in order to transfer the burden of taxation from 'the owners of real property', whether they were rural landlords or urban entrepreneurs, and on to those whose wealth derived from interest, fees, salaries or sales.[34] In Offer's words, Disraeli sought to demonstrate a community of interest between country and city, and also 'to separate the shopkeeper and house-capitalist from the mill-owner and merchant, thus isolating the urban patriciate within its own bastions'.

The tendency of the business and professional middle classes to gravitate towards the Conservatives in the decades after 1870[35] could be seen as a natural response to the slowly developing polarisation of society between capital and labour, and as an anticipation of the twentieth century's 'strange death of Liberal England'. To the extent that that is what it was, Disraeli can hardly be said to have contributed to the process – indeed, his rhetorical gestures to the working classes may even be thought to have hindered it. It may be significant, however, that most social commentators in the 1860s, while they foresaw the rise of 'class' politics, did not expect the Conservatives to displace the Liberals, for they regarded it as axiomatic that 'manufacturing and commercial populations are always the leaders on the side of progress' (i.e. 'liberalism').[36] J. S. Mill, Matthew Arnold,

A. V. Dicey, Leslie Stephen, Goldwin Smith, James Bryce, Frederic Harrison, Thorold Rogers and G. O. Trevelyan all anticipated (with varying degrees of apprehension) the growing power of the trade unions and the demands of working men for a fairer share of the national cake. That is to say, they foresaw the rise of a party of labour, even though they did not know that it would be called the Labour party. They perceived that Britain was moving beyond the stage of vertical politics (town versus country, land versus industry, Protestant versus Catholic, Church versus Dissent) and into the age of horizontal politics (the masses versus the classes, religion versus unbelief). And they inferred from this that all those with wealth – be it landed property, stocks and shares, industrial and business profits or high salaries – would need to come together politically to protect it against confiscation by the masses. In John Morley's famous phrase, 'an extreme advanced party' constituting 'brains and numbers' would lead the attack against all the forces of 'wealth, rank, vested interest, posssession in short'.[37]

Some historians would argue that it is premature to trace the onset of class politics to 1867, and that 'vertical' politics – in particular religious issues – remained resilient. Nevertheless, most pundits in the 1860s seem to have thought that class antagonism was imminent, and, broadly speaking, they were proved correct in so far as the rhetoric of politics did come to be polarised around the theme of capital versus labour during the course of the next sixty years. But if one had asked them what the future held in terms of party politics, it is extremely unlikely that any of them would have predicted the decline of the Liberals, who still seemed to be the natural party of government. The all-important question facing contemporaries was: would politics shift to the 'right' or to the 'left'? If the Liberals developed into 'New Liberals' or Radicals by embracing the interests of the working classes, then there would still be room for a Conservative party, and one more broadly based than the old Tory party had been. But if the Liberals remained true to Gladstone's *laissez-faire* economics, then the radicals would be likely to form a new party of labour and the Liberals to become the party of resistance. In such an event it was expected that the Liberal party would absorb the remnants of the old protectionist Tory party, that the booby squires would gradually drop out of politics while serious Conservatives like R. A. Cross and John Pakington would quietly cross over to the Liberal party.

In fact, of course, the opposite happened, and it was the Conservative party, not the Liberals, who were eventually left to fight the cause of the propertied classes against Labour. In considering why things took this unexpected turn, historians can take either a 'top-down' or a 'bottom-up' perspective. That is to say, they can look either to political events or to underlying social and cultural mentalities. The two types of explanation are not necessarily incompatible but they are drastically different. In politics everything is contingent, outcomes turn on accidents of personality and coincidence, and the unexpected often happens. Mentalities, however, like ocean-going liners, turn round with difficulty, and any unexpected change of direction usually needs to be explained in terms of long-term social and cultural developments.

The most interesting explanation from a 'bottom-up' perspective is to be found in Harold Perkin's essay in cultural Marxism, *The Origins of Modern English Society*. Perkin argues convincingly that the 'entrepreneurial ideal' had swept all before it during the first half of the nineteenth century as it ground the older 'aristocratic ideal' under its foot.[38] Its values were mainly those of religious Dissent, self-help, technology and science, and it was espoused especially by the industrial and provincial middle classes. Aristocrats scuttled before this ideal as it struck successive blows – the Great Reform Act, the Anti-Corn Law League and repeal, the Administrative Reform Association's attack on Crimean War bungling, civil service examinations, the abolition of the purchase of military commissions, and so on. This entrepreneurial ideal, which won the battle for 'the prevailing system of morality' during the mid-nineteenth century, clearly connects with that 'urban vision' which, it was suggested, overtook the country during the 1850s. Indeed, it could be said that for about four decades (1846–86), which were also the decades of the Liberal party's domination of politics, provincial, Dissenting, industrial values were in the ascendant. Most of the great civic and ecclesiastical buildings during that period went up outside London, where there was no architect with the flair and assurance to match Manchester's three 'Ws', Walters, Worthington and Waterhouse. Birmingham and Leeds staged the country's most important music festivals, the Liverpool Philharmonic Orchestra (founded in 1840) and Manchester's Hallé (1858) developed a high culture that was also populist, and these same four cities gobbled up much of the best pre-Raphaelite paintings. During the relatively brief period of the Liberal party's heyday, in other words, it might be said without exaggeration that it was actually *chic* to be provincial. This was in sharp contrast to the way in which the metropolis had dominated national life culturally and architecturally in the earlier decades of the century and would do so again as the 'mother of empire' in the late Victorian and Edwardian periods.

Perkin's story has a sting in the tail. 'By mid-century,' he writes, 'the entrepreneurial class could feel well pleased with the new society which they had created and persuaded the other classes to accept.'[39] However, the subsequent absorption of this new aristocracy of business into county society proved to be 'at once the apotheosis of entrepreneurial society and its demise'.

> From one point of view it celebrated the fulfilment of the entrepreneur's ambition, to be accepted at his own valuation as the natural leader of society and the equal of the landed aristocrats. But from another it marked his transformation into something different, the harbinger of the plutocracy and big business men and great landowners in late Victorian and Edwardian England, in which the old virile, ascetic and radical ideal of active capital was submerged in the still older, supine, hedonistic and conservative ideal of passive property. In a word, the entrepreneurial ideal had triumphed only to throw in its lot with the seemingly defeated aristocratic ideal. This belated capitulation … goes far to explain why Britain, the first to experience the Industrial Revolution, should remain the most traditional and aristocratic of industrialized societies.[40]

Perkin's analysis paved the way for a number of later studies which sought to explain British economic decline in terms of cultural values, the most famous (or notorious) being Martin Wiener's *English Culture and the Decline of the Industrial Spirit* (1981). Leaving the causes of economic decline to one side, it is fairly apparent that culturally the entrepreneurial ideal did go into retreat during the later decades of the nineteenth century. Now it may be (as Perkin seems to suggest) that the seductiveness of the aristocratic ideal had been dimly apparent to entrepreneurs all along, even as they railed against it. That would lessen the element of discontinuity. Again it may be that, whenever a rising class becomes the possessing class, it thereby becomes a conservative one, with a small 'c'. More specifically it may be that particular social developments after 1870 – such as the lure of government and imperial service, or the rapid growth of public schooling for the sons of industrialists and tradesmen – simply readjusted the outlook of a whole generation of the provincial bourgeoisie. Whatever the reasons for the shift, and they cannot be entered into here, it is not difficult to see how it may have made the Conservative party's values seem more attractive to these electors, and this in turn may explain why it and not the Liberal party survived the transition to democratic politics.

On the other hand, it is at least as plausible to explain the Conservatives' success in political terms. Geoffrey Searle has offered a number of mainly political reasons why 'entrepreneurial politics', as espoused by northern industrialists, never developed into a serious force despite its apparent triumph over the repeal of the Corn Laws. For example, its leaders were either ambivalent about entrepreneurial values (Cobden, Bright) or else were bourgeois revisionists and permeationists (Morley, Wilson, Foster, Goschen). Potential allies were more consumer- than producer-orientated (Lowe, Gladstone). The survival of vertical (and especially denominational) antagonisms prevented the expected emergence of a business *class* in politics, and provincial rivalries prevented the formation of a unified urban political culture. Above all, Palmerston got in the way.[41] After that, it could be said, Gladstone made a hash of things, alienating the more conservative (or whiggish) elements among the Liberal coalition with his increasingly wayward impulses, his apparent neglect of the need to safeguard trade routes to the East, his second government's interference with business interests by means of workmen's compensation and railway rates,[42] and above all his sudden *démarche* on Home Rule. (Many historians would argue that the late nineteenth-century Conservative revival was based mainly on Unionism.) Add to this that the Tories organised better and seemed more likely to respond to growing business pressure for fair trade, while the Liberals split disastrously during the First World War, and a political explanation seems fairly compelling.

The point about all such political explanations, as stated above, is that they are essentially contingent – for example, if Gladstone's personality had been different, or if he had not attempted Home Rule, then the Liberal party might never have succumbed to the Conservatives. Even so, the mere fact that the Conservatives beat the Liberals over the long run and not vice versa may in turn have had profound social and cultural effects, because it meant that the

Conservative party's favoured institutions – the monarchy, the Church of England, the Lords, Lord's cricket ground, the empire, the public schools, the ancient universities, the shires, the City – became the main components of a power system whose values seem to have trickled down far more efficiently than any wealth the system may have created. The Church of England has probably exercised a wider influence on the value system of 'middle England' than it did in the nineteenth century, despite a drop in the number of communicants. As for the public schools, which held such a powerful place in popular (and especially middle-class) culture, much ingenious research has gone into showing that they cannot in general be accused of having directly fostered an anti-scientific or anti-competitive ethos in their pupils.[43] However, this research rather misses the point, since the cultural impact of the public schools was felt mainly by those who did not themselves attend them, and it is here in the general culture that their allegedly 'gentlemanly' and anti-entrepreneurial values were most influential. So if it is true that a 'dominant value system' permeates societies at large, thereby reinforcing the hegemony of institutions which spawned those values in the first place, then it may well be that the Conservative party's defeat of the Liberals was a cause rather than a consequence of the decline of that entrepreneurial spirit and provincial Nonconformist culture which had seemed to be ascendant in the early and mid-Victorian periods.

In a characteristically brilliant essay John Vincent has observed that the displacement of Liberals by Labour as the party of the left entailed 'the dropping of power as the central motive in popular politics'. Whereas Labour was prepared to work with the existing system of power and privilege, seeking only to improve the share of resources allotted to working people, Liberals had been moved to attack the system itself, since that was what had galvanised their supporters and provided them with 'emotional subsistence'.[44] To extend Vincent's argument, it is surely the case that if the Liberal party had survived, even as a party of the right, it would have continued to attack symbolic centres of power such as the hereditary peerage and the City, whereas Conservative governments (backed by the BBC) have subtly reinforced them. It is impossible to imagine, for example, a Liberal government doing what Wilson's Labour government did, that is, leaving such symbols of privilege as the public schools untouched while they destroyed the grammar schools as barriers to working-class equality.

It was predictable that the entrepreneurial classes, once they had attained a position of power and influence, should have ceased to be radical and have become defenders of the *status quo*, but it was not to be expected that they would also abandon their traditional values in favour of 'gentlemanly' ones. That they did so may well be explained by the fact that the Conservatives and not the Liberals became the party of the *status quo*, and that in turn may be explained by the many contingencies which shape political outcomes. If so, Disraeli should be accorded a more significant role than he is usually allowed. He did not look to the future and he had little sense of where the party was heading. But simply by defying the laws of political gravity, simply by keeping the Conservative party alive during the 1850s and 1860s, largely through the force of his personality and against all odds, he may have made an indelible mark on the development of British culture. It was in the 1870s and 1880s that all those with different types of wealth and property to protect began to come together politically against the masses. This meant that large sections of the two existing political parties had to join forces against Labour. As it happened (and it might well have happened otherwise) the Conservatve party displaced the Liberals from their position as the natural party of government, and gradually won the support of large elements of the manufacturing, commercial and retailing groups. But the Conservative party was able to do so only because it was still a going force in the 1870s and 1880s. Had it not been, the Liberals would have become the party of wealth and property by default, and the provincial-Dissenting-manufacturing value system described by Perkin might well have persisted. It may be that in this roundabout way 'Young England' succeeded after all. Maybe it is Disraeli who should be thanked for the decline of Britain's industrial spirit.

## Notes

1  N. Gash, *Sir Robert Peel: the Life of Sir Robert Peel after 1830* (London, Longman, 1972), pp. 235–7.

2  For a reappraisal and rehabilitation of Bentinck see Angus Macintyre, 'Lord George Bentinck and the protectionists: a lost cause?' *Transactions of the Royal Historical Society*, 5th Ser., 39 (1989), 141–65.

3  P. Smith, *Disraelian Conservatism and Social Reform* (London, Routledge, 1967), pp. 4, 29. See also Robert Blake, *Disraeli* (London, Eyre and Spottiswoode, 1966), p. 211.

4  Gash, *Sir Robert Peel*, p. 709.

5  Peel to Croker, 15 April 1831, *The Correspondence and Diaries of John Wilson Croker*, ed. by L. J. Jennings (London, John Murray, 1885), ii. 114–15.

6  Ian Newbould, *Whiggery and Reform, 1830–41* (Basingstoke, Macmillan, 1990), pp. 305–11, 320–1; John Wolffe, *The Protestant Crusade in Great Britain, 1829–1860* (Oxford, Clarendon Press, 1991), pp. 97–100.

7  Newbould, *Whiggery and Reform*, p. 321.

8  Peter Ghosh, 'Disraelian Conservatism: a financial approach', *English Historical Review*, 99 (1984), 268–96.

9  Disraeli in the House of Commons, 8 May 1862, *Hansard's Parliamentary Debates*, 3rd Ser. clxvi. 1408.

10  E. H. H. Green, *The Crisis of Conservatism: the Politics, Economics and Ideology of the British Conservative Party, 1880–1914* (London and New York, Routledge, 1995), pp. 4–11, 30–46.

11  As attempted in Gertrude Himmelfarb, 'The politics of democracy: the English Reform Act of 1867', *Journal of British Studies*, 6 (1966), 97–138.

12  Disraeli's comment as quoted in Stanley's diary, 30 April 1866, *Disraeli, Derby and the Conservative Party: the Political Journals of Lord Stanley, 1849–59* (Hassocks, Harvester Press, 1978), p. 250.

13  Likewise he had proposed banning the borough freeholders from county electorates in his Reform Bill of 1859.

14  Sarah Bradford, *Disraeli* (London, Weidenfeld and Nicolson, 1982), p. 254.

15  J. P. Parry, *Democracy and Religion: Gladstone and the Liberal Party 1867–1875* (Cambridge, Cambridge University Press, 1986) pp. 416–17; G. I. T. Machin, *Politics and the Churches in Great Britain, 1832 to 1868* (Oxford, Clarendon Press, 1977), pp. 316–19.

16 Smith, *Disraelian Conservatism*, pp. 12, 16.

17 P. M. Gurowich, 'The continuation of war by other means: party and politics, 1855–1865', *Historical Journal*, 27 (1984), 614–21.

18 This chapter does not discuss the relative roles of Derby and Disraeli in keeping Conservatism alive, though it should be said that attempts made periodically to talk Derby's contribution up have not been entirely convincing.

19 A. J. P. Taylor, *Essays in English History* (Harmondsworth, Penguin Books, 1976), p. 121.

20 David Roberts, *Paternalism in Early Victorian England* (London, Croom Helm, 1979); Alice Chandler, *A Dream of Order: the Medieval Ideal in Nineteenth-Century Literature* (London, Routledge, 1971).

21 R. Arthur Burns, 'A Hanoverian legacy? Diocesan reform in the Church of England *c.* 1800–33' in John Walsh, Colin Haydon and Stephen Taylor (eds), *The Church of England c. 1689–c. 1833: from Toleration to Tractarianism* (Cambridge, Cambridge University Press, 1993), p. 278.

22 Raymond Williams, *The English Novel from Dickens to Hardy* (London, Chatto and Windus, 1970), pp. 9–94, highlights twenty months in 1847–48 during which novels switched from being about 'face-to-face', 'knowable communities' to being about large anonymous towns. He points out that many later novelists (e.g. Eliot, Hardy) who still wished to write about the countryside tended to set their stories in the past.

23 Macintyre, 'Bentinck', pp. 160–1.

24 Disraeli in House of Commons, 12 July 1839, *Hansard's Parliamentary Debates*, 3rd Ser., xlix. 249, 252.

25 Jane Ridley, *The Young Disraeli* (London: Sinclair-Stevenson, 1995), p. 291.

26 After the election of 1880 he might also have claimed to be the first Prime Minister to suffer seriously from a 'feel-bad factor'.

27 Disraeli in House of Commons, 15 July 1867, *Hansard's Parliamentary Debates*, 3rd Ser., clxxxviii, 1609–10.

28 But for the limits of Conservative propaganda here see Miles Taylor, 'John Bull and the iconography of public opinion in England, *c.* 1712–1929', *Past and Present*, 134 (1992), 112–18; Hugh Cunningham, 'The language of patriotism', in Raphael Samuel (ed.), *Patriotism: the Making and Unmaking of British National Identity* (London and New York, Routledge, 1989), i. 57–89.

29 H. C. G. Matthew, *Gladstone, 1809–74* (Oxford, Clarendon Press, 1986), pp. 214–15; Jonathan Spain, 'Trade unionists, Gladstonian liberals and the labour law reforms of 1875', in E. F. Biagini and A. J. Reid (eds), *Currents of Radicalism: Popular Radicalism, Organised Labour and Party Politics in Britain, 1850–1914* (Cambridge, Cambridge University Press, 1991), pp. 109–33.

30 Disraeli to a working-class audience in Edinburgh, October 1867, quoted in Smith, *Disraelian Conservatism*, p. 103.

31 Martin Pugh, *The Tories and the People, 1880–1935* (Oxford, Blackwell, 1985), pp. 70–94; Patrick Joyce, *Work, Society and Politics: the Culture of the Factory in later Victorian England* (Hassocks, Harvester Press, 1980); 2nd edn (London, Methuen, 1982), pp. 268–330; J. Lawrence, 'Class and gender in the making of urban Toryism', *English Historical Review*, 108 (1993), 629–52.

32 James Cornford, 'The transformation of Conservatism in the late nineteenth century', *Victorian Studies*, 7 (1963–64), 42.

33 Macintyre, 'Bentinck', p. 161.

34 There is a striking analysis of how Disraeli's policy on local rates 'helped to forge the modern Conservative party' in Avner Offer, *Property and Politics 1870–1914, Landownership, Law, Ideology and Urban Development in England* (Cambridge, Cambridge University Press, 1981), pp. 167–9.

35 Though Searle has pointed out how much business and commercial Liberalism survived to 1914. See G. R. Searle, 'The Edwardian Liberal party and business', *English Historical Review*, 98 (1983), 28–60.

36 J. S. Mill, 'Opening of the Manchester Reform Club', 4 February 1867, *Collected Works of John Stuart Mill*, ed J. M. Robson (Toronto and Buffalo, University of Toronto Press, 1963–91), xxviii. 127.

37 J. Morley, reviewing *Essays on Reform*, for the *Fortnightly Review*, 1 April 1867, new Ser., ii. 492, quoted in Christopher Harvie, *The Lights of Liberalism: University Liberals and the Challenge of Democracy, 1860–86* (London, Allen Lane, 1976), p. 11.

38 The 'gentlemanly capitalist ideal', identified in P. J. Cain and A. G. Hopkins, *British Imperialism: Innovation and Expansion, 1688–1914* (London, Longman, 1993), corresponds to Perkin's aristocratic rather than to his entrepreneurial ideal, and better describes the values of the landed and upper middle-class Establishment, which mainly supported Peelite politics during the first half of the nineteenth century.

39 Harold Perkin, *The Origins of Modern English Society, 1780–1880* (London, Routledge, 1969), p. 408.

40 *Ibid.*, p. 436. The argument is modified in Harold Perkin, *The Rise of Professional Society: England since 1880* (London, Routledge, 1989), pp. 359–404, where, rather than simply capitulating to the aristocratic ideal, the entrepreneurial ideal is shown as having combined with it to produce a 'professional ideal'.

41 G. R. Searle, *Entrepreneurial Politics in mid-Victorian Britain* (Oxford, Oxford University Press, 1993).

42 Donald Read, *England, 1868–1914: the Age of Urban Democracy* (London and New York, Longman, 1979), pp. 159–61, locates an important Conservative breakthrough in many towns and cities between the 1880 and 1885 elections, before Home Rule. See G. Alderman, *The Railway Interest* (Leicester, Leicester University Press, 1973) p. 225 and *passim*. Paradoxically some businessmen became Conservatives, having been alienated by Chamberlain's policies as President of the Board of Trade in Gladstone's second government (1880–85), only to see Chamberlain gravitate to the Conservative and Unionist party in their wake.

43 H. Berghoff, 'Public schools and the decline of the British economy, 1870–1914', *Past and Present*, 129 (1990), 148–67, and W. D. Rubinstein, *Capitalism, Culture, and Decline in Britain, 1750–1990* (London, Routledge, 1993), pp. 102–39.

44 John Vincent, *Poolbooks: How Victorians Voted* (Cambridge, Cambridge University Press, 1967), pp. 43–50.

## Acknowledgement

I am grateful to Colin Matthew for his customary stimulating advice.

# 4

# Beguiled by France?
# The English aristocracy, 1748–1848

## ROBIN EAGLES

Dr Johnson was not impressed with France. The opening remarks of the journal he kept while accompanying Mrs Thrale on her tour of 1775 leave one in no doubt of his general attitude: 'We saw the École Militaire ... The building is very large, but nothing fine except the council room. The French have large squares in the windows; they make good iron palisades. Their meals are gross.'[1] As far as the cuisine was concerned, Mrs Thrale was equally dismissive.[2] Were one to read these in conjunction with the early diaries of Dr Thomas Campbell, an Irish acquaintance of Johnson, one might be misled into believing that a low opinion of France was common in the late eighteenth century, and that Gallophobia extended far beyond a critical deconstruction of French culinary arrangements: 'Din'd with Lord Dacre ... a lady bridling herself said everyone allows that we have everything better than the French except climate – and I who have spent much of my time in Paris think we have even a better climate.'[3] Campbell himself had never been to France, and when he did finally take the plunge in 1787 he rapidly revised his opinions, but these three remarks might well persuade one that British xenophobia was riding high in the 1770s, and that the great 'Other' propounded by Linda Colley had been firmly established in the minds of the educated as something inferior and even risible.[4]

Colley's view, that from the late seventeenth century onwards England's sense of national identity was compacted into a distinct conception of British as opposed to English or local-orientated nationhood by its rivalry with France has certain attractions, even if it fails to take account of the Anglo-French *entente* of 1716, the Anglo-French understanding of 1830–40 and the considerable periods of peace that intervened (1748–56, 1762–78, 1783–92, and after 1815). However, although it is true that England and France were intermittently at loggerheads over the map of Europe, the succession to the British (and Continental) thrones and colonial aggrandisement, it does not mean that Colley is right in her assertion that these political obstacles resulted in the creation of a particular British identity as a reaction against that projected by rival France. This chapter will attempt to demonstrate the heavily Francophile influences within primarily English society in the second half of the eighteenth century and the first half of the nineteenth, particularly among leading members of the aristocracy. It is the contention of this chapter that one should consider more particularly the influence of the Whig aristocracy, and the effects of the passion for France rife among its members, on English life, both social and political.

Whatever his merits as a lexicographer, Dr Johnson cannot be said to have been a part of the fashionable world of High Whiggery which held sway for much of his lifetime. Nor were his close acquaintances attached to this 'Beau Monde'. When Georgiana, Duchess of Devonshire, met Mrs Thrale in 1778 she was almost as dismissive of her as Mrs Thrale had been of French cuisine: 'Mrs Thrale seems certainly very clever and she entertains me very much, her fault is having a vulgarity about her that seeks to be fine.'[5] It is not from such as Hester Thrale and her coterie, therefore, that one should seek to discover a suitable point of departure for a study of elite culture.

The existence of a Francophile grouping in England is well known. What is less so, despite the work of historians such as Derek Jarrett, is the wider influence of France on every aspect of English life.[6] Charles James Fox admired and emulated France, and consequently passed into society some at least of these Francophile tendencies, whether the jingoists liked it or not, and while it is true that Fox ultimately misinterpreted the course of the French revolution, at its outset hopes were high that the French had succeeded where England had previously, in 1688, and few paid much attention initially to the apocalyptic ramblings of Edmund Burke.[7] Like many of the nobility, Fox knew France well, making trips to Paris and beyond in 1765, from 1767 to 1768, in 1769 and in 1771. He restrained himself from joining the Whig rush to view the effects of revolution in 1789, but resumed his Continental activities in 1802.[8] Horace Walpole was a similarly frequent visitor and for many years an intimate correspondent of Madame du Deffand. The Duke of Norfolk was closely related to members of the French nobility, as was the Duke of Richmond, who was himself a peer of France in his own right as the duc d'Aubigny. Norfolk pursued a property case in France between 1756 and 1768, vigorously assisted by both the French and the English establishments,[9] and, although ultimately unsuccessful in this instance, the importance of the case should not be ignored. The Treaty of Utrecht, the linchpin of his claim was a reciprocal arrangement. Englishmen had the right to claim property in France, as did French-men in England. The two nations were bound by treaty in a partnership that is obscured by overconcentration on the years of hostility.

Interest in France permeated all levels of society, and was instilled early as an essential ingredient of a well rounded education. Writing of the state of Oxford in 1773, Richard Perryn observed that 'Our College [Christ Church] is quite frenchified, most of our members having been this summer.'[10] Indeed, English society could be found fairly insipid after experience of French *politesse*: 'The general appearance of the English was to my eye, fresh from Paris, what it never before had been, strangely awkward and clownish ... The French deserve most richly that character of pre-eminent politeness which they have universally obtained.'[11] Campbell was writing at Brighton, and his observations were made with particular reference to a ball, attended also by the Prince of Wales, the Duke and Duchess of Cumberland, the Duke of Bedford and Mrs Fitzherbert.[12] If these had appeared awkward and clownish, it is hard to imagine the boorish impression that the majority of Englishmen must have made on the foreign observer. It was a common complaint among the French that the English were largely unsuccessful in their aping of French fashions, which they normally acquired when they had ceased to be the vogue in France, and adopted in so heterodox a manner as to lose all the elegance for which they had been prized across the Channel.[13] However, what appears inescapable is that, in an age that was supposedly witness to an increasing sense of national diversity, the highest echelons of English society were ignoring this trend. The concept of two alien and primarily antagonistic nations is certainly in need of serious reappraisal.

The influence of France is especially noticeable in the print satires and cartoons. Government Ministers were accused of French sympathies, and the state of English youth was blamed on the influence of foreign frippery. The fourth Earl of Sandwich was perceived to be selling England to the french, and a print entitled 'Scotch machine on French principles' demonstrated the Earl of Bute and Dowager Princess

1 'England made odious, or the French dressers' (1756), published by Edwards and Darley. This print was the third to appear in a volume of satires entitled *A Political and Satyrical [sic] History of the Years 1756 and 1757*. It depicts the Duke of Newcastle and Henry Fox encumbering Britannia with foolish French attire.

**2** 'The distrest earl of the southern folk prating French to his French servants is by them misunderstood', engraving from *Every Man's Magazine*, 1: 29 (1 August 1771). Suffolk was appointed Secretary of State for the Northern Department on 12 June 1771. His ignorance of French was legendary.

of Wales as riders on a merry-go-round dominated by France.[14] Henry Fox, Lord Holland and the Duke of Newcastle were portrayed decorated with collars and livery coats emblazoned with fleurs-de-lis, pulling down the pillars of the British constitution and even encumbering Britannia herself with French attire in 'England made odious, or, The French dressers' (Plate 1).[15] In all this there was an astuteness on the part of the satirists. Both Holland and Newcastle were reputed Francophiles, and if Charles James Fox became the most notorious Francophile of all, it is understandable in the light of his father's management of his education. He accompanied his father to France whilst still at Eton and strongly identified with the world of the French nobility, later owning a string of race horses at Newmarket in partnership with the duc de Lauzun.[16] The Duke of Newcastle, the Earl of Suffolk and Lord Shelburne employed French chefs and servants, and if this is not an indication of Francophile tendencies it was certainly much commented upon. Suffolk in particular was picked out for abuse in a print entitled 'The distrest Earl of the Southern Folk prating French to his French servants' (Plate 2). Similar doubts surrounded Lord Chesterfield, commonly believed to be the chief culprit in the importation of dubious Continental morality. In the year he resigned as Secretary of State, Chesterfield wrote to Philip Stanhope, 'It must be owned, that the Graces do not seem to be natives of Great Britain ... Since barbarism drove them out of Greece and Rome, they seem to have taken refuge in France, where their temples are numerous, and their worship the established one.'[17] By the 1770s George III himself was advocating alliance with the French, and a commercial pact, something that the British had sought since 1763, the French eventually came seriously to consider shortly before the outbreak of hostilities over the American war.

However, it was not only members of the government who received attention in the press for their determined Francophilia. Georgiana, Duchess of Devonshire, chose France as her home when her many indiscretions finally forced her husband to exile her from England, despite the revolution still raging and death of her close friend the queen, Marie-Antoinette. Fanny Burney, too, lived in France for many years following her marriage to the comte d'Arblay. Such alliances were not rare; Fox's cousin married the niece of the duc d'Orléans, Jane Austen's cousin Eliza the comtesse de la Feuillide, and Lady Mary Howard, daughter of the Earl of Stafford, married the comte du Rohan-Chabot. The phenomenon of France in England (and England in France) went far beyond clothes and chefs.

> The exorbitant impositions of the tradesmen of London ... induced many of the nobility to import goods from France ... Lord Holderness ... with his wife, was, indeed a notorious dealer in prohibited merchandise.[18]

Lady Holderness alone is accredited with illegally importing 114 French gowns. The increased consumption of French products both through the exertions of the Holdernesses and through legal channels (which were limited, as French goods remained contraband until 1786) meant that English society in general was steadily influenced by the Francophile example of the aristocracy. Not only did the last half of the century witness an increase in consumption, though: it also saw an explosion in the number of English of all ranks travelling on the Continent. Yet still, despite this revolution in travelling habits, it remained those who were well placed in society who were best able to appreciate France, and only a minority were wholeheartedly converted without the benefit of elite connections. The reason must lie with the importance of France to the Whigs in particular and with their traditional cultivation of members of the liberal nobility abroad.

Lord Cranborne's *Remarques* demonstrate well that an intimate knowledge of the workings of the world was vital for a true appreciation of Parisian life: 'Visité les Boulevards, un quantité de personnes se promenent en Carosse, à pied lorsqu'il fait beau. Les Jours qu'il y a le plus de Monde sont les Mercredis et Jeudis.'[19] Not being aware that the world went out on Wednesdays and Thursdays could well have been a barrier to the poorly connected seeing the finest sights that Paris could offer. The French were more than pleased to co-operate in welcoming English milords, while salon hostesses such as Madame du Deffand and Madame Geoffrin offered places to *petit-maîtres* at their soirees.[20] What is more significant is that some Englishmen were so concerned by the influence being exerted by France that they felt obliged to speak out.

A particularly alarmist example was the Reverend John Brown, who suggested that the effects of the ties with France were a growth in English effeminacy and a decline in moral stature, and that these tendencies were being encouraged and orchestrated by the French as a means of achieving their revenge for the Treaty of Aix-la-Chapelle in 1748 'We adopt every Vanity, and catch at every Lure, thrown out to us by the Nation that is planning our Destruction.'[21] While the English aristocracy sought to achieve a high standard of culture both for themselves and for their progeny by travel in France and Italy, Brown saw it as the very heart of the problem. Writing in 1757, he was recording these observations at a time when the passion for France was just gaining momentum.[22] The timing is significant. Brown's work appeared the year after Nugent's extremely popular *Grand Tour*, first published in 1749, was reissued in an expanded edition, and at the end of George II's reign when the King was losing interest in the pleasures of the court. The fact that George III failed to inject any new excitement into life at St James's must be considered seriously as an explanation for the aristocracy turning to France. Alarmist he may have been, but Brown showed considerable foresight in his predictions of the increasing influence of France on the higher echelons of society. He also challenges many of Colley's assumptions about the supposedly beneficial effects of British mercantile success. Mercantile wealth, he argued, over-interest in the toys of new worlds and complacency over past successes had diminished the national character and led to a loss of pride and moral rectitude: 'in the State and Period of luxury or Refinement, active religious Principle is lost thro' the attentive Pursuit of Pleasure; as in the commercial State, it is lost thro' the attentive Pursuit of Gain'.[23] Meanwhile, he continued, the French maintained their state of readiness and level of morality, despite their apparent effeminacy, by the 'Principle of Military Honour'.[24] The loss of the wars of the Austrian and Spanish successions had been in some respects a blessing to the French, as it had been instrumental in giving them purpose in the rehabilitation of their military and economy. England, particularly the foppish merchants and Francophile nobility, was being beguiled by France, which prepared for its own revival by the encouragement of dissipated habits among the English and the destruction of any sense of objective morality.

The English aristocracy did not heed Brown and continued to send their heirs to France and Italy for their educations,[25] as the series of prints by Bunbury, the increased output of travel journals and the private correspondence of young *petit-maîtres* and their tutors attest. What it was they sought is explained in part by the Earl of Pembroke, writing to his son, Lord Herbert, in 1780: 'All I entreat ye to do seriously at Paris is this; 13 lessons of dancing ... 13 lessons of Tennis ... and 13 fencing lessons ... De Guines will get ye into Good Company.'[26] Lord Herbert, however, seems not to have appreciated his father's plans for him, all of which were available at any one of the French military academies such as Caen or Angers: 'Lord P. I find has written to Grand, the Banker to take Vestris for me, But I shall and must gett off it somehow, as it would be utterly impossible for me to take a Dancing Lesson, totally so.'[27] Lord Herbert, at least, was not beguiled by the prospect of fencing and dancing lessons in the way Brown believed his countrymen frequently were.

However, one should bear in mind that Lord Herbert was a visitor to a country with which his own nation was still at war, and was himself a serving enemy officer. That this did not prevent him and other Englishmen (he mentions Lord Cobham as one of his acquaintance in Paris) from being there is itself significant. What may seem more bizarre is the eagerness with which the English sought France out in time of war, if their experience was so unfavourable. But this would be misleading. Travel journals carry remarkably similar accounts of the impressions of Englishmen and women, and even the most seasoned traveller found room for improvement. There were, of course, members of the English elite who were critical of French culture and *politesse*. This did not prevent travel in France from being both necessary and instructive. What was most vital was the cultivation of acquaintance and opinion; most English nobles met the same circle of people and did the same things. The names that occur throughout the journals and letters of the Whig elite are strikingly consistent, and they are frequently also to be found both in the letters of notable salon hostesses and of those holding the highest offices of state. Thus the 'world' of the English elite was closely mirrored by that of France. Only by comparison with England can a fuller picture of the attractions of their Gallic cousins emerge.

One common theme in Englishmen's impressions of France is the difference in physiognomy, even just over the Channel, in Calais. Dr Charles Burney was struck by the marked physical difference a few miles succeeded in delineating:

> The difference of complexion in the people is not the least circumstance which on this occasion occasions surprise. The English at Dover are as fair as in any other part of the Kingdom ... but the French at Calais are at least as swarthy of skin and have as black hair as those of Provence ...[28]

This kind of comment is much to be expected; what is rarer, and perhaps was encouraged by the ongoing hostilities, is Lord Herbert's remark with regard to the appearance of Louis XVI and Marie-Antoinette: 'The King looks much like a Castrato, the Queen I saw only at a distance very like her Brother.'[29] Despite this, one should not forget that Herbert's circle in France was that of other less critical members of the Whig elite. He shared the acquaintance of the Duchess of Lauzun, the Comtesse Boufflers and Madame du Deffand with the Countess Spencer, the Duchess of Devonshire and Lord Carlisle, Horace Walpole and Charles James Fox. James Hare was another member of this Foxite-Whig coterie, but he too had his reservations about Paris: 'Lady Jersy has been amazingly good natured to me and carried me to dine at the Duc de Coigny's, when I found myself so ill at my ease, that I made a resolution to which I have adhered ever since, viz, not to go into a French house again –'.[30] Hare complained on his arrival in Paris about the state of his rooms, but his mood improved when that was rectified: 'At my arrival, I was disgusted to the greatest degree with the dirt ... but as I have now got a clean apartment, am very well reconciled to Paris.'[31] An explanation for this dirtiness in French houses is provided by the eccentric travel writer Philip Thicknesse:

the Frenchman is always attentive to his own person, and scarce ever appears but clean and well dressed; while his house and private apartments are perhaps covered with litter and dirt, and in the utmost confusion; – the Englishman, on the other hand, often neglects his external dress; but his house is always exquisitely clean.[32]

This dichotomy is perhaps strange in the context of Anglo-French living habits. The Englishman's main residence and finery were to be found in the country, while he was content to suffer relatively cramped conditions in town for the Season, while the French concentrated their attention on their Parisian homes and considered their country houses as places to be avoided at all costs.[33]

Criticisms such as Hare's were common, though, even to the most staunch Francophile. The Countess Spencer, despite her regular visits, still found an abundance of things about which to complain. All Englishmen and women bemoaned the lack of street lighting and pavements; the equivocal behaviour of the *douaniers*[34] and household servants. Entertainment too received its fair share of criticism, the Opera especially set aside for the most damning remarks. Lady Spencer found that: 'the music and singing [were] equally worse than I could form an idea of without having heard it.'[35] Lord Herbert reckoned it as being 'worse than 10000 Catts & Doggs howling'.[36] Such notices, though, it should be said, tended to be reserved for the Italian Opera, for Herbert returned a few days later with Cobham to hear a French opera: 'Castor and Pollux was the opera, one of a very ancient Date, and in the true French musical taste. However I like it better than Gluck's because there is less musick, and a great deal of Spectacle and dance.'[37] But, however flawed were the delights of Paris, they were as nothing to those of London. Lady Mary Somerset's letters to Georgiana, Duchess of Devonshire in 1774 are particularly revealing in the light of Herbert's abuse of the Paris Opera:

> The amusements here [London] are beginning as the town fills. I have been to two operas and two plays, the former I think not very good, there is but one fine Man singer and the Woman is very Bad, the dancing [is] most abominable; but you know after one has seen that at the grand opera at Paris it is hardly possible to be pleased with any other.[38]

Everything in France was more impressive than in England, and Paris, in particular, dealt solely in superlatives. Lady Mary Somerset was well known (as was Georgiana Devonshire) for her impossible large headdresses, but in Paris they were larger still.[39] Paris, it seems, was capable of anything, even of preventing Lord Herbert from writing his journal: 'I cannot find time to do anything and since my arrival from Versailles, I have not putt Pen to Paper.'[40] This might not rank among Paris's greatest achievements, but Brown would have diagnosed the malady:

> in Contradiction to all known Example, France hath become powerful, while she seemed to lead the way in Effeminacy; and while she hath allowed her neighbour Nations, by her own Example, to drink largely of her circaean and poisoned Cup of Manners, hath secured her own Health by the Secret Antidote of Principle.[41]

Brown had perceived that France was in many respects superior to England, what is apparent is that the Whig elite also understood that there was more to be gained from France than dancing lessons and tall headdresses, and cultivated acquaintance in France for more than purely social ends to offset the deficiencies of life in London.

The reign of George III witnessed a general escalation in the number of Englishmen and women visiting France.[42] It may be argued that this increase was due solely to its coinciding with one of the few lengthy periods of peace that the century witnessed between the two kingdoms. Between 1763 and 1778 there was no open hostility, a period of calm rivalled only by the years 1713 to 1739. However, it has been seen that conflict did not interfere with people of rank travelling. Neither did war prevent Lord Chesterfield from lauding France while he was a Minister and the two nations were at war. These considerations, while important in assessing the increase in numbers among the non-elite, should be laid aside when investigating the lure of France to the English aristocracy. Some other explanation is required of why for the elite too this period was so dominated by Anglo-French contact. Thus one should concentrate attention on the focus of the court in England and France, and the fluctuating fortunes of those among the English nobility who found themselves out of favour, or resenting the lack of a proper centre of opposition. The private correspondence of certain members of the *beau monde*, intimates of Fox and his circle especially, reveals the discontent felt by the Whigs with the state of the court. George III's was a spartan affair, as is attested by Sir William Musgrave, writing to Lord Carlisle in 1768: 'It was whispered that there will be a subscription Masquerade there (the Duchess of Norfolk's) on Monday se'enight which I suppose will be so select as to be very dull – These things have generally been much discouraged by our sober Court—'.[43] The reason why this particular masquerade had to be 'whispered' abroad was that masques in general were forbidden during Lent, and the affair fell within the proscribed period, when mourning was required to be worn at the theatres, and ridottos replaced the more colourful masquerades. It can surely be no coincidence that the reign of George III experienced such heightened interest in the delights of France and Italy (particularly during Lent) when amusements at home were so few and far between. If court was dull, and the houses around St James's cramped, it is understandable that the aristocracy sought their pleasures elsewhere.

The antagonism of the Hanoverian kings towards their progeny, particularly eldest sons, is well known, and this had served to create an alternative court for disillusioned or displaced courtiers. But under George III this system collapsed in the absence of a Prince of Wales of age, or indeed of a royal duke of the political stature of Cumberland after 1765. This vacuum gave an added sense of importance to the cultivation of France and French Enlightenment thought, though this had already been apparent under previous opposition movements. George Bubb Doddington accepted a place in opposition in 1749 under the patronage of Prince Frederick, and his comments demonstrate that already the rival establishment had become a haven for ousted courtiers and French diplomats: 'Kissed the Prince and Princess's hands, as Treasurer of the Chambers. Supped with their Royal Highnesses and Madame de Mirepoix, the French Ambassadress. The Prince pretty eager about opposition.'[44] The connection between opposition Francophiles and members of the diplomatic corps clearly continued. Lord Chesterfield's son, Philip Stanhope, embarked on a career in diplomacy, and the comte de Guines, into whose hands Lord Pembroke delivered his son, had been the French ambassador to London in 1772.[45] Opposition and Francophilia, or at least the establishment of acquaintance in France (Madame de Mirepoix was another intimate of Madame du Deffand) seems to have been a general practice in the second half of the eighteenth century.

It is ironic that, in order to escape the absolutism that some feared George III was seeking to cultivate, the opposition turned to France, the most virulently detested home of all the worst traits of absolutist monarchy. Yet in this they showed considerable foresight. Whether one accepts the view that it was English liberalism that fed the flames of French revolutionary thought, or that it was the French nobility, and even royal family, that was most directly responsible for the progress of the Enlightenment in France, there is much evidence to suggest that it was in the liberal climate of the French salons that the war against absolutism and tyranny was most vigorously waged.[46] English Ministers, though, also joined the opposition Whigs abroad, even in wartime, and it is amusing that Lord Herbert's principal preoccupation as a serving officer in enemy territory was what he should wear. Reasonably enough, he concluded that uniform might not be appropriate and opted instead for mourning.[47] He, too, joined a party at court and, though unimpressed with the physique of the King and Queen, was not averse to attaching himself to the company recommended him by de Guines. Certainly war was no bar to travel or attendance at an enemy court and association with enemy dignitaries. There is a very real sense in which monarchs went to war with each other but not with their subjects.

Equally significant is the question of who was excluded from this Whig 'world' of opposition. The clearer demarcations of French society between the *noblesse* and the lower orders was a further incentive for the English nobility to seek its sanctuary, free from the incursions of nabobs and wealthy merchants at home. The precise times at which society demanded one should be 'seen' mentioned by Lord Cranborne and a fundamental difference in moral values added to the insulation of Whig notables from Linda Colley's triumphant British merchants.[48] However, it must be added that the greater size of French elite society, and the proliferation of guide books and of non-notables travelling abroad meant that even these distinctions were becoming increasingly less obvious and effective as a means of control. That is not to say, though, that distinctions did not remain. If Dr Johnson said of Lord Chesterfield's *Letters* that they taught 'the morals of a whore and the manners of a dancing-master', Georgiana, Duchess of Devonshire commented, 'I should be glad to be better aquainted [sic] with such as his rules for politeness.'[49] Many dancing masters, of course, were French, and the duchess's

attitude towards Laclos's *Les Liaisons dangereuses* impresses one with the extent
to which she was out of step with middling-sort morality. While it was burned
on the streets of Paris as immoral, she merely remarked that 'It is very indecent,
but ... is far from being uninstructive.' [50]

John Moore, writing to his patrons the Duke of Hamilton and Marquess of
Douglas in 1779, summarised the benefits of Paris succinctly: 'the polished mildness
of French manners, the gay and sociable turn of the nation, the affable and easy
conduct of masters to their servants, supply the deficiencies ... of the government'.[51] These also supplied the deficiencies of the English government to the
Whig elite, who, despite their determined isolation from the incursions of
the lower orders of society, still managed to inspire devotion and esteem, none
more dramatically so than Charles James Fox, 'a man completely ruined; yet
beloved by his friends, and admired by Country as much as ever.'[52] Far from
beguiled, the aristocracy of England was itself a beguiling force in politics and
society, and the courting of France must be seen to have been a deliberate advance,
not the result of any sorcery on the part of the Gallic foe.

Many of this Francophile elite were thus initially no less receptive to the cause
of the American revolution, and to the 'bliss' the dawning of the French revolution
appeared to herald, than to the radical voices of Romilly, Wordsworth and Paine.
No great diplomat, the Duke of Dorset's response swiftly somersaulted, but his
reaction to the fall of the Bastille is still significant: 'Nothing could exceed the
regularity and good order with which all this extraordinary business has been
conducted ... From this moment we may consider France as a free country, the
King a very limited monarch, and the nobility as reduced to a level with the rest
of the nation.'[53]

For those who believed that it was only the system of France that made England
and her neighbour necessarily inimical, the prospect of a successful, and moreover
peaceful re-enactment of 1688 was the greatest hope for the anglo-French accord
so desired by, particularly, Foxite Whiggery.[54] The apparently successful outcome
of the revolution for Samuel Romilly meant that thereafter there was no need for
England and France to be considered enemies; that, while France was free, England
would remain free and tranquil;[55] that there would be no excuse for war; and the
real prospect, in the unlikely event of war, that England and France would be
allies, not adversaries.[56]

While one may fling charges of wishful thinking Romilly's way, and quote the
apparently greater perception of Edmund Burke, the attitude of men like Romilly
great at least in part out of the close cultural and intellectual contacts championed
earlier in the century by the elite, and the desire hankered after by many of the
Enlightenment fraternity that England and France's natural amity might be made
real by reformation of the absolutist French State.

Despite the supposed triumph of John Bull over the Francophile tendencies of
the Whigs in opposition, the old iconographies and sentiments died hard. French
remained *de rigueur* in the education of polished young ladies and gentlemen, the
Peace of Amiens provided the Foxites with a chance to test their creed against

that of the consul Bonaparte, and political satire demonstrated the same prejudices as were to be found in the previous century. Just as in the 1750s and 1760s Newcastle and Holland, and Bute and the dowager Princess of Wales, were accused of selling Britannia to France, so in the early years of the nineteenth century the much vilified Addington was accused of attempting to preserve his place by negotiation with Bonaparte.[57]

If the same rhetoric was at work in the political satire of the Napoleonic wars, there is evidence also to refute Linda Colley's assumption that the exterior threat of revolutionary, and later imperial, France had succeeded in establishing irrevocably the position of Britain as the focus of national loyalties. Charles Fox himself suggested that as he was a Scot some might consider David Hume a 'foreigner', and an anonymous tract stated that 'the People of England have remained in utter ignorance upon a point in which all their best interests are involved ... no one ever imputed to them the smallest reluctance to sacrifice to a powerful Enemy any points either of national interest, or national honour'.[58]

The aftermath of the Napoleonic wars found the British love affair with France undiminished, as appears to be demonstrated by a variety of literary sources. Thomas Moore's skittish poem charting the semi-fictional journeyings of the Fudge family through France, and their sojourn in Paris, does little to resolve questions of nationality raised by public reactions to landmarks such as the Peace of Amiens,[59] but the family's ramblings, loosely based on Moore's own trip to Paris in 1817, raise the question of whether Colley is correct that the revolution and Napoleonic wars marked as firm a line under the old ways as she may care to imply.[60]

In unison with Pierre-Jean Grosley, who considered the north of France, and its people, to be more closely related to the English than their southern French countrymen,[61] Biddy Fudge remarks to her correspondent Dorothy —— of the similarity of the countryside beyond Calais and her native Ireland:

> I have seen nothing yet *very* wonderful here;
> No adventure, no sentiment, far as we've come,
> But the corn-fields and trees quite as dull as at home;
> And *but* for the post-boy, his boots and his queue,
> I might *just* as well be at Clonskilty with you![62]

Young master Bob Fudge is seeking fashion in Paris, just as the *petit-maîtres* had done before him. Already dandified, he 'goes now to Paris to study French dishes', while his father plans to pen his Travels in France. The magical name of Sterne is breathed in the first letter, almost in the first stanza, and while Biddy laments that there are so few monks to be seen, and no dying donkeys are apparent on the roads, Dessein's hotel remains a familiar landmark, as Sydney Smith discovered when he too was in Calais following the Napoleonic wars.

The years of conflict had done nothing to dispel the English fascination with French dress, nor the position that France held at the centre of the world of fashion. If revolution and empire consolidated the British into a state of nation-hood, it failed to cure them of their subservience to foreign modes:

> Where *shall* I begin with the endless delights
> Of this Eden of milliners, monkies, and sights –
> This dear busy place, where there's nothing transacting
> But dressing and dinnering, dancing and acting? [63]

However delightful their fashions and way of life, though, less satisfying was the realisation that nothing had been done in the intervening years to improve the standard of the opera. While the ballet and show remained the finest to be seen, it appears that Lord Herbert's description of '10,000 Catts & Doggs howling' was as true as ever, even if Fudge attempted to attribute the row to the excesses of the Jacobin mob:[64]

> – never was known in this riotous sphere
> Such a breach of the peace as their singing, my dear ...
> But, the dancing – *ah, parlez-moi*, Dolly, *de ça* –
> There, *indeed*, is a treat that charms all but Papa.
> Such beauty – such grace – oh ye sylphs of romance! [65]

France then continued to exert its influence, far beyond the parameters estab-lished by Colley, and as late as 1847–48, when Thackeray was publishing *Vanity Fair*, France was still recognised as the arbiter of taste, and a talent for French was an indispensable aid in the infiltration of society:

> When the Potentate from the Danube made his appearance, the conversation was carried on in the French language, and the Lady Bareacres and the younger ladies found, to their further mortification, that Mrs Crawley was much better acquainted with that tongue, and spoke it with a much better accent than they.[66]

Much as faro was introduced from Spa, and quinze from Paris, in the 1820s charades crossed the water to captivate the *ton*: 'At this time the amiable amuse-ment of acting charades had come among us from France: and was considerably in vogue in this country, enabling the many ladies amongst us who had beauty to display their charms, and the fewer number who had cleverness to exhibit their wit.' [67]

Where rivalry existed at foreign courts it remained Anglo-French in character, the fictional court of Pumpernickel a perfect example of the bipartisan politics of eighteenth and nineteenth-century European petty principalities, each faction vying to achieve dominance for the greater glory of either of the 'two greatest nations upon earth'.

> Politics ran very high at Pumpernickel, and parties were very bitter. There was the Strumpff faction and the Lederlung party, the one supported by our Envoy and the other by the French Chargé d'Affaires, M. de Macabau ... it sufficed ... for our Ministers to advance *any* opinion to have it instantly contradicted by the French diplomatist.[68]

Although Thackeray recognised that the closing years of the Napoleonic wars were not ones during which it was well thought-of to rehearse too openly a love for the French nation, in Becky Sharp he created a character who succeeded in spite of her lowly origins because her mastery of French, and her Gallic cunning, enabled her to inveigle her way into society. This despite the fact that at the outset of her progress these, her primary assets, were still frowned upon by simple-minded patriots like Amelia Sedley, though instruction in French remained a vital part of a polite education such as that offered by Miss Pinkerton.[69] There remained an ambiguity in British opinion of things French, as both rival and paramour, that *Vanity Fair* deftly encapsulated.

The aftermath of the wars, however, presented a new situation, and the occupation of Paris an unrivalled opportunity to examine Anglo-French relations, particularly in view of the presence also of Prussians, Austrians and Hungarians.[70] The Prussians had earned the mistrust of the French principally for their rapaciousness on entering the capital, requisitioning art and treasure to which, according to Peel, they had some claim. Peel himself lamented their loss, though not, as he hastened to add, 'on account of the mortification which it will inflict on French vanity' but rather because he feared 'the return of the King will be less popular – than it would have been if he could have preserved entire at least those national monuments and relics which are exclusively French'.[70] This is an interesting attitude, not least because Peel so firmly equates a sense of national pride with memorials which are 'exclusively' the product of that nation. It is a statement which prompts the question which English, or British, memorials Peel might have wished to see preserved had the situation been played out in London. The Prince Regent's principal London residence, Carlton House, for instance, bore little resemblance to anything English. The exterior, though redesigned by English architects, was firmly derived from the Hotel Condé and the Palais Royal, while the interior was decorated almost exclusively by French craftsmen. It must, however, be conceded that Peel's concern for the well-being of the French was at least in part motivated by a political wish not to see France too deeply humiliated.

Ideals of nationality may have begun to embrace ideals of exclusivity, at least to educated men such as Robert Peel, but that does not negate the impression that the Anglo-French reciprocity so apparent before the revolution and the Napoleonic wars remained afterwards, and that the pursuit of Britishness remained with it, but one ideal among several. Neither should it be understood that this pursuit of Francophilia was an elite monopoly, despite J. Goldsworth Alger's assertion that it was only after Amiens that middling-sort travellers were regularly to be seen in Paris, much to the amusement of other Continental visitors.[72] However, it is profitable to consider the influence that the political realignment the Talents Ministry exerted may have had on the later middling-sort attitude to France, characterised as it was by the Foxite ethos of *rapprochement* with Bonaparte, combined with Charles Fox's surprising new-found pro-Hanoverian philosophy.[73] Not least, one should pay attention to Sydney Smith's belief, confided to Lady Grey in 1835, that 'every wife has a right to insist upon seeing Paris', if only because Smith himself (1771–1845) spanned the pre- and post-revolutionary era, and was welcomed into many of the houses of the elite as a noted wit and conversationalist.[74] If 'Liberty and property' was indeed to become the battle cry of the united British peoples, the right to be free to experience travel abroad was no less a fundamental of the national character, and, for most people, 'abroad' meant France.

## *Notes*

1 Dr Johnson, *French Journal, 1775*, ed. Tyson and Guppy (Manchester, Manchester University Press, 1932), p. 169.

2 Mrs Thrale, *French Journal, 1775*, ed. Tyson and Guppy (Manchester, Manchester University Press, 1932), p. 103.

3 Thomas Campbell, *Diary of a visit to England in 1775 by an Irishman*, ed. S. Raymond (Sydney, Waugh and Cox, 1854), p. 63.

4 Linda Colley, *Britons: Forging a Nation* (New Haven and London, Yale University Press, 1992).

5 Chatsworth House MSS, Duchess of Devonshire to her mother, Countess Spencer, Tunbridge Wells, 20 October 1778.

6 Derek Jarrett, *The Begetters of Revolution: England's Involvement with France, 1759–89* (London, Longman, 1973), p. xi.

7 Leslie Mitchell, *Charles James Fox* (Oxford, Oxford University Press, 1992), p. 110.

8 Significantly, one of Fox's purposes on his 1802 visit was to consult the archives in Paris for his volume on the reign of James II, eventually published posthumously as an unfinished work, *A History of the Early Part of the Reign of King James II*.

9 'About a fortnight ago, Lord Hertford presented to the Duc de Pralin [*sic*] a new Memorial in your favour, in which he insisted to have a general Declaration from the King and Council, explaining the Treaty of Utrecht in such a manner as expressly to comprehend your Case.' Arundel Castle, *Howard Letters, 1760–1816*, David Hume to Charles Howard, 20 May 1764.

10 Richard Perryn to Sir James Bland Burges, 1773. Dep. Bland Burges. 18. Bodleian Library, Oxford.

11 Thomas Campbell, *Diary of a Trip to England, 1787*, pp. 102–4.

12 *Ibid.*

13 This is a view particularly propounded by Tobias Smollett in *Travels in France and Italy* (London, 1766), ed. Frank Felsenstein (Oxford, Oxford University Press, 1981), pp. 48–50.

14 *English Cartoons and Satirical Prints, 1320–1832, in the British Museum*, BM 3891 (1763). For a further description see F. G. Stephens and M. D. George, *Catalogue of Political and Personal Satires preserved in the Department of Prints and Drawings in the British Museum*, 11 vols (London, Chadwyck-Healey, 1870–1954). (Numbers prefixed BM hereafter refer to numbers in the *Catalogue*.)

15 BM 3371, 3543.

16 'Je suis toujours Français dans le coeur, et en vérité ce n'est pas merveilleux que je les donne la preference avant un peuple ingrat, commes nous autres.' Quoted in L. G. Mitchell, *Charles James Fox*, p. 16.

17 Lord Chesterfield, *Letters*, ed. David Roberts (Oxford, Oxford University Press, 1992), No. 39, 18 November 1748 (O.S.) p. 115.

18 Horace Walpole, *Journal of the Reign of King George III from the Year 1771 to 1783*, ed. J. Doran, 2 vols (London, Bentley, 1859), May 1772.

19 Hatfield House MSS, Mercredi 9 May 1769, 130–1. Lord Cranborne's *Remarques* is his highly derivative journal of his tour to France and Switzerland between 1768 and 1771.

20 See Bernedetta Craveri, *Madame du Deffand and her World*, trans. Teresa Waugh (London, Halban, 1994).

21 John Brown, *An Estimate of the Manners and Principles of the Times*, 2 vols (London, L. Davis and C. Reymers, 1757) i. 144.

22 It is also significant that it was during 1757, an election year, that the Anti-Gallican society commissioned Louis Boitard to compose his satirical cartoon 'The imports of Great Britain from France', depicting precisely the kind of fashionable and cultural inundation of society complained of by Brown.

23 John Brown, *An Estimate of the Manners and Principles of the Times*, i. 161.

24 *Ibid.*, p. 137.

25 See A. Babeau, *La Vie militaire sous l'ancien régime*, 2 vols (Paris, Firmin Didot, 1889–90). According to Babeau both William Pitt (the Elder) and Arthur Wellesley, future Duke of Wellington, studied at the academy at Angers.

26 Lord Herbert, *Henry, Elizabeth and George, 1734–80: Letters and Diaries of Henry, tenth Earl of Pembroke and his Circle* (London, Jonathan Cape, 1939), p. 369. Wilton House, January 1780.

27 Wiltshire Record Office, Wilton MSS, 2057/F5/6. Lord Herbert's *Diary of a Trip to France*, 29 April 1780. Vestris was much in demand as one of the foremost dancing masters of his day.

28 Charles Burney, *Music, Men and Manners in France and Italy, 1770*, ed. H. Edmund Poole (London, Folio Society, 1969), pp. 1–2.

30 Castle Howard, J14/1/572, James Hare to Lord Carlisle, 15 October 1783.

31 Castle Howard, J14/1/572, 15 October 1783.

32 Philip Thicknesse, *A Year's Journey through France and Part of Spain*, 2 vols (Bath, Cruttwell, 1777), i. 6.

33 Lawrence Stone and Jeanne C. Fawtier Stone, *An Open Elite? England 1540–1880* (Oxford, Oxford University Press, 1984), pp. 295–8.

34 Badminton House MSS, FMK 1/1/2, Diary 2, 21 October 1769 and 30 July 1770.

35 Devonshire MSS, Chatsworth: 5th Duke's Group 2014, 1–11, Countess Spencer's Journal 17 September–17 November 1764.

36 Wilton MSS, 2057/F5/6, 2 May 1780.

37 *Ibid.*, 12 May 1780.

38 Devonshire MSS, letter 48, Lady Mary Somerset to the Duchess of Devonshire, St James's Street, 22 November 1774.

39 Devonshire MSS, letter 52, Paris, 27 November 1774. Lady Clermont wrote to the Duchess of Devonshire describing the scene: 'there is no describing here headdress and of all the young people they sit at the bottom of their coaches as they have not room if they sit on the seat ... Lady Mary Somerset's head is low in comparison ...'

40 Wilton MSS, 2057/F5/6, 19 May 1780.

41 John Brown, *Estimate*, i. 140.

42 Precise figures are difficult to gauge accurately, but the information made available to Louis XV suggested that during the years 1763–65, 40,000 English tourists passed through the port of Calais alone, and that available to William Pitt in 1785 suggested that the same number were by then making the crossing annually. Cited in Jeremy Black, *The British Abroad: the Grand Tour in the Eighteenth Century* (New York, Alan Sutton, 1992), p. 105.

44 Bodleian Library, Diary of George Bubb Doddington, March 1748/9–February 1761, 1 October 1749.

45 Wilton MSS, 2057/F5/6, 13 May 1780. Herbert was taken to court and had his accommodation organised for him by de Guines.

46 See Derek Jarrett, *The Begetters of Revolution*; and Julian Swann, 'The French nobility, 1715–89', in Hamish Scott (ed.), *The European Nobilities in the Seventeenth and Eighteenth Centuries* (London, Macmillan, 1995).

47 Wilton MSS, 2057/F5/6, 20 March 1780. 'Not being able to wear my Uniform in an Enemy's Country I was obliged to take into serious consideration my dress which ... I settled should be mourning, as the cheapest and most convenient ...'

48 For Cranborne see above, note 19.

49 James Boswell, *Life of Johnson*, 2 vols (London, Dent; New York, Dutton, 1906), i. 159; Chatsworth House MSS, Letter 31, Duchess of Devonshire to the Countess Spencer, 14 October 1774.

50 Devonshire MSS, Letter 32, Duchess of Devonshire to the Countess Spencer, 16 October 1782. Queen Marie-Antoinette also had a copy of the book, which was discovered in her private library after the revolution.

51 John Moore, *A View of Society and Manners in France, Switzerland and Germany, with Anecdotes relating to some Eminent Characters* (London, Strahan and Cadell, 1779), pp. 34–5.

52 *Ibid.*, p. 7.

53 Duke of Dorset to Duke of Leeds, Paris, 16 July 1789, cited in John G. Alger, *Englishmen in the French Revolution* (London, Sampson Low, 1889), p. 8.

54 This was certainly the attitude also of the Revolution Society, as expounded by Lord Stanhope in answer to Burke's speech on the French revolution. Earl Stanhope, *A Letter from Earl Stanhope to the Rt. Hon. Edmund Burke, containing a short Answer to his late Speech on the French Revolution* (London, 1790), pp. 13–14.

55 'Public liberty never can be in danger but from the corruption of the people, or from a foreign force; and no force formidable to the liberties of this country can ever exist, while France is free.' Samuel Romilly, *Thoughts on the Probable Influence of the French Revolution on Great Britain* (London, 1790), p. 6.

56 *Ibid.*, pp. 11–12.

57 British Library, Add MSS 41, 856, Grenville Papers, fos 98–9.

58 British Library, Add MSS 41, 856, Grenville Papers, fox 133–4. This unattributed political tract stressed a view that was far from being an isolated opinion. Charles James Fox cited David Hume during his speech in the House of Commons on 3 February 1800, opposing the government motion not to treat with the French Republic as 'A great and justly celebrated historian, whom I will not call a foreigner – I mean Mr Hume – ...'. Charles James Fox, *The Speech of the Hon. Charles James Fox in the House of Commons on Monday, the 3d of February, 1800, on a Motion for an Address to the Throne, approving of the Refusal of Ministers to treat with the French Republic* (London, 1800), p. 12.

59 This is discussed in Angus Macintyre, 'Between two wars: the British in Paris during the Peace of Amiens' (unpublished article).

60 Thomas Moore, *The Fudge Family in Paris*, ed. Thomas Brown the younger (London, Longman, 1818).

61 Pierre-Jean Grosley, *A Tour to London and new Observations on England and its Inhabitants*, trans. Nugent (London, Lockyer Davis, 1765).

62 Thomas Moore, *The Fudge Family in Paris*, Letter 1, p. 2.

63 *Ibid.*, Letter 5, p. 39.

64 *Ibid.*, Letter 5, p. 39, 'That this passion for roaring has come in of late,/Since the rabble all tried for a *voice* in the State.'

65 *Ibid.*, Letter 5, pp. 40–1.

66 William Makepeace Thackeray, *Vanity Fair*, ed. J. I. M. Stewart (London, Penguin, 1985), p. 572. A similar state of affairs is found in *Nicholas Nickleby* with Nicholas engaged to tutor the socially-aspiring Kenwigs children in French. Charles Dickens, *Nicholas Nickleby* (1839), ed. Michael Slater (London, Penguin, 1978), pp. 270–4.

67 Thackeray, *Vanity Fair*, p. 593.

68 *Ibid*, p. 730.

69 *Ibid.*, p. 47.

70 'Paris is surrounded by the troops of the allies and nothing can be more interesting than the present situation of it. The streets are crowded with officers and soldiers of all nations. Cossacks–Russians–Prussians, Austrians, Hungarians, etc. The English are great favourites. The Prussians held in the greatest detestation.' Robert Peel to Lord Whitworth, paris, 16 July 1815, quoted in Vita Sackville-West, *Knole and the Sackvilles* (London, National Trust, 1991), p. 204.

71 Robert Peel to Lord Whitworth, Paris, 16 July 1815.

72 J. Goldsworth Alger, 'British visitors to Paris, 1802–3', *English Historical Review*, 14 (1899), 740. Cited in Angus Macintyre, 'Between two wars'.

73 See Brendan Simms, '"An odd question enough": Charles James Fox, the Crown and British policy during the hanoverian crisis of 1806', *Historical Journal*, 38:3 (1995), 567–96.

74 Quoted in Alan Bell, *Sydney Smith: a Biography* (Oxford, Oxford University Press, 1980), p. 202.

## Acknowledgements

I am grateful to the following owners of manuscript collections for granting permission to reproduce material: His Grace the Duke of Beaufort, His Grace the Duke of Devonshire, the Marquess of Salisbury, the trustees of Wilton Estate. Arundel Castle documents are reproduced by permission of His Grace the Duke of Norfolk, and Castle Howard papers by kind permission of the Howard family. Plates 1 and 2 (BM 4876) are reproduced by permission of the British Museum.

# 5

# 'In the Olden Time': Romantic history and English national identity, 1820–50

## PETER MANDLER

English history-writing in the first half of the nineteenth century is generally seen as an exception to the European (that is, French or German) norm. In France and Germany, it is said, history-writing played a crucial role in the invention (or revolutionary reinvention) of the nation. New nations and new ruling classes required historical pedigrees that were deeply rooted, heroic and inclusive to recruit popular affections and underpin political stability. In France and Germany, therefore, State institutions sponsored and disseminated romantic national histories by the likes of Thierry, Michelet, the Grimm brothers and Ranke.

In England, by contrast, political stability was secured more directly. History-writing had no more to do than add a light gloss by charting the development over time of parliamentary institutions ancient in origin but, more important, successfully adapted to the social changes of the recent past and still thriving in the present. English history-writing in the Romantic period was, therefore, like English politics: cooler, less popular, less nationalist and more elite-driven than its Continental equivalents. There was little State-sponsored history, and the major works of historical writing in this period were produced by a whiggish elite for its own delectation and in praise of its own institutions, with the emphasis on their latest metamorphoses, as in Hallam and Macaulay.[1] This impression has, if anything, been reinforced by John Burrow's marvellous high-intellectual readings of the great texts of Whig history and by Linda Colley's argument that national identity up to 1830 hinged upon the recent development of *British* political institutions. In a different way, it has been reinforced also by recent writing on oppositional history, which has shown how radicals developed their own counter-histories of parliamentary development in order to demand a return to Saxon liberties or some other ancient constitution.[2]

This focus upon history-writing in a constitutionalist idiom captures well the place of history in early Victorian elite culture and politics, but not the place of history *outside* elite culture and politics, especially after 1832. A more capacious view is necessary if we are to grasp the contribution of historical consciousness to a truly national identity.[3] Political historians tend to forget that relative political exclusiveness in Britain was bought at the price of relative cultural openness. In the comparatively democratic market place of culture, identities were constructed that had little or nothing to do with the whiggish world of political institutions. There was here plenty of scope for romantic national history very much on the Continental model: in fact the busy hive of commercial culture in Britain may well have diffused romantic history far *more* widely than any number of State-sponsored or university-based projects in France or Germany.[4] What follows is a sketch of how this romantic English history emerged, what were some of its prominent themes and morals, and what were its longer-term contributions to the making of an *English* national identity in the nineteenth century.

First, what were the dimensions of that 'democratic market place of culture' within which romantic history grew up? Its economic and technical origins are reasonably well known. Most textbooks make some passing reference to the impact of steam printing on the spread of newspapers in the early nineteenth century. Equally significant were technical developments in the printing of images: wood-cuts, which with the development of stereotyping in the 1820s could be combined with text in runs of up to 300,000; the higher-quality steel engravings, which could be produced without text in runs nearly as long, and later with text in the electrotyping processes of the 1840s. These new processes produced the annuals of the 1820s, pocket keepsakes filled with romantic poetry and illustrations in runs of up to 10,000 each, and the first popular illustrated novels, especially Sir Walter Scott's, whose accessibility and illustration overcame the obstacle of expense.

Until the mid-1830s political controversy and the stamp tax placed some con-straints on the popular market for printed text and image. But, after the political settlement of 1832 and reduction of the taxes on knowledge, the popular illustrated press came into its own: penny weeklies such as Charles Knight's *Penny Magazine*, with sales of 200,000 in the mid-1830s, or its Anglican rival the *Saturday Magazine*, with weekly sales of up to 80,000; weightier works issued in cheap parts – novels, histories, topographies, art portfolios (here again Charles Knight was a market leader); and then, at the end of our period, in the late 1840s, even more frankly commercial publications such as those from the presses of George Stiff, Edward Lloyd, G. W. M. Reynolds and John Cassell.[5]

In addition to this flood of print and image there was a related boom in popular spectacle – panoramas, dioramas, magic lanterns, spectacular theatre, *tableaux vivants*, circus and, less well understood, popular tourism. Scholarship on the social history of leisure gives a misleading picture of the early Victorian populace penned up in towns, chained to home or workplace and deprived even of a public park. For a substantial portion of the people this was nothing like the truth. Even before the railway, there was a brisk trade in waggon and charabanc trips into the countryside on Saturdays, Sundays, at Easter and at Whitsun: to take just two examples, thousands were descending by this means from Sheffield to Chatsworth Park and from London to Hampton Court. Steamboats took over 100,000 pas-sengers per annum to Gravesend, Margate and Ramsgate as early as the mid-1830s. A decade later railway excursions would be under way and, a further decade later, would be commonplace.[6]

For all the diversity of genre, a remarkably homogeneous style was emerging in the mass culture industry by the 1830s. This has something to do with the fact that a good deal of print, image, spectacle and even tourist material emanated from London, which alone had the resources to produce cultural matter on such an enormous scale.[7] Because the demand for such material seemed always to be pressing on the supply, there was also a high degree of sharing across genres as material was constantly recycled and transposed for different uses. Scott's novels, for instance, were immediately take up by theatrical impresarios, painters and engravers as well as literary imitators. Royal Academy paintings were engraved and then plagiarised for the penny illustrated press.

Aside from these technical reasons, there were also more conscious, pointed, sometimes nearly political reasons for the homogeneity of mass cultural style. Producers were, of course, keen for commercial reasons to develop a single style that would appeal to the widest possible audience, from the clubman down to the shopgirl and, further, down to the factory floor. There is no doubt that they were highly successful: while their primary market lay in the clerking, shopkeeping and artisanal classes, they reached well up into the middle classes (probably stopping short of the university-educated) and well downwards, too; the *Penny Magazine*, with its peak sale of 200,000, assuredly had more working-class readers than the *Poor Man's Guardian* (sales at best of 15,000) and possibly more than the *Northern Star* (36,000 in 1839).[8] To achieve this broad appeal they had to avoid divisive religious and political matter, and also if possible matter that had an obvious class charge to it: Greek and Latin tags, for instance, or salacious material from the plebeian underworld. More positively, they also tried to cultivate a universally accessible style, a national cultural style. Such a style would have to be popular and democratic in the sense of extending well beyond the bounds of political enfranchisement while at the same time steering clear of politically democratic claims. In short, it had to call into being a cultural nation overlapping with but distinct from the political nation.[9]

History played from the start a highly significant role in the making of this mass cultural style. For one thing, the depths of history provided an inexhaustible well out of which cultural material could be dredged to meet the massive new demand. For these purposes, recent history was less desirable than the more distant past, as recent history was too polite and refined to suit the mass market. The *Saturday Magazine* announced in its very first issue that its primary purpose would be to dig up the great books of the past, buried under dust, remote and inaccessible in libraries, and to reissue them in portable and digestible form, 'for there never was a people whose forefathers planted more deeply and judiciously ... It is now time to pluck up ... to transplant, to graft, to disperse and to multiply the virtues of the ancient stock.'[10]

Beyond the merely technical advantages which history offered, there lay a deeper ideological motive for consulting English history. If the past century or so had been an age of politeness and refinement, when culture had been confined to an elite, then further back might be found a day when culture had been the common property of the English people, created by the people, designed for them, and destined to be restored to them. This was not a matter of looking for a Golden Age, to be recreated in all its features. A consistent characteristic of the mass culture industry is its modernism: a love of technology, an insistence on the extension of opulence, a frank rejection of the nostalgia of a Carlyle or Young England. It was in order to find literary and artistic models suited to this modern age of prosperity and equality that cultural entrepreneurs foraged in the distant past. The last century had witnessed the separation of an exclusive elite from the mass of the people; now the people were catching up, and they needed to rein in their errant, over-cosmopolitan 'betters', reconnecting them with the lost world of a common English culture. A popular and national tradition had to be recaptured, rescued from the dust of ages, and then revivified – continued in a modern, democratic idiom, confirming the commitment to progress and the future. These were uses of history closer to the French and German Romantics than to the British Whigs (or, even, constitutionalist radicals).

In the early phases of the mass culture industry a truly popular approach to history was neither obvious nor easy. Producers were limited by the availability of material. The annuals and early illustrated magazines of the 1820s tended to be omnium gatherums, assembling whatever historical material lay nearest to hand. Much of it came from eighteenth-century antiquarianism and was not obviously suitable for the new market. It was *too* remote – medieval, ancient or even prehistoric – and reflected the aesthetic priorities of a different age and a different market. Most of the historic buildings illustrated in early annuals and popular magazines were picturesque medieval ruins, aimed at evoking the nostalgia, *memento mori* or Gothic thrill beloved of late eighteenth-century virtuosi (although a more modern reason to illustrate ruins was that they were accessible to tourism: among popular tourist sites of this period were the ruins of Netley Abbey, Kenilworth Castle and Fountains Abbey).[11]

More appealing to the modern audience was material from that minority interest of eighteenth-century antiquarianism known as 'popular antiquities', the study of sports, games, costume and customs. The limited amount of this material – much of it derived from the work of two men, Joseph Strutt and John Brand – was eagerly pillaged in the 1820s and early 1830s by painters, engravers and designers such as J. R. Planché, who inspired the first spectacular (and reasonably authentic) productions of Shakespeare in the 1820s. Another pillager was Sir Walter Scott, whose novels drew heavily on eighteenth-century popular antiquarianism. Scott's novels, like the early annuals and magazines, were fairly promiscuous in their historical settings and continued to appeal to older, more exclusive feelings of nostalgia and chivalry. But Scott was also a pioneer in pitching historical material to new mass tastes, emphasising not the exotic and exclusive but the familiar and domestic. It would be the latter parts of his *oeuvre* that the mass culture industry would select out in developing history for the masses in the 1830s.

For in the 1830s, as the mass culture industry matured, learning from its audience what sold but also growing more confident in its ability to shape that audience, a distinct style emerged and with it a specific kind of popular history. Of course, in the great mass of print, image and spectacle one can find bits of everything. But amongst all the flotsam and jetsam there are a central historical motif and a style which were dominant in the popular cultural market from the mid-1830s at least until the early 1850s and in certain respects later. I will call this dominant motif the 'Olden Time', to refer both to a specific period in English history beloved of the early Victorians and to the literary and visual style in which it was represented.

Chronologically the 'Olden Time' began in the late fifteenth century with the advent of the Tudors and ended around the time of the Civil War.[12] The medievalism that had dominated polite antiquarianism and to some extent the mass culture market in its early phases definitely declines in significance in the 1830s. One can see this in the subject matter of Royal Academy paintings, to a great extent dictated by the engravings market, as medieval topics give way to Tudor and especially Stuart ones.[13] One can see it, too, in the sensational popularity of Harrison Ainsworth as a popular historical novelist – by 1840 exceeding even that of Scott. Like the painters, Ainsworth was highly sensitive to market demand and scrupulously avoided medieval settings. The peak of his career was reached in the early 1840s with three novels set in Tudor or Stuart times.[14] The penny press also began to move away from medieval topics and to promote the 'golden days' of 'Good Queen Bess' as more worthy of scrutiny and admiration.

How can we account for the popular market's shift away from medievalism in the 1830s? The Middle Ages had always posed religious difficulties for English antiquarians. In the 1830s, as medievalism was taken up by romantic Tories, it began to pose political difficulties as well: chivalry and courtly romance became too closely identified with hyper-aristocratic high-jinks such as the Eglinton tournament, Young England or Queen Victoria's costume balls. However romanticised, the religious superstition, bloodthirstiness and chivalric exclusivity with which the Middle Ages were inextricably linked could never have made a strong positive appeal to the new popular audiences (though they could be, and were, still used for sensational purposes). The Tudors, on the other hand, offered manifest advantages. While Whig historians were unhappy with the Tudors (as well as the Stuarts) for their authoritarianism and preferred to dwell upon the post-1688 dispensation, popular historians cared less about parliamentary and military history but found much to admire socially and culturally in Tudor England.[15]

First, there was Tudor England as 'Merry England'. While the eighteenth-century antiquarians had clearly identified the origins of many traditional English games and rituals in the Middle Ages, uncomfortably associated with the Catholic Church, their persistence and adaptation in the Tudor period meant that they could still be celebrated as part of the 'Olden Time'.[16] Early Victorian illustrations of games and rituals tend to take them out of their medieval, ecclesiastical settings and transplant them into a Tudor, communal environment (Plate 3). One of the earliest and most imitated of these illustrations was C. R. Leslie's painting of 'May

PLOUGH MONDAY :— Dance of Bessy and the Clown.

BRINGING IN THE YULE LOG ON CHRISTMAS EVE.

**3** Tudor games and rituals, drawn by R. W. Buss for Vol. ii of G. L. Craik and
Charles Macfarlane's *Pictorial History of England*, published in 1839 by Charles Knight.

Day revels in the time of Queen Elizabeth' (1821), partly inspired by Walter Scott and deliberately composed with an eye to the popular engravings market (Plate 4).

> I am in hopes it will be popular [Leslie wrote to his sister] as it is a period that Englishmen are fond of recurring to ... They are also more generally acquainted with the manners of that time than any other, on account of the greater popularity of Shakespeare than any other English writer whatever.[17]

Even more widely reproduced were the representations of sports and revels taking place in and around country houses, depicted by Joseph Nash in his celebrated *Mansions of England in the Olden Time* (1839–49), reprinted immediately upon publication in the *Saturday Magazine* and then liberally copied and miscopied throughout the popular press. Nash's lithographs portrayed nobles and commons carousing together at games of hoodman bind, shovel-board and bowls, and in Christmas revels with morris dancers, hobby-horses and the yule log. There is nothing more feudal than 'tilting at the quintain', an innocent post-chivalric entertainment, and even the craft of arms is mocked with playful attempts at fencing and a little boy parading with helmet and sabre.

Second, as Nash's drawings also illustrate, there is Tudor England as 'Social England' – that is, an England of greater social equality than existed before or after. Medieval romances raised doubts as to whether everyone was really sharing

**4** R. Leslie's 'May Day revels in the time of Queen Elizabeth' (1821), in an engraved version dating from the 1830s.

**5** Christmas festivities at Haddon Hall, from *The Mansions of England in the Olden Time*, i (1839).

in the fun. The general prosperity that was thought to have materialised in the fifteenth century made Tudor romances easier to swallow. With the advent of Henry VII, pronounced one best-selling pictorial history, we find 'the beginning of the same social system that still subsists [today]', 'a condition of progressive amelioration ... the state of things that best keeps a people in spirits, and diffuses most content and enjoyment among all classes'.[18] Even if 'progressive amelioration' in its early phases had hardly begun to touch the cottages of England – a point which the *Edinburgh Review*, in a rare notice, drew sternly to the attention of the popular historians – still the spirit of popular advancement was in the land and, most important, taken to heart by the nation's leaders.[19]

The mansions of England in the Olden Time were of interest precisely because they were interpreted as communal spaces betokening social harmony, places of hospitality, almost of co-residence between the classes. Nash's mansions were intimate, crowded, vernacular, deliberately counterposed to the cold and formal cosmopolitanism of the later neoclassical palaces, emparked behind walls or raised upon eminences (Plate 5). Both Nash and Ainsworth were critical of the eighteenth-century view that the mansions of the Olden Time had been crude and uncomfortable – a view tenable only by modern aristocrats who had got over-refined and distant from the people. The Olden Time was simple, not crude; what the ruling class then lacked in polish it made up for in warmth and common humanity. 'Not harsh and rugged are the ways/Of hoar antiquity, but strewn with flowers,' quoted Nash.[20] Hospitality was particularly valued as a form of sharing more equitable than either the religious charity of the Middle Ages or the philanthropy *de haut en bas* of modern times.[21] Queen Elizabeth's progresses around the country were viewed in the same light.[22] These fascinations do not reflect nostalgia; they formed, rather, part of an argument about the true nature of the English nation, which had been born under the Tudors, had gone astray after the Civil War and could yet be put right.

Third, there is Tudor England as 'Domestic England'. Whatever ferment was taking place in higher political and religious circles in the Olden Time, down among the people peace and harmony permitted the English to cultivate the domestic virtues. It is fashionable nowadays to decry early Victorian domesticity as an instrument of social control, confining workers (especially women workers) to their fireside when they would rather be out revelling or rioting, but in these representations of popular history domesticity has an unbridled, democratic flavour. Combining the themes of Merry England and Social England, the home is portrayed as a place where high and low enjoyed the same 'recreations and pastimes', either separately or (as depicted by Nash) together in the mansion's great hall.[23] The pictorial *style* of Olden Time representations was also domestic, that is, it shrank the Grand Manner of the Georgian artist down to a humbler scale, literally in replacing the painter's canvas with the octavo woodcut, figuratively in replacing the grandeur of classical or picturesque subjects with the small-scale simplicity of the genre scene. It is a commonplace of Victorian art history to associate the democratisation of the art audience in the 1830s and 1840s with the rise of genre painting, and genre painting's two most common subjects were domestic and historical, often in combination.[24] Domesticity in the Olden Time was thus one of the great tropes of early Victorian culture: childish games abound; maids bill and coo with their swains; lutes are plucked in quiet corners, and, less quietly, 'madrigals and glees and songs resound'; simple but hearty meals are served to weary fathers resting from their labours (Plate 6).

Also, books are read: for, finally, there is Tudor England as 'Literary England'. Although the early Victorian emphasis on literacy is also often portrayed as aimed against popular politics, it is the mass culture market's pride in the national vernacular literature that seems to me most aggressively populist. Though the themes of communal festivity and hospitality in the great hall helped to gloss over the problem, early Victorian writers and illustrators were of course aware that Tudor cottages were not yet places of plenty – that was the province and pride of modern times. What the cottage *did* have in common with the mansion, even in Tudor times, was the word. At first the word was metaphysical – that is, it was represented by popular religion in the parish church and not by the physical possession of books. Gradually it became more material. Shakespeare was the greatest glory of the Olden Time because his words were written for and became the common property of all Englishmen, enjoyed by all classes in performance and later in print. Nor was he alone. 'Never in the history of the world, before or since, did great men spring up so numerously,' Charles Knight

**6** Domesticity in the Olden Time: children's games around the hearth, set by Joseph Nash in the gallery over the hall at Knole, from *The Mansions of England in the Olden Time*, ii (1840).

claimed, 'and ... not in the majority of cases for mere temporary purposes.' While spurned in their own lifetime as 'humble servants', these literary heroes would – unlike their haughty patrons – achieve immortality by enlivening the leisure hours of the modern working man. It was for its literary accomplishments, pronounced one popular illustrated magazine in 1847, that the Elizabethan era deserved to be regarded as the most important in English history, 'for a nation without a literary era must ever remain amongst the rude communities from whose barbarous seats of power little save desolating wars can proceed'.[25]

The more radical commentators, like William Howitt (who published with his wife Mary a popular illustrated journal with a peak circulation of 30,000 in the late 1840s), explicitly conjoined the literacy and liberty of the Olden Time. Drawing the usual distinction between the martial arts and power politics, the province of an elite, and social or cultural history that mattered to the people, Howitt forgave the Sidneys for their nobility:

it is by a far higher nobility than that of ancient descent, or martial or political power, that the name of Sidney arrests the admiration of Englishmen. It is one of the great watchwords of liberty. It is one of the household words of English veneration. It is a name hallowed by some of our proudest historical and literary associations; identified in the very staple of our minds with a sense of high principle, magnanimity of sentiment, and generous and heroic devotion to the cause of our country and of men.[26]

Just as Olden Time domesticity contributed a theme and a style to early Victorian genre painting, so the Olden Time vernacular contributed to early Victorian literature. Scott had pioneered the conscious imitation of early English poetry and folk tales in the composition of his early epics. He hoped to use these Olden Time models to transcend the limiting cosmopolitanism and politeness of Augustan literature. By the time of the Howitts the use of these Olden Time forms had become commonplace and clearly marks the poetry and prose of the annuals and the popular magazines as well as of souls on a higher plane like Tennyson.

These four themes – Merry England, social connection, domesticity and vernacular literature – hardly exhaust the uses of the Olden Time by the mass culture industry, but they convey the essential message. Far from carrying a nostalgic and hierarchical meaning, as is alleged on those rare occasions when the subject is even noticed, English romantic history in the early Victorian period aimed at establishing a pedigree and a template for a mass cultural style in the present. Consumers of this history did not want to dance around a maypole, but they did want to honour what the maypole stood for and to imagine what might stand for the maypole in the present. As one popular writer put it,

> It can scarcely be a question whether we – that is, the public – desire to see what is usually called 'the good old times' revivified in reality ... [yet] with all our love of the advantages among which we live, and with all our appreciation of the comforts, social and political, that surround us on every side, we revert with no little pride and pleasure to what our ancestors were, and to what they did ...[27]

This kind of romantic history stressed not the alien and unfamiliar in the past but the intimate and domestic, praiseworthy characteristics of 'our ancestors' that had remained features of popular (but, alas, less so of elite) culture. It was part of a broader movement to build a homogeneous and democratic cultural nation. In this it shared much with French or German romantic history, though without the same explicitly political content.

By 1850 it had reached something of a peak. Thereafter the culture was commercialised further, became too diverse to maintain a homogeneous style, and the mass audience became less tolerant of seriousness and didacticism. Romantic history retained a place at the table but was rather swamped in the diversity of fare available. The novels of Scott and Ainsworth remained popular but represented a particular taste, increasingly associated with youths. Engravings of the Olden Time continued to feature in illustrated magazines throughout the century, but more in the margins, as in the super-illustrated Christmas issues of the *Illustrated London News*. Around 1870 *Punch* was satirising the art world's appetite for the Olden Time as insufficiently racy for the modern audience.

For all that, the Olden Time continued into our own century to embody most English people's idea of the national past, in so far as they had any such ideas at all. The early nineteenth-century cult of the 'Olden Time' was the source of much later thinking about 'Englishness'. Linda Colley may be right that a multi-national ruling class constructed an idea of 'Britishness' during the wars of the long eighteenth century, but in the mass cultural currents considered here there was a pronounced reaction *against* Britishness as reflecting merely constitutional and military preoccupations, the province of an elite. Romantic history issuing from London was nearly always *English*, emphasising the peaceful, cultural and socially inclusive achievements of the English people before the constitutional changes of 1688, 1707 and 1801.

It was, of course, possible to take the early Victorian idea of 'Englishness' and give it all sorts of different spins. After 1850 Kingsley, Froude and Seeley rewrote the Olden Time to emphasise previously neglected racial and imperial themes.[28] Later still, the Arts and Crafts idea of Englishness – also with demonstrable links with the early Victorian cult of the Olden Time – developed both socialist and reactionary variations. But the original idea of the Olden Time also persisted and meant that it remained possible to have a pacific, democratic and culturally defined idea of Englishness – and also that, in preferring 'Englishness' to 'Britishness', one was making a choice for the whole of the people and their cultural heritage *against* the ruling classes, their empty authority and bloodlust.

A single illustration of this persistence may open up an avenue that deserves further research. The notion, planted by the romantic history movement in the 1830s, that the monuments of the Olden Time were part of the national heritage has certainly helped to open up public access to heritage sites, over the resistance of private property interests, just as French and German romantic history did (more effectively) in those countries. Both Hampton Court and the Tower of London were opened to the public commercially in 1839 and quickly became the greatest historical attractions in the metropolis, drawing hundreds of thousands of visitors a year.[29] One of the first historic buildings to be municipalised was Aston Hall, one of Nash's mansions, taken over by Birmingham in 1864 and turned into a people's park and museum. After a disastrous fire in 1871 a public appeal raised the funds to rebuild Warwick Castle, virtually forcing the Earl of Warwick to turn it into a commercial tourist attraction, the first fully commer-cialised stately home, in 1885.[30] Although sentiment about a national heritage for the people may well have been stronger in the 1840s than at any time in the next century, in so far as people *did* continue to cherish an idea of a national heritage it was one built upon the Olden Time and its domestic and literary associations. It is only since the Second World War that the public mind has been opened to a wide variety of alternative heritages. Until then open admiration for the Georgian aristocracy, for example, had been made difficult if not impossible by a lingering awareness of the Victorians' fierce, populist contempt for that effete and cosmo-politan class, and by a lingering attachment to the better men and better days of Good Queen Bess.[31]

## Notes

1 This view is implicit in G. P. Gooch, *History and Historians in the Nineteenth Century* (London, Longman, 1952); less so in Harry Elmer Barnes, *A History of Historical Writing* (New York, Dover, 1962), chs 8–9, but see pp. 185–9 on the differential impact of Scott; Thomas Preston Pear-don, *The Transition in English Historical Writing, 1760–1830* (New York, Columbia University

Press, 1933), esp. pp. 216, 232–3, 271–6; Michael Hunter, 'The preconditions of preservation: a historical perspective', in David Lowenthal and Marcus Binney (eds), *Our Past before Us: Why do we Save it?* (London, Temple Smith, 1981).

2 J. W. Burrow, *A Liberal Descent: Victorian Historians and the English Past* (Cambridge, Cambridge University Press, 1981); on whiggish history by Oxbridge-educated writers, Philippa Levine, *The Amateur and the Professional: Antiquarians, Historians and Archaeologists in Victorian England, 1838–86* (Cambridge, Cambridge University Press, 1986), and Timothy Lang, *The Victorians and the Stuart Heritage* (Cambridge, Cambridge University Press, 1995); Linda Colley, *Britons: Forging the Nation, 1707–1837* (New Haven and London, Yale University Press, 1992); on the mirroring of oppositional and Establishment constitutional history see R. J. Smith, *The Gothic Bequest: Medieval Institutions in British Thought, 1688–1863* (Cambridge, Cambridge University Press, 1987), and James A. Epstein, *Radical Expression: Political Language, Ritual, and Symbol in England, 1790–1850* (New York, Oxford University Press, 1994).

3 Exceptions to the above strictures tend therefore to be cultural rather than political historians, e.g. John Steegman, *Consort of Taste, 1830–70* (London, Sidgwick and Jackson, 1950); Roy Strong, *And when did you last see your father? The Victorian Painter and British History* (London, Thames and Hudson, 1978); Martin Meisel, *Realizations: Narrative, Pictorial, and Theatrical Arts in Nineteenth Century England* (Princeton, Princeton University Press, 1983); Stephen Bann, *The Clothing of Clio: a Study of the Representation of History in Nineteenth Century Britain and France* (Cambridge, Cambridge University Press, 1984), to all of which I am indebted for my starting point.

4 For one political historian's appreciation of this, not followed up, see Olive Anderson, 'The political uses of history in mid-nineteenth-century England', *Past and Present* 36 (1967), 87–105.

5 Richard D. Altick, *The English Common Reader* (Chicago, University of Chicago Press, 1957); Louis James, *Fiction for the Working Man, 1830–50* (Oxford, Oxford University Press, 1963); Celina Fox, *Graphic Journalism in England during the 1830s and 1840s* (New York and London, Garland, 1988); Patricia Anderson, *The Printed Image and the Transformation of Popular Culture, 1790–1860* (Oxford, Clarendon Press, 1991).

6 Bann, *Clothing of Clio*; Michael R. Booth, *Victorian Spectacular Theatre, 1850–1910* (London, Routledge, 1981). There is hardly anything on popular tourism, but see J. A. R. Pimlott, *The Englishman's Holiday: a Social History* (London, Faber and Faber, 1947), 76–93; Ronald Russell, *guide to British Topographical Prints* (Newton Abbot, David and Charles, 1979); Peter Mandler, *The Fall and Rise of the Stately Home* (New Haven and London, Yale University Press, 1997), ch. 2.

7 But for similar kinds of material issuing from Manchester see Patrick Joyce, *Visions of the People: Industrial England and the Question of Class, 1840–1914* (Cambridge, Cambridge University Press, 1991), pp. 173–82. Edinburgh and Dublin also had a popular press which I have not considered here.

8 Anderson, *The Printed Image*, p. 80. For varying opinions on the social character of the 'respectable' penny press see further the citations in note 9 below.

9 These matters arouse controversy. For the traditional view that the mass-culture industry in this period reflected 'middle-class values' aimed at stemming working-class radicalism see R. K. Webb, *The British Working Class Reader, 1790–1848* (London, Allen and Unwin, 1955), ch. 3; Patricia Hollis, *The Pauper Press: a Study in Working Class Radicalism of the 1830s* (Oxford, Oxford University Press, 1970), chs 3–4; Brian Maidment, 'Magazines of popular progress and the artisans', *Victorian Periodicals Review*, 17 (1984), 83–94; Jon P. Klancher, *The Making of English Reading Audiences, 1790–1832* (Madison, University of Wisconsin Press, 1987). For a different view, towards which I lean, which gives more weight to the demand pressures of the mass audience (even in considering the output of Charles Knight) see Scott Bennett, 'The editorial character and readership of *The Penny Magazine*: an analysis', *Victorian Periodicals Review*, 17 (1984), 127–141; Anderson, *The Printed Image*, ch. 2. Altick, *English Common Reader*, esp. pp. 136–40, falls somewhere in between.

10 *Saturday Magazine*, 1 (1832), 'Introduction'.

11 Both the *Penny Magazine* and the *Saturday Magazine* limited their coverage of historic buildings almost exclusively to ruins until the late 1830s, at which point mansions of the Olden Time began to figure.

12 Keith Thomas, *The Perception of the Past in Early Modern England*, Creighton Trust Lecture (London, University of London, 1983), p. 22, suggests in passing that Victorian images of Merry England were 'too vague to be capable of any precise chronological location', but this is not borne out by a systematic survey. I do not mean to suggest that early Victorian evocations of the 'Olden Time' or 'Merry England' invariably referred to the Tudors and early Stuarts – sometimes the fifteenth or the eighteenth century was meant – but only that there was a predominating interest in this period.

13 My calculations from the chronological lists in Strong, *And when did you last see your father?*

14 James, *Fiction for the Working Man*, pp. 89–91; see also the 'Chronology of Ainsworth's romances' in W. E. A. Axon, *William Harrison Ainsworth: a memoir* (London, Gibbings, 1902).

15 George L. Craik and Charles Macfarlane, *The Pictorial History of England*, 4 vols (London, Knight, 1837–41), the best-selling history of its day (issued in monthly parts), was subtitled, 'Being a History of the People, as well as a History of the Kingdom'; see also Charles Knight's insistence that the people's comforts and manners were more important than their constitutional arrangements, in *The Popular History of England*, 8 vols (London, Bradbury and Evans, 1856–62), i. ii–iv.

16 For surveys of the 'Merry England' theme in Victorian culture see Roy Judge, 'May Day and Merrie England', *Folklore*, 102 (1991), 131–48; Rebecca Jeffrey Easby, 'The myth of Merrie England in Victorian painting', in Florence S. Boos (ed.), *History and Community: Essays in Victorian Medievalism* (New York, Garland, 1992); Ronald Hutton, *The Stations of the Sun: a History of the Ritual Year in Britain* (Oxford, Oxford University Press, 1996). These treatments exaggerate the nostalgic and reactionary elements in the 'Merry England' theme by dealing almost exclusively with its elite manifestations. What may have been true of Daniel Maclise, Carlyle, Young England and miscellaneous squirearchical fantasists was decidedly not true of the penny press or the cheap engravings market.

17 C. R. Leslie, *Autobiographical Recollections*, 2 vols (London, John Murray, 1860), ii. 85.

18 Craik and Macfarlane, *Pictorial History*, ii. 268, 899; see also 'The rise and decline of chivalry in England', *Sharpe's London Magazine*, 4 (1847), 183–5; similar sentiments have been found in Victorian schoolbooks by Valerie E. Chancellor, *History for their Masters: Opinion in the English History Textbook, 1800–1914* (Bath, Adams and Dart, 1970), pp. 29–31.

19 'The pictorial history of England', *Edinburgh Review*, 74 (1841–42), 465–72, predictably opting (with Hallam) for the eighteenth century as the truly 'happy age of Old England'. The *Edinburgh*, like *Fraser's* (which also occasionally commented on popular history), looked askance at the genre as unscholarly and sentimental, missing entirely its ideological content.

20 S. M. Ellis, *William Harrison Ainsworth and his Friends*, 2 vols (London, John Lane, 1911), i. 286–7; Joseph Nash, *Descriptions of the Plates of the Mansions of England in the Olden Time* (London, M'Lean, 1849), pp. 1–2; Charles L. Eastlake, *A History of the Gothic Revival* (London, Longman, 1872), pp. 238–9.

21 For just a few representations of social relations between aristocracy and people along these lines see William Hone, *The Every-day Book and Table Book*, 3 vols (London, Tegg, 1831), ii. 1617–26; William Howitt, *The Rural Life of England*, 2 vols (London, Longman, 1838), i. 324–8. Much play was made with the centrality of the great hall in Olden Time mansions such as Penshurst, Knole and Haddon; see, further, Mandler, *Fall and Rise*, chs 1–2. Hospitality and interdependence were also a constant theme in the *Saturday Magazine* reproductions of Nash's *Mansions* in the 1840s.

22 Series on Queen Elizabeth's progresses ran in both the *Saturday Magazine* (January–September 1838) and the *Penny Magazine* (January–December 1843).

23 Praise of the ordinary 'half-timber house' under the Tudors often began on architectural grounds but ended up as social and domestic commentary: see, e.g., *Art Union*, October 1839, p. 156 (including an attack on Pugin for falsely associating these good Protestant homes with the Catholic fifteenth century), *Penny Magazine*, 2 March 1844, pp. 89–91.

24 On the role of Scott in assisting artists across the bridge from the 'Grand Manner' to genre painting see, in addition to Strong, *And when did you last see your father?*, Catherine Gordon, 'The illustration of Sir Walter Scott: nineteenth century enthusiasm and adaptation', *Journal of the Warburg and Courtauld Institutes*, 34 (1971), 297–317.

25 *Old England: A Pictorial Museum* ..., 2 vols (London, Knight, 1845), ii. 127; W. D., 'Eras of English civilisation', *Sharpe's London Magazine*, 4 (1847), 247–8.

26 William Howitt, *Visits to Remarkable Places: Old Halls, Battle Fields, and Scenes Illustrative of Striking Passages in English History and Poetry* (London, Longman, 1840), p. 2. Sidney was also a fixture of the penny press, but almost always in his literary rather than his military guise. Chancellor, *History for their Masters*, pp. 70–5, found that artistic figures predominated over military heroes in schoolbooks until the end of the century.

27 *Art Journal*, July 1857, p. 209; the author was probably the magazine's editor, S. C. Hall.

28 Raymond Chapman, *The Sense of the Past in Victorian Literature* (London, Croom Helm, 1986), pp. 83–100; Lang, *Victorians and the Stuart Heritage*, pp. 187–90.

29 Report of the Select Committee on National Monuments and Works of Art, *Parliamentary Papers* (1841), vi. 440–1, 658–96; Adrian Tinniswood, *A History of Country House Visiting* (London, Blackwell, 1989), pp. 130–7.

30 These episodes are discussed further in Mandler, *Fall and Rise*, ch. 2.

31 Strong, *And when did you last see your father?*, p. 11, sees Victorian history painting as influential until the Second World War; the prestige of Nash, Ainsworth and even Scott seems to me also to fall off thereafter. On the growing appreciation of the Georgian heritage see Mandler, *Fall and Rise*, chs 7–9.

## Acknowledgements

This chapter expands upon themes introduced in chapter 7 of my book *The Fall and Rise of the Stately Home* (New Haven and London, Yale University Press, 1997). I would like to thank audiences at the Victoria and Albert Museum and at the Universities of Warwick, Sussex, Hertfordshire and Oxford for comments on earlier versions.

# 6

## Early Victorian Wales and its crisis of identity

### PRYS MORGAN

In 1770 an intrepid Englishwoman, Elizabeth Baker, came from London to Dolgellau as a mining prospector. Two years later the inhabitants still caused her surprise: 'The people in general are so different from the English one is amazed to think they are subjects to the same Monarchy.' In 1781, seeing a newspaper article suggesting that Welsh should be extirpated and English manners and morals introduced, she exclaimed, 'Whoever wrote it must be a perfect stranger to the Ancient Britons – with pride I confess myself an Englishwoman ... and my wish is they may never lose their language.'[1] By the period from the 1840s to the 1860s things had changed completely. English scorn and hatred for the Welsh had become rampant, despite the sympathetic tone of George Borrow's *Wild Wales* (1862) and Matthew Arnold's *Lectures on Celtic Literature* (1867), and the Welsh had become a people not only of multiple, but of muddled, identities. Hussey Vivian, of Cornish origins, MP for Swansea, told the Swansea Eisteddfod in 1863 that Welsh should be cultivated, of course, but added, 'Remember that you are all Englishmen, though you are Welsh ... Depend upon it, we must consider ourselves Englishmen.'[2] The *Saturday Review* of 4 September 1867 said, 'Kept within proper limits, the worship of Welsh nationality is a harmless one, and may incidentally preserve some useful qualities from merging in the dead level of English society,'[3] but papers such as *The Times* were virulently anti-Welsh. *The Times* of 8 September 1866 stated, 'The Welsh language is the curse of Wales, excluding the Welsh from progress and civilisation,' adding, a week later, that Wales was 'a small country, inhabited by an unenterprising people'. All its progress and civilisation had come from England. 'The sooner all Welsh specialities disappear from the face of the earth the better.'[4] Leaders of Welsh opinion were divided on the question. Such educational technocrats as Hugh Owen and Thomas Nicholas, and even the Celtic scholar, John Rhys, tending to agree with such opinions, while patriotic papers such as *Y Cymro*, *Y Gwron* and *Y Gwladgarwr* were hostile. The public were anxious to learn English and English ways, although adopting with alacrity as national anthem in 1856 *Hen wlad fy nhadau* ('Land of my fathers'),[5] and in 1865 setting up what they intended to be a self-governing Welsh-language 'colony' in Patagonia.[6] John Mills suggested to the national Eisteddfod in 1867 that the Ottoman government was entirely sympathetic to Welsh plans to set up a Welsh 'colony' in Palestine, a notion appealing to those who muddled Welsh identity even more by claiming Welsh descent from the Jews, but nothing came of that.

When Elizabeth Baker wrote in the late eighteenth century, the multiple identities of the Welsh or the British did not deeply matter, since most of the Welsh lived their lives in local communities, only a small minority taking part in politics (which would need a knowledge of English), and the impact of England, or a greater Britain, touched their lives only marginally. But by the middle of the nineteenth century, when Wales was for the first time being integrated into Britain politically and economically, Welsh identity was deeply affected. Could the Welsh be totally integrated into Britain while yet retaining a national identity? It was a matter of debate, causing one of the greatest cultural crises the Welsh had experienced. How the Welsh succeeded in squaring this particular circle is the subject of this chapter.

The Principality of Wales survived as a fiscal unit into the late eighteenth century; the regional government of the Council of Wales and the Marches had disappeared in 1689; the Welsh legal system of the Courts of Great Sessions (set up by the Tudors) was under attack from the 1780s onwards, and was abolished in 1830. Welsh objections to their abolition were brushed aside with disdain, parts of Wales being simply attached to the nearest parts of England. Daniel O'Connell opposed the Bill as a thing of no public utility.[7] The Tudor dynasty had firmly established Anglicanism in Wales but the old loyalty to the Church gradually wore thin in the eighteenth century, with few Welshmen given preferment under the Hanoverians, and with a growing number of the people turning to Methodism or Dissent. The Welsh were still aware of themselves as a distinct language group, but aware too that their culture was moribund, their institutions in a state of decline or dissolution.

Until the 1750s the Welsh were seen by the English as strange and eccentric neighbours, provincials rather than foreigners, too few, too poor and too weak to be threatening – the half-million or so population was only about one-eighth that of Ireland. There was a large market in England almost until the end of the eighteenth century for engravings of comic cartoons of 'Poor Taffy' (and his wife), Welsh men and women who could not afford a horse, shown riding a goat, leeks poking out of their hatbands, round cheeses bulging from their panniers, and parchments of ancient pedigrees sticking out of their pockets.[8]

This image of Wales changed during the eighteenth century. First there was a revival of interest in Welsh history, literature, language and customs, led by the new middle class (such as the Morris brothers of Anglesey) displacing the old gentry patronage.[9] Second, the Welsh, like the other peoples of Britain, began to be seen as slightly less unequal partners in a Britannic struggle against the French.[10] The leading cultural association, the Honourable Society of Cymmrodorion, was founded in 1751 largely by Richard Morris of the Navy Office, Whitehall, and the seventh and eighth verses of the Cymmrodorion anthem lambasted the French and Spanish enemies of Britain.[11] Third, the Romantic movement throughout Europe caused a revaluation of peripheral peoples previously scorned: the extensive literature produced by travellers in Wales from 1770 onwards shows that often the Welsh were admired as children of nature, while reactionaries admired the remoteness of the Welsh from urban luxuries and mob politics. Romanticism also brought about a rediscovery or revaluation of Ancient Britain, the Welsh being cherished by some as extraordinary survivors from that world (hence Elizabeth Baker's 'Ancient Britons') and by others as a link with Caractacus and Boadicea, symbolic of British resistance to Continental foes.[12] The mountainous Welsh landscape, mocked before 1750 as the 'rubbish of Noah's Flood', or the 'Fag-end of Creation', a landscape of which the Welsh were ashamed, thinking it a divine punishment that they had been forced to scrape a living from such unrewarding terrain, came to be admired for its own sake, its stark beauty, its newly discovered mineral riches, its newly found geological interest, and as a fortress of ancient liberties and a bulwark against invaders.[13] Foreign tourists flocked to see sights such as waterfalls, which the Welsh imagined could be found in anybody's back garden, the landscape becoming by the 1830s a matter of national pride – the second verse of the national anthem 'Land of my fathers' (1856) is about 'Old mountainous Wales, paradise of the bards'. A powerful national institution, the Eisteddfod, was revived, its innumerable meetings devoted to the study of Welsh history, poetry and music. Romantic myths about the antiquity of Welsh drove an army of grammarians and lexicographers to study ancient texts, and invent modern vocabularies, so that the burgeoning Welsh popular press could cope, for instance, with modern science and similar subjects.[14]

At the end of the eighteenth century there were signs that Romanticism affected many Welsh intellectuals and early radicals with a dimly perceived national-ism.[15] The myth of Prince Madoc discovering America in the late twelfth century inspired early radicals to organise parties of Welsh emigrants to America, to create free Welsh settlements and perhaps reunite with the long-lost Welsh Red Indians, descendants of Madoc's companions.[16] From 1815 to the 1830s, although ageing radicals such as Edward Williams, 'Iolo Morganwg', were powerful gurus, Welsh Romanticism was dominated by reactionary patriots, including many Anglican clerics, and a group of eccentric and colourful ladies such as Augusta Hall (Lady Llanover), publiciser of the Welsh 'national costume' and Lady Charlotte Guest, translator of the corpus of medieval stories which she called *The Mabinogion*. The Romantic Wales which was created by those three generations of publicists, eighteenth-century antiquaries, radicals and reactionaries remained in the back-ground of Welsh life throughout the nineteenth century, but, even as it was created, it seemed at odds with the emerging reality of early nineteenth-century Wales and, by the 1840s and 1850s, was being relentlessly besieged and attacked.

The most striking difference between image and reality was caused by the coming of industry to what had been one of the most backward regions of Britain. By the late eighteenth century Wales had become a hive of industry, home to some of the largest enterprises of their kind in the world, and to some of the most novel ventures.[17] New links and interconnections were created, the Welsh moving in droves to cities such as Liverpool, while large numbers of capitalists and workers poured into Welsh industrial areas from other parts of Britain. The movement of capital, materials, transport and workers to and fro created a British unity more powerful than the Protestant or anti-French unity forged by the Hanoverians, although it has been observed that industrialisation created a system of regional economic inequality in Britain, emphasising for the Welsh that their economy was a subservient one, serving the needs of mostly English capitalism, thus creating a new kind of difference between the Welsh and English peoples.[18]

The second element making the Romantic image of Welsh life absurd was the instability and violence of Welsh society from the 1790s to the 1840s.[19] Even remote rural counties, such as Montgomeryshire, were in a state of crisis by the end of the eighteenth century,[20] and although rioting was repressed during the great wars, from 1816 onwards Welsh industrial areas were torn by violent strikes; there were dangerous uprisings in Merthyr Tydfil in 1831 and in Newport in 1839, while much of west Wales was drawn into the Rebecca riots from 1839 to 1843. It has been said that by the 1840s, as a result of popular violence, south Wales was the most militarised zone in Britain.[21]

The third reason why Welsh society no longer bore any resemblance to the older image was the growth of religious Dissent. Religious revivals and popular evangelicalism had their origins in the eighteenth century, but it was after 1800 that they made their main impact, with Dissenting meeting houses opening in most parts of Wales at the rate of one per fortnight during the early nineteenth century, so that by the time of the 1851 religious census the great majority of worshippers attended Dissenting meeting houses, by then usually called Nonconformist chapels.[22] Nonconformity was of English origins, but by the early nineteenth century such was its success in converting the Welsh masses and its skill at dealing with what were seen as particularly Welsh problems such as drunkenness, that the movement took on a Welsh colouring.[23] Even in the 1820s there were signs that Nonconformity was beginning to be identified with Welshness, and this became a commonplace by the 1840s. A Welsh journal exclaimed, 'O Wales, where is there a comparable land to thee under Heaven? And what nation under the sun has so many of the marks of religion on it as the Welsh nation? Forget not the gifts of God!'[24] Thomas Stephens, Unitarian scholar and chemist of Merthyr, said that religiosity was a unique feature of the Welsh, and that they were the most religious people in the whole of Europe, save the Scots.[25] One sign of the religious awareness is the urge to send distinctively Welsh missions abroad, to Brittany, Madagascar and (from 1841 onwards) to the Khasi Jaintia hills of north-east India.[26]

The fourth reason why Wales no longer resembled her eighteenth-century self, as seen by the Romantics, was politicisation. The first Welsh radical movement at the end of the eighteenth century had been snuffed out by government repression at the time of the Napoleonic wars, but political discussion returned after 1816, and by 1820 the Welsh journals reported large public meetings, for example to protest against the abolition of the Welsh legal institutions. *The Cambro-Briton* objected, 'But why should not Wales have some institutions of her own, to distinguish her sons, by calling forth their talent and genius, and embodying whatever may give dignity to the descendents [sic] of the primordial Britons?[27] The repeal of the Test and Corporation Acts in 1828, then Catholic Emancipation in 1829, excited Nonconformist interest in politics. In the Merthyr rising of 1831 one of the chief motivations was frustration over the Reform Bill. During the 1830s the Nonconformists began to concern themselves with such questions as anti-slavery agitation, the payment of Church rates, the commutation of tithes, the complex question of working-class education and the question of State subvention for schools. The most powerful Welsh sect, the Calvinistic Methodists, controlled until his death in 1841 by the 'Methodist Pope', John Elias, warned their members against political or trade union involvement, but the younger generation of Methodists swung towards politicisation in the 1840s, one of the most significant shifts in nineteenth-century Welsh life.[28] In the mid-1830s, for example, Caernarfon was already a centre of activism for north Wales radicals, many of them frustrated methodists such as the artist Hugh Hughes and the poet William Williams, 'Caledfryn'. The flavour of their satirical radicalism can be discerned in the journal edited by the Bangor doctor O. O. Roberts, entitled *Figaro in Wales*.[29] The huge growth of population in the early nineteenth century (from about half a million in 1801 to around a million by the 1840s), the increase in the public's spending power, the spread of the railways, the growth of the Welsh press by leaps and bounds from the 1830s to the 1860s,[30] were all factors politicising the Welsh, even if there was little expansion in the parliamentary electorate. Wales's first (bilingual) workers' paper was *Y Gweithiwr* (The Workman), founded in 1834. The industrial, rural and Chartist agitations of the period, combined with all the Nonconformists' complaints, together with the activities of pressure groups such as the Anti-Corn Law League and then after 1844 the association eventually known as the 'Liberation Society' (for Church disestablishment), all combined to give the Welsh a political education.[31] Just as in the mid-eighteenth century a new middle-class leadership had transformed Welsh cultural life, in the 1840s and 1850s a new Welsh middle-class leadership transformed Welsh political life, so that the ground was long prepared for the Liberal advance in the general election of 1868.[32] At a level below that of parliamentary elections these people worked on boards of guardians, municipal councils, church vestries and school boards, to establish their power and influence as well as to improve social conditions.[33] This class, in the country as well as in the now important urban districts, struggled to replace the gentry and the Anglican clergy, and to this end they set themselves up not only as radical leaders but also as distinctly Welsh leaders.[34]

The fifth factor of importance was that by the 1840s and 1850s Welsh Romanticism itself was going out of fashion. It is true that British opinion had oscillated for over a hundred years between those who admired the Celts as noble savages and those who scorned them.[35] But in Wales itself Romanticism had for a whole generation puffed the Welsh up, and had given publicists such as Lady Llanover confidence in popularising Welsh culture. But by the late 1840s the mood was

changing: all over Europe a generation of scholars and scientists appeared, organising for the first time the professional academic sciences of history, archaeology
and philology. J. C. Prichard, a friend of Lady Llanover's, proved conclusively in
1831 that the Celtic tongues were simply parts of the Indo-European family.
Prichard's work was publicised throughout Europe by such scholars as Bopp, who
published his *Die Celtischen Sprachen* in 1839, and Zeuss who published his
*Grammatica Celtica* in 1853.[36] Older Welsh scholars had been instrumental in
founding the Welsh Manuscript Society and the Cambrian Archaeological Association but did not expect that the new sciences would undermine their fantastical
constructs. The chemist Thomas Stephens came to the fore as a severe new critic
of Welsh scholarship in the 1840s, rocking the Eisteddfod world in 1858 by
debunking the legend of Madoc's discovery of America. The prize at Llangollen
Eisteddfod was withheld by the older scholars, led by John Williams, 'Ab Ithel',
on the hilarious grounds that the essay should prove the Madoc legend, not
disprove it. The scandal destroyed the credibility of Welsh Romantic scholarship.[37]
A Continental scholar said of Stephens that 'he scaled the Celtic mythological
heavens and scattered the false gods and goddesses that disported there', and that
Stephens was 'regarded with distrust by Welsh enthusiasts'.[38] The advance of
history, archaeology and philology gnawed at the vitals of Welsh Romanticism,
and at the same time destroyed much of the goodwill for things Welsh and Celtic
created by eighteenth-century antiquaries. Antiquarianism had created a sense of
continuity between the present day and the past of Ancient Britain, the Welsh
seeing themselves as survivors from the world of ancient heroes, bards and Druids,
the substratum of British society. But from the 1770s or 1780s onwards there was
growing suspicion of antiquarianism which coalesced in the early nineteenth
century with the rise of Anglo-Saxonism, a pride in the more recent Germanic
origins of the English. This in turn coalesced with the growing scorn for primitive
peoples caused by familiarity with hordes of natives and aborigines in colonial
climes, which increased the arrogance of white Europeans. The early nineteenth
century, even before the work of Charles Darwin, saw growing interest in racial
theories, and in allied pseudo-sciences such as physiognomy and phrenology,
several English scholars believing that it was possible to prove scientifically the
racial superiority of the Teutons and the corresponding inferiority of the Celts
(and all other 'races'). All these new interests became intertwined at a time, from
the 1840s to the 1860s, when there was growing English suspicion of Welsh
truculence and, above all, fear of Irish immigration and violent nationalism,
expressed in such phenomena as the Fenian outrages.[39] Since the eighteenth century
the Welsh had greatly prided themselves on their unmixed language, considering
English as a tailor's scrapheap of a language,[40] and the land of the bards and
Druids as *par excellence* a land of poetry. But by the 1840s and 1850s English
critics were looking at Wales with the eyes of positivism. Cultures such as that
of Wales which were still stuck at the bardic or poetic stage in the progress of
civilisation were bound to lose the race.
The most important factors have been set out so that it can be seen that by

the 1840s the Welsh had the makings of a serious crisis of identity as they were forced to fit their irregular nationality into the procrustean bed of Anglicising Nonconformist industrial radicalism. The point at which the crisis was reached was the furore of 1847, which by the mid-1850s had become known as the 'Treason of the Blue Books'.[41] Government inquiries, commissions and statistical surveys were of course carried out in all parts of Britain in this period, but the great disturbances in industrial and eventually in rural Wales caused the government to pay attention to the Welsh. The Rebecca riots, which broke out in 1839, lasted until 1843 and suddenly died away, caused the government to institute an inquiry into the causes of the riots, which reported in 1844. It set in motion various commonsense changes to meet the grievances of the rioters over such matters as tollgate charges. But it also noted the persistence of Welsh as the central difficulty of benighted Welsh society, recommending the State to intervene in some way to help the common people learn English. This was a hornets' nest, since Wales in the 1840s was buzzing with all kinds of debates about education, the National and British schools being a battleground between Anglicans and Nonconformists, with yet more debate over the nature of education and training, and over State aid *v.* voluntaryism. The government had burned its fingers badly in 1843 over Sir James Graham's factory Bill, which Nonconformists felt would have handed over the education of the workers entirely to the Church, the ensuing frenzy of petitioning causing the government to drop its plans. A government inspector in Merthyr in 1845 recommended that a band of schoolmasters sent into Wales would be better than a body of police or soldiery. The government did nothing, until in March 1846 William Williams (of Welsh origins but then sitting as MP for Coventry), demanded that the government should set up a Royal Commission to look into the state of education in Wales, especially into the means the Welsh had of learning English. Williams was a Welsh-speaking Anglican, a radical MP and a self-made millionaire, who had voted with Peel on the Maynooth grant and was impressed by the national system of education as developed in Ireland.[42] He told the Commons, 'If the Welsh had the same advantage for education as the Scotch, they would, instead of appearing a distinct people, in no respect differ from the English: could it therefore not be wisdom and sound policy to send the English schoolmaster among them?'[43]

The government set up a commission of the education committee of the Privy Council, the secretary of the committee, (Sir) James Kay-Shuttleworth, appointing three young English barristers later in 1846 to undertake an extensive inquiry into Welsh education. These three produced a vast report in three parts early in 1847, and as a government report it was produced in blue covers.[44] Most of the report consisted of statistical lists describing schools, together with a huge amount of evidence taken from witnesses, but the most readable parts were the three personal reports of the commissioners, Lingen, Symons and Johnson. These short reports presented a damning picture of the Welsh common people, ill treated or neglected by their superiors, gentry, churchmen and industrialists, a people retarded and benighted by their lack of English, fickle, laggardly, unreliable, dishonest, dirty, unresourceful and lacking any methodicality, their womenfolk little better than slatterns and 'universally unchaste', their children bastards more often than not. The country was so poor and lacking in example or leadership, the religious bodies so often squabbling over sectarianism, that no system of schooling would ever arise from Wales itself. The reports drew the conclusion that a State-funded system of education should be introduced to teach English and introduce the Welsh to the world of English progress and civilisation. A great deal of weight was attached to the evidence of Anglican witnesses while that of Nonconformists was often ignored, and since Nonconformity was presented as a force which encouraged the use of Welsh it was shown as one of the main causes of Welsh backwardness. Lingen (writer of the first part of the report) attacked the language as a force keeping the Welsh always 'under the hatches', isolating the common folk from the upper portion of society; Symons (writer of the second part of the report) said, 'the Welsh language is a vast drawback to Wales, and a manifold barrier to the moral progress and the commercial prosperity of the people'. Johnson (who wrote the third part of the report, on north Wales) said much the same thing, and commented in a marginal note which reveals their attitude to the Welsh in the race for progress, 'Imperfect civilisation as seen in the Welsh language'.

The ferocity of the attack, coming as it were from appointees of the government and apparently backed with vast quantities of statistical evidence, took the Welsh by surprise. Many of the Welsh, despite all the factors making for change which have been mentioned earlier, still believed that they were one of the most godly peoples in Christendom, that the language had kept them free from impiety, isolating them from lewd and immoral English literature, and giving cohesion and continuity to the raw and bewildered communities of newly industrialised Wales. The rumpus which followed lasted for several years, beginning with a counter-attack by aggrieved Anglicans, followed by the two-pronged attack of the Nonconformist journalist Evan Jones, 'Ieuan Gwynedd', using satirical ballads and cartoons to pillory the commissioners, and publishing analytical pamphlets showing the statistical and factual foundations of the report to be inaccurate and its conclusions false. The initial reaction of the editors of the Welsh journals, Lewis Edwards in Y *Traethodydd* and David Rees in Y *Diwygiwr*, who had been called by his enemies in Yr *Haul* in 1843 'The Welsh O'Connell', was furiously nationalistic. William Williams of Coventry, who had started the debate, re-entered the fray, assisted by pamphleteers such as Kilsby Jones. Gradually, however, leaders of Welsh opinion began to take a more measured view, and to see that some of the points made were true and that reform was called for. It seems as though other Nonconformists perceived that they could turn the attacks of the Blue Books to their advantage, and emphasise that they were really attacks upon Nonconformity. Evan Jones, 'Ieuan Gwynedd', the bitterest critic of the Blue Books, talked of Wales as a Nonconformist nation, wronged on religious rather than nationalistic grounds. He and the artist Hugh Hughes produced a series of cartoons in 1848 for *The Principality*, the tenth and last of which shows Wales, personified as an old lady hurling the three Blue Book commissioners into Cardigan Bay, but the accompanying text makes it obvious that this is as a result of a wave of protest from Welsh Nonconformity as much as aggrieved nationality (Plate 7). Many of the Welsh believed that the government had deliberately set up the commission in order to vilify the Welsh or the Nonconformists.[45] Local radical

**7** 'Dame Venodotia sousing the spies, or Wales and the late Commission', published by *The Principality* (1848) as No. 10 in a series of ten cartoons 'Pictures for the Million of Wales'. Wales, in the form of an old woman, hurls into Cardigan Bay the three commissioners who compiled the Blue Books on Welsh education in 1847.

leaders in various parts of Wales called public meetings, which were attended by immense crowds, to protest against the libels of the Blue Books. Professor I. G. Jones has observed that these meetings in many cases brought to the fore the radicals who would lead Welsh politics in the 1860s. Henry Richard, for example, was brought back to Wales from London to speak in defence of his 'vilified Fatherland'.[46] The furore took on the sobriquet of 'Treason of the Blue Books' only when the quarrel was subsiding: Robert Jones Derfel, a young radical poet, and an admirer of Kossuth, wrote in 1854 a long satirical play, *Brad y Llyfrau Gleision* (Treason of the Blue Books), showing the whole commission to have been a diabolical plot hatched by Beelzebub in 10 Downing Street. It was a treason or conspiracy, in other words, against Wales. The public understood the historical basis of the satire because in 1853 a Romantic Welsh dramatist, Edward Roberts, 'Iorwerth Glan Aled', had published a play entitled *Brad y Cyllill Hirion* (Treason of the Long Knives), referring to the legend of the first Saxon conquest of Britain, achieved through the plot of Hengist and Horsa to slaughter the Welsh by the secretly concealed long knives.

The impression given so far is that Wales was goaded into a form of nationalist frenzy by the Blue Book controversy, and that is true of many Welsh leaders in the short term. Some of the older Anglican patriots, such as John Williams, 'Ab Ithel', or David James, 'Dewi o Ddyfed', never forgave the attacks of the Blue Books and remained faithful to the Romantic patriotism of an earlier age. Some younger Nonconformist radicals sulked in their tents, such as Michael Daniel Jones, dreaming up plans for escapist Welsh-language colonies overseas.[47] Some of the Welsh-language journals, *Yr Amserau*, *Y Faner* and others, could on occasion be nationalist in tone. William Rees, 'Gwilym Hiraethog', wrote in *Yr Amserau*, in the guise of an old farmer, against the unnecessary use of English and the Anglicisation of the gentry. In a letter of 1851 Rees attacked John Bull for his arrogance, claiming he was hated all over the world – in Jamaica, New Zealand and Ireland, and insisting, despite John Bull's trying to kill off Welsh, it was now to have a new lease of life, the evidence being the flowering of the Welsh press and the rush of English and Scottish publishers to print books for the Welsh market.[48] But the predominant spirit of the 1850s and 1860s in Wales was progressive, positivist, utilitarian, middle-class Anglophiles setting the pace, dragging the Welsh into Victorian respectability, nervously glancing at the English for praise and approval. It is as though the Blue Books, which initially aroused fury and hostility, in the long term produced a sense of national shame and, from shame, a kind of national anxiety as Wales adjusted to the norms of bourgeois Victorian Britain. Recent Welsh historians have approached this great cultural shift either from the political and social side or from the cultural side, and it is essential here to bring the two approaches together.[49]

Lady Llanover and Evan Jones, 'Ieuan Gwynedd', started a magazine for women, *Y Gymraes*, in 1850 to make the Welsh woman less slatternly. Two of the commissioners, Lingen and Johnson, joined Welsh leaders in 1848 to found the Society for the Diffusion of Useful Knowledge in Wales. The first part of Chambers's compendium of useful education for the people appeared as *Addysg i'r Bobl* in 1851, translated by Welsh bards such as Ebenezer Thomas, 'Eben Fardd'. The radical leader and publisher Thomas Gee of Denbigh embarked from 1854 to 1874 on the largest and most successful Welsh-language publishing venture of the century, an immense Welsh encyclopaedia, *Y Gwyddoniadur*, over several years.

The most successful Eisteddfodau of the 1830s and 1840s had been the series, all very colourful and Romantic in spirit, organised by Thomas Price, 'Carnhua-nawc', and Lady Llanover and their friends at Abergavenny, but a new series of Eisteddfodau, on a far larger scale, was held from 1858 to 1868. This is considered to be a barometer of the transformation of Welsh culture from Romanticism to utilitarianism. The Llangollen national Eisteddfod of 1858 was still under the influence of old-fashioned Romantic clerics such as John Williams, 'Ab Ithel', the Gorsedd of Bards (which Iolo Marganwg had associated with the Eisteddfod movement at Carmarthen in 1819) was still active. Ab Ithel and his friends were discredited by the fiasco of the failure to award the prize for the essay on 'Madoc and the discovery of America' to the debunker Thomas Stephens of Merthyr, and they and the Gorsedd bards fell out of favour, especially after the death of Ab Ithel in 1862. Their place was taken increasingly after 1860 by educational tech-nocrats such as the civil servant (Sir) Hugh Owen, college lecturers such as Dr Thomas Nicholas, with their assorted friends, administrators, sympathetic gentry, industrialists and others.[50] Hugh Owen himself had been deeply moved by his visit to the Social Science Association in November 1860, and determined that this was the way forward for the Eisteddfod, by 1862 convincing the Eisteddfod that the highlight of its meetings should be the 'Social Science Section'. The bard John Jones, 'Talhaiarn', Paxton's assistant in building the Rothschild *châteaux*, was at first in despair at the lugubrious dullness of Owen's plans, considering that the Welsh were already be-preached and be-lectured enough, but, like many other survivors of the older Romantic culture, made his peace with the new positivist face of Welsh culture. The 'Social Science Section' began at Caernarfon in 1862, and, although English-speakers must have been hard to find in the area, Owen recommended that the papers should be in English, 'to fix the attention and win the sympathy of onlooking nationalities'.[51] Never had the Eisteddfod been more high-minded, paper after paper dealing with the problems of Wales, especially the improvement of the working classes. The new-found mineral wealth of Wales, naturally enough, gave rise to papers and discussions on geology, a subject of great interest to the Welsh.[52] On occasion, important movements arose from the discussions: the movement to found a university college for Wales arose from a meeting at Aberystwyth Eisteddfod in 1863.[53] Another characteristic mani-festation of the new Eisteddfod was the 'industrial exhibition' held in conjunction with it from 1865 to 1868, and in 1865, 1868 and 1876 large-scale arts and crafts exhibitions were held. It was left to local Eisteddfodau at this period, Ystalyfera 1860 and Flint 1865, however, to encourage photography.

Progressives such as Kilsby Jones complained that bards had kept Welsh in the position of 'the language of national childhood'. Yet the common people idolised them, and even the middle classes could see that bards could massage the injured national ego. The most successful poet to emerge from the Eisteddfod movement of the 1860s was John Hughes, 'Ceiriog', his prize-winning poems 'Myfanwy Fychan' (1858) and 'Alun Mabon' (1861) being amongst the most popular poems ever written in the language. The former is in praise of Welsh womanhood, a picture of womanly virtue as unslatternly and unsullied as it was possible to be; the latter is a song cycle in praise of the honesty and industriousness of the Welsh worker, in this case a shepherd, a pen portrait diametrically opposed to the hateful libels of the workers in the Blue Books.[54]

The Romantic movement had added the cliché of 'Land of Song' to that of 'Land of the Bards'. But the Welsh bourgeoisie, especially the Nonconformists, had misgivings about the Welsh delight in bawdy ballads, comic songs and dances, generally to the accompaniment of harpers. The 1850s and 1860s saw Wales becoming a battleground between old-fashioned musical merriment and the new music of respectability, ordered, disciplined and purposeful. It was also a period when professional entertainers found their way throughout Wales.[55] It was in this period that the temperance movement made great headway, the social reformers gathering Sunday schools into groups for hymn-singing festivals (a festival called in Welsh *Cymanfa Ganu*), which rapidly turned into something of a national tradition by the end of the 1860s. The tonic sol-fa movement, by which thousands could be quickly taught the rudiments of reading a line of music, found its largest number of adherents in Wales. The greater wealth of this period enabled larger chapels to be built, harmoniums or pianos and even organs to be purchased, from which rapidly developed the Welsh choirs, so rapidly indeed that, from humble beginnings in the 1840s, choirs had become a 'national tradition' by the 1870s. A casualty of the rise of the popularity of the pianoforte, and to some degree of the French pedal harp, was the old triple harp, long considered the 'Welsh harp' and a national symbol of romantic Wales. Lady Llanover fought a rearguard action for several decades to defend it, but it survived in the late nineteenth century only on the periphery of Welsh society, in the halls of reactionary gentry and in the caravans of Romany-speaking Welsh gypsies.[56] Just as the harpers were despised by respectable and Nonconformist Wales, so too were the penillion singers, who sang their amusing impromptu verses to accompany the harpers, their elaborate art having had great popular appeal from the 1790s to the mid-nineteenth century. In their place came the brass bands and the pianists, the choirs with an army of Welsh composers writing cantatas, part songs and anthems. For the soloists there were now albums of genteel versions of Welsh melodies, with words by poets such as Ceiriog. Leaders such as Hugh Owen may have been philistines in some ways, but they saw clearly that the Welsh were becoming, through their brass bands and choirs, an ordered, tamed and disciplined people. By 1872 large Welsh choirs were winning great choral competitions in London, and, at home, crowds of 20,000 or more would gather even in the rain merely to listen to them practising, such was the success of this musical revolution.

The decline of the harp and penillion singing was symbolic of the decline of the prestige of the Welsh language in the 1850s and 1860s. One sign of change was the decline of interest in things Celtic in Wales. The Romantic circle of Thomas Price, 'Carnhuanawc', had been deeply interested in things Breton, for example.[57] The leaders of Welsh opinion no longer wished to be associated with Irish culture, despite the radicals' considerable interest in the question of Irish Church disestablishment. They wished to emphasise not the image of 'The Visionary Celt'[58] but, on the contrary, that the Welsh were practical and hard-headed progressives. However, the Welsh in the 1860s had to fight an uphill battle against the growing Celtophobia or Teutonism and Anglo-Saxonism of the English press. No sooner, for example, had Matthew Arnold published his famous lectures on the study of Celtic literature (given in 1865–66)[59] than there was an outburst of furious anti-Celticism and anti-Welshness in the press. It could, of course, have been brushed aside, but for the fact that so many leaders of Welsh opinion were embarrassed by their own Welshness. For example, John Griffith, 'Y Gohebydd', was a fearless radical reporter and critic. But even he was stung by *The Spectator*'s malicious attack on the Swansea Eisteddfod of 1863 to recommend his fellow countrymen to drop all mention of dastardly Saxon oppression or the bravery of the Ancient Britons, and keep welshness for small private gatherings or for oneself.[60] In the later 1860s even Welsh bards and journalists were coming to accept not only the backwardness of Welsh culture, but that it was doomed to die in the near future. By the 1860s (in contrast to his fierce radicalism in the 1840s) David Rees in Y *Diwygiwr* was defeatist about the Welsh language and scornful of the Irish for resisting things British.[61] A crippling fatalism gripped Welsh writers in this period. They were disheartened by the attempt in 1866 to hold a fiercely Welsh and reactionary 'Anti-Eisteddfod', *Eisteddfod y Cymry*, when it was a financial flop. Welsh leaders were most anxious in the 1860s to assure the British that the Welsh had been transformed by then into an outward-looking, progressive people. The metaphor they often used was that they had jumped aboard the great train of progress and civilisation. The defenders of Welshness also saw themselves being crushed by the train of Anglicisation. A cartoon in 1864 in the *Punch Cymraeg* showed Dic-Siôn-Dafydd (slang for an Angliciser) driving a Puffing Billy to crush the Welshwoman on the railway line (Plate 8). One exception perhaps to this fatalistic acceptance of national demise is that radical Nonconformists argued that in future Wales should express her nationality in religious terms, some claiming that Welsh itself would survive inside the walls of the chapel, for religious purposes, while leaving the field outside entirely to the victorious English.

Professor Kenneth O. Morgan, author of the classic work on radical and liberal Wales[62] has observed that the 'deceptively tranquil' period from 1850 to 1870 was the period when the new Wales was being born, a time when a new identity for Wales was being forged, but that it was also a Wales of 'fractured consciousness'.[63]

**8** 'The English train runs over the Welshwoman', from *Y Punch Cymraeg* (1864). The train of Mammon, driven by Dic-Siôn-Dafydd (Anglophile Welshman) crushes the Welsh language (in the form of a woman in national costume). Safe on the mountains behind are the defences of the language, the pulpit and the press.

The local leaders who had come to the surface in 1847 and 1848 in the troubled wake of the Blue Books formed the radical elite of Wales from 1868 onwards. When Henry Richard won the celebrated election in Merthyr in 1868, watched eagerly by the whole of Wales, it seemed an intensely Welsh election. It even seemed that old romantic nationalism was still alive, for the men carrying Richard victorious through Aberdare and Merthyr carried leeks in their caps and sang the national anthem *Hen wlad fy nhadau*, Henry Richard telling the Welsh that they must make their demands 'as a nation'. The old ruling elites of Wales, squires and parsons, were being pushed aside by radicals on the grounds that the old order had been un-Welsh. These radicals were canny enough to see that even *The Times* could not thunder against the rights of the radical Nonconformists of Wales. But if the work of recent political historians of Wales is linked with the work of recent cultural historians – and that has been the chief purpose of this chapter – it is clear that the Wales being presented to the world was a very different country from romantic Wales. From the Blue Books onwards, perhaps because of the great confidence Welsh Nonconformists gained from the religious census of 1851, and certainly from the mid-1860s onwards, the majority of the Welsh came to see themselves as a Nonconformist nation.[64] Henry Richard made such a claim in 1866, and was able to convince Gladstone that the Nonconformists were the people of Wales. The radical elite succeeded for a whole generation and more in uniting under its aegis the middle and working classes of Wales in a populist unity. The Welsh were no longer the backward aborigines of the 1840s, but were now poised, if the plans of the technocrats such as Hugh Owen were perfected with schools and colleges, to take their place, to play a part side by side with the English in that union of multiple identities, Victorian Britain. But this was bought at a cost: several witnesses in the Blue Books had complained in vain that the commissioners were intending to deprive the Welsh of education in their own language. The period from 1850 to 1870 saw the rapid decline of the older indicators of Welshness, history, literature, language. Romantic Welshness remained as a substratum in the culture of radical Wales, but the emergent new Wales was rapidly Anglicising, a land of industrial progress, political involvement and Nonconformist self-awareness. The remaining nationalists were driven to silence or to Patagonia.

## Notes

1 B. B. Thomas, *The Old Order: Based on the Diary of Elizabeth Baker* (Cardiff, University of Wales Press, 1945), p. 44.

2 H. T. Edwards, *Gwyl Gwalia: yr Eisteddfod Genedlaethol yn oes aur Victoria, 1858–68* (Llandysul, Gomer, 1980), p. 348.

3 *Ibid.*, p. 332.

4 *Ibid.*, p. 327.

5 P. Scholes, 'Hen wlad fy nhadau', *National Library of Wales Journal*, 3 (1943), 1–10.

6 G. Williams, *The Desert and the Dream: a History of the Welsh Colonization of Patagonia* (Cardiff, University of Wales Press, 1979); *id.*, *The Welsh in Patagonia* (Cardiff, University of Wales Press, 1990).

7 W. Ll. Williams, *An Account of the King's Court of Great Sessions in Wales* (London, Cymmrodorion, 1916), pp. 75–82.

8 P. Lord, *Gwenllian: Essays in Visual Culture* (Llandysul, Gomer, 1994), esp. p. 10; *id.*, *Words with Pictures: Welsh Images and Images of Wales in the Popular Press, 1640–1860* (Aberystwyth, Planet, 1995), pp. 33–52, 59, 71. W. J. Hughes, *Wales and the Welsh in English Literature from Shakespeare to Scott* (Wrexham, Hughes; London, Simpkin Marshall, 1924).

9 E. D. Snyder, *Celtic Revival in English Literature, 1760–1800* (Cambridge, Mass., Harvard University Press, 1923); P. Morgan, *The Eighteenth Century Renaissance* (Llandybie, Davies, 1981); *id.*, 'From a death to a view: the hunt for the Welsh past in the Romantic period', in E. Hobsbawm and T. Ranger (eds), *The Invention of Tradition* (Cambridge, Cambridge University Press, 1983), pp. 43–100.

10 L. Colley, *Britons: Forging a Nation, 1707–1837* (London, Yale University Press, 1992).

11 R. T. Jenkins and H. Ramage, *History of the Honourable Society of Cymmrodorion* (London, Cymmrodorion, 1951), pp. 239–40.

12 S. Smiles, *The Image of Antiquity: Ancient Britain and the Romantic Imagination* (London, Yale University Press, 1993), pp. 129–64.

13 A. D. Fraser Jenkins, 'The romantic traveller in Wales', *Amgueddfa*, 6 (1970), 29–37; D. Moore, 'The discovery of the Welsh landscape', in D. Moore (ed.), *Wales in the Eighteenth Century* (Swansea, Davies, 1976), pp. 127–51; D. Solkin, *Richard Wilson: The Landscape of Reaction* (London, Tate Gallery, 1982), esp. pp. 77–112.

14 R. E. Hughes, *Nid am un harddwch iaith* (Cardiff, University of Wales Press, 1990), is an anthology of Welsh scientific prose in the nineteenth century.

15 G. A. Williams, 'Druids and democrats: organic intellectuals and the first Welsh nation', in his *The Welsh in their History* (London, Croom Helm, 1982), pp. 31–64; see also his chapter, 'Romanticism in Wales', in R. Porter and M. Teich (eds), *Romanticism in National Context* (Cambridge, Cambridge University Press, 1988), pp. 9–36.

16 G. A. Williams, *Madoc: the Making of a Myth* (London, Eyre Methuen, 1980); *id.*, *In Search of Beulah Land* (London, Croom Helm, 1980).

17 A. H. Dodd, *The Industrial Revolution in North Wales*, 3rd edn (Cardiff, University of Wales Press, 1971); A. H. John, *The Industrial Development of South Wales* (Cardiff, University of Wales Press, 1950).

18 M. Hechter, *Internal Colonialism: the Celtic Fringe in British National Development, 1536–1966* (London, Routledge, 1975), esp. pp. 127–63, 164–207. The pioneer nationalist Michael D. Jones complained already in the 1840s that Wales's position in the British economy was that of a colony.

19 D. J. V. Jones, *Before Rebecca: Popular Protest in Wales, 1793–1835* (London, Allen Lane, 1973); *id.*, *The Last Rising* (Oxford, Oxford University Press, 1985); *id.*, *Rebecca's Children* (Cardiff, University of Wales Press, 1989); I. Wilks, *South Wales and the Rising of 1839* (London, Croom Helm, 1984); G. A. Williams, *The Merthyr Rising* (London, Croom Helm, 1978); D. Williams, *John Frost* (Cardiff, University of Wales Press, 1939); *id.*, *The Rebecca Riots* (Cardiff, University of Wales Press, 1955).

20 M. Humphreys, *The Crisis of Community: Montgomeryshire, 1680–1815* (Cardiff, University of Wales Press, 1996).

21 G. A. Williams, *When was Wales?* (London, Penguin, 1985), p. 196.

22 I. G. Jones and D. Williams (eds), *Religious Census of 1851: Calendar of Returns relating to Wales*, 1, *South Wales* (Cardiff, University of Wales Press, 1976); I. G. Jones (ed.), *Calendar of Returns relating to Wales*, 2, *North Wales* (Cardiff, University of Wales Press, 1981); J. Harvey, *The Art of Piety: the Visual Culture of Welsh Nonconformity* (Cardiff, University of Wales Press, 1995); A. Jones, *Welsh Chapels* (Stroud, Alan Sutton, 1996).

23 W. R. Lambert, *Drink and Sobriety in Victorian Wales* (Cardiff, University of Wales Press, 1983).

24 *Yr Adolygydd*, 3 (1850), 19.

25 *Y Traethodydd*, 13 (1857), 397.

26 N. Jenkins, *Gwalia in Khasia* (Llandysul, Gomer, 1995), p. 208.

27 *The Cambro-Briton*, 2 (1820), 456.

28 Williams, 'Druids and democrats', p. 47.

29 P. Lord, *Hugh Hughes, arlunydd gwlad* (Llandysul, Gomer, 1995), p. 208.

30 A. G. Jones, *Press, Politics and the People: a History of Journalism in Wales* (Cardiff, University of Wales Press, 1993), esp. ch. 4.

31 T. Evans, *The Background to Modern Welsh Politics, 1789–1846* (Cardiff, University of Wales Press, 1936), esp. pp. 191–236; R. Wallace, *Organise, Organise, Organise! A Study of Reform Agitations in Wales, 1840–86* (Cardiff, University of Wales Press, 1991).

32 I. G. Jones, *Explorations and Explanations: Essays in the Social History of Victorian Wales* (Llandysul, Gomer, 1981).

33 I. G. Jones, *Communities: Essays in the Social History of Victorian Wales* (Llandysul, Gomer, 1987), p. 322.

34 M. Cragoe, *An Anglican Aristocracy: the Moral Economy of the Landed Estate in Carmarthenshire, 1830–95* (Oxford, Oxford University Press, 1995); D. Adamson, *Class, Ideology and the Nation: a Theory of Welsh Nationalism* (Cardiff, University of Wales Press, 1991), esp. chs 4 and 5.

35 S. Piggott, *Celts, Saxons and the early Antiquaries* (Edinburgh, Edinburgh University Press, 1967).

36 F. Shaw, 'The background to the Grammatica Celtica', *Celtica*, 3 (1953), 1–17.

37 H. T. Edwards, *The Eisteddfod* (Cardiff, University of Wales Press, 1990), p. 19.

38 T. Stephens, *The Literature of the Kymry*, 2nd edn (London, Longman, 1876), p. xxviii.

39 Smiles, *The Image of Antiquity*, esp. pp. 113–28.

40 E. M. Humphreys (ed.), *Llythyrau 'rhen ffarmwr gan Gwilym Hiraethog* (Cardiff, University of Wales Press, 1939), p. 25, from an article in 1851 by W. Rees, 'Gwilym Hiraethog'.

41 D. Salmon, 'The story of a Welsh education commission, 1846–47, *Y Cymmrodor*, 24 (1913), 189–237; P. Morgan, 'From long knives to Blue Books', in R. R. Davies, *et al* (eds), *Welsh Society and Nationhood* (Cardiff, University of Wales Press, 1984), pp. 119–215; *id.*, 'Pictures for the million of Wales, 1848: the political cartoons of Hugh Hughes', in *Transactions of the Honourable*

Society of Cymmrodorion for 1994 (1995), pp. 65–80; I. G. Jones, *Mid-Victorian Wales: the Observers and the Observed* (Cardiff, University of Wales Press, 1992), esp. pp. 103–65; P. Morgan (ed.), *Brad y Llyfrau Gleision* (Llandysul, Gomer, 1991), is a study of the Blue Books, in Welsh.

42 D. Evans, *The Life of William Williams, MP for Coventry and Lambeth* (Llandysul, Gomer, no date, probably 1939).

43 *Hansard*, 3rd Ser. lxxxiv. 845–59, speech of 10 March 1846.

44 *Reports of the Commissioners of Inquiry into the State of Education in Wales*, 3 parts (London, HMSO, 1847). One-volume synopses of the reports were published in London in 1848 in English and in Welsh.

45 Jones, *Mid-Victorian Wales*, pp. 155–6.

46 *Ibid.*, pp. 162–3.

47 G. Williams, 'The ideological basis of nineteenth-century Wales: the discourse of Michael D. Jones', in G. Williams (ed.), *Crisis of Economy and Society: Essays on Welsh Society, 1840–1940* (London, British Sociological Association, 1983), p. 181.

48 E. M. Humphreys (ed.), *Llythyrau 'rhen ffarmwr* (Cardiff, University of Wales Press, 1939), pp. 31, 41–6.

49 H. T. Edwards, *Gwyl Gwalia: yr Eisteddfod Genedlaethol yn oes aur Victoria, 1858–68* (Llandysul, Gomer, 1980); *id.*, *Codi'r Hen Wlad yn ei Hôl, 1850–1914* (Llandysul, Gomer, 1989); *id.*, *The Eisteddfod* (Cardiff, University of Wales Press, 1990); E. G. Millward, *Cenedl o Bobl Ddewrion* (Llandysul, Gomer, 1991); P. Lord, *Y Chwaer-dduwies: celf, crefft a'r Eisteddfod* (Llandysul, Gomer, 1992); *id.*, *Gwenllian*.

50 Williams, *The Welsh in their History*, pp. 151–70; B. L. Davies, 'Sir Hugh Owen and the Cambrian Education Society', in *Transactions of the Anglesey Antiquarian Society and Field Club* (1973), pp. 137–51.

51 Edwards, *Gwyl Gwalia*, p. 68.

52 D. A. Bassett (ed.), *A Bibliography and Index of Geology and Allied Sciences for Wales and the Welsh Borders, 1536–1896* (Cardiff, National Museum of Wales, 1963).

53 J. G. Williams, *The University Movement in Wales* (Cardiff, University of Wales Press, 1993), pp. 25–6.

54 Edwards, *Gwyl Gwalia*, p. 175.

55 P. Stead, 'Amateurs and professionals in the cultures of Wales', in G. H. Jenkins and J. B. Smith (eds), *Politics and Society in Wales, 1840–1922* (Cardiff, University of Wales Press, 1988), pp. 113–34.

56 Edwards, *Gwyl Gwalia*, pp. 195–210.

57 P. Morgan, 'Thomas Price "Carnhuanawc" et les Bretons', in B. Sellin (ed.), *Parcours: Pays de Galles–Bretagne* (Brest, Université de Bretagne Occidentale, 1995), pp. 5–13.

58 P. Sims-Williams, 'The visionary Celt: the construction of an ethnic preconception', *Cambridge Medieval Celtic Studies*, 2 (1986), 71–96.

59 R. Bromwich, *Matthew Arnold and Celtic Literature: a Retrospect, 1865–1965* (Oxford, Oxford University Press, 1965).

60 R. Griffith (ed.), *Cofiant y Gohebydd* (Denbigh, Gee, 1905), pp. 69–70.

61 I. Jones, *David Rees y Cynhyrfwr* (Swansea, Penry, 1971), p. 244.

62 K. O. Morgan, *Wales in British Politics, 1868–1922* (Cardiff, University of Wales Press, 1980 edn).

63 K. O. Morgan, 'Tom Ellis versus Lloyd George: the fractured consciousness of *fin-de-siècle* Wales', in Jenkins and Smith (eds), *Politics and Society in Wales*, pp. 93–112.

64 Williams, *The Welsh in their History*, p. 88, refers to 'the pseudo-nation of Welsh Dissent'.

# 7

# Sentiment, race and revival: Scottish identities in the aftermath of Enlightenment

## COLIN KIDD

Nineteenth-century Scotland inherited from the Scottish Enlightenment an assimilationist Anglo-British identity. However, between the 1790s and the 1850s – the decade when a Scottish national movement first found institutional embodiment in the National Association for the Vindication of Scottish Rights – this legacy was to be considerably frayed. In the aftermath of the Enlightenment a fragmented intelligentsia, haunted by various social, political and religious anxieties, sublimated its fears in the projection of a new set of Scottish identities. With the escalation of the French revolution during the 1790s, Anglicising measures which had hitherto been welcomed now acquired the taint of reform. As conservatives sought new ways to bolster the *status quo*, the defence of Scottish distinctiveness assumed new ideological significance. On the one hand, romantic Tories sought to recover an indigenous conservative tradition through a sentimental appropriation of Scotland's vivid Jacobite heritage. The Presbyterian past was also exhumed, but to serve the needs of a more proactive style of patriotism. The onset of rapid urbanisation and industrialisation had dented confidence in the transformation of Scotland, provoking the revival of a self-consciously nativist religiosity. Faced with urban *anomie*, the evangelical leaders of the Presbyterian Churches conjured up potent visions of an organic Scottish community of cohesive territorial parishes flourishing under the auspices of the godly commonwealth. However, such shows of assertiveness fell far short of political nationalism. The reforms of 1832–33 confirmed the Presbyterian middle classes of the burghs as the assimilationist heirs of Scotland's expiring Enlightenment. Furthermore, North British absorption in the nascent science of race gave rise to an overarching Teutonist identity highlighting the shared ethnic characteristics of the Saxon English and their Lowland cousins.

Eighteenth-century North Britons had been enthusiastic Anglicisers. They expressed their down-to-earth patriotism in a rigorous critique of Scottish backwardness, from which sprang an illusionless but intense admiration of England's political and economic achievements. Though troubled by the less attractive by-products of modernisation, including the loss of communal cohesion which ensued from the vigorous pursuit of commercial self-interest, the intellectual leaders of the Scottish Enlightenment did not bemoan the disappearance of their own national community or the wearing away of its distinctive feudal institutions.[1] Indeed, their celebrated criticisms of the corrupting effects of commerce and industry owed little to their experience of Scottish society, whose economy was decidedly sluggish until the 1740s.[2] Mid-eighteenth-century Scotland was on the cusp of improvement, a process which appeared to depend upon the 'completion of the Union', the further assimilation of Scotland's institutions, laws and manners to the modern benchmark set by a refined and commercial England.

The main contours of Enlightenment historiography would continue to shape Scottish political culture well into the nineteenth century. Almost nobody questioned the benefit to eighteenth-century Scotland of the Union of 1707, which was widely regarded as the benign euthanasia of a nominal sovereignty and magnate-dominated unicameral legislature. In the first volume of his monumental *Caledonia* (1807) the Pittite historian George Chalmers (1742–1825) celebrated the Union as the 'freeing of the people of Scotland from their parliament'.[3] The Union had anchored Scotland to a more stable and prosperous neighbour, and gained her entry to English and colonial markets. Moreover, the first phase of assimilation, which culminated in the reforms of 1747–48 abolishing wardholding vassalage and most heritable jurisdictions, was welcomed as a sensible and long overdue liberation from the dead hand of feudal localism. This bonfire of feudal controls had been a necessary prelude to the emergence of Scottish civil society. Full legal personality within a national legal system begat security for property, which in turn begat agrarian and commercial improvement. Yet this very consensus of acclaim for the achievements of 1707 and 1747–48 prompted a debate over the utility and propriety of continuing Anglicisation.[4] By the early nineteenth century Scottish social commentators had begun to divide over the issue of further assimilation. Could Scotland benefit from a further wave of anti-feudal reform? Or had the reforms of 1747–48 completed the Union, laying the foundations of a successful Anglo-Scottish partnership based upon shared civil liberties? Might not any additional – and superfluous – reforms be a threat to Scottish social identity, especially given the Anglo-Saxonism displayed in Scottish radical circles during the 1790s?[5]

These arguments resounded in the legal sphere, where whig reformers encountered an emergent Tory resistance. Although Sir Walter Scott, heir to the Enlightenment and a friend of Union, celebrated Scotland's emergence from feudalism and fanaticism to relative peace and plenty, the continuing itch of whigs to reform Scottish legal institutions exasperated him. In 1806 Scott complained to a leading Angliciser, 'Little by little, whatever your wishes may be, you will destroy and undermine, until nothing of what makes Scotland Scotland shall remain.'[6] Whereas Whigs continued to emphasise the common features of Scots and English law, thus minimising the dangers of reform, Tories such as Scott, while mindful of defects in the law, nevertheless began to draw attention to the distinct 'system of jurisprudence, under the protection of which, our native country has advanced from poverty and rudeness, to prosperity and civilization'.[7] Not only did he make plain his disenchantment with 'the cabalistic sound of trial by jury',[8] Scott also worried about the drift of particular reforms, such as the consequences of an efficient system of appeal to the House of Lords: 'the Scottish supreme court will be in effect situated in London. Then down fall – as national objects of respect and veneration – the Scottish bench – the Scottish Bar – the Scottish law herself'.[9]

Such concerns were not confined to the immediate battlefront of legal reform. George Joseph Bell (1770–1843), who established the principles of Scotland's commercial law, stood at the limits of the Anglicising tradition of eighteenth-century Scottish jurisprudence.

> Much caution is to be observed in the adopting of English judgments as authorities in Scotland, [argued the whiggish Bell] and I state this, the rather that I think there has appeared of late some danger lest the purity of this part of jurisprudence, and the integrity of our own system of law, should be impaired by *too indiscriminate* a use of English authorities.

England's advanced commercial experience was not in itself unwelcome, for the law merchant was 'part of the law of nations, grounded upon the principles of natural equity'. However, Bell expressed concern about cases where the 'universal' law merchant and 'municipal law or local custom' had been 'blended together' in such a way that it had been 'difficult to discriminate on what precise ground the decision [had] proceeded amidst these elements of judgment'. Bell acknowledged the irony that contamination in this branch of the law often came in the form of decisions made by an Anglo-Scot, Lord Mansfield.[10] Bell's cautious purism was obviously limited in its inspiration, but so too was Scott's robust championship of legal distinctiveness. Although the organicist jurisprudence of Gustav Hugo (1764–1844) and Friedrich Karl von Savigny (1779–1861) was well received in Scotland through the efforts of John Reddie (d. 1851) and others, a coherent Scots legal nationalism would emerge only in the twentieth century.[11]

Nevertheless, Scott had inaugurated what has variously been described as a 'deformed sub-nationalism'[12] and 'an ideology of noisy inaction',[13] a compound of sentiment, pedantry and defensive particularism, in which Scots law was defended as one of several local barriers against the nightmare of a 'country [made] *tabula rasa* for doctrines of bold innovation'.[14] Oddly, it was the campaign to preserve the Scottish £1 banknote in 1826 which provoked Scott's most eloquent outpourings on the subject of nationality:

> For God's sake, sir, let us remain as Nature made us, Englishmen, Irishmen and Scotchmen, with something of the impress of our several countries upon each! ... The degree of national diversity between different countries is but an instance of that general variety which Nature seems to have adopted as a principle through all her works, as anxious, apparently, to avoid, as modern statesmen to enforce, anything like an approach to absolute uniformity.[15]

Scott actively promoted the memory of Scottish Jacobite loyalty as an antidote to political rationalism. For Scottish conservatives were in something of a quandary. Such was the salience of resistance, revolution and democracy in the established Presbyterian tradition that for many Tories there could be no easy resort to a Kirk-and-King loyalism. Nor was there an indigenous Scottish Tory heritage, other than the cause of the Stuarts. Scott recognised that it was possible to transfer the charisma of the Stuarts to the House of Brunswick now that the cause of the former was decisively lost – indeed, anachronistic in an age of revolution. As master of ceremonies for the visit of George IV to Edinburgh in 1822 Scott invested the Hanoverian dynasty with the mystique of the Stuarts. Though absurdly decked out in tartan and pink stockings, the monstrous figure of George IV projected the patriarchal authority and paternal care of the chief of chiefs.[16] Such creative displacement was a hallmark of the Waverley novels, which engaged with immediate post-revolutionary issues of restored legitimacy and political prudence under the cover of Jacobite romance, and, for those who read more deeply, through metahistorical meditations upon the ambivalence of loss.[17] Could modern civility, whose recent arrival on the North British scene Scott welcomed so enthusiastically, survive a continuing whirl of social change which threatened to leave the Scottish population bereft of any deep rootedness in a communal past?

Scott's death coincided with the passing of the *ancien régime* in Scotland, an event which brought to a head the simmering divisions between enthusiastic Anglicisers and fearful conservatives. From its foundation in 1802 the whiggish *Edinburgh Review* maintained the recognised link between Anglicisation and the liberation of Scotland from feudal oppression, now represented by an electoral system which limited the vote in the Scottish counties to a mere 2,600 landowners holding direct of the Crown in 'old extent', of whom half were the holders of fictitious feudal superiorities. For whigs of the *Edinburgh Review* stamp 1832 was the dawn of a liberal millennium. A hyperbolic Henry Cockburn contended that 'it was impossible to exaggerate the ecstasy of Scotland', though he did: 'it is like liberty given to slaves: we are to be brought out of the house of bondage, out of the land of Egypt'.[18] Yet reform merely exacerbated Tory fears of political rationalism. Although Scottish representation at Westminster had been settled by the Treaty of Union, the nature of the Scottish franchise had been decided by the pre-Union Scottish Estates. Hence 1832 involved not only the rise of democracy but also the passing of the last vestiges of the ancient Scottish constitution. In Scotland liberalism was linked not with nationalism but with Anglicisation. In response, a legalistic defence of the historic Scottish constitution guaranteed by the Articles of 1707 became an important tenet in the creed of Tory reactionaries.[19] Writing in the *Edinburgh Review*, Cockburn met the Tory legalists head on: 'If these unhappy articles had served all the purposes for which they have been employed, the institutions of Scotland would have stood exactly as they did in the year 1707.'[20] The condition of pre-1747 Scotland was, however, not the only weak point in the Tory defence of Scottish nationality. Tory regard for Scottish institutional forms was counterbalanced by a deep-seated fear of the nation itself as a Scots *canaille*. Sir William Rae, the MP for Bute, regretted the extension of the franchise 'because it was well known that Scotchmen seldom came together in a multitude without causing bloodshed, or at least a riot'.[21] The prominent Tory historian Archibald Alison echoed this fear, drawing a sharp distinction between the measured antiquarian pragmatism of the English libertarian tradition and the rootless innovations which had scarred Scottish society during the Reformation and Covenanting eras.[22]

That Alison, the son of an episcopalian clergyman, evidently associated the Presbyterian past with radical politics, highlights the internal contradictions of Scottish conservatism. For Scotland had not one but two conservative intelligentsias committed to the preservation of rival versions of Old Scotland.[23] Most famously, *Old Mortality*, Scott's even-handed but critical interpretation of the Covenanting era, provoked a blistering response from the Reverend Thomas McCrie (1772–1835) of the Auld Licht Anti-Burgher Secession. McCrie's influence extended beyond this traditionalist rump. His biographies of John Knox (1811) and Andrew Melville (1819), though written to counter the voluntarist principles of the New Licht Seceders, inspired a rousing filiopietism within the established Kirk itself. A prominent sub-genre of Scottish art during the first half of the nineteenth century dealt with Knox, the Scottish Reformation and the Covenanters, as, for example, in the works of Sir George Harvey.[24] In literature James Hogg's *The Brownie of Bodsbeck* (1818) and John Galt's *Ringan Gilhaize* (1823) celebrated the heroism of the Covenanters, whilst, in a localist vein, Robert Simpson (1795–1867), United Secession minister of Sanquhar, produced a series of popular works glorifying the martyrdom of the Covenanters, including *Traditions of the Covenanters* (1843), *The Banner of the Covenant* (1847) and the emotively titled *Martyrland* (1861), which traced the civil and religious liberties of modern Scots to the 'toils' of the moorland peasantry of the south-west. There were also monuments galore. During the 1850s Stirling, for example, acquired a series of statues which commemorated the canon of Reformed heroes, whilst in 1858 an obelisk was erected on Wigtown's Windy Hill to the town's celebrated martyrs of 1685.[25]

Yet the Presbyterian community was far from self-confident; indeed, in 1843 the main body of the Kirk would split asunder. The assertive patriotism of the early nineteenth-century evangelicals was intended as a reminder of the Kirk's historic responsibilities and as a clarion call to action in the face of the enormous pressures which threatened to engulf traditional Scottish society. Eighteenth-century Scotland had been the fastest-urbanising society in Europe. In 1700 5 per cent of the population lived in towns of more than 10,000 inhabitants; in 1800 the figure had ballooned to 17 per cent. By the same criteria eighteenth-century England had witnessed significant but less spectacular growth from 13 per cent to 20 per cent. Much of Scotland's urban expansion was concentrated in the industrialising region of Lanarkshire and Renfrewshire. Glasgow, whose population in 1740 was about 17,000, had mushroomed to 83,000 by 1801 and would rapidly expand to 274,000 in 1841.[26] The Kirk's response to the crisis was shaped by the Reverend Thomas Chalmers. Brought up in Anstruther, which had a population of 1,400, educated in the small university town of St Andrews, and inducted to the parish of Kilmany, a Fifeshire village with a population of 800, Chalmers brought to the condition of urban Scotland a vision – historic, utopian and experienced – of idyllic parochial community. In his Glasgow parishes he attempted to recreate the blend of tranquillity, responsible mutuality and sturdy independence found in the small-town and rural parishes of his youth and early manhood. But the genius of Chalmers could not be confined within the discipline of straightforward nostalgic recovery. He radically revised the existing model of parish organisation, persuading the city fathers of Glasgow to grant him an extraordinary parochial laboratory in which he could carry out experiments in welfare, education and ministry. By stimulating the four 'rills' of communal provision – the manners of the local population, the concern of relatives, the sympathy of the rich for the poor, and the sympathy of the poor for each other – Chalmers hoped to restore to Scotland both the parish community and what he identified as its 'traditional' national character, in fact a recently minted notion of self-reliance.[27] It is, however, important to remember that, given Chalmers's vaulting ambition to bestride a British stage, his establishmentarian prescriptions were meant not only for Scotland.[28]

Nevertheless, Chalmers's concern with character and community was widely shared in Scotland. The Reverend Henry Duncan, founder of the savings bank movement, tried to encourage popular thrift at a parochial level, describing his progeny as 'parish banks'.[29] Chalmers's predecessor at Glasgow Tron and later professor of divinity in the same city, Stevenson MacGill (1765–1840), devoted his studies to the relationship between environment and morality.[30] *The Annals of the Parish* (1821), John Galt's account of the experiences of the fictional Reverend Micah Balwhidder, minister of Dalmailing between 1760 and 1820, was a sensitive commentary upon the erosion of clerical authority which accompanied the loss of community.[31] Anxiety about the Scottish character was the catalyst for the first stirrings of a temperance movement in the late 1820s. Shocked by a visit to France in 1828, where he found the morals of the people, despite the obvious handicap of Catholicism, markedly superior to those of his Presbyterian countrymen, the Greenock philanthropist John Dunlop (1789–1868), a proponent of savings banks and popular education, concluded that the effectiveness of Scotland's free Protestant institutions was vitiated by the intemperance of her people.[32] Nor were Presbyterians consoled by the renowned democratic intellectualism of their parochial schools. Confronted with the hydra-headed monster of Reform, the opposition of the voluntaries to religious establishments, and an expanding (and dangerous) industrial population which had overwhelmed the territorial structures of the Scottish parish system, Glasgow Chalmersites formed the Glasgow Educational Association (1834) as a pressure group for the extension of parochial schooling. One of their number was George Lewis (1803–79), editor of the Church defence newspaper *The Scottish Guardian*, which the group had established in 1832. Lewis's eye-catching polemic *Scotland a Half-educated Nation*

(1834) argued that Scotland suffered because only a twelfth of the overall population was in school, whereas in Prussia the figures rose to about a sixth, and higher in New England. Yet beneath this dry exercise in social statistics ran powerful currents of nostalgic pride and self-recrimination. The present generation – the 'degenerate descendants' of Knox and Melville – appeared to be squandering not only Scotland's educational patrimony but the very quintessence of her nationhood: 'In all but our parochial churches and parochial schools, we have lost our nationality. In these alone we survive as a nation.'[33]

The attempt by Chalmers and the evangelicals to reinvigorate a territorial Kirk through the recruitment of an activist ministry and a campaign for Church extension – decried as 'spiritual O'Connellism'[34] – came to fruition in a programme of measures by the General Assembly in 1834. However, a series of adverse legal judgements overturned the Kirk's legislative competence in these areas, exposing the naked subordination of Christ's Church of Scotland to the Erastian powers of Crown-in-parliament. As a result of escalating miscalculations among the ranks of politicians and Kirkmen, the Non-intrusionists withdrew from the Kirk into the Free Church, severing their connection with a corrupt British State, though without disavowing either the establishment principle or the Union itself. The Disruption of 1843 verged on religious nationalism, but the bygone Scotland the Chalmersites wished to recover was not the pre-Union State but the world of the eighteenth-century parish, albeit liberated from the toils of the illegitimate Patronage Act of 1712.

English Erastianism was but one component of the British problem faced by Scottish evangelicals: the immediate problems of Irish immigration and the Popish menace loomed just as large. From the foundation in 1818 of the Glasgow weekly, The Protestant, Presbyterian Scotland responded to the flood of Irish newcomers with a series of anti-Catholic papers and societies. Matters worsened in the 1850s. The 1851 census recorded 207,367 Irish immigrants out of a Scottish population of 2,888,742, which coincided with perceptions of papal aggression over ecclesiastical titles. A tidal wave of anti-Catholicism washed over Scottish culture in the early 1850s, the era of the Scottish Reformation Society, the Scottish Protestant Association and papers such as The Bulwark and The Scottish Protestant.[35]

By the mid-1840s the provocation of Irish Catholic immigration had already contributed to an early manifestation of Scottish nationalism. John Steill (fl. 1840–70) was just as exercised by the baleful effects which he attributed to the Union of 1801 as by those which flowed from the Union of 1707. Scotland's prosperity, according to Steill, was due to the 'intelligence' and 'perseverance' of the Scottish character, not to the Anglo-Scottish Union. Furthermore, the liberal Scots were 'more inclined to take on the impress of democratic institutions than the English'. However, the Scottish character was itself under threat. In his racist jeremiad Scotland for the Scotch Steill despaired of the consequences of mass Irish immigration: an influx of Irish labourers – 'clouds of the vilest specimens of the human animal in the face of the earth' – had made Scots outcasts in their own land, whilst the national fibre had been contaminated through exposure to 'Irish crime,

Irish dirt, Irish disease, and Irish degradation'. The solution lay in 'so thorough and complete an annihilation of the union between the two kingdoms that Ireland shall be left to manage her own affairs socially and politically, as she pleases'. Steill desired an ethnic cleansing of Scotland, yet his racial prejudices were complicated by nationalism. He protested against 'the extermination of the Gaelic race' in the Highlands, arguing that a Scottish legislature would never have allowed the region to become a 'vast experimental garden of misrule and despotism'.[36] A similar tension, though one devoid of nationalist overtones, was a characteristic of the *North British Daily Mail*, which manifested racial hostility to the simian Irish Celt and sympathy for the plight of the indigenous Gael.[37]

Race was part of the common currency of nineteenth-century Scottish political culture, a dubious bequest from the Silver Age of the Scottish Enlightenment. A Teutonic racialist tradition had evolved out of the philological speculations of John Pinkerton (1758–1826) in the 1780s which culminated in the physiological racism advocated by the transcendental anatomist Robert Knox (1791–1862) in *The Races of Men* (1850). Teutonists identified the industrious, liberal Scoto-Saxons of the Lowlands as close relatives of the English. Because the scientific reality of race trumped the artificial distinctions of nationality, these core peoples of mainland Britain were understood to comprise a *natural* community of Saxons.[38] This had repercussions in the treatment of the peripheral non-Teutonic peoples of the British Isles. Scottish Teutonists routinely demonised Celts, whether Irish immigrants or improvident Scottish Highlanders – an attitude apparent in a section of the Scottish press during the relief of the Highland famine of 1846–47.[39] Lowland Scots saw themselves not as an oppressed ethnic group but as an integral part of the dominant British Saxon core of the burgeoning multi-ethnic empire. Pinkerton argued that from Antiquity the majority of the inhabitants of mainland Britain had been of a hardy and libertarian Teutonic stock.[40] Knox, too, proclaimed that 'as a Saxon' he abhorred 'all dynasties, monarchies and bayonet governments, but this latter seems to be the only one suitable for the Celtic man'.[41] Pinkerton and Knox were extreme Teutonic racialists, but a modified Teutonism also appeared within the mainstream of Scottish intellectual life. Several nineteenth-century Scottish historians applauded the central contribution made by incoming Saxon, Norman and Flemish settlers to the making of the medieval Scottish kingdom, the Gothic provenance of whose institutions was evident even to committed opponents of Pinkertonian ethnology such as George Chalmers.[42]

Teutonist attitudes also enjoyed wide dissemination in phrenology, whose citadel in early nineteenth-century Britain was Edinburgh, home not only of its intellectual leader, George Combe (1788–1858), but also to such bodies as the Edinburgh Phrenological Society and the Edinburgh Ethical Society for the Practical Application of Phrenology. Phrenological societies were well established in towns throughout Scotland, such as Glasgow, Aberdeen, Dundee and Ayr, but also in the likes of Peterhead, Rothesay and Forfar.[43] Its naturalistic system threatening to the Common Sense philosophy of Kirk and university, Scottish phrenology combined radicalism with racialism: liberal institutions took their rise from the 'peculiar mental constitution' which a nation 'received from nature'. Combe himself disaggregated nations into racial types, contending that in France, Ireland and Scotland 'the Celtic race remain[ed] far behind the Teutonic in the arts, sciences, philosophy and civilization', whilst it was 'the Scotch Lowland population, which has done everything by which Scotland is distinguished'.[44]

Phrenology was not the only craze sweeping nineteenth-century Scotland. The nation was gripped by a powerful collective memory of her medieval war of independence, whose focus was the cult of William Wallace and, to a lesser extent, Robert Bruce. In the realm of art, for example, Sir William Allan (1782–1850) produced a sprawling 'Bannockburn', whilst David Scott (1806–49) commemorated the war in a triptych comprising 'Sir William Wallace', 'Scottish war: the spear' and 'English war: the bow' (1843). However, Wallace mania was most apparent in the realm of monumental statuary. The radical Earl of Buchan (1742–1829) was responsible for a colossal statue of Wallace overlooking the Tweed (Plate 9). In 1818 there began the first stirrings of the campaign for a major Wallace memorial, though plans for a Glasgow monument proved abortive. Nevertheless within the next two decades a magnificent statue of Wallace was erected in Lanark and the Wallace Tower in Ayr was refurbished, complete with patriotic icon. The erection of a second tower a few miles to the north-east of Ayr at Barnweil in 1855 (Plate 10) may have been part of a regional campaign for the appropriation of Wallace, claimed as a son both by Ayrshire and by Renfrewshire. A National Wallace Monument Committee was established in 1856. Unfortunately its secretary, the Reverend Charles Rogers (1825–92), the chaplain of Stirling Castle, lacked the necessary emollience to complement the energy he expended on behalf of the project. After years of wrangling the campaign achieved a sublime triumph in 1869 with the completion of J. T. Rochead's design: a 200 ft tower atop a massive outcrop of rock near Stirling overlooking the decisive campaign country of the war of independence.[45]

The nineteenth-century appreciation of Wallace needs to be carefully construed, for it bears only a superficial resemblance to the visceral nationalism which Wallace inspires today. Wallace was first and foremost an inspiration to Scottish liberalism, a non-aristocratic native exemplar of the dignity and freedom of mankind. The radical John McAdam (1806–83), a friend of Mazzini, Garibaldi and Kossuth campaigned for a National Wallace Monument which would serve as a shrine to the national movements of Continental Europe, while the Reverend William Anderson (1796–1872) of Glasgow spoke of Garibaldi as the 'William Wallace of Italy'. Contemporary Scotland was awash with paranationalist voluntary associations. Glasgow's citizens, for example, established a Garibaldi Italian Fund, a Working Men's Garibaldi Committee, a Polish Association and a Polish Committee; the ladies of Glasgow had their own Benevolent Association for the Relief of the Sick and Wounded, Widows and Orphans of the Liberators of Italy under General Garibaldi. A company of Scottish Garibaldian volunteers was decked out in a uniform of tartan shirts and bonnets topped with the Scotch thistle. Despite Scottish flirtation with various Continental nationalisms, there is

9 Statue of William Wallace overlooking the Tweed, near Dryburgh.

10 William Wallace tower, Barnweil, near Ayr.

little evidence of any felt need within Scotland for its own modern Wallace. Unlike the historic stateless nations of Italy, Poland and Hungary, nineteenth-century Scotland enjoyed freedom and dignity within a Union of partner States. Above all, Scots enjoyed Protestant freedoms. The popular anti-papal lectures of Alessandro Gavazzo in 1851 had won Scots over to the cause of Italian freedom, while support for Hungary stemmed in part from sympathy with her oppressed Protestants.[46]

The Wallace cult encapsulated the multi-cultural 'blending' which Keith Robbins has identified as a central facet of the nineteenth-century British experience.[47] The matter of medieval Scotland provided literary inspiration beyond the Border. Not only did Robert Southey compose an anti-Plantagenet lament for Wallace, but William Wordsworth in *The Prelude* mentioned the career of Wallace as suitable matter for a projected epic.[48] Jane Porter (1776–1850), born in Durham and brought up in Edinburgh, which she left for London in 1803, wrote her best-selling novel of the wars of independence, *The Scottish Chiefs* (1810), in large part to convey a pan-British message at the height of the Napoleonic wars. While celebrating 'an honest pride in ancestry' which it was then the 'fashion to contemn', she took solace from the union of 'rival nations' which had 'redeemed the peace' of Britain, and 'fixed it on lasting foundations'.[49]

The cult of Wallace provoked at most a sentimental nationalism far removed from visceral blood-and-soil Volkishness. In general the commemoration of the war of independence served to promote a liberal and dignified Unionism, what Graeme Morton has recently described as Unionist-nationalism.[50] True Unionism involved a national component, namely a recognition that Scotland had never submitted to English conquest. The histories of Wallace and Bruce underwrote a Scottish interpretation of nineteenth-century Britain which was, in spite of its single sovereign Parliament, a hybrid union-state rather than a unitary English *imperium*. Joanna Baillie (1762–1851), a London-based Scot, prefaced her 'metrical legend' on the heroism of Wallace with a homily on the Anglo-Scottish partnership:

> The reader, perhaps, will smile at the earnestness with which I estimate the advantage of having been rescued from the domination of Edward, now, when England and Scotland are happily united ... But when we recollect the treatment which Ireland received as a conquered country ... we shall acknowledge, with gratitude, the blessing of having been united to England under far different circumstances.[51]

The unsuccessful proposal of 1859 for a national monument to Wallace and Bruce in Scotland's capital was explicit on this score:

> Intelligent Englishmen know full well the source of Britain's strength and greatness, and that to the independence achieved under Wallace and Bruce, the Union of Scotland with her sister kingdom, on terms satisfying to both, owes not only all its practicality, but the greater portion of its success. Intelligent Englishmen also know that their countrymen from Wallace's day ... not only had no sympathy with the feudal despotism of the Norman kings, but mourned for the Scottish patriot as the forlorn hope against the 'common oppressors of both countries'.[52]

Wallace was seen as a champion of *British* freedom from the Norman yoke. Commemorations of the wars of independence reminded Scots and their English partners that the Union was a partnership of historic sovereign equals. Should this basis of equality be called into question, even the most Anglicised of Scots took offence. John Allen (1771–1843), an Edinburgh medical figure turned metropolitan Foxite historian, produced a *Vindication of the Ancient Independence of Scotland* (1833) in reaction to Sir Francis Palgrave's argument that Scotland had been an English dependency from the seventh century.

Local *pietas*, Unionist nationalism and scientific racism also shaped the emerging cult of the national bard, Robert Burns (1759–96). The Burns cult reinforced the regional identity of the south-west, notably Ayrshire, outside whose county town a magnificent Burns Monument was erected in 1823. Later, at the Ayr Burns Festival of 1844 John Wilson (1785–1854), a professor and journalist of pronounced Tory sympathies, contrived to present the poet's radical patriotism as a pious Unionism.[53] Nor did the vernacular revival stimulated by Burns assume an overtly political form. The Scoto-Saxon dialect of the Lowlander posed no threat to the prevailing ideology of British Teutonism. Thomas Carlyle applauded Burns as 'a piece of the right Saxon stuff: strong as the Harz-rock, rooted in the depths of the world'.[54] Indeed, such was the sway of the new obsession with race and character that the cadaver of the long-deceased poet fell victim to the phrenologists, who had a plaster cast made of his skull in 1834.[55]

Out of this cross-grained *milieu* with its vicarious nationalist interests and Scoto-British Unionism there emerged the National Association for the Vindication of Scottish Rights, the eccentric grandparent of the modern nationalist movement. The Association lasted for only three years, yet it drew considerable public support. Its first public meeting, held in Edinburgh in November 1853, drew a crowd of 2,000, while another the following month in Glasgow attracted a body of 5,000. Though some of the NAVSR's proposals were decidedly obscure, others would resurface in the platforms of the Scottish Home Rule Association. Nevertheless, the NAVSR did not support repeal; its members were true believers in the Union, strict constructionists who felt the English political Establishment had betrayed the original terms and spirit of 1707, most notably by failing to treat Scotland as an equal partner of England in a voluntary union. The NAVSR protested not at oppression but at an amorphous English indifference. In November 1853 the radical *Glasgow Examiner* noted 'proofs of a decided inclination to trifle, if not to treat with contempt, Scotland and her affairs'.[56] Another paper, *The Commonwealth*, while strongly supporting the association, conceded that the campaigns against heraldic irregularities and the use of 'England' as a synonym for the 'United Kingdom' focused on 'sentimental grievances' which 'hurt the feelings rather than the direct material interests of Scotchmen', but they were 'not the less grievances for all that'.[57] Such issues were symbolic of a wider disregard for Scotland and the authentic spirit of Union. There was an element of hurt pride behind the vacuous huffing and puffing of the NAVSR. While a dangerous Ireland needed to be taken seriously, Scotland suffered neglect as a loyal and undemanding province. The movement craved attention, recognition of Scotland's historic status and a strict juridical construction of the Articles of Union.

The NAVSR was the culmination of sentimental nationalism. Despite the roles played by the radical Duncan MacLaren and the Reverend James Begg (1808–83) of the Free Church, the NAVSR was dominated by conservatives whose romantic Toryism, a parody of Scott's, shaded into sentimental Jacobitism and antiquarian pedantry.[58] Indeed, the NAVSR arose out of the campaign of the Grant brothers in 1852 against a most disturbing irregularity in the quartering of the royal arms, a self-evident national scandal against which they appealed to the Lord Lyon. James Grant (1822–87), secretary to the Association, was a second cousin of Scott and a prolific historical romancer on Scottish and military themes, including *The Scottish Cavalier* (1850). This was a subject close to the heart of another prominent supporter, William Edmonstone Aytoun (1813–65), the author of the best-selling *Lays of the Scottish Cavaliers* (1848). The Association's president was the thirteenth Earl of Eglinton (1812–61), the generous host of the much ridiculed neo-medieval Eglinton tournament of 1839.[59] Hugh Scott of Gala, a propagandist for the NAVSR, made explicit the Tory bias of his concern for Scottish 'rights', contrasting these with an 'English democracy [which] carried all before it'. The reform movement of 1831 Scott pronounced to have been 'essentially Anglican. You heard of nothing but the perfection of England and her institutions. Everything national was laughed to scorn. The wisdom of ages was declared to be puerility and folly.'[60] However, romantic Toryism alienated potential radical support. Not only would Eglinton, it was said, 'restore . . . the tournamental ages', but Alison, another Tory vindicator, opposed free trade, and Aytoun, worst of all, loomed large as an enemy of Presbyterian Scotland. What sort of prospect did the NAVSR hold out for liberal Scotland?

> Is it the future of Progress, of parliamentary reform, of free trade, of the abolition of the laws of primogeniture and entail, of separation between church and state, of unsectarian education, of temperance, of peace? . . . It cannot be. Their future is an attempted restoration of the past.[61]

Moreover, the NAVSR suffered from the publicity surrounding its symbolic politics. One pamphleteer noted that 'even ardent Vindicators would meet you with a joke about the Lion's Tail or the Unicorn's Bonnet! and deplore that what they called real Scottish grievances had been mixed up with such matters as flags, banners, ensigns, and armorial bearings'.[62] What were these 'real Scottish grievances'? The Association voiced concern about administrative centralisation[63] and demanded the restoration of the Scottish secretaryship. Scotland's administration was then in the hands of an overburdened law officer, the Lord Advocate, who was nominally supervised by the Home Secretary. The Association also asked for an increase in Scottish parliamentary representation from fifty-three to seventy-one MPs. However, most of the grievances – and much of the pamphlet literature – of the NAVSR related to the distribution of UK expenditure. Most serious of all, the movement was a coalition of marginal men detached from the political mainstream. Alison was a disillusioned protectionist; Begg was disenchanted by the growing authority of Robert Candlish within the Free Church; MacLaren had been rejected by the voters of Edinburgh at the general election of 1852.[64] Nor was Anglicisation a dead letter. As Iain Hutchison notes, the Glasgow Law Amendment Society, which concluded on commercial grounds that the time had come 'when the laws of the two divisions of the island should be gradually assimilated', enjoyed much wider support during the 1850s, receiving the backing of thirty-six newspapers, compared with twenty for the Scottish rights campaign.[65]

Nevertheless, the NAVSR did reflect a real shift of opinion in nineteenth-century Scotland. In the opinion of Cockburn, the great whig Anglicizer of the 1830s, the NAVSR was a ridiculous pantomime; yet, he conceded, there were certain changes which a 'sensible Scotchman may naturally lament', such as centralisation and excessive English 'disregard' of things 'dear to us, merely because they are not English'. Above all, Cockburn, who fiercely denied that 'age' had made him a Tory, was deeply concerned by the 'now almost complete abolition of every official thing connected with our ancient monarchy and political state, which is not necessary for modern purposes'. However, as the old reformer now realised, there were 'some things that are useful for the public, though not necessary, and the difficulty lies in distinguishing between these two'.[66]

Mid-nineteenth-century Scotland rested securely within Britain's union of multiple identities. Renewed pride in Scotland's culture and history was variously channelled into sentimental particularism, assertively Scottish brands of liberalism and strict constructions of Union as a partnership of equals. The dominance of Liberalism within Scotland embedded the nation within the British party system and acted as a surrogate nationalist ethos. Moreover, the influence of Saxonism and phrenology served to inhibit the nationalist potential of radical causes. Nor had the assimilationist train quite reached the buffers. The eighteenth-century critique of Scottish feudal backwardness and oppression remained a prominent feature of the nineteenth-century Scottish liberal landscape. Begg, for example, who blamed the ills of contemporary Presbyterianism upon the Union, was also active in the reform of Scots land law as a means of remedying deficiencies in Scotland's appalling housing situation.[67]

Protestantism was not quite the uncomplicated integrative glue identified by Linda Colley;[68] yet neither was the assertive Presbyterian revivalism of the Chalmers era the fuel of political nationalism. Its communitarian rhetoric focused as much upon parish as on nation, whilst its anxious and defensive explorations of national character fell far short of ethnic nationalism.

Awash with a variety of sentimental substitutes for nationalism proper, nineteenth-century Scotland missed out on the real thing. However, it would be a mistake to assume Scottish innocence of the rise of nationalism, whether in Ireland or on the continent of Europe. The former provoked jealousy of the high seriousness accorded Irish matters by the British political elite: indeed, for Scotland the

Irish problem and its consequences for the mainland dwarfed minor frictions in the Anglo-Scottish Union. On the other hand, Scots were active in promoting the national movements of Italy, Hungary and Poland. Proud of their history, freedoms, religion, Saxon origins and equal partnership with England, mid-nineteenth-century Scots could happily endorse the Shilling Subscription for European Freedom,[69] oblivious of any constraints upon their own liberal nationality.

## Notes

1  C. Kidd, *Subverting Scotland's Past* (Cambridge, Cambridge University Press, 1993).

2  T. C. Smout, 'Where had the Scottish economy got to by 1776?' in I. Hont and M. Ignatieff (eds), *Wealth and Virtue* (Cambridge, Cambridge University Press, 1983).

3  G. Chalmers, *Caledonia*, 3 vols (London, Cadell and Davies/Constable, 1807–24), i. 866.

4  Kidd, *Subverting Scotland's Past*, chs 7, 9, 10.

5  J. Brims, 'The Scottish Jacobins, Scottish nationalism and the British Union', in R. Mason (ed.), *Scotland and England, 1286–1815* (Edinburgh, John Donald, 1987).

6  J. G. Lockhart, *Memoirs of the Life of Sir Walter Scott, Bt* (Edinburgh, Cadell, 1837), ii. 110–11.

7  Walter Scott, 'View of the changes proposed and adopted in the administration of justice in Scotland', *Edinburgh Annual Register for 1808* (1810), i. 372

8  *Ibid.*, i. 365.

9  Walter Scott, *Journal*, ed. W. E. K. Anderson (Oxford, Oxford University Press, 1972), 9 June 1826, pp. 156–7.

10  George Joseph Bell, *Commentaries on the Law of Scotland and on the Principles of Mercantile Jurisprudence* (Edinburgh, Constable 1810), preface.

11  John Reddie, *Historical Notices of the Roman Law, and of the Recent Progress of its Study, in Germany* (Edinburgh, Tait, 1826); J. Cairns, 'The influence of the German historical school in early nineteenth-century Edinburgh', *Syracuse Journal of International Law and Commerce*, 20 (1994), 191–203; C. Harvie, 'Legalism, myth and national identity in Scotland in the imperial epoch', *Cencrastus*, 26 (1987), 35–41.

12  T. Nairn, *The Break-up of Britain* (1977, London, Verso, 1981 edn), p. 156.

13  N. Phillipson, 'Nationalism and ideology', in J. N. Wolfe (ed.), *Government and Nationalism in Scotland* (Edinburgh, Edinburgh University Press, 1969), p. 186.

14  Scott, *Journal*, Tuesday 14 March 1826, p. 113.

15  Walter Scott, *Letters from Malachi Malagrowther on the Proposed Change of Currency*, ed. P. H. Scott (Edinburgh, Blackwood, 1981), pp. 143–4.

16  J. Prebble, *The King's Jaunt: George IV in Scotland, 1822* (London, Collins, 1988).

17  F. Robertson, *Legitimate Histories: Scott, Gothic and the Authorities of Fiction* (Oxford, Oxford University Press, 1994), pp. 8–10, 254.

18  M. Dyer, *Men of Property and Intelligence: the Scottish Electoral System prior to 1884* (Aberdeen, Scottish Cultural Press, 1996), p. 23.

19  Harvie, 'Legalism, myth and national identity'; Dyer, *Men of Property*, p. 5.

20  Henry Cockburn, 'Parliamentary representation', *Edinburgh Review*, lii (1830), 220.

21  Dyer, *Men of Property*, p. 26.

22  Archibald Alison, *History of Europe during the French Revolution*, 10 vols (Edinburgh and London, Blackwood and Cadell, 1833–42), i. 38.

23  B. Lenman, *Integration, Enlightenment, and Industrialization: Scotland, 1746–1832* (London, Arnold, 1981), pp. 147, 166.

24  D. Macmillan, *Scottish Art, 1460–1990* (Edinburgh, Mainstream, 1990), pp. 186–9, 191–2.

25  C. Rogers, *Monuments and Monumental Inscriptions of Scotland*, 2 vols (London, Grampian Club, 1871–72), i. 349; ii. 41.

26 T. M. Devine, 'Urbanisation', in T. M. Devine and R. Mitchison (eds), *People and Society in Scotland*, i, *1760–18* (Edinburgh, John Donald, 1988).

27 S. Mechie, *The Church and Scottish Social Development, 1780–1870* (Oxford, Oxford University Press, 1960), ch. 4; S. J. Brown, *Thomas Chalmers and the Godly Commonwealth* (Oxford, Oxford University Press, 1982); S. J. Brown, 'Thomas Chalmers and the communal ideal in Victorian Scotland', in T. C. Smout (ed.), *Victorian Values* (London, British Academy, 1992); J. McCaffrey, 'Thomas Chalmers and social change', *Scottish Historical Review* 60 (1981), 32–60.

28 D. Hempton, *Religion and Political Culture in Britain and Ireland: from the Glorious Revolution to the Decline of Empire* (Cambridge, Cambridge University Press, 1996), p. 67; K. Robbins, *Nineteenth Century Britain: Integration and Diversity* (Oxford, Oxford University Press, 1988), p. 71; A. C. Cheyne, 'Introduction', in *id*. (ed.), *The Practical and the Pious: Essays on Thomas Chalmers, 1780–1847* (Edinburgh, St Andrew Press, 1985), p. 23.

29 Mechie, *Church and Scottish Social Development*, p. 39.

30 Stevenson MacGill, 'On provision for the poor', in *id.*, *Discourses and Essays on Subjects of Public Interest* (Edinburgh, Waugh and Innes, 1819).

31 A. R. Divine, 'The changing village: loss of community in John Galt's *Annals of the Parish*', *Studies in Scottish Literature*, 25 (1990), 121–33.

32 E. King, *Scotland Sober and Free: the Temperance Movement, 1829–1979* (Glasgow, Glasgow Museums and Art Galleries, 1979), p. 7.

33 George Lewis, *Scotland a Half-educated Nation both in the Quantity and Quality of her Educational Institutions* (Glasgow, Collins, for the Glasgow Educational Association, 1834), pp. 20, 75; D. Withrington, 'Scotland a half-educated nation in 1834? Reliable critique or persuasive polemic?', in W. Humes and H. Paterson (eds), *Scottish Culture and Scottish Education, 1800–1980* (Edinburgh, John Donald, 1983).

34 Hempton, *Religion and Political Culture*, p. 66.

35 J. Handley, *The Irish in Modern Scotland* (Oxford, Oxford University Press, 1947), pp. 24–5, 43, 47, 94, 99–105, 112.

36 John Steill, *Scottish Independence* (1844, 2nd edn Edinburgh, 1845); Steill, *Scotland for the Scotch: and Reasons for Irish Repeal* (Glasgow, Stewart, 1848?), pp. 6, 8, 10; Steill, 'Letters to Newspapers in defence of the Highlanders, 1854–64', Glasgow University Library Sp. Coll. Mu 38-h. 2.

37 Handley, *Irish in Modern Scotland*, p. 108; L. P. Curtis, Jr, *Apes and Angels: the Irishman in Victorian Caricature* (Newton Abbot, David and Charles, 1971), p. 98; T. M. Devine, *The Great Highland Famine* (Edinburgh, John Donald, 1988), p. 130.

38 C. Kidd, 'Teutonist ethnology and Scottish nationalist inhibition, 1780–1880', *Scottish Historical Review*, 74 (1995), 45–68.

39 Devine, *Great Highland Famine*, p. 130.

40 Kidd, 'Teutonist ethnology', 53.

41 Robert Knox, *The Races of Men: a Fragment* (London, Renshaw, 1850), p. 27.

42 Kidd, 'Teutonist ethnology', 54–5.

43 R. Cooter, *Phrenology in the British Isles: an Annnotated, Historical Bibliography and Index* (Metuchen, Scarecrow Press, 1989), appendix D.

44 George Combe, 'Phrenological remarks', in Samuel Morton, *Crania Americana* (Philadelphia, Dobson, 1839), p. 271; Combe, *A System of Phrenology*, 5th edn, 2 vols (Edinburgh, Maclachlan and Stewart, 1853), ii. 359.

45 H. Hanham, 'Mid-century Scottish nationalism, romantic and radical', in R. Robson (ed.), *Ideas and Institutions of Victorian Britain: Essays in Honour of George Kitson Clark* (London, Bell, 1967), p. 145; Macmillan, *Scottish Art*, pp. 205–6; C. McWilliam, *Scottish Townscape* (London, Collins, 1975), p. 135; J. Mackay, *William Wallace: Brave Heart* (1995, repr. Edinburgh, 1996), pp. 16–17; Rogers, *Monuments*, i. 234, 504.

46 J. Fyfe (ed.), *The Autobiography of John McAdam* (Scottish History Society, 4th Ser., 16, 1980), p. 196; J. Fyfe, 'Scottish volunteers with Garibaldi', *Scottish Historical Review*, 57 (1978), 168–81; O. and S. Checkland, *Industry and Ethos: Scotland, 1832–1914* (1984, new edn Edinburgh, 1989),

p. 74; A. Wilson, *The Chartist Movement in Scotland* (Manchester, Manchester University Press, 1970), p. 260.

47  Robbins, *Nineteenth Century Britain*.

48  Robert Southey, 'The Death of Wallace' (1798), in *The Poetical Works of Southey* (London, Longman, 1845), p. 128; William Wordsworth, *The Thirteen-Book Prelude i*, ed. M. L. Reed (Ithaca, Cornell University Press, 1991), p. 112, Bk. I, lines. 214–20. I am indebted to Fiona Stafford for this reference.

49  Jane Porter, *The Scottish Chiefs*, 5 vols (London, Longman, 1810), i, preface, vii–viii.

50  G. Morton, 'Unionist nationalism: the historical construction of Scottish national identity, Edinburgh 1830–1860', Ph.D. thesis, Edinburgh University, 1993, p. 13; L. Paterson, *The Autonomy of Modern Scotland* (Edinburgh, Edinburgh University Press, 1994), p. 60.

51  *The Dramatic and Poetical Works of Joanna Baillie* (London, Longman, 1851), pp. 707–8.

52  R. J. Morris and G. Morton, 'The remaking of Scotland: a nation within a nation, 1850–1920', in M. Lynch (ed.), *Scotland, 1850–1979: Society, Politics and the Union* (Historical Association Committee for Scotland and the Historical Association, 1993), pp. 16–17.

53  A. Noble, 'Burns and Scottish nationalism', in K. Simpson (ed.), *Burns Now* (Edinburgh, Canongate Academic, 1994), pp. 170–2.

54  Thomas Carlyle, *On Heroes, Hero-Worship and the Heroic in History* (with *Sartor Resartus*) (London, Everyman, 1908), p. 416.

55  I. McIntyre, *Dirt and Deity: a Life of Robert Burns* (London, Harper Collins, 1996), p. 416

56  Wilson, *Chartist Movement in Scotland*, p. 259.

57  *Scottish Grievances Analysed*, from *The Commonwealth*, 10 December 1853.

58  Hanham, 'Mid-century Scottish nationalism'; W. Ferguson, *Scotland, 1689 to the Present* (1968, repr. Edinburgh, Mercat Press, 1987), pp. 319–21.

59  M. Girouard, *The Return to Camelot* (New Haven, Yale University Press, 1981), ch. 7.

60  Hugh Scott, *The Progress of the Scottish National Movement*, i (Edinburgh, Bell and Bradfute, 1853).

61  *Reasons for Declining to Join the National Association for the Vindication of Scottish Rights* (Edinburgh, Thomas Grant, 1854), pp. 8–9.

62  *John Buchanan, *Scotland Insulted! or, The Heraldic Outrage at the Glasgow Post Office* (Glasgow, Bowie and Glen, 1856), preface.

63  G. Morton, 'Scottish rights and centralisation in the mid-nineteenth century', *Nations and Nationalism*, 2 (1996), 257–79.

64  I. G. C. Hutchison, *A Political History of Scotland, 1832–1924* (Edinburgh, John Donald, 1986), pp. 92–3.

65  *Ibid.*, pp. 94–5.

66  Cockburn, *Journal*, 2 vols (Edinburgh, Edmonston and Douglas, 1874), ii. 291–2.

67  Mechie, *Church and Scottish Social Development*, pp. 120–1.

68  L. Colley, *Britons: Forging the Nation, 1707–1837* (New Haven and London, Yale University Press, 1992).

69  For the Shilling Subscription of 1852 see Fyfe, *Autobiography of John McAdam*, 'Biographical appendix', p. 203.

## Acknowledgement

I should like to acknowledge indebtedness to my colleague John McCaffrey, a sure guide in the under-explored labyrinth of nineteenth-century Scottish politics.

# 8

# Integration or Separation?
# Hospitality and display in Protestant
# Ireland, 1660–1800

## TOBY BARNARD

In 1788 a leading Irish newspaper lamented that 'what is called hospitality swallows up everything: eating, drinking and rural sports fills up the whole of our Irish country gentlemen. The principal point of ambition is to outdo his neighbours in hospitable profusion.'[1] These criticisms elaborated a theme already beloved by censorious visitors and local moralists. Throughout the eighteenth century, hospitality and display interested observers chiefly for what they told of the cultural backwardness of Ireland.[2] Although the island seemed better integrated into the politics and economy of Britain, the idiosyncratic manners of many of its inhabitants diverged worryingly from metropolitan norms. These quirks of individual and collective behaviour were long interpreted as symptoms of the insecurity of the Protestants lately established in Ireland. Recently such traits, instead of being treated as evidence of psychosis, are thought merely to reveal 'the uneven penetration of a provincial elite by the standards of metropolitan society'.[3] From this perspective Hanoverian Ireland varied rather than diverged wildly from what was happening as consumption and consumerism gathered pace throughout Britain and the American colonies.

Both the reconstruction of patterns inside Ireland and comparison with developments outside are hampered by sparse evidence. Some essentials in changing cross-Channel and international trade have been delineated.[4] It is clearer how rapidly Ireland's population grew, probably doubling between 1706 and 1791. At the same time Dublin's inhabitants increased from about 45,000 in 1685 to perhaps 182,000 by 1798; Cork's from maybe 17,595 in 1706 to 57,033 in 1796. Other ports and provincial towns also expanded.[5] An enthusiastic, even precocious embrace of fashions, shipped into Dublin and other harbours usually from Britain but sometimes from continental Europe, has been sketched.[6] However, the trends, in themselves conjectural, are hard to link convincingly with Irish society because so much about its structures is still unknown. In consequence, most accounts of social habits derive, both in conception and in detail, from the memorable characterisation by W. E. H. Lecky in the 1890s. Lecky blended together the miscellaneous notes of eighteenth-century reporters – prescriptions as often as descriptions – into an argument in which Irish practices of hospitality and display demonstrated the material and moral failings of those who dominated eighteenth-century Ireland. He also believed that the all-important landowning order was internally stratified. A 'small gentry', normally tenants enjoying estates on long and favourable leases, was differentiated from its social betters both by more recent date of settlement and by the connected characteristic of uncouthness. Among 'this harsh, rapacious and dissipated class' 'an insolent, reckless and unprincipled type of character was naturally formed. Drunkenness and extravagance went hand in hand among the gentry, and especially among the lesser gentry, and the immense consumption of French wine was deplored as a national calamity.'[7]

Since Lecky wrote, the 'lesser' or 'small' gentry, if not wholly rehabilitated, have been allowed a more useful role in diffusing agricultural innovations and new tastes. Regional variegation in origins and circumstances has been noticed. Also, from the 1760s onwards, thanks to the greater profitability of agriculture, *rentiers* and urban speculators in leases became more conspicuous.[8] Confusingly, these gentlemen, or would-be gentlemen, comprehended both the cadets and mobile among the Protestant elites and the hardy survivors and aggressive opportunists from the Catholic community.[9] If some of the economic impact of these proprietors is now considered more favourably, their culture awaits sympathetic scrutiny. Certainly, when the material life of eighteenth-century Ireland is occasionally discussed it is generally refracted through the experience of landowners, the only group readily documented. But contradictions and inconsistencies abound. Ireland, although it possessed a parliamentary peerage modelled after and with much the same (limited) powers as England's, was an apparently meritocratic and 'open' society.[10] Nevertheless, it is allowed that late eighteenth-century Dublin was dominated physically – and, by implication, culturally – to a greater degree than either contemporary Edinburgh or London by the houses of its resident aristocrats: a situation little altered by the Act of Union after 1800.[11] Dublin, notwithstanding its size (throughout this period the second city of the Hanoverians' empire) and its magnetism for Irish provincials, has yet to distract attention away from a tiny segment of the landed. The importance of the merchants, artisans and populace in the politics of the Dublin municipality with its 3,000 freemen is being appreciated only slowly.[12] But the reverberations from studies of material and consumer culture in Britain, France and North America, where often the urban, professional, trading and middling sorts first welcomed and then spread novelties, have yet to be felt in Ireland.[13]

How Irish Protestants (and Catholics) dressed, ate, drank and entertained may reveal dependence on or independence from Britain. The deeper and wider circulation of 'baubles of empire', if traced, may show Ireland being subordinated and assimilated to British standards. Goods also stimulated other values and loyalties, many local, others remote. Consumers in Ireland selected according to need, availability, fashion and utility. A rigorously statistical approach to what was imported or manufactured locally, the prerequisite for any account which moves beyond Lecky and his followers, may miss the qualitative effect of single objects on individual lives. When an Irish grand tourist sent home a mysterious Parmesan cheese it was passed quickly between honoured recipients, each fearful of the novelty. Yellow glass rosary beads sent from Rouen and bought at a pattern, a torn mezzotint picked up at a local auction, even the vivid designs of delft plates pilfered from a mansion, enabled their humble owners to enter new worlds of imagination and pleasure.[14] Objects of this kind, glimpsed fleetingly, lead us beyond Protestant gentlemen (at most 1 or 2 per cent of Ireland's inhabitants) towards women, children, servants, townspeople, professionals, traders, artisans and the 'middling sort'. For most, their possessions, while they embodied something of the contested relationship between Ireland, Britain and Europe, seldom appealed primarily for patriotic reasons.

In Ireland, modes of living, eating and entertaining had long carried social and ethical meanings. Since the twelfth century, if not earlier, conquerors had ridiculed indigenous ways. In consequence, even the luxury and excesses of the newcomers could be excused, not just because they created work, but because they assisted the pacification, enrichment and Anglicisation of Ireland. By the same token, Gaelic customs were equated with barbarism. Moreover, those who clung to, or degenerated into, the older ways signalled a wish to reject both the culture and the rule of the English.[15] Thus the backward and vicious habits spotted in eighteenth-century Ireland amongst Protestant settlers dismayed observers, since they recalled unruly behaviour. The oppressive guesting and feasting of the Gaelic chiefs were continued by their Protestant successors in provincial Ireland.[16] As a result, the vocabulary of description and condemnation hitherto reserved for the indigenes lampooned the more recently established. But, just as the liberality and ostentation of the now displaced Irish had been rooted in local conditions, so their successors strengthened a sometimes precarious position by adopting customary practices of hospitality and display. However, newcomers, when they defended themselves against detractors, represented their own behaviour not as rational responses to tricky local conditions but as evidence of their continuing Englishness. The seemingly disorderly expansiveness of the Gaelic lineages when continued by their Protestant successors in the eighteenth century was extolled as 'the old English hospitality in Queen Elizabeth's days', which had now retreated from lowland England to the Irish provinces.[17]

The institution designed to speed the cultural as well as political integration of Irish Protestants into the British system, the viceroyalty in Dublin, failed to do so.[18] The impact of successive lords lieutenant varied according to temperament, resources and wives. Holders of the post recognised how the monarch's reputation was bound up with their own. The latest fashion from England (or Europe) was added to the armoury to overawe their numerous critics in Dublin. In the 1670s the Earl of Essex ordered lace cuffs and cravats 'of the fashion now used' and the Duchess of Ormonde commanded feathers for a state bed 'according as they are now used'.[19] Responses to styles which emanated from the Castle veered from doting imitation to angry denunciation. In a familiar pattern, the court could be blamed for importing decadence and debauchery into a hitherto robust society. Thus, for example, in the 1750s, a moment of heightened Irish patriotism, the standard stereotypes of moderate English and libidinous and wild Irish were reversed. It was insisted that the viceroy, Bedford, had led his retinue in drunken antics, while not one Irishman had been seen drunk.[20]

Guests bidden to the viceroy's fêtes at Dublin Castle might be excited into frenzied exhibitionism. Extra forces were added to those already powering the Dublin dress trade. From time to time the craze of dressing Irish was promoted. As early as the 1660s the lord lieutenant, Ormonde, and his sons patronised such a campaign in retaliation for an embargo on exports of Irish cattle imposed by England. Whether or not they kitted themselves out at Charles II's court in suits of prickly Irish frieze, the vogue did not take.[21] Again, in the 1720s, as waves of anti-English feeling and worries over the domestic economy swept through Irish Protestant notables, Irish textiles were pushed. In 1729 the funerals first of Colonel Groves and then of Speaker Conolly saw the distribution of Irish linen scarves in a bid to popularise the manufacture.[22] The two queen bees of Dublin, the vicereine Lady Carteret and Conolly's wife Katherine, vied with one another to encourage embroidery and quilting with Irish materials. Mrs Conolly, the more continuous presence in Ireland, exerted the greater influence. In 1729 she congratulated herself that she had 'set all the idle ladies at work' and that 'all Dublin ladies [had] fallen aknotting'.[23] But eventually even she had to resign herself to the fickleness of fashion. In 1741 she mused, 'it's strange that the people in England should be so fond of Irish things when here they all run after English poplins to a degree of madness'.[24]

The pull of the imported and exotic was acknowledged by the artificers who had to cater to it. One Dublin dressmaker resorted to industrial espionage in the 1720s to keep ahead of her rivals. She was abetted by the wife of the landowner for whom her own husband acted as agent. Samples of the latest in dresses and cuffs were despatched from London. This particular *modiste* built up a lucrative business on her own account which usefully supplemented the income of the household. In 1725 she boasted how she dressed thirty-five ladies for the recent ball at the Castle in 'very fine clothes, most of them trimmed and embroidered with silver'.[25] The smart accomplice in London was told frankly, 'the name of having my patterns from your ladyship brings me more business than I could possibly expect if I had them from any other hand'.[26] Those within the ambit of the Castle budgeted and dressed accordingly. In 1733, for example, the County Longford squire Richard Edgeworth allowed his wife £20 to buy a suitable gown for the viceregal celebrations on the sovereign's birthday.[27]

Men as well as women arrayed themselves for these public events. In 1728 a peer from the backwoods of Galway, in demand suddenly as a dancing partner for Lady Carteret, procured himself 'a fine suit of clothes for the birthday, trimmed with gold'.[28] The prevalent fashions of each season constituted a kind of uniform. But subtle variations in the quality and cut of the cloth, the patterns, colours and trimmings allowed individual statements through which superior taste and wealth could be read. As a trend to greater restraint intensified, so the skills of tailors and the discernment of customers were more severely taxed. Formal uniform gained ground. But once more the ways in which the regimentals of an officer were dyed, tailored and embellished or the materials from which the gowns of the clergy and lawyers were cut constituted minute calibrations on a gauge through which social differences could still be measured. Recognising this, a Church of Ireland dean who aspired to a bishopric in 1780 ordered 'two new fashionable gowns ... of such materials as are not to be got in Ireland, notwithstanding our boasted manufactures'. These had to be made in London 'by one of the best and fashionable gownmakers', following the pattern 'always worn by dignified clergymen and bishops'.[29]

The Castle, and its denizens, stimulated but did not originate demand in the Irish clothing as in other local industries. The same could be said of the 300 Members of Parliament, in the 1790s each alleged to spend £1,400 annually in the capital. The hectic round of conviviality and emulative spending, and the shoppers' paradise of Dublin, reflected the unusual concentration of functions and people in the Irish capital. Of these the viceregal establishment and the Parliament were no more than a minor part, so that the city was little affected by the institutional changes which followed the Act of Union.[30]

Beyond the ambit of the Castle, and only tangentially connected with smart Dublin, lived Nicholas Peacock in the 1740s. Peacock, cadet of a Yorkshire family which had settled in the vicinity of Limerick in the mid-seventeenth century, can stand for those newcomers who, snatching at the opportunities of leases, purchases, agencies and parochial offices, scrambled into the ranks of Lecky's reviled 'small' gentry.[31] Peacock dwelt in a modest house, probably of a single storey and thatched with reeds, with two principal rooms. He enjoyed the society and favour of local gentry, from whom he learnt habits. On occasion, when their effects were sold, he also picked up some of their belongings. At this time he lived on the fringes rather than as a member of the local Protestant elite.

In more than a decade he journeyed to Dublin twice, and then only for a few days. When he returned the first time he noted glumly, 'Nothing to show but a pair of pumps, 4s 4d, and a pair of buckles, 10d.'[32] Both were articles he could buy as readily in the port of Limerick, which supplied the bulk of his wants. A second visit to the capital in 1745 brought two mementoes which may have expanded his mental as well as material universe. His employer presented him with a silver cup. Hitherto he had used only treen and pewter. These habits were not changed by the showy gift, so that the sense of its difference from the everyday items in his house remained. In Dublin he also spent £4 15s. on a watch.[33] His encounters with the mechanisation of time, because not altogether happy, were remembered. Already when a clock entered the house its pendulum was promptly broken by a servant. The Dublin watch was quickly mislaid when Peacock went to the Limerick assizes. A servant was accused but it was rapidly rediscovered in Peacock's own pocket. Meanwhile the clock was sent to a neighbouring gentleman for expert attention, and was set going only when the neighbour came to dine.[34] These seemingly inert objects, sometimes invested with powerful anthropomorphic features by Irish silversmiths and cabinetmakers, enlivened domestic settings. Furthermore, such novelties, endowed with animism and gender, joined an existing world in which natural objects and familiar utensils already radiated strong personalities.

Peacock's home was not sparsely equipped. Like so many of his contemporaries, outside as well as inside Ireland, the bulk of his assets consisted in livestock or linen. 'The invention of linen' gripped eighteenth-century Ireland, a prime producer, no less than France.[35] Twice Peacock returned home from business in the district for a clean shirt. He had twenty-six from which to choose: a circumstance for which he thanked God.[36] His most regular and costly purchases in Limerick city were of cloth for his own and his servants' apparel. Often this was then made up at home by itinerant tailors whom he paid, partly in kind. Hats and wigs, cheaper than those from Dublin or London favoured by the gentry, also came from Limerick. A hint of personal vanity surfaced only when he was about to marry. The scarlet and blue of the fabrics which he bespoke from his regular supplier in Limerick conformed to the jaundiced dismissal by Lady Orrery of rustic squires 'with blue coats, red waistcoats and cockades in their hats' but not to her sententious rider, 'with no money in their purses'.[37] Nevertheless, Peacock's extravagance was as nothing to the dazzling rig which Squire Edgeworth, who prided himself on his moderation, procured for his wedding in 1732. The silver buttons on Edgeworth's wedding suit cost nearly as much as Peacock's entire wardrobe.[38] Whereas Edgeworth regularly bought his wigs for £5 in London, Peacock contented himself with the 7s 6d versions to be had in Limerick.[39] The speed with which artificers in Dublin and the Irish provinces improvised local equivalents of imported luxuries, adjusting them to modest customers, may have speeded imitation but lessened the cost and soon introduced considerable provincial variations from the metropolitan originals.

Peacock in his dress struck a figure closer to the gentry with whom he consorted than to the servants and farming neighbours with whom he dealt daily. Contrary to what some contemporaries and later Lecky contended about grandiose mansions devoid of basic comforts, Peacock's house remained the same modest size even after he had married and started a family, but its contents were increasingly diverse. Often he sat reading; when the chance came he bought engravings at nearby auctions; chairs, tables, chests and beds were made by local craftsmen. If there was a hint of archaism in so much of his substance being tied up in animals and linen, the arrival of a wife introduced changes. Six knives and forks were bought shortly before he married, and teapot, cups and tea soon afterwards.[40] As a bachelor his needs had been modest, and his resources, farming in an area of notable fertility, adequate. A physical circuit, normally bounded by the city of Limerick and the fairs and markets of the vicinity, was stretched beyond the hilly frontier into County Cork by his marriage. Already, thanks to his links with the gentry, he had ventured to Dublin. Moreover, through the newspapers from

Limerick he learnt of wars and rumours of war.[41] In 1745 he had obeyed his commission as a cornet in the militia and went to a rendezvous, only to find no one else there.[42] Through worship in the established Church and participation in the vestry and local courts he was part of Ascendancy Ireland and so, at least vicariously, of the Hanoverian State. Generally, though, his daily life was articulated by the predictable rhythms of the agricultural seasons and the ritual calendar of his Catholic servants and neighbours. These pretexts for neighbourly commensality were supplemented by the unexpected rites of passage.

Sometimes these occasions required special raiment, even if only a black hatband or scarf.[43] More common as an object of extra spending was the festal fare. Peacock usually noted what he had eaten only on special days: a shoulder of mutton when the vestry met; at Michaelmas, roast and boiled goose; on Twelfth Night, beef, pork, potatoes, pudding and roast turkey, all washed down with whiskey and cider, at a neighbouring gentleman's.[44] He turned the christenings of his sons into parties. Eager to strengthen his bonds with the local gentry, he persuaded some to stand as godparents. This may have spurred him to provide claret, whiskey, shrub and Lisbon wine, together with beef and wheaten bread, all procured from Limerick. Closer to home he found lobsters and asparagus. More durable acquisitions were a cradle and punch ladle.[45]

Weddings, by comparison, could be quieter, often solemnised in a private house rather than in church.[46] Spending tended to be concentrated on the apparel of bride and groom. Not only did Peacock deck himself out brightly, he bought jewellery and bespoke a side-saddle for his intended.[47] Sometimes this finery dazzled a larger audience. An account of the wedding in Kinsale of the daughter of the mayor dwells on the *al fresco* feasting and dancing, with 200 guests served with 100 different dishes. This amplitude may have been connected with the public function of the parent, particularly at a moment – 1713 – of excited political partisanship. A statement of loyalism seemed to be intended, as the English shoes of the bride and the English ensign fluttering overhead throughout the merry-making were emphasised.[48]

Marriage permanently altered patterns of spending. Peacock now ordered a wider range of clothes, haberdashery and groceries from Limerick. Others modernised, enlarged or rebuilt their houses; exchanged cramped Dublin lodgings for more extensive and expensive accommodation, and furnished them with previously unknown elegancies.[49] Then, as children departed or a spouse died, expenditure lessened. But funerals were themselves costly events, often preceded by a period of high spending on medicines, medical services and health fads. In Ireland, as elsewhere, the cult of health fuelled consumerism. So, too, did mourning, manipulated by the textile and dressmaking trades. For the financially straitened a sudden death, such as that of Queen Mary in 1694 or of a distant relative, with the requirement to don black, could overwhelm. Rich kinsfolk might be touched for a subvention.[50] Ingenuity was also exercised to evade the obligations. In 1728 a Westmeath squire contended that, having just dyed the liveries of his servants green, his sister's death need not bring any fresh expense. 'As she was not known to many people, I believe my not appearing in closest mourning will not be remarked.'[51] As the accessories of dress multiplied, with cuffs, fringes, girdles, buttons, belts, buckles, ribbons, necklaces and rings, so the need for them to be appropriate to mourning added to costs.[52] For the vain there was the further mortification of being constrained to wear 'one's old rusty clothes'. In 1738 an arbiter of Dublin fashion declared that, once the lord lieutenant embarked, most cast off their deep mourning for Queen Caroline. However, this commentator, as an Englishwoman, despised such local deviations. Instead she proclaimed, 'I think one owes it to oneself to conform to the court in such a trifle as dress, tho' one may be tired of it.' Conformity to English court etiquette probably came more naturally to an English aristocrat temporarily in Ireland than to a habitual resident.[53]

Once more it was Mrs Conolly rather than the English viceroy who set the standard of ostentation in the arrangements for her dead husband, the Speaker. Not only had 800 linen scarves been distributed to mourners in an effort 'hereafter [to] fix that custom in Ireland', all the rooms and stairs of their Dublin house were hung with grey and black.[54] Although Mrs Conolly had been advised in this dramatic display by the vicereine and Ulster King of Arms, some felt that the grieving widow had been gulled by tradesmen. Others whispered that, yet again, she had overstepped the mark, such mourning 'being usual only to persons of the first quality', and that 'it does not belong to her to do what even a duchess could not have pretended to'.[55] Rich Irish Protestants like Mrs Conolly who arrogated to themselves the right to break or make conventions exemplified that Irish disregard of English customs deplored by English observers.

In general Mrs Conolly's idiosyncrasies were more gossiped about than copied. In most respects Irish funerals, like christenings and marriages, varied rather than overthrew English habits. Restraint and economy warred with the urge to advertise the rank and riches of the deceased. Thoughtful testators anticipated some of the costs, and either bequeathed money specifically to buy mourning and keepsakes like rings and gloves, or enjoined simplicity.[56] The quality, and so the cost, of coffins and shrouds could be adjusted to resources.[57] The Presbyterians of one Belfast congregation adopted a Scottish economy by keeping a stock of black cloaks to be hired to the bereaved.[58] Censure awaited those who in death, as in life, violated sumptuary conventions and were buried with unfitting pomp.[59] As in England, heavy spending on funerals was discouraged, especially since so often, channelled into drink, it led to slights being given and offence taken. Reformers in Ireland also worried about the persistence of indigenous customs, notably the wake, which by the late seventeenth century had retreated in Britain to the uplands and peripheries.[60] The wild demonstrations of sorrow struck the rational Protestant and self-consciously polite English as at best bizarre and at worst outlandishly pagan. Furthermore, as the keening was stylised and sometimes commercialised, the Catholic Church also championed restraint.[61] Yet numerous Protestant landowners assisted the families of the dead not just with the burial but also by paying for the tobacco, pipes and music at the wakes.[62] Indeed, some were so fully assimilated to the locality that they were themselves waked: a sign to the hostile of how far newcomers might degenerate from the English civility which they were in Ireland to uphold.[63]

Public celebrations other than funerals revealed how ambivalently the new landowners viewed the reform of traditional Irish culture. When they organised races and games, or commanded music and song, they may have displayed that attitude of *de haut en bas* which seemingly characterised elites across Europe after they had themselves withdrawn from spontaneous enjoyment of demotic fun.[64] If some of the supposedly popular pastimes of eighteenth-century Ireland resulted from the interventions and inventions of the prosperous, others still suggested the reciprocal processes of acculturation. Willy-nilly, members of the new ruling order learnt from those among whom they lived and by whom they were nursed, reared and served. Music, a common accompaniment to much of the sociability, while it exploited the virginals, harpsichords, chamber organs and spinets imported, together with printed songs and airs, from overseas, still employed the traditional harpers, fiddlers and pipers.[65] Exponents of the older modes switched rapidly to new patrons, adopted novel idioms and adapted to altered requirements.[66] Gentry patrons may have enlisted such traditional services to buttress their still rickety position. However, some seem to have appreciated and enjoyed what was locally available. Lord St George, encountered already as a modishly attired escort of the vicereine in the 1720s, was eulogised as a discerning connoisseur of the Irish pipes by a leading Irish performer.[67] Indeed, St George, like so many others in Protestant Ireland whose activities can be reconstructed in something more than hazy outline, mocked the cultural stereotyping of later observers. Sprung from stock once notorious for rapacity, he shunned the rack renting of some neighbours in the 1720s.[68] With his lofty paternalism, it sometimes seemed as if he was being corrupted by the soft west. Yet in his house there he copied the latest London and Dublin fashions, and was regarded by the Whig regime after 1714 as reliable enough to be elevated to the peerage.[69]

Some public display occurred at events that were thought of as peculiarly Irish, such as wakes, or varied from the habits current in lowland England. Much of the activity in Ireland was neither slavishly imitative nor markedly wayward. Often it was linked with the pursuit or exercise of power: in Parliament, the locality or the family. Reputation could be enhanced or tarnished irreparably by public behaviour. However, the distinction between liberality, excess and parsimony, always finely drawn, might shift arbitrarily and inconsistently. In the conventional humanist *topos* the outward mirrored the inner person. As a result care over dress, deportment, conversation and gesture was urged. But moralists also feared that the use of these denominators increased the risks of imposture. The growing consumerism provoked calls for the resurrection of the old sumptuary inhibitions, without which the inferior and undeserving could easily buy the accoutrements of gentility and pass for what they were not. An extreme illustration of the dangers in this materialism was offered in 1719. A newcomer, by renting one of the most expensive houses in Dublin and hiring thirty footmen, all of them 'handsome fellows' and therefore costly, was accepted as a German prince. When he absconded with bills unpaid, he was unmasked as a nobody from the Irish provinces.[70] Less sensational but in the longer term more subversive was the conduct of Katherine Conolly, whose wealth allowed her to remake conventions. Deep in her widowhood in 1744, she was still criticised for the showy regime in her County Kildare palazzo. At dinner she provided three separate tables. 'This many ridicules her for and friends grieve for her doing anything that is not very proper.'[71]

Mrs Conolly had reached an eminence where she could do what she pleased. Others calculated more conventionally. In 1686 a substantial landowner in County Cork begged a wealthier neighbour to lend him a splendid saddle and horse furniture so that he could ride out to greet the itinerating judges looking 'very fine and sparkish'.[72] Such strategies continued among those who aspired to or occupied public office. In the 1720s the owner of Castle Durrow shook himself out of an almost Virgilian retirement and exerted himself to secure election to the Dublin Parliament. He heeded the counsel of an affluent uncle in England, that 'there is no making show without money. Money is always best spent where one makes the best figure'.[73] True to this philosophy, the most whimsical expenditure could be defended: hiring opera singers for private concerts, laying out lavish grounds and embellishing houses or simply furnishing 'a spit of beef' for the local garrison because 'it will make a grand figure'.[74] Flower, master of these arts, prepared 'to begin his grand figure in Dublin', with the object of wooing the new lord lieutenant.[75] He succeeded to the extent that he was added to the Irish Privy Council and elevated to the peerage.

Less satisfactory was the outcome of the otherwise similar campaign of Michael Smythe from Portlick. Smythe, keen to crash through the closed doors of County Westmeath society, dressed for the task. Like Flower contriving 'my grand parade', Smythe deputed a cousin in Dublin to buy for him a crimson velvet saddle and trappings fringed with gold for his horse. £30 was set aside for this commission, which, it was specified, should follow a model used by the lord chief justice. Other articles which he requested Smythe left to the 'genteel fancy' of his more cosmopolitan cousin, insistent only that 'all' should be 'in the most fashionable way'.[76] After the assizes, he announced happily that 'everybody who saw them admired the choice'.[77] Yet the illusionism practised by Smythe, his style and grandeur filched from others, did not so beguile the gentry and freemen of Westmeath as to secure his election for Athlone. Moreover, the counterfeiting went beyond Smythe's borrowed plumage. Desperate to be nominated as a commissioner for the projected turnpike in his area because 'the common people here imagine my not being named as a kind of slur or discredit', he decided to bribe the parliamentary printer to include him in the published Act. In the end, Smythe's unfulfilled ambitions wasted his estate and wrecked his marriage.[78]

The anxiety of women to cut a figure was less obviously motivated by public responsibilities. Nevertheless, some wished to proclaim the rank of brother, husband or parents, as well as their own. But acute sensitivity to what was fitting in dress, decor and behaviour was not always matched by resources. Women, even of gentle birth, had difficulty in commanding an income commensurate with their gentility.[79] A young visitor from Mayo in the 1750s confessed her predicament. 'I believe you know people in Dublin can't make visits without money in their pockets and tolerable clothes to appear in, of which I had neither.' Her circuit contracted until even church going proved impossible for want of suitable apparel.[80]

Another indicator of Irish Protestant extravagance, the amount of wine drunk in eighteenth-century Ireland, is less readily explained. By the 1720s recorded imports totalled a startling 12·4 million gallons annually. However, by 1791 this volume had increased by only 15 per cent, whereas the population may have doubled.[81] Tastes were turning to locally distilled spirits, better for the economy if not for the health of Ireland. Contemporaries deplored examples of alcoholism. In 1735 the head of a Dublin dynasty of office-holders killed himself by drinking drams in the morning and claret at night.[82] Another of comparable status was drunk three times a day, sleeping between each binge.[83] In the Edgeworth family, which cultivated moderation, the example of a neighbouring reprobate was held up as a warning. When a career of profligacy had brought the estate into Chancery, the judge, astonished by the size of the wine merchant's bills, averred that even had the carriage horses quaffed claret the consumption was impossible to understand.[84] The cautionary tale did not make Richard Edgeworth stint himself. His many bottles were, however, counted carefully in and out of his cellar.[85]

A closer look at individual and collective encounters with alcohol weakens explanations which rest on notions of Irish Protestant insecurity driving the privileged to drink or of the moist climate inducing a pathological need. Some Irish Protestants blamed the viceroy and his Castle set for corrupting local manners. Also, as clubs, voluntary societies and meetings proliferated, so sociability increased. Already the festivities decreed by the Protestant State, some common to the Hanoverians' scattered possessions, others unique to Ireland, expanded the ritual year of corporations, trade guilds and the Established and Roman Churches. Largesse was distributed by, and came to be expected from, landlords, bishops, parliamentary candidates and employers. Thereby freeholders and tenants glimpsed objects and sampled luxuries normally beyond their ken. Some literally carried away lasting remembrances from these celebrations. A dinner for freeholders at Carlingford in 1760 saw vanish a tablecloth, a pewter serving dish, seven pewter plates, five knives, seven forks, two pewter spoons and thirty-two glasses.[86]

Such bacchanals, not notably worse than those which accompanied electioneering in England, shaded into the unruliness which could arise at private entertainments. But any rigid distinction between the public and private in hospitality was hard to maintain. Liberality was a duty which both Christian and humanist teaching enjoined on the propertied.[87] So, while the intimacies of conjugal and family relationships and friendship were cherished, obligations to expansiveness persisted. Few houses in eighteenth-century Ireland were designed for privacy. While the pressures from Protestant doctrine and economy, in Ireland as elsewhere, constricted the traditional largesse, not all abandoned it. However, those who kept open house or allowed long trains of kinsfolk and dependants under their roofs were thought guilty not just of bad housekeeping but of falling into the parasitism of Gaelic society.[88] In this matter, as in so much else in Ireland, the promptings of social and economic utility were complicated by ideology. Yet, while the openhandedness was condemned for blending the indiscriminate doles of the Catholics with the oppressive coshering of old Irish chiefs, some Irish Protestants defended it as a relic of better times when their own English ancestors had practised *noblesse oblige*.[89]

A dangerously febrile quality could attach to Irish Protestant festivities. At a Limerick tavern in 1711, for example, five Whiggish army officers downed seven bottles of claret and two or three pints of sherry before staging an impromptu hunt around the Tory bishop's palace. The incident occurred on 23 October, a day consecrated by the Protestant State to thanksgiving and feast, at a moment of political excitability and in a city where the ruined defences still reminded of the two epic sieges which had helped to decide the fate of Ireland.[90] Protestant Limerick continued to be punctuated by agitations in which drink featured. A less frenetic conviviality lubricated the disputes of the 1740s. Disgruntled freemen met regularly at a vintner's to scheme over a bottle of wine, and the gentlemen of the neighbouring counties gathered for similar purposes in a club.[91] The huge garrison in Limerick – more than 10 per cent of the total army in Ireland – gave the place a distinctly boozy atmosphere. Through the barracks and garrisons into which the soldiery were coralled, both the society and economy of the locality were affected: once again it seemed that those sent from Britain to uphold in fact subverted order and decency.[92]

On 28 August 1741 a young Protestant farmer fell in with neighbours at Corofin in County Clare, spent 6s 8d on wine at the tavern and stayed out all night. This lapse was, however, unique in a record which covered more than a year, and coincided with elation (and coin in the pocket) once the harvest had been safely gathered.[93] Four years later, the better-off son of a Meath gentleman joined local officers at an inn. There he drank, as he admitted, 'to be sick'. This self-indulgence, freely confessed and one of two in a diary for eighteen months, occurred on 4 November 1745: a date which resonated even before a Jacobite victory was rumoured.[94] Peacock in County Limerick, like these other diarists, appeared frank about his escapades. He noted as a discovery, 'when I have drink I find people come to drink it'.[95] Meetings for business with local gentlemen might terminate with a modest number of bottles of wine. Workers were baited with food and drink at the end of their labours. Trips to nearby markets and fairs or into Limerick were refreshed with a dram of spirits or a mug of cider. In the summer of 1744 Peacock recorded how he drank with two male companions 'until drunk'. He added, 'I do not know how they scaped but I slept the day and night.' The following day, he acknowledged, 'I was cow sick and loitered about.'[96] Otherwise only on Twelfth Night and then in the house of a gentleman did he note that after dinner 'we drank till 7, then went to bed almost drunk'.[97] These obsessive accountants and introverted diarists, for whom their diurnals paralleled spiritual tally-keeping, uncover only one kind of experience. The profligate fail to chart either their material or their spiritual descent down the primrose path. Even so, Peacock's chronicle shows both the routine social uses of alcohol and the experimentation as he learned from others, sampled what was newly available and adapted his own hospitality in response not only to his own altered circumstances but to the expectations and status of his guests.

Tea-drinking with its special utensils seems to have been introduced to Peacock by his wife. It supplemented rather than replaced alcohol. Its appearance testified to the widening range and cheapening of goods in the provinces. The cost of tea, indeed, seems to have been halved by some Irish suppliers within a couple of decades of the eighteenth century.[98] Its use suggested the integration of Irish provincials into international trade and culture.[99] Associated particularly though not exclusively with women, it added rituals which complemented the ribaldry unleashed by the punchbowl and decanter. Unfortunately, as the prices of tea were lowered, so too was its social cachet. Now the fashionable had either to abandon the despised bohea or find new ways in which to express their superior taste.[100]

Tea required special equipment. This demanded a fresh vocabulary as well as skills. In 1710 the housekeeper of one grand establishment struggled to find the right words which which to describe a tea kettle and stand.[101] The problem recurred with other articles, notwithstanding the tuition offered by newspapers and neighbours. The enlarged choice of commodities, and shopping for them, created new relationships. Kinsfolk and acquaintances undertook commissions in London and Dublin. Retailers were trusted to send goods on approval or choose what they deemed best.[102] Since the instructions were often simply to buy the 'fashionable', misunderstandings did arise. An Ulster squire rebuked his son in Dublin, 'I think the hat you sent me too narrow in the brims, and must desire you get me a hat made such as Mr. Dowlin wears.'[103] In the 1750s a Dublin emissary of a family in Westmeath hesitated to purchase 'a sowing cane' and 'capuchin cheese toaster' because, without a pattern, she could not recognise the first and did not know the right price of the second. A commission to procure cowhide was equally frustrating, 'because you did not tell me what use it was for I was at a loss, for the people laughed at me to call for a thing I did not know the use of'.[104]

Few goods were monopolised for long by the Protestant gentry. Even if the originals were not cheapened, popular versions soon appeared. As early as 1701 a Dublin ironmonger kept a vast stock, supplied from Ireland, England and Holland. More than 500 customers had accounts with him. They ranged from Trinity College in Dublin, through peers and squires to a much more numerous contingent of city craftsmen, traders and householders.[105] Throughout the century Dublin offered a unique variety of specialists. In 1711 the visitor who climbed Cork Hill to the Castle would pass periwig makers aplenty, two toyshops, milliners, gunsmiths, a woollen draper, makers of pattens, shoes and razors, a brazier, a pewterer and a shop which sold silver lace.[106] Yet the provincial could find staples and exotics closer to hand. By 1720 an inland town like Birr boasted a general store which stocked an impressive array of textiles, haberdashery, groceries and even books, some home-produced, others imported.[107]

In 1743 a recently landed English judge reported from Dublin, 'the common manner of living in respect of eating and drinking, and entertainments from house to house, is not such as squares with my inclinations'.[108] His view was widely shared: so widely, even among those permanently resident in Ireland, that it cannot be discounted. Fashions in furnishings, foods and finery changed over the century.[109] Each commodity, as it spread and was popularised, revealed the intricate social and economic stratigraphy of Protestant Ireland. For the observant such indicators told not only of the cultural gulf between capital and provinces, the urban and rural, the urbane and bucolic, the fashionable and the outmoded, but enabled the lettered, leisured and active to differentiate themselves from the idle and ignorant. Much of the detail of what was happening remains elusive, but the trend towards greater materialism is clear. Attitudes to these developments varied from ecstasy at the resultant acceleration of Anglicization to regret at the erosion of old (and English) ways. Irish champions of modernisation might deploy the arguments of Davenant, Mandeville and Adam Smith, but often the transformations were incorporated into traditional ideas.[110] All that altered was that newcomers replaced natives as targets for criticism.

By the late seventeenth century Gaelic Ireland was losing much of its capacity to horrify strangers.[111] Once sinister customs were now viewed as friendly and generous. The lavish hospitality seemed an ethnographical oddity, anomalous by English standards but part of the charm of Ireland.[112] Observation of how the respected guest was feasted might still expatiate on what looked incongruous to English eyes: the disparity between the plentiful food and drink and the spartan setting.[113] But by the mid-eighteenth century the circumstances of most Irish Catholics, even those of gentle status, were too straitened for dramatic consumption. Instead a sober and politic frugality attended their lives. They husbanded resources to pay over the odds to rent land, stock farms and shops, and set up children.[114] In consequence, they came to be regarded as dangerous because they exhibited the industry, restraint and thrift once thought to be Protestant attributes.[115] Worse still, as the familiar traits were transposed, the Protestant settlers, far from being industrious paragons, were enervated by Irish ease and fell into the barbarous ways of those whom they had ousted.

Just as the image of the feckless and menacing Gael had been constructed to frighten immigrants and sanction English conquest, so the transfer of many of these features to the Protestant squirearchy served topical needs. Into this fabrication also went the unease, far from specific to Ireland, about enslavement to fashion and the economic and moral harm inflicted by obsessive consumerism. Depending on the angle from which they were approached, the gusto with which the new proprietors undertook the obligations of hospitality indicted them as wastrels, commended them as public-spirited or simply linked them with the habits of the prosperous and important the world over. Nor was the contrast between them and their predecessors as absolute as some imagined, Catholic Ireland did not stay innocent of these developments. Its inhabitants participated, as producers, retailers and consumers.

Through what they bought and used Irish customers resembled more closely their contemporaries in Britain, Europe and North America. In part, obedient to cross-channel and international fashions, they willed this greater integration. Sometimes, when they purchased fabrics, pottery, glass or furniture of Irish making, they selected what declared a distinct Irish identity.[116] A sharper sense of Irishness did not necessarily exclude an equally strong attachment to Britain. But the Protestants of provincial Ireland, like Peacock, not endlessly shuttling between England, Dublin and their country homes, had limited budgets and choices. Selecting from the huckster's stall, the pedlar's pack, the shopkeeper's shelves or retailer's advertisements, they picked what they needed and fancied, little bothered whether the object had originated in and still evoked Rouen, Canton, Malabar, Paris, Birmingham, Burslem, Belfast or Waterford.

## Notes

1 *Finn's Leinster Journal*, 26–9 November 1788, quoted in K. Whelan, 'An underground gentry? Catholic middlemen in eighteenth-century Ireland', *Eighteenth-Century Ireland*, 10 (1995), 32–3, now reprinted in *id.*, *The Tree of Liberty* (Cork, Cork University Press, 1996), p. 25.

2 S. J. Connolly, *Religion, Law and Power: the Making of Protestant Ireland, 1660–1760* (Oxford, Oxford University Press, 1992), p. 66.

3 L. E. Cochran, *Scottish Trade with Ireland in the Eighteenth Century* (Edinburgh, John Donald, 1985); L. M. Cullen, *Anglo-Irish Trade, 1660–1800* (Manchester, Manchester University Press, 1968); T. M. Truxes, *Irish-American Trade, 1660–1783* (Cambridge, Cambridge University Press, 1988).

4 D. Dickson, C. Ó Gráda and S. Daultrey, 'Hearth tax, household size and Irish population change, 1672–1821', *Proceedings of the Royal Irish Academy*, section C, 82 (1982), 156; D. Dickson, 'The demographic implications of Dublin's growth', in R. Lawton and R. Lee (eds), *Urban Population Development in Western Europe* (Liverpool, Liverpool University Press, 1989), pp. 178–87; *id.*, 'An Economic History of the Cork Region in the Eighteenth Century', Ph.D. thesis (Trinity College Dublin, 1977), ii. 420.

5 T. C. Barnard, 'Art, architecture, artefacts and Ascendancy', *Bullán*, 1:2 (1994), 17–34; *id.*, 'The political, material and mental culture of the Cork settlers, c. 1650–1700', in P. O'Flanagan and C. G. Buttimer, *Cork: History and Society* (Dublin, Geography Publications, 1993), pp. 309–65; D. Fitzgerald, Knight of Glin, 'Early Irish trade-cards and other eighteenth-century ephemera', *Eighteenth-Century Ireland*, 2 (1987), 115–32; S. Foster, 'Going shopping in eighteenth-century Dublin', *Things*, 4 (1996), 33–61.

6 W. E. H. Lecky, *History of Ireland in the Eighteenth Century*, new edn (London, Longman, 1912), i. 284, 287.

7 D. Dickson, 'Middlemen', in T. Bartlett and D. W. Hayton (eds), *Penal Era and Golden Age* (Belfast, Ulster Historical Foundation, 1979), pp. 162–85: K. Whelan, 'Settlement and society in eighteenth-century Ireland', in G. Dawe and J. W. Foster, *The Poet's Place* (Belfast, Institute of Irish Studies, 1991), pp. 45–62.

8 L. M. Cullen, 'The hidden Ireland: reassessment of a concept', *Studia Hibernica*, 9 (1969), 7–47

(reprinted Dublin, Lilliput Press, 1988); *id.*, 'Catholics under the Penal Laws', *Eighteenth-Century Ireland*, 1 (1986), 23–36; *id.*, 'Catholic social classes under the Penal Laws', in T. P. Power and K. Whelan (eds), *Endurance and Emergence: Catholics in Ireland in the Eighteenth Century* (Dublin, Irish Academic Press, 1990), pp. 57–84; Whelan, 'An underground gentry?', 3–56.

9 A. P. W. Malcomson, *John Foster: the Politics of the Anglo-Irish Ascendancy* (Oxford, Oxford University Press, 1978), pp. 193–208; F. G. James, *Lords of the Ascendancy: the Irish House of Lords and its Members, 1600–1800* (Dublin, Irish Academic Press, 1995).

10 L. M. Cullen, 'The growth of Dublin, 1600–1900: character and heritage', in F. H. A. Aalen and K. Whelan (eds), *Dublin: City and County* (Dublin, Geography Publications, 1992), pp. 262–5; D. Dickson, 'The place of Dublin in the eighteenth-century Irish economy', in T. M. Devine and D. Dickson (eds), *Ireland and Scotland, 1600–1850* (Edinburgh, John Donald, 1983), pp. 185–6.

11 D. Dickson, 'Centres of motion: Irish cities and the origins of popular politics', in L. Bergeron and L. M. Cullen (eds), *Culture et pratiques politiques en France et en Irlande, XVIe–XVIIIe siècles* (Paris, Centre de recherches historiques, 1991), pp. 101–22; J. R. Hill, 'Corporate values in Hanoverian Edinburgh and Dublin', in S. J. Connolly, R. A. Houston and R. J. Morris (eds), *Conflict, Identity and Economic Development: Ireland and Scotland, 1600–1939* (Preston, Carnegie Publishing, 1995), pp. 114–24.

12 J. Barry, 'Provincial town culture, 1640–1780: urbane or civic?', in J. Pittock and A. Wear (eds), *Interpretation and Cultural History* (Basingstoke, Macmillan, 1991), pp. 119–23; J. Brewer and R. Porter, *Consumption and the World of Goods* (London, Routledge, 1993); C. Carson, R. Hoffman and P. J. Albert, *Of Consuming Interest: the Style of Life in the Eighteenth Century* (Charlottesville and London, Virginia University Press, 1994); P. Earle, *The Making of the English Middle Class* (London, Methuen, 1989); C. Shammas, *The Pre-industrial Consumer in England and America* (Oxford, Oxford University Press, 1990); L. M. Weatherill, *Consumer Behaviour and Material Culture in Britain, 1660–1760* (London, Routledge, 1988).

13 B[ritish] L[ibrary], Add. MS 46938, f. 148v; N[ational] A[rchives, Dublin], Chancery Pleadings, 'Unidentified Material', box 14, sale at Little Grange, 27 October 1749; *ibid.*, box 27, schedule of 15 July 1700 (I am grateful to Dr Jane Fenlon for directing me to this source); N[ational] L[ibrary of ] I[reland, Dublin], MS 4919, f. 128v.

14 This material is surveyed in D. B. Quinn, *The Elizabethans and the Irish* (Ithaca, Cornell University Press, l966); E. MacLysaght, *Irish Life in the Seventeenth Century* 3rd edn (Shannon, Irish University Press, 1969); C. Maxwell, *Country and Town in Ireland under the Georges* (Dundalk, Tempest, 1949).

15 T. C. Barnard, 'Reforming Irish manners: the religious societies in Dublin during the 1690s', *Historical Journal*, 35 (1992), 805–38; *id.*, 'The Hartlib circle and the cult and culture of improvement in Ireland', in M. Greengrass, M. Leslie and T. Raylor, *Samuel Hartlib and Universal Reformation* (Cambridge, Cambridge University Press, 1994), pp. 281–97; *id.*, 'Improving clergymen, 1660–1760', in A. Ford, J. McGuire and K,. Milne (eds), *As by Law Established: the Church of Ireland since the Reformation* (Dublin, Lilliput Press, 1995), pp. 136–51.

16 K. Simms, 'Guesting and feasting in Gaelic Ireland', *Journal of the Royal Society of Antiquaries of Ireland*, 108 (1978), 67–100.

17 *The Letters of Lord Chief Baron Edward Willes to the Earl of Warwick, 1757–62*, ed. J. Kelly (Aberystwyth, Boethius Press, 1990), pp. 96–7.

18 T. C. Barnard, 'The viceregal court in Dublin under the later Stuarts', in E. Cruickshanks (ed.), *The Stuart Court* (Stroud, Alan Sutton, forthcoming).

19 Bodleian [Library, Oxford], Add. MS C. 34, f. 97v; Historic Manuscripts Commission, *Ormonde Mss.*, New Ser., iii. 454.

20 N. L. I., MS 20389.

21 Birr Castle, Co. Offaly, MS A/16, D. Johnson to E. Pilsworth, 1671; Kent Archive Office, Maidstone, Sackville MSS, U 269/ C18/6.

22 N. L. I., PC 435, J. Bulkeley to J. Bonnell, 4 April 1721; *The Order of Proceeding to the Funeral of the Rt Hon. William Conolly, Esq.* (Dublin [1729]); J. Trusler, *The Tablet of Memory* (Dublin, 1782), p. 175.

23 P[ublic] R[ecord] O[ffice, London], C 110/46/729; N. L. I., PC 434, K. Conolly to J. Bonnell, 16 March 1728[9], 27 May 1729, 26 August and 3 December 1734.

24 *Ibid.*, same to same, 7 March 1740[1].

25 P. R. O., C 110/46/327, 362, 404, 414, 419, 496, 729.

26 *Ibid.*, C 110/46/916.

27 N. L. I., MS 1510, p. 82.

28 P. R. O., C 110/46/470, 475, 528.

29 N. L. I., PC 875, envelope 7, W. C. Pery to Mrs. Clayton, 7 March 1780; Purdon MSS, Cloverhill, Co. Cavan, diary of John Pratt, 1 February 1745[6]; A. P. W. Malcomson, 'Speaker Pery and the Pery papers', *North Munster Antiquarian Journal*, 16 (1973–74), 40.

30 Dickson, 'The place of Dublin', pp. 185–9; S. Foster, 'Going shopping in Georgian Dublin: luxury goods and the negotiation of national identity', M. A. thesis (London, Royal College of Art, 1995), p. 7; T. Mooney and F. White, 'The gentry's winter season', in D. Dickson (ed.), *The Gorgeous Mask: Dublin, 1700–1850* (Dublin, Trinity History Workshop, 1987), pp. 1–16.

31 J. B. Burke, *A Genealogical and Heraldic History of the Landed Gentry of Ireland*, ed. A. C. Fox-Davies (London, Burke, 1912), p. 552; S. Lewis, *A Topographical Dictionary of Ireland* (London, 1837), ii. 87.

32 N. L. I., MS 16091, 6 May 1744.

33 *Ibid.*, 23 May–2 June 1745.

34 *Ibid.*, 9, 22 December 1743; 28, 29 May 1744; 8, 9 August 1745; 25, 28, 29 April 1751.

35 W. H. Crawford, 'The political economy of linen in Ulster in the eighteenth century', in C. Brady, M. O'Dowd and B. Walker (eds), *Ulster: an Illustrated History* (London, Batsford, 1989), pp. 134–57; D. Roche, *The Culture of Clothing* (Cambridge, Cambridge University Press, 1994), pp. 151–83.

36 N. L. I., MS 16091, 1 June 1741, 19 November 1743, 25 January 1744[5], 26 June, 1, 29 September 1745, 30 October 1746, 16 February 1746[7].

37 *Ibid.*, 18 April 1747; [E. Boyle], Countess of Cork and Orrery, *The Orrery Papers* (London, Duckworth, 1903), ii. 240.

38 N. L. I., MS 1510, pp. 19, 35.

39 *Ibid.*, MS 16091, 10 April 1742, 22 July–10 November 1743, 19 April 1750; MS 1508, pp. 140, 148; MS 1509, p. 118; MS 1510, p. 35; MS 1513, p. 68; MS 4919, f. 64; MS 14468, 7 August, 3 October 1713; Purdon MSS, Pratt diary, 15 May 1746; Lawder of Bunnybeg MSS, Great Rissington, Glos., Account Book 1759–71, pp. 12, 62 (I am grateful to Captain Richard Turner for allowing me to read this).

40 N. L. I., MS 16091, 29 April 1747, 27 January, 10 February 1747 [8].

41 *Ibid.*, 6, 8 March 1743 [4], 18 May, 7 August 1744, 8 January 1744 [5], 15–17 May, 19 July, 23, 26 October 1745; R. Munter, *The History of the Irish Newspaper, 1685–1760* (Cambridge, Cambridge University Press, 1967), pp. 136–8.

42 N. L. I., MS 16091, 25 November 1745.

43 *Ibid.*, 5, 7 October 1742, 15 November 1743, 1 August 1744, 11 August 1745.

44 *Ibid.*, 3 September 1744, 6 January 1744 [5], 9 June, 29 September 1745.

45 *Ibid.*, 4, 6 May 1748, 15 September, 5 October 1749, 18 August 1750.

46 *Ibid.*, 9 May 1747; MS 3855, 3 December 1762, 9 August 1764.

47 *Ibid.*, 18 April 1747; MS 1510, pp. 19, 35.

48 University College Cork, U55, Kinsale Manorial Papers 1698–1764, H. Hawley to E. Southwell, 17 July 1713; Birr Castle, A/16, disbursements at A. Stokes's wedding, 18 September 1669; N. L. I., MS 4918, p. 2; MS 4919, f. 83.

49 N. L. I., MS 16091, 20 June 1747, 27 January, 10 February 1747 [8], 17 August, 27 September 1748, 13–15 August, 8 December 1749, 1 August, 16 November 1750; T. C. Barnard, 'The worlds of a Galway squire: Robert French of Monivae 1716–79', in G. Moran and R. Gillespie (eds), *Galway: History and Society* (Dublin, Geography Publications, 1996), pp. 275–89.

50 Christ Church, Oxford, Evelyn MSS, J. Evelyn to J. Evelyn, Sr, 12 January, 26 February 1694 [5].

51 N. L. I., PC 448, M. Smythe to W. Smythe, 9 March 1727 [8].

52 *Ibid.*, MS 12938, pp. 24–7.

53 B. L., Add. MS 22228, f. 162v ; Dromana, Co. Waterford, Villiers-Stuart MSS, T 3131/B/1/31, 33; Newport Public Library, Gwent, Delany MSS, 2, letter of Mary Delany, 13 October 1747; N. L. I., PC 434, K. Conolly to J. Bonnell, 20 December 1737; Genealogical Office, Dublin, MS 17, p. 39; *The Synge Letters*, ed. M. L. Legg (Dublin, Lilliput Press and Irish Manuscripts Commission, 1996), pp. 275, 294, 490.

54 N. L. I., PC 434, K. Conolly to J. Bonnell, 9 December 1729, 3 April, 25 November 1740; PC 435, J. Bulkeley to J. Bonnell, 13 December 1729, 24 January 1729 [30]; T. Pierson to same, 30 October 1729; F. Burton to same, 9 November 1729; P. R. O., C 110/46/733.

55 N. L. I., PC 434, K. Conolly to J. Bonnell, 28 November 1741; PC 435, F. Burton to same, 9, 13, December 1729; 26 January 1729[30].

56 N. L. I., PC 876, 22/35, 40; N. A., Sarsfield-Vesey MSS, no. 155; P. R. O., PROB. 6/644/132; P. R. O. N. I., D 1449/1/33; D 3406/D/2/2/1C; T. 2954/2/6; 'Abstract of Wills', *Irish Ancestor*, 5 (1973), 55, 59; 6 (1974), 118; 7 (1975), 95; R. Hayes, 'Some old Limerick wills', *North Munster Antiquarian Journal*, New Ser, 2 (1940), 71; T. U. Sadleir, 'Manuscripts at Kilboy, Co. Tipperary', *Analecta Hibernica*, 12 (1943), 147; E. W. Waters, *The Waters or Walter Family of Cork* (Cork, Guy and Co., 1939), p. 71.

57 Birr Castle, A/16, account with executors of Elizabeth Vincent, *c.* 1669, and 9 April 1675; N. L. I., MS 3000, p. 10; MS 10276/7; MS 16091, 5 October 1742; N. A., Chancery Pleadings, box 1, accounts of executors of Dudley Joynte, Edward Brenan, *c.* 1750; J. D. White, *History of the Family of White of Limerick* ... (Cashel, printed privately, 1887), unpaginated (will of Thomas Scaife, 1749).

58 J. Agnew (ed.) *Funeral Register of the First Presbyterian Church of Belfast, 1712–36* (Belfast, Ulster Historical Foundation, 1995), p. 1; P. R. O. N. I., T. 2954/2/6.

59 Dromana, Villiers-Stuart MSS, T 3131/B/1/9.

60 J. Addy, *Death, Money and the Vultures: Inheritance and Avarice, 1660–1750* (London, Routledge, 1992), pp. 37–8; F. Heal, *Hospitality in Early Modern England* (Oxford, Oxford University Press, 1990), pp. 365, 371–6.

61 Bodleian, MS Locke C 31; John Loveday, *Diary of a Tour in 1732* (Edinburgh, Roxburghe Club, 1890), p. 44; *Letters of Willes*, p. 85; S. J. Connolly, *Priests and People in pre-Famine Ireland, 1780–1840* (Dublin, Gill and Macmillan, 1982), pp. 148–74; Maclysaght, *Irish Life*, pp. 6, 162, 286, 318, 349; Maxwell, *Country and Town*, pp. 144, 154–5; S. O'Suilleabhain, *Irish Wake Amusements* (Cork, Mercier Press, 1967).

62 N. L. I., MS 1522, p. 143; MS 1535, p. 143; MS 1593, account with John Kelly; T[rinity} C[ollege] D[ublin], MS 10528, f. 184v.

63 *Ibid.*, p. 3, volume reversed, pagination from back; N. L. I., MS 4199, 24 September 1761; PC 438, F. Walsh to W. Smythe, 19 October 1735.

64 S. J. Connolly, 'Approaches to the history of Irish popular culture', *Bullán*, 2:2 (1996), 83–100; *id.*, 'Popular culture: patterns of change and adaptation', in Connolly, Houston and Morris, *Conflict, Identity and Economic Development*, pp. 103–13; Whelan, 'An underground gentry?', 34–7.

65 Birr Castle, MS A/1/143; N. L. I., MS 1510–1533, *passim*; MS 4919, p. 77; MS 14836, 14 December 1686; Barnard, 'Cork settlers', p. 329; *id.*, 'Land and the limits of loyalty: the second Earl of Cork and first Earl of Burlington, 1612–98', in T. Barnard and J. Clark (eds), *Lord Burlington: Architecture, Art and Life* (London, Hambledon Press, 1995), p. 191.

66 B. Boydell, 'The Earl of Cork's musicians', *Records of Early English Drama*, 18 (1993), 1–15; B. Breathnach, 'The dancing master', *Ceol*, 3:4 (1970), 116–17; D. O'Sullivan, *Carolan: the Life, Times and Music of an Irish Harper* (London, Routledge, 1958), ii. 5–108.

67 Thady Lawler, *An Apology for Pipes and Pipers* [Dublin, *c.* 1730].

68 P. R. O., C 110/46/51; T. C. Barnard, 'The Protestant Interest, 1641–60', in J. H. Ohlmeyer (ed.), *Ireland from Independence to Occupation 1641–1660* (Cambridge, Cambridge University Press, 1995), p. 229.

69 B. L., Add. MS 61639, fos 62v, 66; P. R. O., C 110/46/332, 340, 410; Brabazon MSS, private collection, London, box III, O. O'Malley to A. Brabazon, 14 May 1722.

70 Bodleian, Ballard MS 36, fos 109–9v ; P. R. O. N. I., D 2707/A1/11/37.

71 N. L. I., PC 434, K. Conolly, to J. Bonnell, 31 July 1744; PC 435, M. Jones to same, 27 October 1744.

72 B. L., Add. MS 46962, f. 240.

73 N. L. I., MS 11478, Lord Palmerston to W. Flower, 8 October 1728.

74 *Ibid.*, MS 11478, same to same, 30 April 1730, 16 December 1731.

75 *Ibid.*, MS 11478, same to same, 19 August 1731; MS 11475/1, J. Jeffreys to Lord Castledurrow, 2 September 1735.

76 *Ibid.*, PC 448, M. Smythe to W. Smythe, 16 February 1727 [8], 21 July 1728.

77 *Ibid.*, PC 448, same to same, 9 March 1727 [8], 15 May, 2 August 1728.

78 *Ibid.*, PC 448, same to same, 15 February 1733 [4]; J. Sheehan, *South Westmeath: Farm and Folk* (Tallagh, 1978), pp. 67–8. He was included in the Act: *Statutes at Large ... Ireland* (Dublin, 1786–1804), vi. 220.

79 N. A., M 2663, E. Houghton to J. Howlin, 12 July [1751]; N. L. I., PC 434, K. Conolly to J. Bonnell, 4 February 1729 [30]; *ibid.*, PC 448, S. Povey to W. Smythe, 6 August, 26 October 1748, 27 January 1753, 24 June 1758, 7, 27 May 1760, 18 December 1762; *ibid.*, PC 449, James Smythe to W. Smythe, 7 March 1752; E. J. A. Impey, *A Roberts Family, quondam Quakers of Queen's County* (Birmingham, published privately, 1939) pp. 78, 87–92.

80 Brabazon MSS, box I, M. Moore to M. Moore [December 1759]; same to J. Moore, 11 December 1759. (I am grateful to Mrs Eileen Barber for permission to read these manuscripts.)

81 E. Malcolm, *'Ireland Sober, Ireland Free': Drink and Temperance in Nineteenth Century Ireland* (Dublin, Gill and Macmillan, 1986), pp. 22–3; Cullen, *Anglo-Irish Trade*, p. 205.

82 N. L. I., MS 875, M. Coghill to E. Southwell, 24 April 1735.

83 *Ibid.*, PC 434, K. Conolly to J. Bonnell, 28 November 1741.

84 *Memoirs of Richard Lovell Edgeworth, Esq.* (London, 1820), i. 38–9.

85 N. L. I., MSS 1514, p. 139; MS 1518, p. 227; MSS 1519–24; MS 1533.

86 *Ibid.*, MS 10276/3, George Curphy's bill, 10 January 1760; N. A., Sarsfield-Vesey MSS, Accounts, No. 54.

87 F. Heal, 'The idea of hospitality in early modern England', *Past and Present,* 102 (1984), 66–93.

88 Petworth House, West Sussex, General Series, 30, L. Beecher to Dowager Countess of Orrery, 25 May 1685; H. T. Crofton, *Crofton Memoirs* (York, published privately, 1911), pp. 108–9; *Memoirs of Edgeworth,* i. 38–9; L. F. McNamara, 'Some matters touching Dromoland', *Journal of the North Munster Antiquarian Society,* 28 (1986), 67, 70; W. H. Maxwell, *Wild Sports of the West of Ireland* (London, Simpkin Marshall, 1892), p. 318.

89 N. L. I., MS 7361, pp. 185–6; 'An autobiography of Pole Cosby of Stradbally, Queen's County, 1703–37 (?)', *Journal of the County Kildare Archaeological Society,* 5 (1906), 90–1, 429; *Letters of Willes,* p. 96.

90 T. C. Barnard, 'Athlone, 1686, Limerick, 1711: charivaris or religious riots?' *Studia Hibernica,* 27 (1993), 71–5.

91 C. Massy, *A Collection of Resolutions* (Limerick, 1769), pp. 10, 16, 20, 31.

92 Dromana, Co. Waterford, Villiers-Stuart MSS, T 3131/B/1/47; Church of Ireland Rectory, Youghal, Co. Cork, Register 'B'; J. L. Darling, *St. Multose Church, Kinsale* (Cork, Guy and Co., 1895), p. 42; P. McSwiney, 'Eighteenth-century Kinsale', *Journal of the Cork Historical and Archaeological Society,* 43 (1938), 75–95; M. Quane, 'Tour in Ireland by John Harden in 1797', *ibid.,* 58 (1953), 84–6.

93 N. L. I., MS, 14101, 28 August 1741.

94 Purdon MSS, diary of John Pratt, 4 November 1745, 27 June 1746.

95 N. L. I., MS, 16091, 27 January 1742 [3].

96 *Ibid.*, 7, 8 June 1744.

97 *Ibid.*, 6 January 1745 [6]. Cf. 19, 31 December 1745.

98 Damer House, Roscrea, Co. Tipperary, J/3, bill of R. Bull, 26 October 1711; J/2, T. Fitzgerald to Lady Vesey, 17 April 1713; N. L. I., MS 4919, f. 78v; MS 13991, opening 8; Cork Archives Institute, U 229/box 105, 10 July 1769; H. F. Berry, 'Notes from the diary of a Dublin lady in the reign of George II', *Journal of the Royal Society of Antiquaries of Ireland,* 5th Ser., 8 (1898), 151.

99 J. Ovington, *An Essay upon the Nature and Qualities of Tea* (Dublin, 1732); S. Madden, *Reflections and Resolutions proper for the Gentlemen of Ireland* (Dublin, 1738, reprinted 1816), pp. 47–48; Cullen, *Anglo-Irish Trade*, p. 52; Barnard, 'Cork settlers', p. 331.

100 H. C. Mui and L. H. Mui, *The Management of a Monopoly: a Study of the East India Company's Conduct of its Tea Trade, 1784–1833* (Vancouver, University of British Columbia Press, 1984), pp. 47–48.

101 Damer House, Roscrea, de Vesci MSS, J/8, M. Nichols to Mrs Fitzgerald, 11 August 1709.

102 Brabazon MSS, London, box III, G. Fitzgerald to M. Brabazon, 17 April 1728; C. Lyon to same, 15 February 1728[9]; Roscrea, Damer House, Lady Vesey to T. Fitzgerald, 9 January 1708 [9]; M. Nichols to Mrs Fitzgerald, 19 May 1710; Abbey Leix, Co. Laois, J/8, same to same, 10 July 1710; Dromana, Villiers-Stuart MSS, T 3131/B/17; N. L. I., MS 11481, C. Warren to Lord Castledurrow, 2 December 1732; J. Fitzpatrick to same, 15 March 1734 [5]; *ibid.*, MS 20388, T. Caulfield to K. O'Hara, 19 March 1702 [3], 9 December 1703; PC 434, 25 October 1731, 28 February 1732 [3]; P. R. O. N. I ., D 2092/1/3/17, 230; *ibid.*, D 2860/11/56, 67, 68.

103 *Ibid.*, D 695/63.

104 N. L. I., PC 446, M. Ledwidge to Mrs Smythe, 20 March 1745 [6], 20 May 1751, 20 February 1755; *ibid.*, MS 20277, E. O'Hara to K. O'Hara, 12 May [1717].

105 N. A., Chancery Pleadings, 'Unidentified Materials', box 14, inventory of Alderman William Stowell, 1701.

106 Pearse Street Public Library, Dublin, Gilbert MS 195, p. 16.

107 B. L., Add. MS 31881, f. 295. Cf. Barnard, 'Cork settlers', pp. 345–7; W. H. Crawford, 'A Ballymena business in the late eighteenth century', in J. Gray and W. McCann (eds), *An Uncommon Bookman* (Belfast, Linen Hall Library, 1996), pp. 23–33.

108 B. L., Add. MS 35, 587, f. 182v.

109 N. L. I., MS 20389; M. Dunlevy, *Dress in Ireland* (London, Batsford, 1989); *Letters from an Armenian in Ireland* (London, 1757), pp. 36–7, 85–7, 113.

110 D. Castiglione, 'Excess, frugality and the spirit of capitalism: readings of Mandeville on commercial society', in J. Melling and J. Barry (eds), *Culture in History* (Exeter, Exeter University Press, 1991), pp. 106–63; F. Hutchinson, *A Letter to a Member of Parliament, concerning the Imploying and Providing for the Poor* (Dublin, 1723), p. 16; P. Kelly, 'Industry and Virtue versus Luxury and Corruption: Berkeley, Walpole and the South Sea Bubble crisis', *Eighteenth-Century Ireland*, 7 (1992), 57–74; N. L. I., MS 20397; T. Rundle, *A Sermon Preach'd ... the 23rd of October, 1735* (Dublin, 1735), pp. 32–4.

111 D. W. Hayton, 'From barbarian to burlesque: English images of the Irish, c. 1660–1750', *Irish Economic and Social History*, 15 (1988), 5–31.

112 R. Gillespie and G. Moran (eds), *Longford: Essays in County History* (Dublin, Lilliput Press, 1991), p. 209; J. Logan, 'Tadhg O Roddy and two surveys of Co. Leitrim', *Breifne*, 4 (1971), 333; MacLysaght, *Irish Life*, pp. 332, 345; H. Piers, 'A chorographical description of the county of Westmeath', in C. Vallancey (ed.), *Collectanea de Rebus Hibernicis* (Dublin, 1770), i. 113; *Letters of Willes*, pp. 37, 61, 96–7, 120.

113 Connolly, *Religion, Law and Power*, p. 67.

114 Cullen, 'Catholic social classes', pp. 57–84; Cullen, 'Catholics under the Penal Laws', 23–36; Whelan, 'An underground gentry?', 37–41.

115 D. Dickson, 'Catholics and trade in eighteenth-century Ireland: an old debate revisited', in Power and Whelan (eds), *Endurance and Emergence*, pp. 85–100; M. Wall, *Catholic Ireland in the Eighteenth Century* (Dublin, Geography Publications, 1989), pp. 61–92; Wall, 'Catholic manufacturers and traders in Dublin, 1778–82', *Reportorium Novum*, 2 (1960), 298–323.

116 Foster, 'Going shopping in Georgian Dublin', 88–103; P. Francis, 'The Belfast Potthouse, Carrickfergus clay and the spread of the Delftware industry', *Transactions of the English Ceramics Circle*, 15 (1994), 267–82; D. Fitzgerald, Knight of Glin, *A Directory of the Dublin Furniture Trade* (Dublin, Irish Georgian Society, 1993).

# 9

# O'Connell's ideology

## OLIVER MACDONAGH

Many years after the death of Daniel O'Connell (1775–1847), Gladstone paid tribute to his political versatility.

> He was an Irishman, but he was also a cosmopolite. I remember personally how, in the first session of my parliamentary life [1833], he poured forth his wit, his pathos, and his earnestness, in the cause of negro emancipation. Having adopted the political creed of Liberalism, he was as thorough an English liberal, as if he had no Ireland to think of. He had energies to spare for Law Reform, for Postal Reform ... for secret voting, for Corn Law Repeal, in short for whatever tended in the political sphere, to advance human happiness and freedom.[1]

Gladstone had put his finger on the leading paradox of O'Connell's political ideology: that he was at once a universalist radical, a life-dedicated Irish nationalist and a leading member – in many causes, the leading member – of the British left in Parliament.

The foundation of O'Connell's universal radicalism was laid in 1796, when he was twenty years of age and reading for the bar at Lincoln's Inn. He was deeply impressed by William Godwin's novel, *Caleb Williams*, a fictional tract on human perfectibility, and still more by Godwin's *Political Justice*, which argued that, by the continuous exercise of reason, man would eventually attain intellectual and moral perfection and complete control both of his own nature and of the outside world. From *Political Justice* O'Connell derived his three fundamental principles of active politics: first, that violent means were *always* to be rejected, because of their intrinsic evil and because, whatever they achieved, it would not be the object originally sought; second, that public opinion, properly marshalled and controlled, would, sooner or later, however laboriously or distantly, achieve any reform in view; and thirdly, that civil rights were at once absolute and universal, irrespective of religion, race, colour or condition. For all his gross demagoguery and tactical twists and turns, O'Connell was to adhere to his three tenets with remarkable fidelity throughout his long political career.

O'Connell's abhorrence of violence in politics was heavily reinforced by early experience. When a schoolboy of seventeen at Douai College, in northern France, he fled in terror from the advance of the revolution. Soon after the Wexford rebellion of 1798, in which he himself might well have been a victim or a reluctant participant, he wrote in his private journal, 'A great deal of innocent blood was shed on the occasion. Good God! What a brute man becomes when ignorant and oppressed! Oh liberty, what horrors are perpetrated in thy name. May every virtuous revolutionist remember the horrors of Wexford.'[2] Emmet's insurrection, he declared in 1803, 'merits and will suffer the severest punishment ... pity would be almost thrown away upon the contriver of the affair ... A man who could coolly prepare so much bloodshed, so many murders – and such horrors of every kind has ceased to be an object of compassion.'[3] This remained a fixed attitude in O'Connell. He might laud rhetorically, and take sides emotionally with, Bolivar in South America, the Belgian and Polish revolutionaries of 1830, or Irish feats of arms 'in far foreign fields from Dunkirk to Belgrade' in the remote past, but the pike and gun were anathema to him in modern Ireland. The same was true of conspiratorial methods. As a member of the landowning class and one whose life had been gravely endangered by his association with United Irishmen in 1798, he was an unremitting public and private enemy of all secret societies.

Conversely, O'Connell spent a political lifetime in the development and deployment of 'opinion'. In this he was an unrivalled practitioner, endlessly fertile and inventive, an unwearying accumulator of resources, both human and financial, an artist in aggregating and controlling mass support, and the true begetter of mass Irish constitutional agitation against British domination. In 1830, for the benefit of Thomas Attwood, who had just set up the Birmingham Political Union, he translated Godwin's visionary philosophy into the language of the workaday agitator:

> There are two principal means of attaining our constitutional objects which will never be lost sight of. The first is the perpetual determination to avoid anything like physical force or violence and by keeping in all respects within the letter as well as the spirit of the law, to continue peaceable, rational, but energetic measures so as to combine the wise and the good of all classes, stations and persuasions ... The other is to obtain funds by the extension of a plan of collection ... The multiplication of small sums, of very small sums, should be the proper as it would be the efficacious popular treasury ... The people should incessantly call for reform until their cry is heard and *felt* within the walls of Westminster.[4]

With nearly half a century of adherence to this creed behind him, O'Connell told a popular Irish audience in 1843 that his principle had ever been that all political improvements were attainable by peaceful means, and that none was attainable by forcible means except at the cost of much greater evil than it cured. O'Connell's 'peaceful' did not of course exclude the impression of violence barely held in check!

Godwin's leading idea, the utmost possible freedom from restraint, virtually summarised a whole range of O'Connell's political objectives. It also classified O'Connell's type of early nineteenth-century radicalism. It was not by chance that, from the late 1820s on, he was commonly named 'liberator' or 'emancipator' by his admirers. These terms described exactly how O'Connell himself saw his reforming role – as the unshackling of people from the fetters imposed by inequities and tyrannies of every kind. His was, by contemporary standards, an extreme programme of individual rights – essentially negative in that it was a grand procession of 'freedoms from', but positive in pursuing civil equality on every front. Typical was his persistent advocacy of Jewish 'emancipation'. As he assured the leader of English Jewry, Isaac Goldsmid, in 1829, 'you will find in me the constant and active friend to every measure that tends to give the Jews … a perfect unconditional equality. I think every day a day of injustice until that civil equality is attained by the Jews'.[5] He lived up to his promise. Although Jewish relief was a highly unpopular cause even among many of the British radicals of the day, including Cobbett, O'Connell was foremost in support of the Bill to secure it in the House of Commons in 1830. His claim to be a universal egalitarian was important, for at times he represented his struggles to achieve parity for Catholics and for the Irish as mere particular manifestations of a general, all-embracing aspiration.

If he consistently opposed racial discrimination with cold reason, colour prejudice and slavery provoked his most passionate and savage denunciation. He would never visit the United States or even shake the hand of an American who was 'contaminated' by residence in a 'bond' state. His earnestness in all this cannot be doubted. Although international support was vital to his Repeal campaign of the 1840s, he persisted in his public execration of American slavery, ultimately at the cost of destroying his entire support structure in the United States. The Young Ireland faction, and indeed many others within the home movement, argued that Ireland's need for overseas sympathy and resources should be paramount, but O'Connell would have none of it. He would, he said, recognise no one as an Irishman who failed to repudiate the tainted institution. Moreover, his 'brotherhood of man' embraced all victims of Western colonialism. In his speech to the Aborigines Protection Society in 1840, for example, he denounced colonialism in Australia and New Zealand as carrying ruin and genocide in its train; 'no other human event led to evils so multitudinous'.[6] O'Connell's hatred of supremacism and servitude was moreover of long standing. Since early in the century he had been a leading figure in the main European abolitionist organisation, the British and Foreign Anti-slavery Society; and he hailed the West Indian 'emancipation' of 1833, to which he had himself contributed, as 'one of the glorious acts of nineteenth-century civilisation, a symbol of the inevitable progress of man'.[7] All this accorded thoroughly with the optimistic, generalised humanism of the 1790s, but it may also have been driven by O'Connell's own resentments. The Jewish situation in the British State was in many respects analogous to the Catholic – at any rate, before 1829; and (in common with other radical or reformist movements of the day) O'Connell's used the powerful comparison of black slavery to drive home the claim of unjust powerlessness or subjection.

There was no difficulty in O'Connell's adopting 'perfect liberty' of conscience in religious matters during his Deist phase, which lasted from 1793 or 1794 to some time about 1808. When he returned to the practice – and an increasingly devout and rigorous practice – of Catholicism, however, he was swimming against the anti-liberal ecclesiastical tide of his day. Nonetheless, he adhered to his original position, as when he wrote publicly in 1841 that the 'respect' which each person would claim for his own [religious] opinion would require him to treat with equal justice the opinion of others'.[8] His normal state of bitter struggle with 'Orangeism' and the established Church in Ireland was, he claimed, only opposition to a political ascendancy based on confessional allegiance. This seems to have been true enough. In sect-torn Irish society he himself employed a Protestant attorney, a Protestant land agent and a Protestant manservant. He was also a tireless advocate of the English Dissenters' causes, from the removal of religious tests for office to the abolition of Church rates. 'Friend O'Connell,' the Quaker veteran, Joseph Pease, once told him, 'I have for many years watched thine actions closely; I have kept mine eye upon thee, and I have never seen thee do aught that was not honest and useful.'[9] As an individual O'Connell was a hot religious partisan, eagerly counting up converts and exulting that Catholicism was 'daily making progress'.[10] But rarely, if ever, did he deviate from public impartiality and mag-nanimity.

For a nineteenth-century Catholic, he was as remarkable for his commitment to the total separation of Church and State as for his virtually unqualified defence of the individual's liberty of conscience. It was on this ground of religious inde-pendence that he hailed enthusiastically, for example, the Orleanist revolution of 1830: 'the Bourbons had placed religion in a false position. Catholicity in France was situate somewhat as Protestantism has been, and to a certain extent still is, in Ireland. It was considered to be the enemy of the people and of liberty.'[11] Such a stance – publicly manifest since at least 1815 when he declared that he would as soon take his politics from Constantinople as from Rome—had long rendered O'Connell a hero to the nascent Catholic liberal movements of the Continent. Yet when these were condemned roundly by Gregory XVI in his encyclical *Mirari vos* in 1832 (in particular, freedom of conscience and of expression and the separation of Church and State were anathemised) O'Connell remained unscathed and unchanged in his opinion. How did he escape? First, he was a layman; he was devout; he had long struggled for, and ultimately won, the most famous Catholic victory of the age; he was genuinely, as well as prudentially, deferential to the Irish Church; and the majority of the Irish bishops were on most occasions his warm supporters. Second, the liberal 'error' most severely denounced in *Mirari vos* was religious 'indifferentism', and here O'Connell was unquestionably ortho-dox. He fully accepted the precept 'no salvation outside the Church', even if, characteristically, he also held that no one had a 'right to judge his neighbour's conscience'[12] or to suggest that a rejection of Catholicism might not be serious and sincere.

During his last years there were distinct signs of clericalism in some of his public stances. These were largely the product of circumstances. The large O'Connellite section within the Irish episcopate (on whom he depended politically from 1840 onward) was also doctrinally the narrowest and most truculent. More-over, Peel's Ministry (1841–46) deliberately raised divisive religious issues in the hope of alienating the 'moderate' Irish Catholic bishops from O'Connell and the repeal agitation. In such circumstances O'Connell had to bend a little before the rising ultramontanist wind. He was also led into sectarian asperities in 1845–46 by Young Ireland insinuations that he was heading a 'priests' party' and that some of his lieutenants at least were planning a Catholic ascendancy in Ireland. On the whole, however, even in his final phase, he adhered remarkably to his earliest definitions of individual rights and institutional limitations in all matters of religion.

O'Connell applied the radical individualism that underlay his principles of human rights and religious freedom quite as confidently to the field of economics, and especially to its industrial and commercial aspects. He was a doctrinaire free-trader and strongly opposed to all restraints on commerce. He was equally opposed to 'artificial' interference with the supply of labour, even though this, at certain junctures, gravely endangered his hold on the Dublin artisans, a vital component of all his movements. He accepted trade unions *per se*, but only because of his general commitment to freedom of contract and personal liberty of choice and action. The same principle, that every individual had the right to make his own wage contract, explains his strong support of the Trade Unions Act of 1825, which prohibited 'intimidation', 'protestation', 'obstruction', the 'closed shop' and even peaceful picketing. While it was fair for the workers to combine, O'Connell declared in 1838, 'the moment they attempted to coerce others ... that instant crime commenced, and they were not only guilty of a crime in the eye of the law, but also of a moral crime, and they inflicted a robbery upon others'.[13] Restrictive labour practices were inimical to employment, and thereby ultimately to wages too. 'They [workers] were not entitled to wages out of capital; they were only entitled to them out of profits, and if their employers made no profits the wages must decrease.'[14] O'Connell carried such reasoning to the point of being ambivalent, at best, on the issue of factory reform.

Before 1830 O'Connell's economic rationalism was delivered at a distance and was of little practical effect. But from then on it had considerable influence on the course of reform in Britain by reason of his parliamentary leadership and close alliances with both the middle class and artisan radicals. When it came, however, to what was still much the largest economic concern of all, land, O'Connell stopped short. By upbringing and (after 1825) inheritance he was a lesser Irish landlord of the non-improving, uncommercial kind. He occasionally supported minor reforms in the tenants' interest but practically speaking he had no clear policy towards landed property beyond his own particular brand of kindly but slovenly paternalism. It would scarcely be an exaggeration to approximate his landed philosophy to the Dickensian 'spirit of Christmas'. At the same time, he did not look back to any rural Golden Age, after the fashion of his contemporaries Wordsworth and his Lake Country dalesmen, or Cobbett and his yeomen of Old England. If anything, O'Connell's Golden Age lay in the early Christian era, with Ireland the supposed Isle of Saints and Scholars. His 'dreamy boyhood', he wrote, dwelt on the 'glories of that land which preserved literature and

Christianity when the rest of now civilised Europe was shrouded in the darkness of godless ignorance'.[15] In his fifties he confessed that even still 'in my day-dreams I revisit the brighter period of Irish history when Erin was the hotbed of saints and Science'.[16]

Thus O'Connell's romanticism – or perhaps we should say, sentimentality – was a far cry from the Golden Ages of the Irish Revival movements of the late nineteenth century which glorified either the pagan Celts or the traditional peasant culture. He might flatter his popular audiences by proclaiming them 'the finest peasantry in the world', but he would otherwise jog along comfortably with their actual way of life. He had no illusions about the virtues of either his people or their habits. They were the breathing and moving part of the landscape to which he wholly belonged, and in which he completely fitted – no more, no less.

O'Connell differed from many belonging to later forms of Irish nationalism in being completely at ease in his own sense of nationality. The questions that were to trouble the Young Irelanders – 'What is Irishness? Who am I?' – would never have crossed his mind. If perchance they had, the answers would have seemed to him (reared first in a herdsman's cottage where Irish was the only language, and then growing up in a remote, still thoroughly Gaelicised corner of County Kerry) self-evident. Being Irish was merely being himself. Totally assured in his national identity, he was quite indifferent as to whether any of his attitudes or notions might be labelled British. It was simply not an issue. They were his own, and he knew exactly who he was. Correspondingly, he readily and large-heartedly extended Irish national identity to all the inhabitants of his island – whether Catholics, Protestants and Dissenters, in Wolfe Tone's historic phrase. So far from wishing to impose his native culture on his fellow countrymen of different traditions, he regarded the decline of Gaelic with equanimity: 'although the Irish language is connected with many recollections that twine around the hearts of Irishmen, yet the superior utility of the English tongue, as a medium of modern communication, is so great, that I can witness without a sigh the gradual disuse of Irish'.[17] Ireland would be no less a nation without its own language. To O'Connell, the utilitarian, a 'diversity of tongues is of no benefit'.[18]

As all this suggests, O'Connell, for all his modernity, even prophetic modernity, in many fields, was a man of the past in others, especially by the 1840s. Ideologically he had been bred, as we have seen, a rationalist and a universalist, with an essentially atomistic view of society. Certain trends in Ireland, and to some extent in Britain, worked against all three during his later years. First, extra-rational politics broke the surface. If only obliquely, several of O'Connell's fundamental presuppositions came under challenge. The Germanic type of romanticism and idealism which infused the more ardent element in Young Ireland placed the emphasis on the race rather than the person, the group rather than the individual, cultural rather that constitutional liberation, and a subjective and creative rather than a formal and negative concept of independence. Secondly, in part because of the passion generated by such a view of nationality, but also because there were few left who, like O'Connell, had had direct experience of the French revolutionary turmoil and the Irish risings of 1798 and 1803, doctrines of armed resistance – if only in hypothetical form – began to circulate again in Ireland before he died. To him these were, as always, both dangerous and deplorable. Thirdly, the new concept of 'the nation' was accompanied by a new notion of its supremacy. For O'Connell the Irish nation meant simply all the inhabitants of Ireland, as an aggregate. Politically it would exist to ensure self-rule, equality before the law and equal civil rights for all its members, whatever their religious denomination. But 'the nation' conceived of as a spiritual entity demanded much more of its component individuals, and this was to become of increasing importance as the public domain expanded in the third and fourth decades of the nineteenth century. Would 'the nation' develop a quasi-religion of its own, inculcating 'national' values in the young? This was by no means what O'Connell meant in calling for denominational neutrality in the State. Nor, for that matter, was the surreptitious advance of collectivism in the 1830s and 1840s something that O'Connell would applaud or even very clearly comprehend. To the end, his idea of the State was confined largely to the staples of late eighteenth-century government – national defence, national revenue, foreign affairs, constitutional arrangements and law and order in their largest aspects.

Although O'Connell's failure to hear some of the early whispers of the future was to lead him into unaccustomed political difficulties during his final years, 1844–47, his command at home was never seriously threatened, and the ideal which he adumbrated for Ireland still held until the day he died. In one sense this ideal was both simple and single. He had entered public life dramatically on 13 January 1800 when, as a young and unknown barrister, he had played the leading part in organising a Catholic protest meeting against the impending Act of Union between Great Britain and Ireland. This was in itself extraordinary. The Catholic hierarchy and the great majority of educated Irish Catholics, including O'Connell's own uncles and brothers, supported the Union, in the belief that their 'emancipation' would follow if it were enacted, but would fail if the Ascendancy-dominated Irish Parliament remained intact. Essentially, O'Connell argued that Catholic interests should be subordinated to 'Irish'; 'let every man who feels with me proclaim', he told the meeting,

> that if the alternative were offered to him of union, or the re-enactment of the penal code in all its pristine horrors, that he would prefer without hesitation the latter, as the lesser and more sufferable evil; that he would rather confide in the justice of his brethren, the Protestants of Ireland, who have already liberated him, than lay his country at the feet of foreigners.[19]

Although this was his first public declaration of his political faith, its roots lay as far back as the 1780s, when Washington and Grattan were his early boyhood heroes, and it was his dream (as he later put it) to have it said of him too, 'He found his native land a pitiful province of England. He left her – Oh Glorious destiny! – an independent and mighty nation.'[20] Thus O'Connell could, and for nearly half a century did, express his leading political idea most baldly and briefly as nothing more or less than repeal of the Act of Union. Nor did he ever lose completely the visionary dimension of this aim. As a working politician, however, he used the elemental phrase in a great variety of ways and contexts.

Let us begin by asking what O'Connell could have meant by calling for the mere abolition of the Act. Literally interpreted, his reiterated demand for the 'simple repeal' of the statute was nonsensical. He could scarcely have desired the reconstitution of the eighteenth-century Irish constituencies, controlled, as almost all had been, by Crown, patrons, proprietors or bribes. He surely could not have accepted the reimposition of those Roman Catholic disabilities which he himself had done so much to have removed statutorily in 1829. Yet both these 'safeguards' had been preconditions of the Irish Parliament's 'independence' before 1800. In fact the Union had come about, so far as the great majority of Irish Protestants were concerned, precisely because they had come to feel that even these defences were too flimsy for the maintenance of Protestant Ascendancy, or even Protestant security. Furthermore, as the Repeal movement developed in the early 1830s, it was closely linked, by and through O'Connell, with the full radical reform pro-gramme – manhood suffrage, vote by ballot, triennial Parliaments, equal electoral districts and no property qualifications for MPs. Isaac Butt was surely right in asserting that 'Repeal was a revolution ... the proposition was not to return to any state of things that previously existed in Ireland – not to adopt the constitution of any European state, but to enter on an untried and wild system of democracy.'[21]

If then, O'Connell could not have intended what he often formally proposed, the turning back of the constitutional clock to 1799, why did he present the issue in such terms? Certainly, it testified to extraordinary political consistency. Throughout his twenty-year campaign for Catholic civil rights he had always stressed its secondary nature, that religious liberation was ultimately meaningful only in the context of Repeal. When, therefore, at the close of 1832 he committed himself, at last, to a direct assault upon the Union, the mature man of fifty-seven may have looked back to the young man of twenty-five and told himself that in his beginning was his end. The very Act which he had opposed in 1800 he still opposed in 1832; all that he had ever sought was the restoration of the *status quo*. He could moreover claim consistency with his original radical principles, and through these reconcile his personal ambitions and his grounding in the ideology of the Enlightenment. Lifelong, he resented the condition of inferiority into which he had been born as an Irish Catholic, and his consequent passion for parity could be readily articulated in terms of civil equality. As we have seen, he was the complete egalitarian in the formal senses in which contemporaries under-stood the word. Thus, O'Connell could honestly present his drive for political equality for Irish Catholics within the United Kingdom as a particular manifes-tation of a general and absolute principle. Repeal fitted with similar neatness into his universalist radicalism. The demand for legislative independence could be paraded as the very apotheosis of equal rights between the nationalities.

In the actual contest of nationalities, however, O'Connell had to work within the political system of the United Kingdom. He had to move British opinion, a British Ministry and a British House of Commons – to say nothing of further forces of resistance – and to do so with only popular and parliamentary pressures at his command, and with violence specifically disavowed. In the best of circumstances this would have been a daunting journey. But had he proclaimed that his real objective was to advance to a novel state of things which, whatever its constitutional form, implied democracy and disestablishment, it would have been pointless for him ever to begin. Hence the great value of the political ideas and imagery inherent in the very term 'Repeal'. Nothing could have been more conducive to countering the British 'great fears' – of revolution, of popery and of separation. It suggested, so far as any conceptual representation of his objectives might, that O'Connell's programme was moderate almost to the point of being reactionary. 'Simple repeal', often accompanied by invocations of 'Grattan's Parliament' and '1792', could scarcely be bettered as a device not only for exciting Irish nationalist enthusiasm but also for allaying British alarms. It conveyed, as it was meant to, the ideas of restoration and of Protestant security, if not of actual Protestant domination. The repeated use of the name of Grattan and the words 'College Green' (where the old Irish Parliament had stood) in O'Connell's repeal oratory suggested mere colonial nationalism and even perhaps renewed Ascendancy leadership, if freed from its former sectarian oppression. The backward references also commonly included the comforting incantation of 'King, lords and commons', the most solemn of all conjunctions in the liturgy of high-and-dry constitutionalists. Moreover, fervent, not to say servile, expressions of adherence to the Crown (of Ireland, of course, as well as of Great Britain) were from first to last a leading feature of each O'Connellite campaign. Thus, taking advantage of happy accidents of history, O'Connell tailored his constitutional ideology carefully for the British market.

Practically speaking, therefore, Repeal constituted, in O'Connell's view, the safest means of exerting mass, extra-parliamentary pressure, and represented the highest opening bid that an Irish agitation of the 1830s and 1840s could safely make. For, despite appearances, it would seem that O'Connell was not putting forward a serious specific proposal when he called for the 'simple' erasing of the Act of Union from the statute book. What he probably intended in making this demand, and backing it with the utmost Irish demonstration of 'peaceful' strength, was to elicit a counter-proposition from the British government. Repeal was only an apparent demand. In reality it constituted an attempt to open up negotiation; in lawyers' language, it was an invitation to treat rather than a firm offer. Its true counterpart, in terms of nineteenth-century Anglo-Irish business, was not so much Catholic Emancipation, or tithe abolition, or the disestablishment of the Church of Ireland, as Parnell's 'Home Rule'. Like O'Connell, Parnell avoided, so far as possible, the specification of his national objective. Like O'Connell, Parnell's pressure appears to have been designed to force out some British response, which might then be closed on, rejected or used as a start for beginning.

The artful ambiguities of O'Connell's position are excellently illustrated by this extraordinary passage towards the end of the great Mansion House debate of 1842 on the desirability of Repeal:

> a Parliament inferior to the English Parliament I would accept as an instalment if I found the people ready to go with me, and it were offered to me by competent authority. It must first be offered to one – mark that – I will never seek it. By this declaration I am bound thus far, that if the period should come when I am called upon practically to act upon it I will do so; but I will not give up my exertions for the independent legislation [*sic*] until from some substantial quarter that offer is made ... Upon this subject I must not be mistaken, I will never ask for or look for any other, save an independent legislative [*sic*], but if others offer a subordinate parliament, I will close with any such authorized offer and accept that offer.[22]

Although O'Connell hedged in his initial qualifications, 'an instalment' and 'the people ready to go with me', he was showing more of his hand than Parnell would ever do. But this was a mere difference of political style and generational mode. One's tactic was garrulity and an ostensibly uncomplicated single step, Repeal; the other's, silence and an ambiguous and amorphous name, Home Rule. Each, however, was really seeking to force a declaration from a British party while making none specifically himself. They were at one in being 'comparative separatists' who recognised that the degree of separateness would be ultimately determined in Great Britain, and who committed themselves to no abstraction or ideal form of State.

Nevertheless, it is doubtful if O'Connell's vision would ever have embraced total separation from Great Britain. It is true that he never wrote or spoke (or, we may safely add, thought) of himself or his fellow countrymen as British. There were innumerable occasions on which he expressed himself in a contrary or antithetical sense. On 20 July 1810, in his first major anti-Union speech after his initial declaration of 1800, he bitterly denounced the faithlessness of British politicians as revealed since 1801. 'What sympathy can we, in our sufferings, expect from these men? ... What are they to Ireland or Ireland to them?' The 'British' allegiance of the Irish supporters of the Union was to be explained by Britain's unremitting practice of 'divide and conquer' through religion: thus 'the enemies of Ireland have created, and contained, and seek to perpetuate [dis-union] amongst ourselves, by telling us off, and separating us into wretched sections and miserable subdivisions'. The 'enemies of Ireland' were clearly successive British government; and against these O'Connell – as always – pitted a concept of Irish nationality which was essentially locational, to be determined solely by Irish birth or residence, dwarfing every difference of class, interest, culture, language or even religion. Britain's ambition rather than their own 'wicked and groundless animosities' was the final obstacle to 'that greatest of all political blessings, an Irish King, an Irish House of Lord, and an Irish House of Commons'.[23]

The anti-British vein kept on appearing in O'Connell's speeches and correspondence throughout his political career. Although if anything a Francophobe, he greeted the tidings of Bonaparte's escape from Elba ecstatically. On 17 March 1815 he wrote to his wife, 'and then, love, the public news, the public news!! I can scarce draw my breath. Good God, how I die with impatience for the next packet.'[24] He was correspondingly despairing when he heard of Waterloo. 'I am horribly out of spirits. There is all the bad news confirmed beyond our fears ...'.[25] Ten years later, O'Connell measured himself in imagination against his 'foes', the leading British politicians whom he heard or encountered for the first time during a visit to London in 1825. 'Darling,' he told his wife, 'they think themselves great men, but the foolish pride of your husband would readily make him enter a contest with them. I have not the least fear of being looked down on in Parliament.'[26] Of course, Irish rabble-rousing – even of rabbles composed of the mercantile and professional classes – often dictated denigration of Britain, and in particular the English. One example was O'Connell's abuse in 1830 of Sir Henry Hardinge, the chief secretary, who was merely the formal signatory of a repressive proclamation:

> I arraign that paltry, contemptible little English soldier [Hardinge], that had the audacity to put his pitiful, and contemptible name to an atrocious Polignac Proclamation (loud cheers) – and that too in Ireland, in my own country – in this green land – the land of Brownlow – the country of Grattan ... the land of Charlemont and the 70,000 volunteers – the heroes of the immortal period of '82 (cheers). In that country it is that a wretched English scribe – a chance-child of fortune and of war, urged on by his paltry pitiful lawyerships – puts his vile name to this paltry proclamation putting down freemen (cheers).[27]

Later in his diatribe O'Connell excoriated 'the English Major-General' and his officers as 'our enemies'. Similarly, he chose for the epigraph of his book, *Memoir of Ireland, Native and Saxon* (1843), Thomas Moore's braggart lines,

> On our side is Virtue and Erin,
> On theirs is the Saxon and guilt,

which, every Irish reader would have known, followed directly

> But onward! – the green banner rearing,
> Go flesh ev'ry sword to the hilt.

As usual, O'Connell's most savage outbursts were inspired by his hatred of colonial oppression. 'There,' he exclaimed in December 1839, 'are your Anglo-Saxon race! Your British blood! your civilizers of the world ... the vilest and most lawless of races. There is a gang for you! ... the civilizers, forsooth, of the World!'[28]

None of these, however, necessarily implied a deep-rooted Anglophobia. To turn back to some of our examples, O'Connell bewailed the outcome of Waterloo not because he admired Bonapartist France but because of his conviction that his hopeful campaign for Catholic Emancipation depended for its success on Britain's being embroiled again in a dangerous Continental war, and hence more amenable to Irish pressure. The scurrility of his attack on Hardinge was a mere smokescreen to conceal the fact of his total, humiliating surrender to the vice-regal proclamation. His use of Moore's bloodthirsty lines was designed as a momentary popular intoxicant to inspirit without the peril of action: the martial reference was to a gallant, distant past, not – horror of horrors! – to modern violence. Even the tirade against Anglo-Saxon imperialists had its own offset in O'Connell's wild and unmeasured ferocity whenever the cruel or conscienceless treatment of native populations or coloured people came under his attention.

The truth is that O'Connell was, all round, a poor hater, and certainly no inveterate hater of the English. (Almost always it was the 'English', and not the 'British', whom he assailed when tactics or taunts launched him into an attack.) Nor is this surprising. During his most active decade of politics, the 1830s, he looked to the 'English democracy' as his natural ally and, commonly, their cause as his. In terms of parliamentary business, he was as fully an 'English' as an Irish force in the House of Commons: almost all the 'reform' causes were as much his as those of British radicals and advanced liberals. Publicly at least, he was as perfervid a supporter of the monarchy as any two-bottle squire or parson. His Repeal platform never so much as mentioned the abolition of the vice-royalty in Ireland. After all, even 'Grattan's Parliament' had not considered such a move, and O'Connell's own relations with lords lieutenant were not always disharmonious or unprofitable.

Nor did O'Connell ever repudiate the British empire. Rather was it his purpose (we may infer) to have it clearly recognised as an Irish as well as a British exercise of far-flung sovereignty. Certainly he used the imperial structure to provide careers for Irish friends and clients and to facilitate the establishment of Catholicism as an equal faith, as well as the establishment of civil liberties in general, in the new communities. He even spoke of 'conciliating the Irish nation and strengthening the British empire'[29] as two faces of a single coin. Given his own time frame, and given his own mind set, tasks and experience of struggle, the question of total separation from Great Britain was not an issue. Nor did this matter much. It was not in O'Connell to care for constitutional forms if only he could get the constitutional substances that he desired.

Perhaps O'Connell came closest to specifying his idea of the most satisfactory practicable Anglo-Irish relationship in a speech delivered to the reformers of Bath in 1832 and in the subsequent exchanges. He was eager to lead British radicals on from making common cause on parliamentary reform to making common cause on the constitutional rearrangement of the British Isles – minimising, of course, the unpalatable consequences of the rupture that would follow the repeal of the Act of Union. He was reported as saying:

> The Irish have been accused of wishing to have a separate Legislative, and to be divided entirely from England. Nothing can, however, be more untrue than this. We are too acute not to be aware of the advantages which result particularly to ourselves from our union with this country. We only want a Parliament to do our private business, leaving the national business to a national assembly; for it is well known to all who are acquainted with the subject that the private business of the House of Commons, if properly attended to, is quite enough to occupy its entire consideration. Each of the twenty-four States of North America has its separate Legislature for the dispatch of local business, while the general business is confined to a national assembly, and why should not this example hold good in the case of Ireland?[30]

O'Connell was immediately accused at home of betrayal of the Repeal cause. His phrase 'our union with this country' (Great Britain) was seized on as an abject and absolute surrender. He may well have spoken loosely or carelessly in using these particularly terms, just as his references to 'national business' and 'private business' were dangerously ambiguous. But the context establishes that in no sense was he arguing for the maintenance of the Act of Union; altogether the reverse. In any event, he claimed, as is commonly the case with politicians, to have been misreported. According to his later public letter of explanation, addressed to 'the People of ireland', the word he had used was, not 'union' but 'connexion'.

The public letter went on to make it clear that he saw Repeal as issuing in a form of federation between Great Britain and Ireland. He proposed that each country should have a domestic legislature, consisting only of a single chamber, a House of Commons. These legislatures were to meet in the last quarter of every year, and deal with such issues as law and order, agriculture and commerce within their respective territories. Then in the following January and February an imperial parliament should meet in London to determine matters of common concern to Ireland and Great Britain – among them, war and peace and imperial and foreign relations. Despite its lack of detail and obvious impracticalities in the machinery, O'Connell's proposal is not only intrinsically interesting but also most revealing of his ideology of the Irish–British relationship.

At first sight, his domestic legislature may appear a very limited objective, especially when he had employed, in his Bath speech, the direct analogy of the states of the American union. It seemed to fall far short of genuine parliamentary independence. But the independence of 'Grattan's Parliament', the holy grail of the Repeal movement, had been largely illusory. The British government, effectively in control of the Crown, the Irish executive and, normally, the majority of votes in both House of the Irish Parliament, had been the ultimate authority in Ireland throughout the period 1782–1800. Moreover, O'Connell's domestic legislature was meant to have *exclusive* power over the areas of administration that concerned him most: the economy, the civil service, local government, issues of public order, and the legal and police systems. Overall, this was a bid for a higher degree of autonomy than either of Gladstone's Home Rule Bills purported to provide.

Secondly, and perhaps still more important in O'Connell's thinking, his proposal reduced Great Britain to the same formal constitutional level as that of his own country. The British domestic legislature would have no greater range of business, no larger powers, than its Irish counterpart, under his ideal. The equal footing of the two was further emphasised by O'Connell's proposed joint parliament for imperial affairs – or, as he would have said, affairs of equal interest to both nations – for instance, external and colonial relations, and everything that bore on them, such as the armed forces, import duties and regulations, navigation and the foreign service. It is true that this would have been, in actual terms, a mock equality. The imperial parliament would have been absolutely dominated by its British members – to say nothing of its embracing the current House of Lords, unchanged. Nonetheless, its very theory, the mode of composition and the types of duties of the new body could be taken to imply that Ireland was no less a mother country, no less a nation than Britain itself. No less than the domestic assemblies might O'Connell's concept of an imperial parliament serve as a symbol and, as it were, international assertion, of political equality.

The proposal probably expressed O'Connell's fundamental purposes throughout his Repeal campaigns, and even from the opening of his political career. His notion of 'internal' affairs may have been ill defined and certainly did not come to grips with the problem of how economic policy and the levels of taxation and public expenditure should be determined. It was also antiquated in its very limited view of the State's sphere of action. Nevertheless, O'Connell's general intent as to the division of business was clear enough. Ireland should govern itself alone, and so should Britain. In matters that concerned the outside world – physically speaking – he was prepared to allow Britain the substantial power, provided that Ireland was allowed to appear formally as an equal partner. Parity was the key to all his thinking on Repeal, as it had been to all his thinking on Catholic Emancipation and indeed on civil rights in general. The great driving force of his politics was revolt against inferiority of condition – in the negative sense in which the Enlightenment had understood such terms.

O'Connell was ever the pragmatist. After his Bath speech and its fall-out had drawn from him a comparatively specific avowal of his real ambition for a settlement, he never again allowed himself the indulgence of detailed speculation, but rather used Repeal *sans phrase* as a popular rallying cry, a mode of intimidating governments and a hoped-for bargaining counter. At the same time, all but his most delphic later references made it clear that what was subsequently to be called Dual Monarchy lay at the centre of his constitutional ideology. 'The Crown,' as Professor Rose has written, 'is an idea, not a territory ... it is a Crown of indefinite domain,'[31] compatible, that is, with an Irish as well as with a British Parliament of virtually any scope. This fitted both O'Connell's retrospective idealisation and his workaday politics to a nicety. After all, even extreme nineteenth-century Irish nationalists could follow him to the point of acquiescing in a common sovereign. As the Fenian leader, John O'Leary, put it, 'Let England cease to govern Ireland, and then I shall swear to be true to Ireland and the Queen or King of Ireland, even though that Queen or King should also happen to be Queen or King of England.'[32] As to attaining particular stages on the road to Dual Monarchy, O'Connell was always the lawyer-politician as well as the unvarying ideologist. He was ready to compound (*pro tem.*, at least) whenever that seemed the advantageous course. There would always be another day in court.

## Notes

1 W. E. Gladstone, 'Daniel O'Connell', *Nineteenth Century*, 25; 143 (January 1889), 156–7. The present chapter draws freely on Oliver MacDonagh, *The Hereditary Bondsman: Daniel O'Connell, 1775–1829* (London, Weidenfeld and Nicolson, 1988), and *id.*, *The Emancipist: Daniel O'Connell, 1830–1847* (London, Weidenfeld and Nicolson, 1989).

2 A. Houston, *Daniel O'Connell: his early life and Journal, 1795–1802* (London, Pitman, 1906), p. 235, 2 January 1799.

3 O'Connell to (his wife) Mary O'Connell, 18 November 1803, M. R. O'Connell (ed.), *The Correspondence of Daniel O'Connell* 6 vols (Dublin, Irish Academic Press and Blackwater Press, 1972–80), i. 99.

4 O'Connell to Attwood, 16 February 1830, *ibid.*, iv. 129.

5 O'Connell to Goldsmid, 11 September 1829, *ibid.*, iv. 95.

6 *Liberator*, 7 August 1840, quoted in Gilbert Osofsky, 'Abolitionists, Irish immigrants, and the dilemmas of romantic nationalism', *American Historical Review*, 90: 4, 893.

7 *Ibid.*, 891.

8 M. F. Cusack (ed.), *The Speeches and Public Letters of the Liberator* (Dublin, McGlashan and Gill, 1875), ii. 285.

9 W. J. O'N. Daunt, *Personal Recollections of the late Daniel O'Connell, M.P.* (London, Chapman and Hall, 1848), i. 78.

10 *Ibid.*, 156.

11 O'Connell to (his son-in-law) Christopher FitzSimon, 11 September 1830, O'Connell, *Correspondence*, iv. 204–5.

12 Daunt, *Recollections*, i. 75.

13 13 February 1838, *Hansard* 3rd Ser., xl. cols 1085–6.

14 *Ibid.*, col. 1086.

15 O'Connell to W. S. Landor, 4 October 1838, W. J. Fitzpatrick (ed.), *Correspondence of Daniel O'Connell the Liberator* (London, John Murray, 1888), ii. 151.

16 O'Connell to Bishop James Doyle, 6 August 1829, O'Connell, *Correspondence*, iv. 87–8.

17 Daunt, *Recollections*, i. 14–15.

18 *Ibid.*

19 J. O'Connell (ed.), *The Select Speeches of Daniel O'Connell, M.P.* (Dublin, Duffy, 1867), i. 8–9.

20 O'Connell to J. H. Payne, 22 May 1829, O'Connell, *Correspondence*, iv. 70–1.

21 *Nation*, 4 March 1843.

22 J. Levy (ed.), *A Full and Revised Report of the Three Days' Discussion in the Corporation of Dublin on the Repeal of the Union* (Dublin, Duffy, 1843), pp. 191–2.

23 O'Connell, *Selected Speeches*, i. 20–4.

24 O'Connell to Mary O'Connell, 17 March 1815, O'Connell, *Correspondence*, ii. 19.

25 O'Connell to Mary O'Connell, 12 July 1815, *ibid.*, ii. 53.

26 O'Connell to Mary O'Connell, 17 March 1825, *ibid.*, iii. 141–2.

27 *Freeman's Journal*, 23 October 1830.

28 *Liberator*, 6 December 1839, quoted in Osofsky, 'Abolitionists, Irish immigrants, and the dilemmas of romantic nationalism', p. 892.

29 O'Connell to Lord Campbell, 9 September 1843, O'Connell, *Correspondence*, vii. 224.

30 *Freeman's Journal*, 10 May 1832.

31 Richard Rose, *Understanding the United Kingdom: the Territorial Dimension in Government* (London, Longman, 1982), p. 49.

32 J. O'Leary, *Recollections of Fenians and Fenianism* (London, Downey, 1896), i. 27.

# 10

# Nationalist mobilisation and governmental attitudes: Geography, politics and nineteenth-century Ireland

## K. THEODORE HOPPEN

The Act of Union of 1800 constitutes a defining moment in the modern history of Britain and Ireland. It created a new constitutional entity – the United Kingdom – with a new and increasingly demanding political agenda. If – on the British side, at least – its comparatively uncontroversial passage at first seemed to suggest quiet times ahead, this was to prove a profoundly misleading impression. For its part, Irish political culture became more and more obsessed, not just by the British connection, but by Britain (or more often 'England') as such. England came to be perceived, not simply as the dominating and dominant power (which, of course, it was), but as the yardstick against which all things should be measured – prosperity, social development, liberty, political sophistication. Only very occasionally did Irish political or cultural leaders raise their eyes much beyond London or take into account the possibility that interesting worlds might exist beyond Dover.[1] In particular, the politicians of the second half of the nineteenth century – Charles Stewart Parnell prominent among them – confined themselves to horizons determined exclusively by British, Irish and (in a very particular and defined manner) American imperatives.

While in certain respects much of this was natural enough – after all, England did indeed loom very large as far as nineteenth-century Ireland was concerned – yet its exclusive and all-pervasive character is nonetheless surprising, given that Ireland shared so many important social and economic experiences with parts at least of continental Europe. As John Stuart Mill put it in a speech to the House of Commons in May 1866:

> Irish circumstances and Irish ideas as to social and agricultural economy are the general ideas and circumstances of the human race; it is English circumstances and English ideas that are peculiar. Ireland is in the main stream of human existence and human feeling and opinion; it is England that is in one of the lateral channels.[2]

In addition, the kind of nationalism which, throughout the last quarter of the nineteenth century, began to dominate the political life of Catholic Ireland (and in turn helped to create new types of Unionism in Protestant areas) included many characteristics of a distinctly 'British' nature. Its political programme was one which many English radicals would have found acceptable, though some might have thought it conservative. Irish culture too, in its broadest sense, was becoming steadily more and more 'modern'. Certainly the Gaelic Revival, in all its linguistic, social and sporting forms, was a profoundly modern phenomenon, dependent, above all, on the nostalgia which only the collapse of traditional Gaelic society could have engendered. Nineteenth-century Irish nationalism, in other words, owed as much to British as to Hibernian influences.

Prominent among the forces which enabled this increasingly vociferous and Janus-faced nationalism to manifest itself was the growing homogeneity and integration of the various regions which made up what can best be described as 'Catholic Ireland', that is, the area in which Catholics constituted the largest religious element.[3] This does not mean that by 1921, let alone by the end of the nineteenth century, all parts of Ireland outside the Protestant and industrial north-east had coalesced into bland uniformity; far from it. Nonetheless, there can be no doubt that the very dramatic internal differences of the period before about 1850 diminished thereafter and that with the diminution came a new kind of nationalist mobilisation. In other words, as the Catholic peripheries gradually lost the extreme distinctiveness they had once possessed, so Irish political life began to adopt a new and more clearly focused character.

Before the Great Famine of the 1840s the western regions of Ireland were seen by many almost as another country where the people spoke a different language, farmed differently, maintained different customs, almost perhaps (at least in the eyes of modernising bishops) followed a different and degenerate form of Catholicism. And certainly the levels of attendance at mass in the 1830s were much lower in the Gaelic west than in the Anglicised east of the country.[4] 'I was now,' wrote Henry Inglis in an account of a journey in 1834, 'about to leave for a while the more civilized part of Ireland ... and travel through Cunnemara [sic] and Joyce's Country'. Eight years later the novelist Thackeray talked in much the same way of 'this stony, dismal district' and 'most woeful country'.[5] However, within a decade or two conditions of this kind, in which different districts were 'almost as unlike each other as any two countries in Europe' and in which disappointed nationalists could, in the 1840s, come across parts of western counties like Leitrim and Sligo where the very name of O'Connell was almost unknown, began to pass inexorably away.[6]

There is no need to embrace any strict form of economic determinism before accepting that economic – and especially agrarian – developments lay behind many of these changes. Pre-Famine rural society was – in numerical terms, at any rate – dominated by landless agricultural labourers and by 'cottiers' who rented small potato plots on a tolerably regular basis from farmers and paid for them in part by labour services. Together these two groups constituted about 76·5 per cent of all adult males in rural districts in 1841. Tenant farmers (most of whom rented less than twenty acres of land) were therefore at this time in a minority – as, of course, were the landlords themselves.[7] However, the effects of the Great

Famine as regards both mortality and emigration were felt especially by those without land. This, together with other agrarian developments such as the continuing decline of tillage after 1850[8] and the consequent fall in the demand for hired help, produced dramatic changes in the social structure of rural Ireland and, above all, in that of Connacht, where the proportion of the total occupied agricultural population consisting of tenant farmers and their 'assisting relatives' more than doubled during the forty years after 1841 – from a minority of 35·7 per cent to a clear majority of 73·3 per cent.[9]

Now, no one would deny that Connacht remained, by almost any measure, the poorest and most backward province in Ireland. However, the economic and social changes which it experienced proved sufficiently great to enable the peripheral western region to move from a position of comparative political quiescence to one involving a significant degree of integration into national political processes in general. Especially important in a political context were the profound changes which took place in the economic standing of voters (three-quarters of whom were tenant farmers) in the thirty-two county constituencies which together returned more than three-fifths of Ireland's members of Parliament. Whereas in 1840 almost a third of farmer voters occupied holdings valued under £15, by 1866 only a fifth did so, with the result that, in economic terms, the electorate became notably more homogeneous than it had been before.[10] Of course, regional economic differences remained strong. But there can be no doubt that post-Famine agricultural developments – particularly the spread of a sophisticated livestock economy into the west – meant that living standards improved throughout rural Ireland as a whole.[11] Not only that, but Irish income *per caput* rose from about two-fifths to nearly three-fifths of British levels between 1845 and 1914.[12] While no one any longer accepts the notion that a rigid 'dual' economy existed in pre-Famine Ireland, consisting of a commercialised maritime zone and a mainly subsistence area elsewhere, it remains the case that the economic changes which occurred after 1850 served to accelerate the process by which the various parts of Catholic Ireland drew more closely together.[13]

The erosion of the west of Ireland's peripheral status can also be detected in a variety of more broadly cultural developments. The history of the Irish language encapsulates a series of important changes. Already in the 1830s, though the language's ultimate retreat to the remotest parts of the west still lay a few decades away, most of what one might call the major domains of linguistic practice had already become dominated by English speech and images, notably the worlds of government, courts, garrisons, fairs and markets, the print media, the churches and the schools. Only the domains of the home and the neighbourhood remained Irish-speaking, and then only in a few comparatively small districts.[14] Having already become the language of the poor, Irish was then also pushed – partly by the consequences of the Great Famine – further and further into the geographical peripheries of Irish life. In 1851 some 23·3 per cent of the population could speak Irish (4·9 per cent nothing but Irish), though in Connacht 50·8 per cent could still do so. Within twenty years these figures had fallen to 15·1 per cent and 39·0 per cent respectively, and they were to continue to fall thereafter. By 1891 only 38,121 people in the whole island were still monoglot Irish-speakers.[15]

In addition, while the related phenomena of literacy (in English) and educational provision recorded remarkable upswings in all parts of the country, this was especially so in the west. Whereas in 1841 the proportion of those aged five and over 'able to read' in Connacht stood at just over half the national average (27·9 per cent, compared with 47·3 per cent), by 1881 it stood at above four-fifths (62·1 per cent compared with 74·8 per cent). And much the same was true of school attendance, with the proportion of those aged six to fifteen attending in Connacht rising from 14·1 per cent in 1841 to 45·4 per cent forty years later (when the national figure had reached 57·1 per cent).[16] People were becoming not only more literate but financially more sophisticated as well. Banks greatly extended their operations, and the number of full branches for every 100,000 people rose more rapidly in Connacht than elsewhere – from 1·8 to 6·0 in the twenty years after 1859.[17] At the same time the extension and improvement of transport facilities had a profound impact upon people's consciousness of distance and of place. Between 1849 and 1879 the number of miles of railway track rose from 428 to 2,285 and the number of passengers carried each year from 0·8 to 3·1 per head of the population.[18] Not only that, but a wider set of family and business contacts was also made possible by the enormous growth in postal services. The average annual number of letters posted by every inhabitant rose from 2·9 in the period 1841–45 to 17·3 in 1881–85, by which time large numbers of packets and postcards were also being sent.[19]

Denominational religion too experienced changes which encouraged both Catholics and Protestants to fashion themselves into more homogeneous – but also more separated – communities. The first half of the nineteenth century witnessed energetic attempts to align Irish Catholicism more closely with the kind of purified ultramontane practices increasingly favoured by the papacy and to rid it of that popular religiosity – interest in the celebration of seasons, belief in magical cures, holy wells, the evil eye – which had long given many of its manifestations a distinctly unorthodox flavour.[20] Before the Famine, however, efforts to introduce religious modernisation were confined almost entirely to dioceses in the eastern and southern parts of the country, with the result that the west became, for a time, even more clearly peripheral as regards the character of its Catholicism than before.[21] Only from the 1850s onwards did this begin to change, and it was not until the 1870s that the major western diocese of Tuam moved decisively into the mainstream of a new Irish Catholicism now more and more clearly shorn of the demotic 'extravagances' of the past.[22]

And just as Catholic Ireland was becoming more integrated along geographical as well as ideological lines, so Irish Protestants – partly in response to the evangelical awakening of the eighteenth century and partly in response to the increasingly energetic Catholicism which surrounded them – began to abandon the deep political and other differences which had formerly divided the episcopal Church of Ireland from the (largely) Calvinist Presbyterian Churches. Under the leadership of Church of Ireland evangelicals, on the one side, and Presbyterians like the Reverend Henry Cooke, on the other, the majority of Protestants came together from the 1830s onwards in unambiguous political and religious opposition to the forces of Catholic nationalism.[23] Election contests, especially in religiously mixed areas, became increasingly sectarian in character. The era of fierce urban rioting was inaugurated in 1832 as working-class Protestants and Catholics – often with open encouragement from their genteel co-religionists – took to the streets at the first Belfast election held after the Reform Act of that year. As territorial imperatives now more and more shaped the ways in which different religious groups regarded one another, so the supporters of both Orange and Green began to march (or, as they usually put it, to 'walk') through the streets in order to establish citadels, taunt opponents and raise the temperature all round.[24]

At more or less the same time, therefore, the various fault lines which ran through Irish society were being redrawn and relocated. On the one hand, what had, in the eighteenth century, been at least a partially coherent eastern core, separated from the less developed west, now fell apart under the impress of rising sectarian tensions into distinct northern and southern parts. On the other hand, the once clearly peripheral character of the west underwent substantial erosion. Connacht and other western areas, though still 'backward', were no longer almost foreign countries. Instead they became no more than somewhat less developed sub-regions within a gradually integrating whole. Religious rather than economic and social criteria were becoming the prime generators of divisions within Ireland. As the west became less and less obviously peripheral, so Catholic Ireland could – during the last third of the nineteenth century – begin to sustain political movements and a political culture more coherent, broadly based and dynamic than before.

During the first half of the nineteenth century the campaigns led by Daniel O'Connell for Catholic Emancipation and repeal of the Union represented, as regards the numbers involved and the methods employed, an entirely new departure in world, let alone Irish, politics. Yet even they were subject to certain debilitating constraints, most obviously those imposed by the restricted social and spatial character of the various forces at O'Connell's disposal. Not only, indeed, did O'Connell face almost insuperable problems when trying to identify the precise location of his electoral 'centre of gravity', he also found that support for his campaigns was still largely (though not exclusively) based upon the old eastern and southern axis which had underpinned the revolutionary mobilisation of the 1790s. Attendances at the enormous meetings called in 1843 to demand repeal of the Union were substantially above the national average in Leinster and Munster, somewhat below it in Connacht.[25] More striking still, O'Connell raised a far higher proportion of his 'Repeal Rent' in the same year from counties in the east and the south than can be accounted for by the comparative poverty of the west.[26] Clearly, therefore, the major areas of support for O'Connellism were to be found where the Catholic middle classes (urban as well as rural) were strongest and where communications and the appurtenances of a commodity culture had become most extensive and advanced.

The evaporation of this stark economic, social and political dichotomy between the east and the west and its replacement by even sharper distinctions between the north-east and the rest of the country were among the most significant of the changes which occurred in Ireland during the seventy years after the Great Famine. The important social and economic developments already mentioned helped make the western peripheries less isolated. Equally, the Irish Franchise Act of 1850 completely altered the basis upon which the right to vote was defined so as to render the electorate economically and spatially very much more uniform than before.[27]

The impact of such developments was not, of course, felt immediately. Connacht's post-Famine social and economic shift towards a situation in which the western province became more closely integrated into a broader national framework was necessarily slow. But, while the west remained poor, developments after 1850 gradually diminished the intensity of the isolation which had once characterised its political life. In much the same way the changes brought about by the Franchise Act took time to affect the attitudes of a political class whose outlook and *mores* had been substantially moulded by the experiences of the O'Connellite era. Indeed, the absence of any dominant national political leader in the 1850s, 1860s and early 1870s meant that the inherently strong predisposition of Irish political culture to operate in localist and fissiparous terms was allowed to flourish in notably luxuriant ways.[28]

In other words, distinct, though brief, 'lags' occurred, first, between the changes introduced in 1850 by the Franchise Act and the materialisation of a cohesive electorate in the Catholic south open to mobilisation along national lines, and, secondly, between the appearance after the Famine of certain integrative socio-economic developments and the creation of a new political consciousness in the peripheral west. Before the Famine, Connacht had been relatively uninvolved, not only in O'Connell's agitations but also in those movements more directly related to questions of land tenure, land occupation, and the payment of land taxes and rents. 'It was,' as O'Connell himself noted in 1839, 'the province from which the Emancipation struggle we received [sic] the least and the last assistance and now that the rest of Ireland is engaged, more or less, in another movement [for repeal of the Union] ... Connaught omits to join.' Similarly, during the violent popular protests of the same period against the payment of tithes to support the Church of Ireland, Connacht had actually paid tithes more readily than Ulster, 'Protestant as it is ... whilst in Leinster and Munster, the resistance' had been 'universal'.[29] And even during the first post-Famine decade this kind of agrarian quiescence still tended to pervade the west. Particularly notable was the way in which Connacht experienced the highest eviction rates of all four provinces during the period 1851–60 but generated the least amount of agrarian crime. By the 1860s and the 1870s, however, all this had changed. Eviction levels in Connacht remained relatively high but were now matched by the highest levels of crime, whether agrarian or otherwise.[30] The west's quiescence was coming to an end.

This spread of social and economic protest to formerly peripheral regions was accompanied by an equally striking geographical extension of both formal and illegal political activity. The members of the Irish Republican Brotherhood, founded in 1858, who were arrested under the Habeas Corpus Suspension Act of 1866 came not only from Munster and Leinster but – to a significant degree – from Connacht also.[31] As the agricultural depression took hold from the mid-1870s onwards, so protests against evictions and rent levels began to increase. But, on this occasion – in contrast to all previous occasions of a similar nature – they made themselves manifest particularly in the western parts of the country and above all in the province of Connacht itself. Already in 1878 a number of large organised demonstrations were held in Counties Galway and Mayo. These continued until August 1879, when a National Land League of Mayo was set up after a meeting at Castlebar. Two months later it was transformed into the Irish National Land League under the joint leadership of Michael Davitt and the most formidable of the new Home Rule MPs, Charles Stewart Parnell.[32]

The Land War of 1879–82 which these meetings set in motion constituted the most intense period of agrarian and political agitation in Ireland during the whole of the nineteenth century. Its success in combining land reform and Home Rule as twin objectives gave it a power and drive which previous movements had lacked. Not only that, but in this instance the land question had, for the first time, been placed upon the agenda of events by actions in Connacht – in, that is, an area which had formerly possessed a distinctly peripheral character in politics as in everything else.[33] The general context of this unprecedented occurrence was supplied by those broad post-Famine developments which have already been discussed and, more immediately, by the post-Famine appearance in parts of the west of a sophisticated livestock-based capitalist economy together with its associated farming and trading elites. Indeed, the spatial patterning of the new economy helps to explain the geographical dimensions of the agitation within Connacht itself and even within particular counties, for disturbances were not distributed evenly or randomly but were concentrated especially in the rich plains and their surrounding areas 'where the livestock economy and its accompanying social and political changes were most evident'.[34]

In all but the short term the Land War and the other agrarian agitations of the 1880s proved unable to sustain the comparatively united character with which they began. The more substantial farmers of Munster and Leinster did not always want the same things as the poor farmers of the west. And even in Connacht the preliminary excitements of 1879–80 succeeded only briefly in disguising the fact that two ultimately irreconcilable agrarian revolutions were being agitated: one by large farmers who wanted to be free of rents and landlords so they could take full advantage of the market, and one by small tenants who wanted protection from eviction and equitable access to the land.[35] Yet the Land War's failure to retain its original unity, though important enough as regards the overall history of late nineteenth-century Ireland, does not in any way affect the fact that, in spatial and social terms, Catholic Ireland achieved greater integration during these years than it had ever achieved before. Having once become involved in a powerful set of political movements in 1879–82, Connacht did not meekly return to its former isolation. When in 1898 another major land agitation broke out, it too began in County Mayo. It too produced another impressive organisational manifestation, this time in the shape of the United Irish League, which everybody (not least its own leaders) realised was most effective as an agrarian and intimidatory body in the counties of the west.[36]

Henceforth nationalist or nationalist-type political movements were able to function throughout Catholic Ireland as a whole. Sometimes one region would be more prominent, sometimes another. But if any geographical pattern of political action could be said to have existed during the last decade before the Anglo–Irish Treaty of 1921 it was one in which Connacht was more rather than less prominent: it had more United Irish League members per head of the population in 1913 and in 1916, more Sinn Fein members in 1919, and the highest Sinn Fein representation on county councils in 1920.[37] Indeed, a comprehensive index of nationalist 'organisational density' for the years 1916–19 places Connacht first, Leinster second, Munster third and Ulster (which, of course, contains many Catholic areas) a respectable fourth.[38]

If, therefore, the island of Ireland remained a periphery within the United Kingdom throughout the whole of the period between 1800 and 1921, the various constituent parts which, as it were, made up this Irish periphery experienced substantial internal rearrangement and change. In 1800 the discontinuities in Irish society and politics tended to lie between east and west. By 1921 they clearly lay between the north-east and the rest of the country. Over these years, therefore, the divisions *within* both Catholic and Protestant Ireland were substantially reduced, to be replaced by deep divisions between the two.[39] This enabled nationalism to mobilise throughout the whole of Catholic Ireland in new and more effective ways. Equally, it drove Unionism back into a north-eastern fortress-like periphery where alone it could sustain itself by those injections of sectarian solidarity which were becoming increasingly necessary to political survival in all parts of Ireland.

But while the character of nineteenth-century Irish political culture undoubtedly owed much to core–periphery changes within Ireland itself, equally important from a broader UK perspective were certain deep transformations that were taking place in the ways in which Ireland and the Irish Question were perceived by those in power in London, transformations which, though obviously not unconnected with party affiliations or immediate contingencies, moved to drumbeats of a slower, more lasting but no less effective kind.

The first thirty years under the Union were – from a governmental perspective – a period both of Tory dominance and of aggressive (if not always very efficient) attempts at iron-fisted control. The idea behind this approach was that 'Ireland was different', that it was a place where – at least for the foreseeable future – tender-hearted English notions of 'freedom' and 'rights' had best be applied to an altogether lesser degree. As Viscount Whitworth (Liverpool's Irish viceroy between 1813 and 1817) put it in 1814:

The great object is not to lose sight of the Distinction to be made between England and this part of His Majesty's Dominions ... The Character and Spirit of the governed are completely different ... It is only by a protecting force that the magistrates can be encouraged to do their Duty, and by an imposing one that the lower orders can be kept down.[40]

In similar vein, Whitworth's chief secretary, the young Robert Peel, demanded special measures for Ireland precisely because its condition was 'so different' from that of England.[41] And it was above all for this reason that the establishment of the new Irish Peace Preservation Force in 1814 (the forerunner of the Royal Irish Constabulary) attracted so little opposition from MPs who would have reacted very differently had a police force organised along unambiguously military lines been proposed for any other part of the United Kingdom.[42] Even so, Peel himself would have liked to go further still, believing, as he then did, that 'an honest despotic Government would be by far the fittest Government for Ireland'.[43] For his part, Liverpool excluded Ireland altogether from the community of modern civilisation, noting in 1816 that its people were simply 'not influenced by the same principles as appear to affect mankind in other countries'.[44] Just so – though in a very different context and with very different aims in view – did Gladstone in 1881 dismiss those who criticised his second Irish Land Bill on the grounds that it undermined English principles of freedom of contract with the assertion that English notions of that sort were no more relevant to the Irish than they would be to 'the inhabitants of Saturn or Jupiter'.[45]

These assessments by Liverpool and Gladstone of Ireland as a 'special place' with distinct requirements were not, however, connected by a half-century of general agreement that such was indeed the case. Instead – from the early 1830s until the late 1860s – the predominant perceptual framework among the governing classes in London as regards Ireland depended on the belief that the overall stability of the United Kingdom would best be served if Irish conditions were very rapidly altered so as to match the political, social and economic norms widely held to be characteristic of Britain itself. Although this shift in opinion clearly coincided with the end of Tory and the beginning of Whig/Liberal hegemony at the centre, it was not wholly party-political in nature. Nor was it exclusively a direct product of Whig attempts to bind Ireland to the union by conciliatory rather than coercive means.

The new approach which emerged in the 1830s involved, indeed, far more than the application of large doses of friendly legislation designed to isolate those Irish politicians most eager to overthrow the settlement of 1800. It amounted rather to something like a programme by which Ireland should either be treated more or less exactly like the rest of the kingdom or, where that was not yet possible, in a fashion designed to eliminate its distinctiveness in as short a time as possible. Apart from an abortive attempt to provide a loan for the development of Irish railways, the Whigs' legislative agenda for Ireland in the 1830s depended upon the conviction that Irish problems – albeit more difficult politically – were fundamentally the same as English problems and therefore required either similar solutions or solutions specifically designed to liberate those latent similarities still disguised beneath superficially distinct appearances. Some Whigs, like Viscount Howick (in Melbourne's Cabinet 1835–39 and – as third Earl Grey – in Russell's 1846–52) even went so far as to argue that the requirements of equality dictated that Roman Catholicism should become the established religion in Ireland, 'since the Establishments in each of the three divisions of the United Kingdom could then be supported on the irresistible grounds of their practical utility to the great bulk of the population'.[46]

Though Howick rather naively recorded Melbourne's (dissimulating) agreement with his views,[47] few Whigs were prepared to go quite so far in their search for pan-UK evenhandedness. They were, nonetheless, often prepared to go a very long way indeed. Having, for example, reformed English municipal corporations in 1835, Melbourne's government – caring little that Irish urban conditions were very different from those of England – introduced a series of almost identical Bills for Ireland which were only ground down into insignificance by problems in Parliament.[48] Far more striking still was the government's success – with somewhat uncertain support from O'Connell's Repeal Party, which had entered into a compact with the Whigs in 1835 – in transferring to Ireland in 1838 an exact replica of the New Poor Law unveiled in England four years before. Totally ignoring the recommendations of an Irish Poor Law Commission (which had declared the English model quite unsuitable), Ministers sent over an English expert, who, after a few weeks, returned with the 'correct' recommendation that not a moment should be lost in giving Ireland workhouses and 'less eligibility' in all their recent Anglo-Saxon glory.[49] And even when in 1831 Ireland was provided with a national education system which had no parallel in England, the stated aim behind the enterprise was to reduce religious tensions and thus bring to Ireland the blessings of British good feeling and up-to-date modernity.[50]

Lord John Russell was perhaps the chief proponent of such views. Determined that Ireland should be treated just like England in matters of municipal reform, he was equally determined to detach as many as possible in Ireland from the 'partisans of separation' and recruit them into 'the ranks of Order and British Connexion'.[51] In 1837 he rounded upon those in Parliament who took a different view: 'Scotland is inhabited by Scotchmen, and England by Englishmen, yet, because Ireland is inhabited by Irishmen, you will refuse them the same measure of relief that you have applied to Scotland and to England'.[52] Whether, when it came to the Great Famine, Russell consistently stuck to his aim of treating Ireland as he would have treated English counties had their inhabitants been starving or as he was actually treating the famine-stricken Scottish Highlanders is of course very much open to doubt.[53] What is not in doubt is that, having been Prime Minister during the Famine years, Russell and his closest associates became determined to do all they could to refashion the social and economic circumstances of the Irish countryside (to which they largely attributed the disaster of the 1840s) along English lines. What this amounted to was little less than a massive project of social engineering: small farmers and cottiers were to be allowed to fall into their 'natural' position of labourers, labourers were to be paid money wages, a prosperous middle class of shopkeepers and merchants would then spring up to service their needs and Irish counties would become bucolic Hibernian versions of Hampshire, Suffolk and Kent.[54]

The so-called Gregory clause in the Poor Law Amendment Act of 1847 barring from public relief anyone holding more than a quarter of an acre of land was to be the sovereign means to achieve this *bouleversement* in Irish society – and a powerful means, too, considering that 335,535 of the 681,794 persons being relieved in the week ending 4 July 1847 would thereby have been denied help.[55] If at the same time many Irish landlords (men the Whigs thought generally exploitative and inefficient) were also to go to the wall, so much the better. Irish property, it was widely believed in government circles, should exculpate its past transgressions by being made to pay for Irish poverty (no matter that this was far beyond its capacity).[56] And just as the Gregory clause was supposed to solve the problem at the lower end of the scale, so the Encumbered Estates Act of 1849 – which provided unprecedented legal machinery for selling bankrupt estates to (it was hoped) commercially-minded and probably Catholic entrepreneurs – was designed to do so at the upper end.[57]

Such grand, ambitious, not to say chilling, aspirations were to be only very partially fulfilled. Cottiers and labourers did indeed suffer immediate and conti-nuing numerical attrition after the Famine, but largely for structural reasons which had little to do with clauses in the Poor Law Amendment Act.[58] And while many landed properties were sold under the provisions of the legislation of 1849, most were bought not by new-style commercial men but by those old-style (and over-whelmingly Protestant) landowners who had weathered the Famine storms and were now in a position to benefit from the economic upswings that characterised the third quarter of the nineteenth century in the Irish no less than in the English countryside.[59] Complications like this did not, however, produce any sudden reduction in the ardour of political leaders wishing to recreate Irish rural life along the most approved English models. Palmerston, who did not agree with Russell on many things, agreed with him on this – that is was 'useless to disguise the Truth, that any great Improvement in the Social System of Ireland must be founded upon … a long continued and systematic ejectment of Small Holders and of squatting Cottiers'.[60] Indeed, given the fact that 'tenant right' in Ireland involved far more than mere compensation for improvements, Palmerston's fa-mous aphorism that tenant right was 'equivalent to landlords' wrong'[61] was merely another way of saying that English rules should apply equally on both sides of the Irish Sea. And it was under Palmerston's prime ministership in 1860 that the two most unvarnished legislative attempts to align Irish tenurial principles with those of England were passed into law. What is known as Cardwell's Act (23 and 24 Vict., c. 153) extended landlords' powers in certain important respects, while Deasy's Act (23 and 24 Vict., c. 154) specifically provided that 'the relation of landlord and tenant shall be deemed to be founded on the express or implied contract of the parties, and not upon tenure or service'.[62] 'Let the owner and the tenant,' Palmerston told the Commons in 1863, 'settle their own affairs. Give to each fully liberty to do so.'[63]

While the Whigs undoubtedly constituted the chief apostles of treating Ireland along English lines, mid-century Conservatism was not – as regards Ireland – the simple unyielding Toryism of earlier times. However much Peel at first tried to maintain a reputation as the hammer of Ireland, the granting of Catholic Emancipation by a Tory administration in 1829 had rendered his protestations less convincing than before. Eventually, indeed, in the mid-1840s, he suddenly began to follow a different line entirely, a line designed (almost as if on Whig principles) to make Ireland more stable and peaceful – and therefore a kind of candidate for promotion to English status – by conciliating moderate Catholic opinion. A Charitable Bequests Act in 1844, a substantial increase in the grant to the Catholic seminary at Maynooth in 1845, and the establishment of a system of higher education for Catholics in 1845–46 (though the bishops soon rejected it) formed the cornerstones of the new policy.[64] And even after the Conservative split over the Corn Laws in 1846, the majority protectionist element – occasional flurries of Protestant rhetoric notwithstanding – showed few signs of hard-core recidivism so far as Ireland was concerned, Derby's distrust of Catholicism being, in part at least, balanced by Disraeli's urgent desire to seek political allies, even, if necessary, Catholic and Irish ones.[65] Not that mid-century British politicians were slow to insist that their policy of 'integration' (if so it may be called) must necessarily involve Ireland in new duties as well as in new rights. Thus when in 1842 Peel revived the income tax he exempted Ireland on technical grounds only, and it was Peel's fiscal disciple, Gladstone, who eventually extended the tax to Ireland, in his budget of 1853.[66]

However, at some time in the 1860s the agenda introduced more than thirty years earlier of treating Ireland as if it were – or could rapidly be transformed into – a sort of smaller England began to be abandoned. The reasons are complex and not yet well understood. Certainly shifts in the broad intellectual climate of the time played a part, in particular a move away from classical political economy with its emphasis upon immutable general principles and towards a greater sympathy for historicist views which emphasised cultural relativism, envisaged social phenomena as historically determined, and displayed a profound respect for traditions of almost every kind.[67] Historicist ideas had undoubtedly begun to appeal to Gladstone, now the rising man of the Liberal party. In particular, certain writings which offered comparisons between traditional tenurial systems in India and in Ireland influenced the preparation of Gladstone's first Irish Land Act of 1870.[68] But, whereas the early nineteenth-century notion of Ireland as another country where things should be done differently had been coercive in character, its revival in the 1860s was – at least at first – conciliatory both in intention and in tone. Nor (again) was it confined to the Liberals. Indeed, as early as October 1869 a recent Tory Cabinet Minister and future party leader (Stafford Northcote) told the Social Science Association that

the facts are stubborn and cannot be bent ... [The Irish] national idea of the relations of landlord and tenant is something totally different from the national idea in England ... It is one so rooted in the Irish mind that it is impossible to remove ... [therefore] you must provide for it accordingly.[69]

From then until the Anglo–Irish Treaty of 1921 (and beyond) British politicians of all parties effectively based their Irish policies upon the axiom that Ireland should be treated as a special case. Of course Gladstone's main intention regarding disestablishment in 1869 (then unique in the United Kingdom), the Land Act of 1870, the second Land Act of 1881 (in which he deliberately ignored the advice of the Bessborough Commission that 'the same Land Laws should prevail ... in every part of the Kingdom')[70] and the Home Rule Bill of 1886 may well have been to defuse discontent and so ultimately strengthen the connection between Britain and Ireland: it was, after all, in that sense that he saw Home Rule as a conservative rather than a radical affair.[71] But the inevitable effect of the new approach was to encourage notions of difference and eventually perhaps even of separation. If in 1820 Ireland had been something like a *de facto* colony, to be kept in check, fifty years later it was being regarded as a kind of colony again, as a place needing special forms of treatment rather than the broadly English remedies that had been supplied in the intervening years. Save in unusual cases (such as the Scottish Land Act of 1886) the sauce now considered suitable for the Irish goose was no longer that thought appropriate for the British gander. Not only Gladstone, but the Unionists too, had become convinced that this was so – hence the expensive land purchase schemes introduced by Tory and Unionist administrations from 1885 onwards. What, after all, were such schemes if not an 'Irish solution to an Irish problem'?

If changes in the intellectual climate had something to do with inaugurating the great shift in attitudes towards Ireland which begins to appear in the 1860s, then so also perhaps did the arrival of a new generation of Prime Ministers. Between 1830 and the 1860s governments of all stripes had largely been led by men with substantial personal knowledge of Ireland, as chief secretaries, as landlords or as frequent visitors. Melbourne, Russell, Peel, Derby and Palmerston all fall into this category. However, when Disraeli and Gladstone both reached the top of the greasy pole in 1868 it ceased to be the case. The former never visited Ireland, while one of the latter's two visits lasted less than twenty-four hours. Neither Salisbury, Rosebery, Asquith nor Lloyd George had much personal knowledge of Ireland, and Balfour, who had some, did not let it stop him from seeing Ireland as a wild and foreign country deserving wild and foreign remedies for its ills.

Thus, during the 121 year history of the United Kingdom of Great Britain and Ireland, not only did the character of the Irish periphery change out of all recognition, but so too did the governing ideas of the British governing class. Those who knew Ireland most intimately had been anxious – for all sorts of reasons – to see that country as an integral and largely undifferentiated part of a united polity. Their successors, with fewer direct experiences to hand, felt differently. For them – Liberals and Unionists alike – Ireland had once again become a place of special measures and special solutions. But this new version of an old song turned out to be no neutral melody (however much the singers might sometimes argue otherwise) because reintroducing 'special solutions' as an item on the Anglo–Irish menu inevitably made it more rather than less difficult to resist the most special solution of all – independence for Ireland and the break-up of the Union itself.

## Notes

1 J. Lee, *Ireland 1912–1985: Politics and Society* (Cambridge, Cambridge University Press, 1989), especially pp. 511–687.

2 *Hansard*, 3rd Ser. clxxxiii, 1088 (17 May 1866).

3 The 1861 census recorded Protestant majorities in only four counties: Antrim, Armagh, Down and Derry. In another two – Tyrone and Fermanagh – Protestants constituted more than 40 per cent of the population: W. E. Vaughan and A. J. Fitzpatrick (eds), *Irish Historical Statistics: Population, 1821–1971* (Dublin, Royal Irish Academy, 1978), pp. 51–3.

4 E. Larkin, 'Church and State in Ireland in the nineteenth century', *Church History*, 31 (1962), 294–306; D. W. Miller, 'Irish Catholicism and the Great Famine', *Journal of Social History*, 9 (1975), 81–98.

5 H. D. Inglis, *A Journey throughout Ireland, during the Spring, Summer, and Autumn of 1834*, 5th edn (London, Whittaker, 1838), p. 219; W. M. Thackeray, *The Irish Sketch Book of 1842* (London, Smith Elder, 1879), p. 149.

6 T. N. Brown, 'Nationalism and the Irish peasant, 1800–48', *Review of Politics*, 15 (1953), 403, 434.

7 J. S. Donnelly, Jr, 'The social composition of agrarian rebellions in early nineteenth-century Ireland: the case of the Carders and Caravats, 1813–16', in P. J. Corish (ed.), *Radicals, Rebels and Establishments, Historical Studies* xv (Belfast, Appletree Press, 1985), p. 152.

8 The ratio of acreage in tillage to acreage in grass (that is, in animal production) shifted from 1:1·90 in 1851 to 1:3·23 in 1880 and 1:4·16 in 1910 (K. T. Hoppen, *Ireland since 1800: Conflict and Conformity* (London, Longman, 1989), p. 87).

9 K. T. Hoppen, *Elections, Politics, and Society in Ireland, 1832–1885* (Oxford, Oxford University Press, 1984), p. 105. The increase for Ireland as a whole was from 40·3 per cent to 60·1 per cent. See also D. Fitzpatrick, 'The disappearance of the Irish agricultural labourer, 1841–1912', *Irish Economic and Social History*, 7 (1980), 66–92.

10 Hoppen, *Elections, Politics, and Society in Ireland*, p. 27. In 1840 54·8 per cent of those Irish county voters with agricultural holdings occupied farms valued at £20 and above, but only 26·1 per cent did so in Connacht. By 1866 these proportions had moved much closer – to 56·3 per cent and 48·2 per cent respectively.

11 S. Clark, *Social Origins of the Irish Land War* (Princeton, Princeton University Press, 1979), pp. 110–11.

12 C. Ó Gráda, *Ireland: a New Economic History, 1780–1939* (Oxford, Oxford University Press, 1994), p. 272.

13 *Ibid.*, pp. 40–1. The dual economy theory was first proposed in P. Lynch and J. Vaizey, *Guinness's Brewery in the Irish Economy, 1759–1876* (Cambridge, Cambridge University Press, 1960), pp. 9–36.

14 W. J. Smith, 'The making of Ireland: agendas and perspectives in cultural geography', in B. J. Graham and L. J. Proudfoot (eds), *An Historical Geography of Ireland* (London, Academic Press, 1993), pp. 420–7.

15 *The Census of Ireland for the Year 1851*, vi, *General Report*. H[ouse of] C[ommons Paper] 1856 [2134], xxxi, p. xlvii; *Census of Ireland 1891*, ii, *General Report*, H.C. 1892 [C. 6780], xc, table

155 (p. 571), which gives figures for 1871, 1881 and 1891. (Those for 1881 are less reliable than the others.)

16 *Report of the Commissioners appointed to take the Census of Ireland for the Year 1841*, H.C. 1843 [504], xxiv, 432–3 (literacy), 150–1, 260–1, 362–3, 428–9 (schools); *Census of Ireland, 1881, General Report*, H.C. 1882 [C. 3365], lxxvi, 343 (literacy, giving data for 1841–81 inclusive), 344–53 (schools). School figures are based on attendances (not enrolments, which are higher) during the weeks ending 5 June 1841 and 14 May 1881.

17 *The Banking Almanac, Directory, Year Book, and Diary for 1860* (London, Waterlow, [1860]). In 1879 the national figure was 7.8 full branches per 100,000 people.

18 *Thom's Official Directory of the United Kingdom of Great Britain and Ireland for the Year 1916* (Dublin, Thom, 1916), p. 811.

19 T. W. Grimshaw, *Facts and Figures about Ireland*, i (Dublin, Hodges Figgis, 1893), p. 52; B. R. Mitchell, *British Historical Statistics* (Cambridge, Cambridge University Press, 1988), pp. 563–4.

20 S. J. Connolly, *Priests and People in pre-Famine Ireland, 1780–1845* (Dublin, Gill and Macmillan, 1982), pp. 135–74.

21 D. J. Keenan, *The Catholic Church in Nineteenth Century Ireland: a Sociological Study* (Dublin, Gill and Macmillan, 1983), *passim*.

22 E. Larkin, 'The devotional revolution in Ireland, 1850–75', *American Historical Review*, 77 (1972), 625–52; Hoppen, *Elections, Politics, and Society in Ireland*, pp. 211–24.

23 D. Bowen, *The Protestant Crusade in Ireland, 1800–70: a Study of Protestant–Catholic Relations between the Act of Union and Disestablishment* (Dublin, Gill and Macmillan, 1978), pp. 29–80; F. Holmes, *Henry Cooke* (Belfast, Christian Journals, 1981), pp. 115–16; F. Holmes, 'Ulster Presbyterianism and Irish nationalism', in S. Mews (ed.), *Religion and National Identity*, Studies in Church History, xviii (Oxford, Blackwell, 1982), pp. 535–55.

24 S. E. Baker, 'Orange and Green: Belfast, 1832–1912', in H. J. Dyos and M. Wolff (eds), *The Victorian City: Images and Realities*, 2 vols (London, Routledge, 1973), ii. 789–814; I. Budge and C. O'Leary, *Belfast, Approach to Crisis: a Study of Belfast Politics 1613–1970* (London, Macmillan, 1973), pp. 41–100; K. T. Hoppen, 'Grammars of electoral violence in nineteenth-century England and Ireland', *English Historical Review*, 109 (1994), 597–620.

25 K. T. Hoppen, 'Politics, the law, and the nature of the Irish electorate, 1832–50', *English Historical Review*, 92 (1977), 746–76; 'Confidential Print' concerning repeal meetings, 7 March to 1 October 1843, in British Library, Peel Papers Add. MS 40540.

26 D. G. Pringle, *One Island, Two Nations? A Political Geographical Analysis of the National Conflict in Ireland* (Letchworth, Research Studies Press, 1985), pp. 156–7; S. J. Connolly, 'Mass politics and sectarian conflict, 1823–30, in W. E. Vaughan (ed.), *A New History of Ireland*, v, *Ireland under the Union*, i, 1801–70 (Oxford, Oxford University Press, 1989), p. 90.

27 Hoppen, *Elections, Politics, and Society in Ireland*, pp. 16–33.

28 K. T. Hoppen, 'National politics and local realities in mid-nineteenth-century Ireland', in A. Cosgrove and D. McCartney (eds), *Studies in Irish History presented to R. Dudley Edwards* (Dublin, University College, Dublin, 1979), pp. 190–227.

29 O'Connell to Archbishop MacHale, 3 January 1839, *The Correspondence of Daniel O'Connell*, ed. M. R. O'Connell, 8 vols (Dublin, Irish Academic Press and Blackwater Press, 1972–80), vi. 204; Lord Anglesey to Lord Grey, 28 November 1832, Public Record Office of Northern Ireland, Anglesey Papers MS D619/28A.

30 W. E. Vaughan, *Landlords and Tenants in mid-Victorian Ireland* (Oxford, Oxford University Press, 1994), pp. 236, 282, 284.

31 H. H. van der Wusten, *Iers verzet tegen de staatkundige eenheid der Britse Eilanden, 1800–1921* (Amsterdam, Sociaal-geografisch Instituut University of Amsterdam, 1977), p. 90.

32 Clark, *Social Origins of the Irish Land War*, pp. 246–7.

33 *Ibid.*, p. 256.

34 D. E. Jordan, Jr, *Land and Popular Politics in Ireland: County Mayo from the Plantation to the Land War* (Cambridge, Cambridge University Press, 1994), p. 5.

35 *Ibid.*, p. 8.

36 P. Bew, *Conflict and Conciliation in Ireland, 1890–1910: Parnellites and Radical Agrarians* (Oxford, Oxford University Press, 1987), p. 79.

37 D. Fitzpatrick, 'The geography of Irish nationalism, 1910–21', *Past and Present*, 78 (1978), 138–9; van der Wusten, *Iers verzet tegen de staatkundige eenheid der Britse Eilanden*, p. 209.

38 Fitzpatrick, 'The geography of Irish nationalism', pp. 138–9.

39 As regards Protestant Ireland in this period, see I. d'Alton, *Protestant Society and Politics in Cork, 1812–44* (Cork, Cork University Press, 1980); Hoppen, *Elections, Politics, and Society in Ireland*, pp. 278–332; P. Gibbon, *The Origins of Ulster Unionism: the formation of Popular Protestant Politics and Ideology in Nineteenth Century Ireland* (Manchester, Manchester University Press, 1975); A. Jackson, *The Ulster Party: Irish Unionists in the House of Commons, 1884–1911* (Oxford, Oxford University Press, 1989); id., *Colonel Edward Saunderson: Land and Loyalty in Victorian Ireland* (Oxford, Oxford University Press, 1995); P. Buckland, *Irish Unionism*, 2 vols (Dublin, Gill and Macmillan, 1972–73); P. Bew, *Ideology and the Irish Question: Ulster Unionism and Irish Nationalism, 1912–16* (Oxford, Oxford University Press, 1994).

40 Whitworth to Sidmouth, 21 April 1814, B. Jenkins, *Era of Emancipation: British Government of Ireland, 1812–30* (Kingston and Montreal, McGill-Queen's University Press, 1988), pp. 101–2.

41 *Hansard*, 1st Ser. xxviii, 172 (23 June 1814).

42 G. Broeker, *Rural Disorder and Police Reform in Ireland, 1812–36* (London, Routledge, 1970), pp. 55–70.

43 Peel to W. Gregory, 15 March 1816, C. S. Parker, *Sir Robert Peel from his Private Correspondence*, 3 vols (London, John Murray, 1891–99), i. 215.

44 N. Gash, *Mr Secretary Peel: the Life of Sir Robert Peel to 1830* (London, Longman, 1961), p. 176.

45 *Hansard*, 3rd Ser. cclx, 895 (7 April 1881).

46 Howick to Sir J. Graham, 9 March 1835, I. Newbould, *Whiggery and Reform, 1830–41: the Politics of Government* (London, Macmillan, 1990), pp. 284–5.

47 *Ibid.*, p. 378.

48 A. Macintyre, *The Liberator: Daniel O'Connell and the Irish Party, 1830–47* (London, Hamish Hamilton, 1965), p. 260.

49 Newbould, *Whiggery and Reform*, p. 293.

50 R. Brent, *Liberal Anglican Politics: Whiggery, Religion, and Reform, 1830–41* (Oxford, Oxford University Press, 1987), pp. 222–3.

51 J. Prest, *Lord John Russell* (London, Macmillan, 1972), p. 112.

52 *Hansard*, 3rd Ser. xxxvi, 207 (7 February 1837).

53 J. S. Donnelly, Jr, 'The administration of relief, 1846–47', 'The soup kitchens', 'The administration of relief, 1847–51', in Vaughan, *A New History of Ireland*, v, *Ireland under the Union*, i. pp. 294–306, 307–15, 316–31.

54 Russell to Bessborough, 6 November 1846, Prest, *Lord John Russell*, p. 236.

55 *Ibid.*, p. 251.

56 J. S. Donnelly, Jr, '"Irish property must pay for Irish poverty": British public opinion and the Great Famine', in C. Morash and R. Hayes (eds), *'Fearful Realities': New Perspectives on the Famine* (Dublin, Irish Academic Press, 1996), pp. 60–76.

57 Russell to Clarendon, 13 December 1847, Prest, *Lord John Russell*, p. 275.

58 Hoppen, *Elections, Politics, and Society in Ireland*, pp. 98–105; Fitzpatrick, 'The disappearance of the Irish agricultural labourer', pp. 66–92.

59 J. S. Donnelly, Jr, *Landlord and Tenant in Nineteenth Century Ireland* (Dublin, Gill and Macmillan, 1973), p. 51; id., *The Land and the People of Nineteenth Century Cork: the Rural Economy and the Land Question* (London, Routledge, 1975), p. 131; M. Turner, *After the Famine: Irish Agriculture, 1850–1914* (Cambridge, Cambridge University Press, 1996), pp. 196–216.

60 Memorandum of 31 March 1848, Prest, *Lord John Russell*, p. 286.

61 *Hansard*, 3rd Ser. clxxvii, 823 (27 February 1865).

62 R. D. Collison Black, *Economic Thought and the Irish Question 1817–70* (Cambridge, Cambridge University Press, 1960), pp. 45–6.

63 *Hansard*, 3rd Ser. clxxi, 1375 (23 June 1863).

64 D. A. Kerr, *Peel, Priests, and People: Sir Robert Peel's Administration and the Roman Catholic Church in Ireland, 1841–46* (Oxford, Oxford University Press, 1982), pp. 110–15.

65 K. T. Hoppen, 'Tories, Catholics, and the general election of 1859', *Historical Journal*, 13 (1970), 48–67.

66 *Hansard*, 3rd Ser. lxi, 444–8 (11 March 1842); W. E. Vaughan, 'Ireland, *c.*1870' in Vaughan, *A New History of Ireland*, v, *Ireland under the Union*, i. pp. 784–7. I owe the former reference to the kindness of David Eastwood.

67 C. Dewey, 'Celtic agrarian legislation and the Celtic Revival: historicist implications of Gladstone's Irish and Scottish Land Acts, 1870–86', *Past and Present*, 64 (1974), 30–70.

68 E. D. Steele, 'Ireland and the empire in the 1860s: imperial precedents for Gladstone's first Irish Land Act', *Historical Journal*, 11 (1966), 64–83; S. B. Cook, *Imperial Affinities: Nineteenth Century Analogies and Exchanges between India and Ireland* (New Delhi, Sage, 1993), pp. 39–62.

69 Steele, 'Ireland and the empire', p. 77.

70 *Hansard*, 3rd Ser. cclx, 906–6 (7 April 1881).

71 H. C. G. Matthew, *Gladstone, 1875–1898* (Oxford, Oxford University Press, 1995), p. 234.

## Acknowledgement

This chapter was written while the author held a British Academy research readership. He is grateful to the Academy for its support.

# 11

# National and regional identities and the dilemmas of reform in Britain's 'other province': Hanover, c. 1800–c. 1850

## MICHAEL JOHN

In the early summer of 1860 the weekly journal of the liberal German National Association published a pair of articles attacking the policies of the Hanoverian government and particularly its Minister of the Interior, Count Wilhelm Friedrich Borries. Borries's approach to government since 1855 was, it was claimed, defined by its absolute dependence on the bureaucracy and its absolute power over the people. Noting that Borries had recently threatened to ally with foreign powers should a unified central power in Germany be established, these articles drew explicit comparisons with seventeenth-century English politics. Borries had, it was claimed in the first article, acted with 'the unbearable arrogance of Stuart politics' and there was a strong possibility that he was becoming 'a second Lord Strafford'. The second piece moved the comparison forward in time by noting that James II had become Louis XIV's vassal in order restore an unrestricted royal prerogative and claimed that Borries's system was inspired by similar motivations.[1] The following March, the same journal argued that the particularism and sense of national quasi-separateness in Hanover had their roots in the eighteenth-century English link. That link had, on the other hand, at least prevented the worst excesses of governments in other German States until the accession of King Ernest Augustus in 1837. As a result, so it was claimed, the German question did not exist in the State until that year.[2]

These reflections provide a few examples of the ways in which political debates in mid-nineteenth-century Hanover were shaped by an understanding of English history and by acute awareness of the long-term significance of the English link. As will be seen below, the position adopted by the National Association by no means exhausted the possibilities inherent in this political appropriation of English influences. But in order to understand the complex effects of this approach to problems of government and politics, it is first of all necessary to understand the peculiarities of Hanover's situation during and after the Napoleonic wars. At one level, early nineteenth-century Hanover faced a range of problems to be found elsewhere in the German-speaking lands. Among the typical difficulties confronting Restoration governments and politicians were the corrosive effects of the changes generated by the French revolutionary and Napoleonic periods, which were particularly marked (perhaps paradoxically) in those States that may be regarded a 'winners' in the large-scale territorial reorganisations that arose out of the dissolution of the Holy Roman Empire in 1801–6. Put briefly, the victors in these changes were faced with the problem of integrating extensive new territories, with few if any traditions of loyalty to their ruling houses and often divergent confessional identities, into those of the dynastic heartlands. As is well known, the principal decision-makers at the Congress of Vienna, who ratified many preceding territorial decisions while also introducing new ones, were guided largely by strategic and political considerations which frequently took scant account of the nature and diversity of the territories to be governed in the future. In these respects the newly elevated kingdom of Hanover was no exception, acquiring the bishopric of Hildesheim and the principality of Osnabrück (both with substantial Catholic populations and a decidedly ambiguous relationship with the Guelph ruling house), the province of East Friesland in the north-west which had been a Prussian territory from 1744 and 1806 and which was never happy with its incorporation into the Hanoverian State, and a number of other territories. These changes made Hanover the fourth largest German State after 1815 but gave it an extremely distinctive shape, with the western provinces (Osnabrück, the Emsland and East Friesland) joined to the eastern provinces solely by a 6 km long strip of territory. In the words of a central figure in the politics of this period, Johann Carl Bertram Stüve, Hanover was a land containing a 'wealth of different relationships and sharp contrasts'.[3]

In effect, Hanover underwent a similar process to that experienced by the southern States of Bavaria, Württemberg and Baden, which had also expanded rapidly after 1801 and had been elevated to the status of monarchies (or, in Baden's case, a grand duchy) for the first time. Yet Hanover also approached the problems of the post-Restoration period in a fundamentally different way from that adopted in the south. There the years after 1815 saw moves to create recognisably 'modern' constitutional institutions that were largely seen by their bureaucratic creators as answers to the pressing problems of integration and State formation generated by the new European order.[4] Since about 1800 these southern States had seen bureaucratic elites promoting constitutions, attempting to codify laws and to dismantle local corporate privileges – traditions of behaviour that, broadly speaking, continued after 1815. These States essentially retained gains made during the early Napoleonic wars before 1805. Hanover, on the other hand, had seen much of its territory incorporated into the Napoleonic kingdom of Westphalia, which, like the Grand Duchy of Berg, was abolished when the French empire collapsed. Hanover was thus a restored State (albeit on a considerably expanded basis) and the process of restoration was marked by a thoroughgoing campaign, arguably unparalleled anywhere in West Elbian Germany, to reverse the socio-economic and political changes of the revolutionary period. As a result, both the primary institutions of seigneurialism *and* the power of provincial political institutions that underpinned noble hegemony in the State were to a large extent restored.

Although a State-wide political assembly (the Allgemeine Ständeversammlung) was created in 1819, it existed alongside surviving provincial Estates, had decidedly little power *vis-à-vis* both the bureaucracy and those provincial Estates, and was in any case constructed in such a way that noble dominance was virtually certain. It was this constellation of forces, connecting deficient State-wide integration at an institutional level with the increasingly contested issue of noble rights and privileges, that determined the political history of the kingdom of Hanover for the fifty years between the Congress of Vienna and the annexation by Prussia in the summer of 1866.[5]

The most significant aspects in that political history were: (1) the mounting social and economic crisis of the late 1820s and early 1830s, which led to the emancipation of farmers from servile dues and the passage of a constitution in 1831–33; (2) the revocation of that constitution by the new king, Ernest Augustus, in 1837 and the ensuing bitter constitutional conflicts; (3) a period of decidedly moderate reform carried through between 1848 and 1850 by Hanover's 'March Ministry'; and the revocation of many of these reforms in the aftermath of a second *coup* in 1855 that was once again backed by the desire of nobles to restore privileges which were seemingly incompatible with even the most modest reform proposals.[6] Throughout these vicissitudes the key issue was clearly twofold. In the first place, they involved the rights accorded to a nobility that, in contrast to its Prussian counterpart, did not hold extensive land as a basis for the exercise of power relatively independent of the State, and which therefore needed continued control over the State apparatus as a vital condition the survival of its influence. The second aspect was the connection between these noble aspirations and the desire of the kings of Hanover after 1837 to develop a thoroughgoing monarchical-restorationist absolutist project for the first time in Hanover's modern history.[7]

Contemporaries were in no doubt whatsoever that these conditions posed particular problems of modernisation in Hanover which had no precise equivalent anywhere else in the German-speaking lands. As one account of German political and constitutional thought put it on the eve of the second *coup* in 1854:

> In no German State will it be so difficult to convert historically rooted, but in part extremely inappropriate, conditions of a country which has come together gradually into the unified, self-conscious State of the modern period. The particular, admittedly in many respects very admirable, stubbornness of the Lower Saxon tribe, and the repeated difficulties placed in the way of the aforementioned development – sometimes by the government, sometimes by the nobles – compete to produce this outcome, and it is hard to say when things will come to a firm conclusion.[8]

In understanding why this should have been the case, there seems little doubt that key influences were at work in Hanover that went back well beyond the Napoleonic period and the ensuing political debates of the Restoration. Above all, it was the character of the English link and, in particular, the absence of the monarch from any direct presence in Hanoverian life after 1760 that ensured this outcome. In contrast to most of the other States that may be considered victors in the Napoleonic redistributions, there had been no meaningful attempt at princely centralisation of powers in the late eighteenth century. By 1800 there were nine administrative units (principalities, counties, etc.) and the extent of administrative integration between them was minimal. The government was carried on by a bure-aucracy dominated by nobles and a so-called 'secretarocracy' of nobles and upper commoners, which tolerated and indeed encouraged the survival of provincial political institutional and local peculiarities. In consequence, the State that was created and/or recreated in 1814 after the collapse of the kingdom of Westphalia had no meaningful tradition of enlightened absolutism to influence its develop-ment.[9] As James Whitman has recently suggested, this was the neglected third Germany, 'where neither Prussian State reformism nor Western constitutionalism had succeeded in displacing the old legal order'.[10]

Furthermore, the English link was highly influential at an intellectual level as well. That archetypal creation of the Hanoverian monarchs of England – the University of Göttingen – functioned as the primary conduit by which Burkean ideas of organic historical development, respect for local and regional peculiarities, and hostility to natural-rights and other 'abstract' political doctrines divorced from the concrete realities governing people's lives, entered German political thinking.[11] To a figure such as the conservative politician and scholar August Wilhelm Rehberg, 1688 and England's subsequent constitutional development showed the possibility of reforms by the State which would prevent a repetition of the excesses experienced in France after 1789, a Whiggish view which could almost certainly not have developed in any German State other than Hanover.[12] The approach to politics broadly associated with this body of thought was undoubtedly of the first importance in informing all significant contributions to the controversies that bedevilled Hanoverian political life in the early nineteenth century, and that significance is incomprehensible without the existence of the English connection.

Paradoxically however, this approach became most important at the precise moment at which that English connection was formally severed, in 1837. As Wolf D. Gruner has convincingly shown, geopolitical considerations associated with the need for a strong Hanoverian territorial State played a central role in both British and Hanoverian policy-making at the Congress of Vienna. The main Hanoverian figure at the congress, Count Ernst Friedrich Herbert zu Münster, sought in principle a return to a modified version of the old imperial constitution and, when such a move proved impractical, attempted to insist on a federal confederation in which the larger German States other than Prussia and Austria would have a meaningful say in German affairs.[13] Quite apart from the thorny question as to whether this second vision was practicable, Münster's whole approach pointed to a real problem which was to return with a vengeance in subsequent decades. In essence, that problem involved the relationship between a post-revolutionary order in which all sorts of historical institutions and traditions had been overturned for ever and the primacy accorded to historical justifications for any significant political programme. To that extent, Münster was *the* pivotal figure in the political history of Hanover in the decade and a half after 1815 until his fall in the aftermath of popular disturbances in provincial Hanoverian towns such as Osterode and Göttingen in 1831.

Those disturbances came after an extended period of growing social distress in the late 1820s and a rapidly swelling movement calling for fundamental reforms – a movement which came to cast Münster himself as the figurehead of a reactionary nobility determined to prevent any material or institutional progress that might restrict its unjustified privileges.[14] Yet in the tense and difficult years immediately after the July revolution in France, which saw the legislation removing servile dues, a move away from the outright bias towards nobles in the distribution of civil service posts, and the eventual passage of a constitution in 1833, the lead was taken in the reform movement by decidedly moderate figures – men like Friedrich Christoph Dahlmann and the long-serving mayor of Osnabrück, Johann Carl Bertram Stüve – who to all intents and purposes shared key elements of the quasi-Burkean world view adopted by their opponents. They would, for example, have had little difficulty in accepting the validity of Münster's preference (in a reply to his critics published in 1831) for specifically German-style Estates-based constitutions as opposed to constitutions rooted in 'modern theories'.[15]

Men such as Dahlmann and Stüve, who played the leading role in the opposition to the forced removal of the 1833 constitution in 1837, shared with their noble and reactionary opponents a conviction of the necessity of basing all important political institutions on allegedly 'organic' historical developments, and a deep suspicion of those forms of liberalism which they associated with suspicious French tendencies towards centralisation and the levelling of local and provincial traditions. This fact helps to explain why the prime movers behind the 1833 constitution – once again Dahlmann and Stüve – should not have seriously considered abolishing the provincial Estates which were in fact the major power bases of their reactionary noble opponents. It also explains the primary characteristics of their long-running, in the short term essentially fruitless, campaign against the 1837 *coup* – a campaign during which Hanover's internal affairs for the first time became the object of serious scrutiny across Germany in connection with the treatment of the so-called 'Göttingen Seven'. Despite frequent assertions to the contrary, the Göttingen Seven affair was not primarily a question of the battle between antagonistic liberal and conservative principles and groups. Instead, it was really a contest within a predominantly historically-minded, political culture about *which* lessons for future development should be derived from the fractured history of the Hanoverian peoples and about *which* social groups the beneficiaries of those lessons should be.

That such was the case can be demonstrated by a necessarily brief discussion of the constitutional conflict provoked by King Ernest Augustus's revocation of the 1833 constitution. As Duke of Cumberland the new king had made no secret of his belief that he was not bound by a constitution to which he had not personally agreed and had made contact with the leadership of the reactionary nobility well before his accession. As modern students of these events have shown, there was a clear distinction between Ernest Augustus's motives – which stressed the restoration of monarchical rights – and those of noble leaders such as Georg von Schele whose real goal was to preserve a society in which noble interests would be uppermost. But in the context of 1837 these divergent aspirations could come together as Schele sought to convince Ernest Augustus that a restored monarchical sovereignty could in practice be based only on a recreated system of noble rights and privileges.[16] For tactical reasons the royal *Patent* of 1 November 1837 abrogating the 1833 constitution proceeded from two fundamental, but rather different, arguments: first, that the 1833 constitution was invalid because it had not been concluded legally on the basis of an agreement between prince and Estates; second, that it was in any case invalid because no prince could bind his successor to any act which inalienably revoked the latter's sovereign privileges and rights.[17] The first of these arguments was designed to secure the support of the confederation for the *coup*, a strategy devised by Schele well before the new king's arrival in Hanover; the second mirrored the arguments of Charles X of France in the run-up to the 1830 revolution – a point that was not lost on contemporaries. But, for our purposes, the key point was that the *coup* was justified through forms of argument best described as 'historico-legal' in nature.

Even more significant, however, was that the actions of the *coup*'s opponents are best described in similar terms. The immediate refusal of the seven Göttingen professors to sign an oath of loyalty was in the first place justified by their moral sense of obligation to their previous oath of allegiance to the 1833 constitution. At all significant points in the controversies arising out of their speedy dismissal, they denied that they were acting from a political standpoint hostile to that of the new king and asserted that the only point at issue was whether the king had the legal and moral right to revoke the constitution one-sidedly, without the agreement of the Estates. Time and again the leading members of the Seven, particularly Dahlmann and the brothers Grimm, reiterated their view that their actions had been guided by their consciences, that their protest was moral rather than political in nature.[18] Moreover, their actions and those of their leading supporters in Hanover – men like Stüve who orchestrated the long-running campaign against the legality of the king's move – were marked by studied moderation, involving the avoidance of actions likely to lead to significant breaches of the peace or disturbances, and a marked preference for seeking legal forms of redress. In a highly revealing comment by Wilhelm Eduard Albrecht – one of two of the Göttingen Seven whose academic specialism was law – this moderation came clearly to the fore: 'The only thing that lies close to our hearts is to defend our behaviour in terms of its conformity with the law (legality) and above all against the charge that it represented a revolutionary step,'[19] while other members of the Seven, notably the brothers Grimm, were even more insistent on their lack of 'political motives' and their contempt for 'liberals' who sought to make political capital out of the events. The closeness of the Grimms to men like Friedrich Carl von Savigny – founder of the far from liberal Historical School of Law and sympathiser with the predicament of the Seven[20] – should leave no doubt as to the true nature of these controversies. What was really at stake was whether a 'reform conservatism' (to use Epstein's phrase), built on Burkean historicist precepts and prioritising recourse to law as a means of underpinning organic development without succumbing to the twin dangers of bureaucratic, centralising despotism and popular revolution from below, could provide stability in the Hanoverian context. The evidence of the recurrent constitutional and political crises in post-1815 Hanover suggested that it could not. Faced with a determined monarch, and deliberately eschewing tactics which might move popular opinion in the direction of illegal action, the opponents of the 1837 *coup* were reduced to impotence once the confederation had refused to come to their aid in the summer of 1839.[21]

Yet for all the power of English influences on the political understanding of Hanoverians in this period, there was a further feature of this story that assumed increasing significance as time went on. That feature concerned the existence and nature of a specifically Hanoverian 'national' character and its relationship with a broader German culture. The question of specific regional identities and their connection, if any, with larger political and cultural entities was a thorny one, especially in view of the parallel development of the idea of a 'Lower Saxon' identity. The rhetoric surrounding 'Lower Saxon-ness' had emerged well before 1815; indeed, since the later seventeenth century the term 'Lower Saxon' had increasingly been used to reach a broader public in north-western Germany than would have been possible by a simple concentration on the dynastic fortunes of one or other of the princely houses. Justus Möser's work in the late eighteenth century idealised Saxon traditions as the acme of Germanic freedom, and his assertion of a dialectical relationship between local corporate structures and centralising monarchies marked an important stage in the elaboration of this rhetoric.[22] But one of Möser's major concerns was to see Saxon virtues embodied in Westphalia (of which his home town of Osnabrück was a part). Considerable reformulation was thus required after 1815, when Osnabrück was brought into the Hanoverian State.

Stüve put this point well in his comments concerning the lack of distance between true 'Lower Saxon' Hanoverians and the Westphalians of his native Osnabrück and in his conviction that the government's policies were not designed to overcome the lack of common identities in what was effectively a new State.[23] At this point, the idea that 'Lower Saxons' embodied certain positive characteristics – personal reserve, attachment to inherited customs, independence, obstinacy, and so on – rapidly gained ground. The essential conservatism of the Lower Saxon 'tribe' (*Volksstamm*) was widely accepted by 1789, as it was to be a century later,[24] but this perception could be put to a number of different political uses. From the 1820s onwards, circles connected with the court consciously sought to promote the link between the Lower Saxon cause and the interests of the Guelph ruling dynasty. When a historical association for Lower Saxony was set up with the patronage of the viceroy, the Duke of Cambridge, in 1835 its scope was deliberately restricted to the lands between the rivers Weser and Elbe and especially to those areas that made up the heartland of the ruling house. The initial uncertainty about whether the association should include the words 'Lower Saxony' or 'Braunschweig and Hanover' in its title was in itself highly sympto-matic of the unstable relationship between regional identities and dynastic interests. Moreover, the fact that Stüve had played a leading role in calling for such an association since 1827 should remind us that the political motivation behind such projects was never unambiguous. It was thus possible for the association to include both liberals and conservatives in its membership.[25] The monarchy's attempts to link the fortunes of the dynasty with the idea of Lower Saxony continued, and indeed intensified after the accession to the throne of King George V in 1851,[26] but so too did alternative visions. This point was amply demonstrated in 1851, when Franz Wilhelm Miquel (brother of the later leading National Liberal politician, Johannes) called for the teaching of Lower Saxon history in elementary schools as a means of *overcoming* dynastic particularism. A relatively unified concept of 'Lower-Saxon-ness', equipped with its symbolism of oak trees and so on, survived throughout the nineteenth century but it did so in large part because it provided a framework within which political disagree-ments were fought out.[27]

An analogous point may be made concerning shared ground in political debate between moderate liberals and conservatives. Both sides shared a deep-rooted suspicion of the phenomenon of bureaucracy and centralised government and tended to see them as incompatible with 'true' German freedoms. Thus Rehberg's 'reform conservative' vision saw Hanover's avoidance of absolutism as an ex-pression of such freedoms, in marked contrast to Prussian bureaucratic centralisation. In the 1830s the association of hostility to bureaucratic centralisa-tion and hostility to liberalism was a major part of the ideological offensive waged by noble reactionaries such as Georg von Schele – a leading figure in the events surrounding the 1837 *coup*.[28] Yet a liberal-reformist variant of the same position developed very rapidly after 1830 and the emphasis on provincialism and 'justified [local] peculiarities' was anything other than a conservative/reactionary monopoly by the middle of the century, as Stüve's lifelong hostility to bureaucratic centrali-sation and doctrinaire liberalism showed. Only thus can one explain Stüve's belief that bureaucratic absolutism and doctrinaire liberalism shared common vices, above all the tendency towards ahistorical, rationalist 'levelling' which destroyed the sense of independence and freedom characteristic of the medieval local com-munity. In Stüve's opinion, modern constitutions created a situation in which 'the naked arbitrariness of the majority was allowed to bind the minority' and he continued: 'Lasting freedom and legal certainty can never arise out of a constitution of this sort, which is only a link in the constitutional circle running from monarchy to aristocracy, aristocracy to democracy, and then back round into despotism.' The year 1848 had, he believed, confirmed the negative social and political effects of doctrinaire liberalism:

> Universal suffrage and elections according to classes of taxpayers; freedom of movement and lack of membership of a community; the 'mobilisation' of landed property and

freedom to pursue a trade are parts of one and the same system; and this system ends only in anarchy or despotism.[29]

As has been suggested, there were two immediate reasons for this failure – the intransigence of the kings of Hanover and the intransigence of an intrinsically weak but nevertheless privileged nobility. Hanover was not the only place in Europe in which uncertainties in the post-revolutionary political order and in particular the relationship between a restorationist nobility and a restorationist monarchy caused great political problems. France in the years leading up to 1830 is an obvious case in point and here, as in Hanover, that regime was replaced by one whose leading statesmen were clearly guided by the experience of eighteenth-century England (or what they believed that experience to have been). Indeed, Orleanism, with its pursuit of the *juste milieu* as a middle way between reaction and popular revolution and its distinctive blend of liberalism and authoritarianism, was very close to the positions adopted by Dahlmann or Stüve. Moreover, when Guizot wrote, 'Je suis grand partisan de la race des country-gentlemen,'[30] he was expressing sentiments that would have been immediately familiar to the 'organic liberals' who led the campaign against the revocation of the 1833 constitution.[31] Stüve's political career as the leading figure in Hanover's 'March Ministry' after 1848 was in large part guided by his desire to reconstitute Hanoverian political life on the basis of the active public involvement of property owners, and particularly *landed* property owners, irrespective of whether they happened to possess a noble title or not. Such a project involved recognisably 'English' aspects such as the development of vibrant organs of local self-administration,[32] which would foster the self-reliance and public-spiritedness of property owners and provide a modernised form of the stability which Stüve believed to have characterised the pre-1806 Holy Roman Empire before it had been swept away by the twin forces of bureaucratic centralisation and French-style popular mobilisation. But all such visions in Hanover foundered on the reversion to monarchical and noble intransigence and their characteristic political expression – a monarchically led, noble-backed *coup* in 1855. That experience, coupled with the fact that the second *coup* was explicitly supported from the start by the confederation persuaded the next generation of Hanoverian reform-minded liberals to draw conclusions that were arguably implicit in the events of the late 1830s; that given the prevailing conditions, no sustainable solution of the 'Hanoverian question' was achievable without the prior solution of the 'German question'.[33]

The second *coup* had one further important consequence in that it forced out into the open something that had remained hidden after the 1837 crisis. The extreme nature of George V's reactionary views as Crown Prince had alienated even members of the nobility in the 1840s but, as in the 1830s, the coincidence of essentially different strategies of monarchical absolutism and noble restorationism concealed these differences for a while after 1848.[34] But while the similarities with the post-1837 situation were clear, so too were the differences. This time the success of the *coup* depended not on the confederation's inactivity but on its positive response to the monarch's appeal for support, for which the king's advisers had carefully laid the ground since 1853–54. This, coupled with the escalating use of absolutist practices of government and the growing isolation of the king's court in Herrenhausen from many of its erstwhile noble supporters, introduced a fundamentally new element into Hanoverian politics. By 1859 the opposition was relatively united for the first time since 1848 and considerable noble opposition to the king's Minister of the Interior, Count von Borries, was becoming clearly evident. As George's much-hated adviser, Oskar Meding, later pointed out, the interventionist nature of the Borries Ministry came to infringe the inherited rights of the nobility, and the constant stream of administrative regulations – especially regarding domains policy, the reorganisation of local government, the judicial system, and hunting rights – gradually undermined the coherence of the alliance that had brought about the 1855 *coup*.[35] The distance between monarchical absolutism and noble politics was now out in the open – a fact noted with great satisfaction by the government's opponents. As the National Association's weekly put it in 1860–61, 1837 had destroyed the possibility of a coherent Hanoverian identity by dividing the new and old provinces. The Borries system had compounded this problem by alienating the nobility, delaying the development of a true conservatism among that section of society and doing great harm to the monarchical principle in Hanover.[36]

At this point the relevance of the neo-Burkean approach of a Stüve to problems of government and reform seems to have declined sharply, though some aspects of that inheritance – the concern with local government rights and justified local peculiarities, for example – seem to have lived on in the minds of younger liberals such as Bennigsen.[37] But the larger failure of the 'organic' approach to encompass the changes in the political system after 1848 emerged clearly when Hanover was annexed by Prussia in the summer of 1866. The annexation acted as a major caesura in the political history of the area, leaving a sense of bitterness and resentment between those who, however reluctantly, accepted it as a new beginning and those who would never accept it that lasted for generations. Yet it was among the 'losers' in this process – the pro-Guelph particularists who formed the German-Hanoverian party – that the influence of that line reaching back though Stüve to Rehberg and Möser was most apparent. This lineage was clearest in one of the key texts of this movement, Baron Heinrich Langwerth von Simmern's *Hanoverian Particularism* (1867), which mobilised the idea of Lower Saxony as a medium through which people's love for the nation was expressed and laid the ground for rejecting that Prussia had any particular national mission in Germany.[38] Time and again in the late nineteenth century Guelph propaganda reiterated those themes, with Langwerth von Simmern once again articulating them most clearly in his reflections on the relationship between German traditions and foreign policy just after the turn of the century. The current Anglophobia evident in Germany was, he believed, an expression of the Prussianisation of Germany, whereas true 'Germanness' would find its reflection in a positive attitude towards England, a State that had developed precisely those institutions – local self-government, the avoidance of bureaucratic excess, etc. – that lay at the heart of Germanic freedoms.[39] That sort of language would have been instantly recognisable to a Stüve, even if he might have come to somewhat different conclusions.

By this time the unpopularity of Langwerth's support for Britain during the Boer War was clear. Indeed, the link felt by most Hanoverians with British models and patterns of thought was becoming ever more indirect even before the annexation. Arguably, the experience of the first three decades of the nineteenth century suggested that even then the advantages to be derived from maintaining the English link were limited. The experiences of occupation by Prussia and France after the early 1800s and English impotence in the face of those expansionist powers taught important lessons that were not forgotten. Those lessons were only to a very limited extent counterbalanced by the territorial gains achieved before 1815, which were in any case largely the result of deals done from 1807 onwards between Britain and Prussia, deals that were connected with Britain's desire to ensure Prussia's survival as a great power in the post-Napoleonic world.[40] Yet, of the more significant medium-sized German States to survive after 1815, Hanover through its geographical position was uniquely threatened by Prussian territorial ambitions, and recent history suggested that Britain would be a very uncertain supporter in the event of those ambitions coming into the open. These strategic and geographical considerations effectively hamstrung Hanoverian policy in German affairs even before 1837 – the refusal of Hanover to enter Prussia's *Zollverein* in the 1830s and the profound controversies surrounding its entry in 1851–54 being a case in point – and led directly to the disastrous decision to enter the 1866 war on Austria's side.

Yet this final political error merely confirmed what had been clear for at least thirty years – that, despite the continued influence of modes of political thought derived in large part from eighteenth-century Britain, the British link was effectively irrelevant in the Hanoverian context and that Hanover's fortunes were now indissolubly linked with the unfolding events in the dying German Confederation. To that extent, the process leading to Bismarck's decision to annex Hanover in the summer of 1866 merely confirmed what had been implicit since 1837 if not since 1815. In view of the scale of the historical caesura generated by the French revolution and Napoleon's reordering of the map of central Europe, no appeal to historical traditions modelled on what were thought to be English examples and cautious 'organic' development could possibly withstand the temptation to resort to political violence that was the most likely outcome of the conditions of the post-revolutionary world.

## Notes

1  'Die Verdienste des Herrn von Borries', *Wochenschrift des Nationalvereins*, 3 (15 May 1860), pp. 18–19; and 'Hannover und der Nationalverein', *ibid.*, 6 (8 June 1860), pp. 42–4.

2  'Die Entwicklung der nationalen Idee in Hannover', i, *Wochenschrift des Nationalvereins*, 48 (29 March 1861), pp. 398–9.

3  Stüve, 'Hannover', in J. C. Bluntschli and K. Brater (eds.), *Deutsches Staats-Wörterbuch*, 4 (Stuttgart and Leipzig, Expedition des Staats-Wörterbuchs, 1859), 700.

4 See in general H. Gollwitzer, 'Die politische Landschaft in der deutschen Geschichte des 19./20. Jahrhunderts. Eine Skizze zum deutschen Regionalismus', *Zeitschrift für bayerische Landesgeschichte*, 27 (1964), 523–52; H. Berding, 'Staatliche Identität, nationale Integration und politischer Regionalismus', *Blätter für deutsche Landesgeschichte*, 121 (1985), 373–6; L. E. Lee, 'Liberal constitutionalism as administrative reform: the Baden constitution of 1818', *Central European History*, 8 (1975), 91–112; V. Press, 'Landstände des 18. und Parlamente des 19. Jahrhunderts', in H. Berding and H. -P. Ullmann (eds), *Deutschland zwischen Revolution und Restauration* (Düsseldorf, Athenäum/Droste, 1981), 133–57.

5 The most important sources for this paragraph are E. von Meier, *Hannoversche Verfassungs- und Verwaltungsgeschichte 1680–1866*, i (Leipzig, Duncker und Humblot, 1898), pp. 368–97, 461–98; H. -J. Behr, *Politisches Ständetum und landschaftliche Selbstverwaltung. Geschichte der Osnabrücker Landschaft im 19. Jahrhundert* (Osnabrück, Wenner, 1970), pp. 5–36; R. Oberschelp, *Niedersachsen 1760–1820. Wirtschaft, Gesellschaft, Kultur im Land Hannover und Nachbargebieten*, i (Hildesheim, August Lax, 1982), pp. 11–12, 44–8; R. Oberschelp, *Politische Geschichte Niedersachsens 1803–1866* (Hildesheim, August Lax, 1988), pp. 46–91; W. Wittich, *Die Grundherrschaft in Nordwestdeutschland* (Leipzig, Duncker und Humblot, 1896), pp. 426–31.

6 The best recent general account of these events is Oberschelp, *Politische Geschichte Niedersachsens 1803–1866*. On the second royal *coup* see also R. Wöltge, 'Die Reaktion in Königreich Hannover 1850–1857. Die Rückbildung des Verfassungsgesetzes und die Reformversuche an den Provinziallandschaften,' Diss. phil. (Tübingen, 1932), and M. L. Anderson, *Windthorst: a Political Biography* (Oxford, Oxford University Press, 1981), pp. 69–76.

7 For a contemporary liberal critique of these connections see [A. Lammers], 'Hannovers Reactionsjahre', *Preussische Jahrbücher* 3 (1859), 505–40.

8 [Anon.], 'Neuere deutsche Leistungen auf dem Gebiete der Staatswissenschaften', *Deutsche Vierteljahres-Schriften* iii (1854), 47.

9 Apart from the sources cited in note 5 above, see H. Heffter, *Die deutsche Selbstverwaltung im neunzehnten Jahrhundert. Geschichte der Ideen und Institutionen* (Stuttgart, Koehler,1950), pp. 202–4.

10 J. Q. Whitman, *The Legacy of Roman Law in the German Romantic Era: Historical Vision and Legal Change* (Princeton, Princeton University Press, 1990), p. 113.

11 K. Epstein, *The Genesis of German Conservatism* (Princeton, Princeton University Press, 1966), ch. 11; cf. W. R. Röhrbein and A. von Rohr, *Hannover im Glanz und Schatten des britischen Weltreiches. Die Auswirkungen der Personalunion auf Hannover von 1714–1837*, 2nd edn (Hanover, Hennes und Zinkeisen, 1977), p. 30, on the link between Hanover's political peculiarities and the attractions of Burkean thought.

12 A. Michaelis, 'Die ideologische Auseinandersetzung mit der Französischen Revolution. Edmund Burke und August Rehberg', in H. N. Rohloff (ed.), *Großbritannien und Hannover. Die Zeit der Personalunion* (Frankfurt am Main, Fischer, 1989), pp. 360–6.

13 W. D. Gruner, 'England, Hannover und der Deutsche Bund 1814–1837', in A. M. Birke and K Kluxen (eds), *England und Hannover* (Munich, etc., Saur, 1986), pp. 81–126.

14 On these disturbances and their aftermath see H. G. Husung, *Protest und Repression im Vormärz. Norddeutschland zwischen Restauration und Revolution* (Göttingen, Vandenhoeck und Ruprecht, 1983), pp. 74–94.

15 See, for example, the *Erklärung des Ministers Grafen von Münster über einige in der Schmähschrift 'Anklage des Ministeriums Münster' ihm persönlich gemachte Vorwürfe, sowie über seinen Austritt aus dem Königlich-Hannoverschen Staatsdienst* (Hannover, no publisher, 1831), pp. 10–11.

16 H. -J. Behr, *Georg von Schele, 1771–1844. Staatsmann oder Doktrinär* (Osnabrück, Wenner, 1973), pp. 132–45.

17 The *Patent* is reprinted in W. Real (ed.), *Der hannoversche Verfassungskonflikt* (Göttingen, Vandenhoeck und Ruprecht, 1972), pp. 11–17.

18 See, for example, F. C. Dahlmann, 'Zur Verständigung' (1838), in *F. C. Dahlmann's Kleine Schriften und Reden* (Stuttgart, Cotta, 1886), p. 267; Wilhelm Grimm, quoted in A. Saathoff, *Geschichte*

*der Stadt Göttingen seit der Gründung der Universität* (Göttingen, Vandenhoeck und Ruprecht, 1940), p. 190. J. Grimm, 'Über meine Entlassung' (1838), in J. Grimm, *Reden und Aufsätze. Eine Auswahl*, ed. W. Schoof (Munich, Winkler, 1966), pp. 34–63. For a similar argument to the one presented here see G. Dilcher, *Der Protest der Göttinger Sieben. Zur Rolle von Recht und Ethik, Politik und Geschichte im Hannoverschen Verfassungskonflikt* (Hanover, Hennes und Zinkeisen, 1988).

19 [W. E. Albrecht], *Die Protestation und Entlassung der sieben Göttinger Professoren*, ed. F. C. Dahlmann (Leipzig, Weidmann, 1838), p. 4.

20 For the closeness of the Grimms, especially Jacob Grimm, to Savigny and the latter's support for the Göttingen Seven see W. Schoof and I. Schnack (eds), *Briefe der Brüder Grimm an Savigny* (Berlin and Bielefeld, Schmidt, 1953), pp. 390–6; A. Stoll, *Friedrich Karl von Savigny* (Berlin, Neymann, 1929), ii. 500–9.

21 On the events leading up to this decision see Oberschelp, *Politische Geschichte Niedersachsens 1803–1866*, pp. 143–9.

22 See J. Knudsen, *Justus Möser and the German Enlightenment* (Cambridge, Cambridge University Press, 1986), pp. 102–6; 150–9.

23 See Stüve to Fromann, 31 December 1822, 22 April 1825 and 4 September 1829 in W. Vogel (ed.), *Briefe Johann Carl Bertram Stüves*, i (Göttingen, Vandenhoeck und Ruprecht, 1959), pp. 68, 87, 102.

24 See the quotations from Ernst Brandes assembled in F. Thimme, *Die inneren Zustände des Kürfürstentums Hannover unter der französisch-westfälischen Herrschaft 1806–13*, i (Hanover and Leipzig, Hahn'sche Buchhandlung, 1893) pp. 30–1, and Thimme's own similar comments in *ibid.*, ii (Hanover and Leipzig, Hahn'sche Buchhandlung, pp. 1895) 652–3.

25 See 'Verkündigung der geschehenen Errichtung des historischen Vereins für Niedersachsen', in *Vaterländisches Archiv für hannoversch-braunschweigische Geschichte 1834* (Lüneburg, 1835), pp. 162–3; cf. M. Hamann, 'Überlieferung, Erforschung und Darstellung der Landesgeschichte in Niedersachsen', in H. Patze (ed.), *Geschichte Niedersachsens*, i (Hildesheim, August Lax, 1977), pp. 75–6; Hamann, 'Die Gründung des Historischen Vereins für Niedersachsen', in W. Maurer and H. Patze (eds), *Festschrift für Berent Schwineköper* (Sigmaringen, Thorbecke, 1982), pp. 569–82; A. Kroker, 'Niedersächsische Geschichtsforschung im 19. Jahrhundert. Zwischen Aufklärung und Historismus', *Westfälische Forschungen*, 39 (1989), 83–113.

26 D. Brosius, 'Georg V von Hannover – der König des monarchischen Prinzips', *Niedersächsisches Jahrbuch für Landesgeschichte*, 51 (1979), 259–61. Brosius correctly notes that George V's historical interests were directly related to his belief in divinely ordained, patrimonial kingship.

27 See, above all, D. Lent, 'Der Niedersachsenbewußtsein im Wandel der Jahrhunderte', in C. Haase (ed.), *Niedersachsen. Territorien – Verwaltungseinheiten – geschichtliche Landschaften* (Göttingen, Vandenhoeck und Ruprecht, 1971), pp. 39–50.

28 Behr, *Georg von Schele*, pp. 103–8 and *passim*.

29 Stüve, *Wesen und Verfassung der Landgemeinden und des ländlichen Grundbesitzes in Niedersachsen und Westphalen* (Jena, Frommann, 1851), pp. 108, xv.

30 Guizot to Sainte-Aulaire, 11 March 1842, cited in D. Johnson, *Guizot: Aspects of French History 1787–1834* (London and Toronto, Routledge, 1963), p. 78.

31 For a good treatment of the historically rooted 'organic liberalism' of men like Dahlmann, and its connection with the swelling nationalist movement, see E.-W. Böckenförde, *Die deutsche verfassungsgeschichtliche Forschung im 19. Jahrhundert. Zeitgebundene Fragestellungen und Leitbilder* (Berlin, Duncker und Humblot, 1961), ch. 3. Note also the similarities between Guizot's analysis of the Hanoverian constitutional crisis – i.e. that it revealed apathy and 'universal impotence' – and those of the Hanoverian government's opponents; see Guizot to Dorothée de Lieven, 9 September 1838, in *Lettres de François Guizot et de la Princesse de Lieven*, i (n.p., Mercure de France, 1963), pp. 192–3.

32 These aspects of Stüve's programme and their connection with Rudolf von Gneist's later attempt to reform Prussian local administration by converting nobles into what he believed to be English-style gentry are stressed by Heffter, *Selbstverwaltung*, p. 199. Stüve believed that any such project must

involve the removal both of the nobles' exclusive right to representation in the local Estates and the First Chamber in Hanover and of the nobles' much-prized tax exemptions. See C. V. Graf, 'The Hanoverian Reformer Johann Carl Bertram Stüve, 1798–1872', Ph.D. thesis (Cornell University, 1972), chs 13, 15.

33 This was the conclusion drawn by those liberal opponents of the government led by Rudolf von Bennigsen who played a leading role in the formation of the German National Association in 1859. See F. Frensdorff, *Gottlieb Planck, deutscher Jurist und Politiker* (Berlin, Guttentag, 1914), p. 220.

34 Brosius, 'Georg V von Hannover', pp. 258–9, 265–70.

35 O. Meding, *Memoiren zur Zeitgeschichte* (Leipzig, Brockhaus, 1881), i. 20–4; [Lammers], 'Hannovers Reactionsjahre', pp. 514–16, 520–34; H. Frhr. Langwerth von Simmern, *Aus meinem Leben. Erlebtes und Gedachtes*, i (Berlin, Behr, 1898), p. 184. For an admirable analysis of the ambivalent relationship between George V's absolutism and the Hanoverian nobility, emphasising industrial policy, see R. Ott, *Kohle, Stahl und Klassenkampf. Montanindustrie, Arbeiterschaft und Arbeiterbewegung im Osnabrücker Land 1857–1882* (Frankfurt am Main and New York, Campus, 1982), pp. 26–31.

36 'Zur hannöverischen Frage II', *Wochenschrift des Nationalvereins*, 20 (12 October 1860), pp. 187–9. 'Die Entwicklung der nationalen Idee in Hannover', II, *ibid.*, 50 (12 April 1861), pp. 398–9. 'Die Verdienste des Grafen Borries', *ibid.*, 51 (19 April 1861), pp. 422–3.

37 On this point see the perceptive analysis in H. Barmeyer, 'Die hannoverschen Nationalliberalen 1857–1885', in *Niedersächsisches Jahrbuch für Landesgeschichte*, 53 (1981), 65–86.

38 [H. Fhr. Langwerth von Simmern], *Der 'Hannöverische Particularismus'. Eine oratio pro domo* (Mannheim, Schneider, 1867). On the significance of this pamphlet see Lent, 'Niedersachsenbewußtsein', pp. 44–5; cf. Langwerth von Simmern, *Aus meinem Leben*, i. p. 206.

39 See the writings collected in H. Frhr. Langwerth von Simmern, *Deutschtum und Anglophobie*, 2 vols (Wiesbaden, Brocking, 1903/4).

40 Röhrbein and Rohr, *Hannover im Glanz und Schatten*, pp. 40–1; Gruner, 'England, Hannover und der Deutsche Bund', pp. 86–7.

# Conclusion

# From dynastic union to unitary State: The European experience

## DAVID EASTWOOD, LAURENCE BROCKLISS AND MICHAEL JOHN

It is a historical commonplace to think of English State formation as exceptional. In a wonderfully suggestive essay Edward Thompson introduced us to the peculiarities of the English, while, in very different ways, Gerald Alymer, Derek Sayer and Philip Corrigen have probed the peculiarities of English State formation.[1] More recent work has begun to delineate the peculiarities of the British.[2] Much of this work has focused either on describing the making and meaning of Britishness or on mapping the shifting matrix of local, national and British identities which arose in these islands in the eighteenth and nineteenth centuries.[3] As a consequence our understanding of the processes through which the kingdom was united and of the meanings of Britishness in the Hanoverian and Victorian periods is vastly richer. Sophisticated readings of Britishness contrast with sometimes still relatively underconceptualised accounts of British State formation. Here British exceptionalism is perhaps best understood in terms of wider typologies of State formation. If one compares the British experience with those of France, or the German Reich it is clear that the problems which led to the forging first of Britain and later of the United Kingdom were not unique. Dynastic rulers and their constitutional successors frequently found themselves governing multi-ethnic States within which local enmities ran deep. What was distinctive was the way in which Britain sought to reconcile national, cultural and ethnic identities within a supranational State.

The British State, as formed in 1707, and the United Kingdom, forged through the Act of Union in 1800, are best thought of as Unionist States.[4] In both instances constitutional instruments were used to translate existing dynastic unions into a parliamentary Union. British Unionism exploited both the capacity and the flexibility of Parliament, relying on a reconfigured pattern of parliamentary representation serving as a political framework through which differences could be accommodated or contested. Thus in 1707 Anglo–Scottish parliamentary integration was regarded as a sufficient basis for Union, despite radical differences in Church establishment, law and education. In the same way, the Act of Union with Ireland eventually stood despite the failure to resolve the question of Catholic rights and the persistence of separate financial institutions for Britain and Ireland.

As the unification of the British and Irish Treasuries in 1816, the eventual passage of Catholic Emancipation in 1829 and the disestablishment of the Church of Ireland in 1869 demonstrated, legislative Union did not presuppose fixed arrangements in other central institutions in Church and State.[5] The 1536 and 1543 Acts of Union with Wales achieved substantial uniformity by remorselessly displacing Welsh institutions and Anglicising Welsh public life. Nevertheless even here the Welsh Great Sessions continued to 1830, giving Wales one unique public institution.[6] Given Parliament's ability to reform itself, the constitutional arrangements of this Unionist State proved remarkably plastic, especially when compared with the comprehensive constitution-making which elsewhere characterised post-Enlightenment European State formation. From the French constitution of 1791, and arguably from the constitution of the United States in 1787, constitution-making was hugely ambitious, seeking precise mechanisms to regulate the distribution of power, rights and entitlements. In this sense both unitary States, such as the post-revolutionary French State, and federal states, such as the United States of America or Bismarckian Germany, were much more precisely constructed and much more rigidly regulated through constitutional prescription than was the British Unionist State.

The nature of Unionism was crucial to the development of the British State. Despite party and political contestation, Parliament constituted a strongly integrative element within these Unions. Within and beyond Parliament political spaces remained within which separate cultural identities might be asserted and religious and national differences contested. This is not to deny that there were strong centralist tendencies within the British State: both the response to the 'Forty-five' in Scotland and the broad thrust of British policy towards Ireland in the thirty years after the 1800 Act of Union amply attest a preference for greater uniformity. Nevertheless the restricted constitutional language embodied in British Unionism permitted shifting patterns of development.[7] Thus the Welsh language could be castigated as an instrument of barbarism by the notorious 1847 Royal Commission on the state of education in Wales but positively encouraged by some school inspectors in Wales a generation later.[8] Similarly national education resulted in English displacing Gaelic in Ireland in the half-century after 1830, but the triumph of the English language did not undermine the authority of the Catholic establishment, nor did it inhibit the further marginalisation of Anglo–Irish identities in the second half of the nineteenth century. Moreover, for much of the United Kingdom, industrialisation, internal migration and the move to mass communications were far more potent promoters of the English language than official policy.[9] In the same way, the United Kingdom was, by the 1851 religious census, reconciled to religious pluralism, with different religious establishments in England and Scotland, full tolerance for Irish Catholics, and Nonconformity fast emerging as the demotic national religion of Wales.[10]

To this extent at least, the Unionist State was formally a union of multiple identities which made precisely limited demands on British subjects. Loyalty to the Crown, obedience to Parliament, tolerance of Church establishment, and acceptance of English as the primary public language constituted the principal pillars of the Unionist State. Crucially there was no formal attempt to make Britishness a primary cultural identity. Of course, Britishness had meaning, or rather meanings. The political basis of the Union demanded allegiance to a limited range of British political institutions. War between 1707 and 1815, as Colley has argued, could help fashion a peculiarly British patriotism.[11] But even here one should beware of pushing the argument too far. There were moments of British unity in war; there were national heroes, from Admiral Vernon, through Lord Nelson to the Duke of Wellington.[12] Nevertheless wars were nationally divisive. The Tories swept to victory in the 1710 election on a peace platform, whilst the War of the Austrian Succession created the circumstances not only for Walpole's fall but for the 'Forty-five'. The American War of Independence was hardly a patriotic struggle or a focus of national unity, whilst war with revolutionary France in the 1790s saw the British nation still more openly divided. One should not confuse a patriot rhetoric of Britishness, forged or deployed in wartime, with a pervasive or persistent sense of Britishness as a primary or normative identity. British Unionism worked precisely because it depended not on the creation of a hegemonic British identity but on the availability of institutions and symbols which offered a means of identifying with Britain. If we are to understand the forging of Britishness as a process, it is a process perhaps better understood in Keith Robbins's elegant formulation of 'the blending of Britain'.[13] Although this kind of formulation risks blurring the real cultural frictions in eighteenth and nineteenth-century Britain, it captures something of the widely ramified cultural interactions through which a symbolic supranational identity was improvised. Robbins has suggested that 'we need to ask more precisely what we mean by "culturally distinct peoples", on the one hand, and, on the other, what we mean when we talk of a country "coming into being"'.[14] One might go some way towards resolving this problem by drawing attention to a British State's coming into being through legislative Unions which acknowledged that political frameworks were being constructed through which 'culturally distinct peoples' could coexist.

There were, of course, profound limits to the cultural spaces permitted within the British State. Peasant cultures, especially Catholic peasant cultures, were culturally and economically squeezed. Languages of economic modernity, markets and superior cosmopolitan moralities underpinned the Highland clearances in Scotland and the Whigs' brutal response to the Irish famine in the later 1840s. The Whigs were certainly wrong to think that a depopulated, economically modernised Ireland would fit better into the Union, but they thought it none-theless.[15] However, the plasticity of Unionist arrangements was clearly demonstrated in the later nineteenth century, when the tone of policy towards the periphery and minorities began to change. The most dramatic shift was British Liberals' willingness to embrace Home Rule for Ireland, and even to risk dramatic instability within the Union to carry it through between 1912 and 1914.[16] Other measures modified the Union without formally rewriting its terms as Home Rulers intended. The 1881 Irish Land Act went a long way towards recognising fundamental differences not just in Irish land holding but also in Irish economic culture. The Crofters' Act of 1886, a modest atonement for the Clearances, was a similarly conceived attempt to recognise and reconcile a peripheral culture within the British State.[17] Similarly the 1881 Welsh Sunday Closing Act, the first public legislative Act since 1543 to treat Wales separately from England, was significant in its recognition that Welsh religious and moral distinctiveness might require Wales to be accorded a marginally different status within a legislative Union stretching back to 1536.[18]

Thus the British State was able to function without Britishness ever having been a necessary primary identity, and without new constitutional and institutional instruments being forged. The United States in 1787, the French repeatedly after 1789, the Italians in 1861 and the Germans of *Kleindeutschland* in 1871 all constructed new States in terms of new constitutional and institutional arrangements. Even the Habsburgs in the 1780s and the 1860s sought to strengthen the sinews of their multi-ethnic empire through major constitutional, cultural, and structural reform.[19] British Unionism rested, fundamentally, on an extension of the domain of the English Crown and the English Parliament. Here again British peculiarities were crucial. The upheavals of the sixteenth and seventeenth centuries had resulted in an important separation between the monarchy as a personal institution and the Crown as a constitutional concept. British monarchs might be intermittently popular and occasionally personally effective, but their personal authority mattered increasingly less. Yet precisely because the authority of the Crown rested after 1689 and 1701 on legal and constitutional formulations, rather than on personal or dynastic authority, its role could be redefined and refined within a British State as a symbol of frequently changing relations within both the Union and the empire. Similarly Parliament, especially from the 1760s onwards, offered a theatre in which different constituencies within the Union could organise. For as long as radicals, Chartists, Irish Home Rulers, Welsh Nonconformists and latterly Scottish nationalists were prepared to work through parliamentary means the political blending of British Unionism could continue. The moment they challenged Parliament, they challenged the Union itself, as when the Irish Home Rule Party came to be eclipsed by Sinn Féin during the First World War.[20]

This is not to say that the Unionist State worked happily, simply that it worked. If the century and a half after 1707 saw a hesitant attempt to manufacture a tighter political union, the century and a half after 1850 has witnessed an equally hesitant loosening of the Union, with much of Ireland recovering its independence and Gaelic identities finding greater space to explore, recover and remake their identities. In the process British Unionism may have run its course, at least in the particular parliamentary and monarchical forms envisaged in 1707 and 1800. The formal devolution of power constitutes a formidable challenge to older ideas of legislative Union. More strikingly still, the English language has persistently proved able to sustain, and even nurture, cultures which came to challenge the English and their political arrangements. This happened first in 1776, and later in Ireland and the empire. Perhaps the final irony is that the capacity of English-inspired

Unionism to tolerate diversity continues to be subverted by the capacity of the English language to promote political and cultural diversity.

Unlike the United Kingdom, the nineteenth-century French State was not the amalgam of three ancient, relatively independent kingdoms unified over time under one Crown. The boundaries of the French State after 1815, especially with the loss of Alsace-Lorraine to the new State of Germany in 1871, resembled closely the boundaries of the kingdom of France established in 843 by the Treaty of Verdun on the break-up of Charlemagne's empire. Nevertheless, the kingdom of France on the eve of the revolution was far from being a unitary State of the kind long established in England at least. Although the boundaries of the kingdom had remained relatively fixed for a thousand years, the ability of the French king to exert even minimal control over large swathes of his realm had been continually questioned until the end of the sixteenth century. As a result, the French State ruled over by the Bourbon dynasty consisted of a central, relatively homogeneously organised core based on Paris and a hotchpotch of peripheral provinces formerly under the control of independent dukes and counts, which had been allowed to retain their idiosyncratic traditions and privileges when the territories had been brought back under royal control through war or dynastic accident. France in many respects in 1789 was a geographical expression: there was no uniform system of taxation, no common legal system and no common language. Rather than a unitary, it was a corporative, State where not only individual provinces but particular social categories, individual towns and specific occupational groups within those towns enjoyed various fiscal, judicial and trade privileges.[21]

The calling of the Estates General in 1789 led to the rapid creation of the most developed unitary State that Europe had ever known. In the course of two years the revolutionaries swept away the corporative edifice of the *ancien régime* and established a uniform system of administration, taxation and justice that was meant to ensure that every Frenchman (and in many ways -woman) was equal before the law. This was a political, administrative and social revolution. The king became a constitutional monarch subject to the people's representative and the people became citizens rather than subjects. The traditional provincial boundaries of France disappeared and the country was divided into eighty-three departments of roughly equal size, christened according to local physical features, and subdivided into 5,400 cantons and 36,000 communes. Finally, group privileges of all kinds were removed, both the fiscal and judicial privileges enjoyed by the nobility, clergy and State officials, and the commercial and occupational monopolies enjoyed by professional men and artisans. The new France was in theory an open competitive society, where the talented would succeed and the lazy would go to the wall. It was also a secular society. Although the special place of the Catholic Church in French life was recognised, the revolutionaries nationalised ecclesiastical property, redrew diocesan boundaries to be territorially congruent with the departments, destroyed the Church's administrative hierarchy by introducing elections into appointments, and guaranteed civil and religious rights to

Protestants and Jews. Every attempt was made – even before the overthrow of the monarchy and the declaration of the republic in August 1792 – to stress that this was a new State, completely different from its *ancien régime* predecessor. Uniformity was achieved not by extending existing institutions or practices to the rest of the realm but by inventing new ones: hence the new decimal currency and the new decimalised system of weights and measures with their newfangled names.[22]

Of course, the revolutionaries were unable to put every piece of the unitary French State in place in two short years. Above all, they left to their successors a uniformly organised but highly decentralised polity with little bureaucratic structure. Before the revolution the French bureaucracy had been the largest in Europe, counting some 80,000 officials, over half of whom could not be dismissed without compensation because their office had been purchased. Decommissioned by the revolutionaries, who naively believed that the new State would live at peace with its neighbours, this bureaucratic Leviathan (shorn of venality) was only gradually reconstructed in a larger and more pervasive form after the outbreak of war in April 1792. In the Napoleonic era it was structurally perfected, with the removal of any vestiges of the electoral principle from the departmental administration and the introduction of the eagle-eyed figure of the prefect.[23] It was Napoleon, too, who completed the other unfinished piece of revolutionary business, the promulgation of a uniform law code. Historically the south of France operated under Roman law, the north under a variety of different customs. Attempts had been made since the reign of Louis XIV to bring all Frenchmen under a single code, but it was only under the Directory that the process of codification, apart from procedural law, was seriously begun.[24]

The structure of the new unitary French State erected in the revolutionary and Napoleonic eras was hardly touched thereafter. Although regimes came and went in the course of the nineteenth century, constant experiments were made with extending and curtailing the franchise, and the State's servants were frequently purged on the occasion of each revolution, the same system underpinned the Third Republic as had sustained the First Empire. In an important respect, then, the history of the modern French State is one of singular continuity. Only in the recent past has some attempt been made to introduce a more decentralised system of administration. The modern French State has also been a remarkably successful instrument. If its record as a war machine, after the glorious Napoleonic interlude, has been as disastrous as that of its eighteenth-century Bourbon predecessors, it has been notably more successful than its traditionally more decentralised and less unitary British counterpart in winning and retaining the loyalties of its citizens. Except belatedly, with the struggle for Corsican independence, France has experienced no secessionist moves by disgruntled provincials anxious to establish an independent State or attach themselves to another. Above all, while the Catalonians and Basques have been a continual thorn in the Spanish national flesh, their ethnic cousins on the French side of the Pyrenees seem to have had no difficulty in adopting a Gallic identity.[25] Admittedly, the new French State had one significant advantage over its British neighbour. As it was not the construct of three previously independent kingdoms but the heir to the western part of the Carolingian empire, it had powerful historical legitimacy. The advantage should not be exaggerated. The survival of France as an entity was continually in doubt until 1600, while Frenchness even in 1789 was still a very underdeveloped identity. Not only was the French State in the nineteenth century a novelty; so too was the French nation.

Prior to the revolution, it is difficult to judge the extent and depth of a sense of Frenchness among the Bourbons' subjects. Thanks to the military and cultural *élan* of the reign of Louis XIV, doubtless most educated and well-to-do eighteenth-century Frenchmen, except the non-Francophone on the recently integrated eastern frontier, not only distinguished themselves from but considered themselves superior to the members of other European nations. Indeed, the growing pressure for an end of the absolute monarchy in the final two decades of the *ancien régime* owed much to a sense of national frustration born out of continual failure in war. However, there was little informing this sense of national pride beyond a belief in the prowess of French arms and the sublimity of the French language. There was nothing akin to the English Protestant conviction that the nation was God's chosen people and little sign that this sense of French nationality was widely shared by ordinary Frenchmen. Even among the elite the strength of this French identity outside the capital was compromised by a deep-rooted provincialism. The corporative structure of the French State ensured that for the most part its members were raised, educated, worked and relaxed in their native province, and that their cultural ambitions were fulfilled through membership of their local academy of arts and sciences.[26] This was particularly true of professional men. Although by and large entry to all three traditional professions required a much more formal education than was ever the case in the British Isles in the eighteenth century, the constraints of the corporative system guaranteed that most professional men, even the well connected and ambitious, had to study at a local college or regional university, then enter a corporation or accept a cure in their native town. Robespierre enjoyed a scholarship to the University of Paris but he practised as a barrister in his home town, Arras.[27]

Provincial identities in France at the end of the eighteenth century, then, were pervasive. Although they could scarcely be described as national identities in the manner of Englishness, Scottishness or Irishness, they could not be ignored by the revolutionary State-builders and their successors. Decisions had to be taken as to the best way of ensuring that these residual loyalties did not undermine allegiance to the new revolutionary State. The nineteenth-century British State's response to the problem of powerful alternative spatial identities appears to have been (with certain important exceptions) to appease them. Nothing was done to eradicate traditional national loyalties; sometimes they were even encouraged. It was as if Britain's governing class thought the best method of cementing allegiance to the State of the United Kingdom was to let traditional loyalties coexist in healthy competition like houses in a public school. That was not the French way. As the administrative reconstruction of France in the years 1789 to 1791 made clear, provincialism was identified with the *ancien régime*. In the first half of the nineteenth century the French State took significant steps towards ensuring that provincial loyalties would die out.

The key to the erosion of provincialism in France lay in large measure in the successful construction of an elite whose primary (perhaps even total) identity was French. This was done firstly through the establishment of a common pattern of secondary education for all members of the elite, whatever their future occupation. A national network of secondary schools was already in place in eighteenth-century France which boasted some 300 colleges for the study of the Latin and Greek humanities and/or philosophy, chiefly run by the regular orders. On the eve of the revolution these schools were in better shape than their British counterparts, the grammar and burgh schools, though they too suffered competition from a growing number of private academies that offered a more modern and 'enlightened' curriculum of mathematics, science and modern languages.[28] The colleges were eventually closed during the revolution and their property was confiscated, but Napoleon reopened them in a new guise in 1802 when he endowed France with a smaller network of state *lycées* (later supplemented by municipal colleges). Although before the 1850s the *lycées* still devoted the lion's share of their time to teaching the classics and philosophy, they successfully countered the appeal of the private schools by at least making some effort to teach a broader range of subjects and by offering specialist teaching in mathematics, if not natural science, outside the main curriculum.[29] Significantly, not only did the *lycées* provide a common, State-funded general education that virtually all members of the nineteenth-century elite would have enjoyed, apart from diehard members of the old aristocracy,[30] but until the Third Republic the courses were predominantly taught by teachers who had had a similar formation in Paris at the Ecole Normale Supérieure, established in 1808. The Ecole Normale was an institution which recruited nationally on the basis of a competitive examination and provided free board and lodging and tutorial teaching while prospective teachers studied for their teaching diploma or *agrégation*. The Ecole Normale was an institution completely unknown in the British Isles, where teaching-training remained completely haphazard, and it ensured that the *lycées* were filled with non-local, suitably metropolitan-orientated teachers.[31]

The breakdown of provincial loyalties within the all important sub-group of the elite formed by members of the professions was further accentuated by the creation of a new nationally organised process of admission to these careers. In the first years of the revolution the corporative system of professional organisation was abolished. The universities and other specialist schools that provided professional training were closed down, local professional corporations lost their monopolistic privileges and all entrance requirements to the professions were lifted, on the grounds that limiting access to a career to those with certificates of entertainment was a restraint on trade. With the fall of the Jacobins in the summer of 1794, however, the trend was reversed and a new professional structure erected. The starting point was the opening of the Ecole Polytechnique in late 1794.

This was a school based in Paris which trained scholarship boys from all over the country in mathematics and science for entry to specialist schools serving the engineering and artillery corps.[32] It was the first of many similar *grandes écoles* that sprang up in the nineteenth century offering high-quality formal training for entrants to State careers. Before 1815 the emphasis was on finding first-class recruits for the army and navy officer corps, but thereafter new *écoles* were gradually established governing entry to other parts of the State apparatus. In 1848, at a time when the British were only beginning to contemplate demanding any sort of educational qualification for civil servants, an Ecole d'administration was founded, albeit temporarily, for training high-flying bureaucrats.[33] The *grandes écoles* were *the* national integrative mechanism. Recruiting by competitive examination, like the *Ecole Normale Supérieure* (which should be included within their number), they offered a prestigious meal ticket for the ambitious and talented provincial who was inevitably led to see service to the State of France as the route to fame and fortune. The *écoles* similarly ensured that the French military and bureaucracy were staffed with dedicated French nationalists.[34]

Early in the 1800s the process of restructuring was extended to the traditional private professions of law and medicine. The universities were not reopened but a small number of law and medical schools were established in Paris and other large towns providing a standardised curriculum.[35] Henceforth students in law and medicine who had studied at a State law or medical school for a set period of time and passed the relevant examinations were free to set up their stall where they wished.[36] This reform in 1802–03 not only allowed lawyers and medical men to operate nationally, it also tended to suck them into the Paris faculties and away from the provinces. On the eve of the revolution only 100 of the 500 trainee physicians were registered in the Paris faculty; by the 1820s there were 2,000 medical students in the capital.[37] The Paris faculties had a larger staff and better facilities, especially for medicine, but what drew students to the capital in addition was the greater opportunities of professional mobility that had opened up. Professional men now could have wider horizons. Yet, even if entering on a private career, lawyers and medical men were always closely under the State's eagle eye. The faculties were government bodies, not private corporative institutions, and from 1808 the law and medical faculties, along with the newly founded arts and science faculties, were placed under the umbrella authority of the Université impériale. This was an embryonic Ministry of Education. It kept close control over faculty professors and played a decisive role in their appointment.[38]

By the mid-nineteenth century, therefore, a large proportion of the French professional elite, and the elite as a whole, were raised and worked in an all-French environment and had almost certainly developed a deep-rooted French identity.[39] The wider French population, especially given the slow pace of French industrialisation and the continued size of the peasantry, inevitably had narrower, often still local horizons, but they too were beginning to experience a wider, very French world. Their baptism in Frenchness as a lived identity had generally been involuntary and unpleasant, when they were called to the colours in the conscript

armies of the revolutionary and Napoleonic periods. The evidence suggests, however, that the peasantry had got used to the responsibility of dying for the *patrie*
by 1810 and the survivors of the *Grande Armée* seem to have helped to create
and keep the myth of Napoleon alive among the ordinary people.[40] From 1815 to
1889 France was less demanding of its humbler citizens. If the State continued to
intrude into the lives of ordinary Frenchmen as the century wore on, it did so
less in the form of recruiting officers than as tax officials, health and safety
inspectors, and teachers. As early as 1833 – forty years before similar developments
in the British Isles – the State had become anxious that peasant children should
have access to primary education and legislated for the introduction of a school
in every commune. Although it would be 1886 before State primary schools had
to be staffed by laymen, the *loi Guizot* also required the establishment of a
State-run *école normale* in every department to train elementary schoolteachers
to the same standards. By the end of the century the results were impressive: in
1914, the military records reveal, less than 2 per cent of conscripts were illiterate.[41]
By the outbreak of the First World War the large majority of Frenchmen had
experienced a similar institutionalised acculturation that left them able to write
in the same hand and know the same past: only in areas that had suffered
extraordinarily in the Terror of 1793–95, notably the Vendée, was a different
version of history kept alive orally.[42]

Indeed, so successfully had a French nation been created in the course of the
Third French Republic that the State could afford to relax the screw a little:
provincialism was allowed to rear its head in the anodyne form of antiquarian
societies devoted to exploring the 'world we have lost'. Essentially, however,
Frenchmen retained their provincial identity in what they ate and drank, but little
else.[43] The comparative success of the French and British unitary States in creating
a French and a British nation remains poignantly expressed on the gravestones
of the hundreds of thousands of soldiers who were killed in the Great War. Britons
on the western front died ambiguously 'for King and Country'; their allies further
down the line died 'pour la France'.

To some extent the creation of not only a unitary but a national State of France
in the century and a quarter after the revolution was inevitable in the context of
the history of the *ancien régime*. The Bourbons may not have been successful in
creating a linguistically and culturally homogeneous State, but they had constantly
backed Gallicisation from the moment Francis I made French the official language
of the administration and the law. More important, the persistent drive to erode
provincialism after 1789 was determined by the potentially destructive concept
on which the new order was built – the sovereignty of the people. If, in consequence, the State was there only for the people's convenience, there could be no
theoretical objection to the aggrieved inhabitants of a peripheral province declaring
independence. The disintegrative force of the concept had already been seen in
the American revolution. The territorial integrity of France post-1789 was most
easily maintained by making its citizens think themselves one nation and their
collective fate indissolubly connected. The discontented might subsequently seek

to change the government at the centre in the name of the French people, but revolutionary violence from below would not harm the territorial configuration of the *patrie*. In this respect the French situation was very different from that of the United Kingdom, where political discourse was broadly built around the assumption that Parliament, not the people, was sovereign. As long as the inhabitants of the British Isles accepted the very English idea that change could occur legitimately only if sanctioned by the British Parliament, there was a limited need to foster unity by State-sponsored acculturation. The British were united by their political culture, regardless of their national or other divisions, and Parliament (especially after 1832) was the nodal point of the Union State where interest groups (national, class or religious) jockeyed for advantage. It may have been naive of the British ruling elite to assume that the belief in parliamentary sovereignty would always pertain – after all, the Americans had already found their way out of the ideological straitjacket – but the definite pervasiveness of the idea helps to explain why there was little British interest in the positive promotion of Britishness.

Neither the British nor the French case provided an acceptable model of development for the central European area approximately encompassed until 1806 by the Holy Roman Empire of the German Nation and after 1815 by the German Confederation. This was the case despite the enormous importance of Burkean patterns of thought and the discernible similarities between the approaches of at least some Germans to the political problems associated with the post-revolutionary era and those of the French Orleanists of the 1830s and 1840s. The defining feature of the 'German question' in the late eighteenth and nineteenth centuries – and one could argue that this has remained true to the present day – lay in the fateful intersection of three overlapping, but distinct, problems. The first was the absence of clarity concerning the territorial boundaries of 'Germany'. The second was the problematic accommodation of multiple levels of State formation within a wider nation-building project. The third was the tendency to define German nationality through blood lineage (the *jus sanguinis*) and more generally through language and culture – a tendency that reached its high point in the 1913 Citizenship Law.

Despite extensive recent research on this subject, there is still arguably insufficient awareness of the energies devoted by the post-Napoleonic German States to the process of State-building. As has been seen in Chapter II, States such as Hanover with their substantial *ancien régime* residues and their powerful tendencies towards a genuine restoration of the old order in the post-1815 period were in some respects the exception. Elsewhere a varying combination of fiscal problems, the need to integrate new territories, and (particularly after 1830) pressing difficulties associated with the provision of poor relief in an increasingly migratory age[44] pushed statesmen and bureaucrats in the direction of reforms which conclusively broke with the institutions of the early modern *Ständestaat*. The precise manner in which different statesmen responded to the changes varied dramatically from State to State, with a markedly less centralised, French-influenced response

noticeable in the north and east than in the States that had formed the core of
Napoleon's satellite system in the south and west. But some type of response
involving the codification of citizenship rights and moves towards constitutions
and modern parliamentary institutions was evidently on the agenda by 1850
virtually everywhere in Germany, with the exception of the two Mecklenburgs.
As a crucial part of this process, States such as Bavaria also engaged quite
consciously in attempts to promote a specifically Bavarian 'State nationalism',[45]
a project that was imitated with varying degrees of success elsewhere. It was
highly telling that the first, generally underestimated, attempt to organise a conservative mass movement in Prussia in 1848 should have taken as its slogan 'For
prince and fatherland' (*Für Fürst und Vaterland*).[46] In Germany as elsewhere, the
liberal language of the *patrie* was capable of multiple political uses.

The major consequence of these projects was that the concept of the modern
State was realised in Germany in the early nineteenth century, which made the
building of a wider German nation-State far more difficult to accomplish than it
otherwise would have been. Apart from anything else, what at first sight seems
to be a reasonably homogeneous political culture was fractured into a number of
contradictory, essentially regional, political cultures. In a process analogous to
the 'provincialisation' of regions that arose out of the first stages of industrial
development,[47] Germany was in all probability less homogeneous politically in
1850 than it had been in 1815. As Heinrich Best has shown, it was this fact that
above all else condemned the Frankfurt Parliament's attempts to construct a viable
nation-State in 1848–49, posing the well-nigh insoluble question of whether a
*kleindeutsch* or a *grossdeutsch* Germany was to be created.[48] For a related reason,
1848 also saw the completion of the process by which the term 'particularism' –
a key aspect of the polemics surrounding unification in the 1860s and 1870s –
shed its localist or provincial connotations as it came to be attached to the fortunes
of the individual States and dynasties.[49]

A further aspect of this story lay in the often tense and ambiguous relationship
between the developing idea of the modern State in Germany and the fortunes of
the princely houses. Time and again the problems associated with the role of the
dynasties arose and in many respects the problems were papered over rather than
resolved in the Bismarckian State. How else is one to explain the view of that
State's foremost constitutional lawyer, Paul Laband, that the princes rather than
the German people were the true basis (*Substrat*) of the empire and that citizenship
operated in a direct relationship to those princes, not to the empire as such?[50]
Here, as elsewhere, Bismarck and his allies in the process of unification were
forced, as their predecessors had also been forced, to recognise the major, paradoxical consequence of the impact of the French revolution on Germany – the
strengthening of those dynasties that survived the dramatic, brutal territorial
reorganisations of the period after 1801. This fact underpinned almost every
important decision that Bismarck made in the unification process, from his insistence on maintaining the maximum appearance of institutional continuities
across the caesura of 1866 to his determination that the Prussian king should be

granted the title of Emperor against the serious misgivings of the Prussian king himself. It was precisely because of Bismarck's determination to avoid anything that looked like an excessive removal of the sovereign powers of the princes that the post-1871 German State was equipped with such a remarkably limited array of constitutional powers and functions, and even fewer uncontested symbolic attributes of nationhood. As has frequently been pointed out, the continuous intertwining of dynastic and national ideals meant that the 1871 constitution could never become an effective symbol of nationhood, while the national flag was clearly less significant than it was elsewhere. Before the 1890s Germany did not even have an official national anthem.[51]

None of this should be taken as meaning that mid-nineteenth-century Germany lacked a powerfully articulated nationalist ideology. According to one recent study, by 1848 perhaps 250,000 Germans were organised into the singing, gymnastics and other ostensibly apolitical associations that played such a vital role in the development of an 'organised societal nationalism' in Germany.[52] At least by the 1860s, nationalism was arguably *the* hegemonic political discourse among educated Germans, if by that is meant that virtually all significant groups could agree that some form of closer union of the German States was a pressing necessity. Yet in practice this elementary level of agreement meant very little and operated mainly as a framework within which different, contradictory programmes for German unification were argued out. Even the notably *kleindeutsch* National Association (Nationalverein) had serious difficulties when it came to discussing the precise constitutional form of its proposed nation-State, and it did not come close to monopolising the national issue.[53] This analysis should not, then, be understood as supporting the attempts of recent historians to debunk German nationalism as a minority pursuit for a small and unrepresentative group of privileged, educated intellectuals.[54] But it does indicate that, however strongly that nationalism was articulated, it was essentially weakly defined and probably incapable of providing conclusive outcomes when the time came to construct the institutions of the new State. As has often been argued, the decision to adopt a federal approach to unification had probably become an emotional necessity by 1866 despite the remarkable failure before that date to develop any convincing theoretical analysis of how a federal system might work in practice.[55] But a major reason for the emotional necessity of federalism lay in the existence of the princely houses and the States they governed.

In no other case of nineteenth-century European nation State formation did that problem pose itself to anything like the same extent. But it was compounded by another, perhaps more familiar, aspect of the German national question – the emphasis on language and culture as the defining characteristic of Germanness. From the Romantic period onwards, the assumption that the *Volksgeist* was to be found primarily in language, culture and the historical development of the law may be termed one of the central foundational myths of the German national movement. Yet that cultural emphasis sat very uneasily indeed with the fact that nation-building was so intimately bound up with the struggle between two multi-national States, Austria and Prussia, for hegemony within the German Confederation. Moreover, the methods adopted by Bismarck as that struggle reached its conclusion in the mid-1860s undoubtedly exacerbated the problem very greatly, for the outcome was the construction of a German State which in linguistic or ethnic terms was considerably less 'German' than the German Confederation had been. Prussia's Polish subjects were now deemed to be subjects of the German State, whereas before 1866 they had overwhelmingly lived in those eastern provinces of Prussia that lay outside the Confederation. The war against Denmark in 1864 resulted in the inclusion in the new State of a significant number of Danes in northern Schleswig. Even more important, of course, was the effect of the Franco-Prussian War and the consequent annexation of Alsace-Lorraine, which brought in another troublesome minority who were not, despite the views of Heinrich von Treitschke, meaningfully German. And, most important of all, the major consequence of the Austro-Prussian War of 1866 was the exclusion from Germany of large numbers of people who were beyond any shadow of a doubt in nineteenth-century terms ethnically German.[56] The following excerpt taken from a particularist pamphlet circulated during the February 1867 election campaign in Hanover may be faulted on grounds of taste but not for failing to adhere to the basic assumptions of nineteenth-century cultural nationalism:

> [The man to be elected] must be a true Hanoverian who wishes to work in the Reichstag for the development of the whole of Germany, in which every German man can retain his individuality, rather than for the creation of a Greater Prussia, in which everything is arranged uniformly and in which the two million Polacks in Posen and Silesia count as German brothers, because they are Prussian subjects, but on the other hand the nine million Franks, Swabians and Bavarians are counted as foreigners ...[57]

Bismarck's understanding of the nation-building process, with its well known 'Greater Prussian' statist assumptions simply could not contain the aspirations which were becoming common among the more radical sections of nationalist opinion as early as the 1860s[58] and which assumed a much more overt form in bodies such as the Pan German League after 1890. The radical nationalism of the late nineteenth and early twentieth centuries took a number of different forms but common to almost all its variants were the convictions that the 1871 State was 'incomplete' in terms of the inner, emotional integration of its citizens and that a core part of any nationalist programme was involvement in the rights of ethnic Germans irrespective of where they happened to reside. Both these major features of German radical nationalism – that most disruptive political force in the late nineteenth and twentieth centuries – were recognisably stimulated by the limitations of the Bismarckian project.

Ultimately, it was the contradiction between the scale of nationalist aspirations and the perceived deficiencies of the State to which those aspirations were attached that generated the febrile and eventually highly (self-) destructive tendencies in German nationalist politics. To paraphrase Max Weber, the problems associated with a form of federalist, dynastically orientated State-building in a time of unprecedently rapid social transformation cried out for a form of politics rooted in the 'ethic of responsibility'. Yet the ways in which German statesmen over-whelmingly attempted to deal with these problems tended to clothe what sense of responsibility they possessed in the opposing ethic of 'conviction'.[59] But then how could a responsible nationalist tradition be plausibly expected to develop when a highly respected periodical directed at Germany's educated classes could seriously suggest that the brewing and drinking of lager expressed the essence of Germanness and of the German people's love of their country? As the (fortunately) anonymous author concluded:

> The cultural-historical mission of German lager has been recognised and there is no longer any doubt that this is the actual vehicle of the German spirit, that German culture (*Bildung*) and German beer go hand-in-hand, that they are two good comrades, who will truly help each other to conquer the whole world.[60]

The thrust of this book has been to emphasise that in the course of the eighteenth and nineteenth centuries a modern semi-unitary modern State was created in the British Isles out of a people of multiple allegiances whose primary identity was seldom permanently, if at all, British, if British is taken to mean something more profound and visceral than the acceptance of the legitimacy of certain political and administrative arrangements. The Union State was not then a national State but a State of three and increasingly four separate nations, whose inhabitants lived relatively happily together but continued to see themselves principally as English, Scots, Welsh and Irish. Even a cursory glance at the history of State- and nation-building in two of the largest Continental countries on the eve of the first World War – France and Germany – emphasises the distinctiveness of the British experience. Indeed, were the analysis extended to a survey of other European States, this conclusion would be only confirmed. Although Spain and the Habsburg empire were similarly States whose inhabitants were divided into a number of self-conscious national groups, some of ancient provenance, the history of their nineteenth-century modernisation bore little resemblance to Britain's. Spain, true to its eighteenth-century Bourbon inheritance, developed a centralised liberal polity along French lines that paid no attention to ethnic diversity. The Habsburg empire, too, toyed with the French unitary model in the 1850s, only to abandon it after the disasters of the Italian war for an ultimately flawed system of condominium where two nations, the Austrians and the Hungarians, were allowed to lord it over the rest.[61]

Historians, then, who have stressed the peculiarity of the English or British experience have been right to do so. There *was* a British *Sonderweg*. On the other hand, once the history of British State and nation formation begins to be studied comparatively in its wider European context, the peculiarity of this British ex-perience loses much of its traditional resonance in that it quickly becomes apparent that there was no Continental norm from which Britain differed. On the Continent, too, as the history of France and Germany so clearly reveals, each country trod its own singular path to modernisation. Britain in the nineteenth century was a semi-unitary State of multiple nations; France a unitary nation State erected on the inclusive principle of popular sovereignty; Bismarckian Germany a federalist nation State built on the exclusive concept of the *Volk*. Where Britain did differ strikingly from its Continental neighbours was in the experience and management of empire, which at the end of the nineteenth century became a force for the creation of a much more positive British identity than that which the Union State's structures had hitherto encouraged.

Yet if the nineteenth-century experience of every European State was peculiar, this does not gainsay the fact that the same forces were making for modernisation everywhere: demographic growth, industrialisation, the development of the public sphere, secularisation, liberalism, and so on. The peculiar and idiosyncratic ways in which the individual State coped with these forces reflected its past history, its positive or negative exposure to the Napoleonic winds of change, and the policy choices (among a range of alternatives) adopted by its political leaders. The multifarious nature of the European State- and nation-building experience, therefore, can in no way justify the continued study of the development of the British, or any other State, in isolation. This book has primarily explored the richness and plasticity of specifically British national identities. It is intended to be a starting point for a more sensitive and nuanced exploration of national feeling in the Union States created in 1707 and 1800 than has so far been attempted. This concluding chapter makes it clear that State and nation formation in the British Isles can be understood only in a comparative context. As a number of historians of Britishness have already begun to realise, it must never be thought that the infamous fog in the English Channel which left the Continent isolated from time to time was a permanent blanket that separated Britain from the rest of Europe for the century after 1815 and created two distinct and rival historical experiences.

## Notes

1 E. P. Thompson, 'The peculiarities of the English', in *id.*, *The Poverty of Theory and other Essays* (London, Merlin Press, 1978); Philip Corrigan and Derek Sayer, *The Great Arch: English State Formation as Cultural Revolution*, new edn (Oxford, Blackwell, 1991); G. E. Aylmer, 'The peculiarities of the English State', *Journal of Historical Sociology*, 3 (1990), 91–108.

2 Notably Hugh Kearney, *The British Isles: a History of Four Nations* (Cambridge, Cambridge University Press, 1989); Keith Robbins, *Nineteenth Century Britain: Integration and diversity* (Oxford, Oxford University Press, 1988); Linda Colley, *Britons: Forging the Nation, 1707–1837* (New Haven and London, Yale University Press, 1992); Alexander Grant and Keith J. Stringer (eds), *Uniting the Kingdom? The Making of British History* (London, Routledge, 1995).

3 Particularly suggestive works are Gerald Newman, *The Rise of English Nationalism: a Cultural History, 1740–1830* (London, Weidenfeld and Nicolson, 1987); Colin Kidd, *Subverting Scotland's Past: Scottish Whig Historians and the Creation of an Anglo-British Identity, 1689–c.1830* (Cambridge, Cambridge University Press, 1993); Prys Morgan, 'From a death to a view: the hunt for the Welsh past in the Romantic period', in Eric Hobsbawm and Terence Ranger (eds), *The Invention of Tradition* (Cambridge, Cambridge University Press, 1983), pp. 43–100; Oliver MacDonagh, *States of Mind: a Study of Anglo–Irish Conflict, 1780–1980* (London, Allen and Unwin, 1983).

4 I use the terms 'Britain' and 'British' to refer to England, Wales and Scotland and their inhabitants before 1800 and England, Wales, Scotland and Ireland thereafter.

5 W. A. Speck, *The Birth of Britain: a New Nation, 1700–10* (Oxford, Blackwell, 1994); Roy Foster, *Modern Ireland, 1600–1972* (Harmondsworth, Penguin, 1988), pp. 282–302, 395–6; Brian Jenkins, *Era of Emancipation: British Government of Ireland, 1812–30* (Kingston and Montreal, McGill-Queen's University Press, 1988); Norman Gash, *Mr Secretary Peel*, new edn (London, Longman, 1985), pp. 108–12.

6 Glanmor Williams, *Renewal and Reformation: Wales, c. 1415–1642* (Oxford, Oxford University Press, 1993), pp. 263–78; John Davies, *A History of Wales* (Harmondsworth, Penguin, 1994), pp. 237, 364.

7 S. J. Connolly, 'Varieties of Britishness: Ireland, Scotland and Wales in the Hanoverian State', in Grant and Stringer (eds), *Uniting the Kingdom?*, pp. 193–207.

8 Prys Morgan, 'From long knives to Blue Book', in R. R. Davies, R. A. Griffiths and K. O. Morgan (eds), *Welsh Society and Nationhood* (Cardiff, University of Wales Press, 1984), pp. 199–215; Prys Morgan, 'Pictures for the million of Wales, 1848: the political cartoons of Hugh Hughes', *Transactions of the Honourable Society of Cymmrodorion*, new ser., i (1995), 65–80; David Howell, 'A "less obtrusive and exacting" nationality: Welsh ethnic mobilization, 1850–1922', in David Howell (ed.), *Roots of Rural Ethnic Mobilization* (Dartmouth, New York University Press, for European Science Foundation, 1993), pp. 51–98.

9 Robbins, *Nineteenth Century Britain*, pp. 29–57; Joseph Lee, *The Modernization of Irish Society, 1848–1918* (Dublin, Gill and Macmillan, 1973), pp. 27–34; Foster, *Modern Ireland*, pp. 516–20.

10 David Hempton, *Religion and Political Culture in Britain and Ireland* (Cambridge, Cambridge University Press, 1996); Matthew Cragoe, *An Anglican Aristocracy: the Moral Economy of the Landed Estate in Carmarthenshire, 1832–95* (Oxford, Oxford University Press, 1996), pp. 191–246.

11 Colley, *Britons*, esp. pp. 17–18; Linda Colley, 'Britishness and otherness: an argument', *Journal of British Studies*, 31 (1992), 309–29. For a critique see Gerald Newman, 'Nationalism revisited', *Journal of British Studies*, 35 (1996), 118–27.

12 Kathleen Wilson, *The Sense of the People: Politics, Culture and Imperialism in England, 1715–1785* (Cambridge, Cambridge University Press, 1995); Gerald Jordan and Nicholas Rogers, 'Admirals as heroes: patriotism and liberty in Hanoverian England', *Journal of British Studies*, 28 (1989), 211–24; David Eastwood, 'Robert Southey and the meanings of patriotism', *Journal of British Studies*, 31 (1992), 265–87.

13 Keith Robbins, 'An imperial and multinational polity: the "scene from the centre", 1832–1922' in Grant and Stringer (eds), *Uniting the Kingdom?*, pp. 244–54, esp. p. 249; *id.*, *Nineteenth Century Britain*, esp. pp. 5–6, 183–6.

14 'An imperial and multinational polity', p. 249.

15 T. M. Devine, *Clanship to Crofters' War: the Social Transformation of the Scottish Highlands* (Manchester, Manchester University Press, 1994); Angus Macintyre, *The Liberator: Daniel O'-Connell and the Irish Party, 1830–47* (London, Hamish Hamilton, 1965), pp. 290–2; John Prest, *Lord John Russell* (London, Macmillan, 1972), pp. 269–71, 285–6; Jonathan Parry, *The Rise and Fall of Liberal Government in Victorian Britain* (New Haven and London, Yale University Press, 1993), pp. 195–8.

16 D. G. Boyce, *The Irish Question and British Politics, 1868–1996*, 2nd edn (London, Macmillan, 1996), pp. 49–65; *id.*, *Nationalism in Ireland*, 2nd edn (London, Routledge, 1991), pp. 259–94; *id.*, *Nineteenth Century Ireland: the Search for Stability* (Dublin, Gill and Macmillan, 1990), pp. 213–41.

17 Kearney, *The British Isles*, pp. 222–3.

18 K. O. Morgan, *Rebirth of a Nation: Wales 1880–1980* (Oxford, Oxford University Press, 1981), pp. 36–7; Gareth Elwyn Jones, *Modern Wales: a Concise History*, 2nd edn (Cambridge, Cambridge University Press, 1994), p. 250.

19 T. C. W. Blanning, *Joseph II* (London, Longman, 1994); Charles Ingrao, *The Habsburg Monarchy, 1618–1815* (Cambridge, Cambridge University Press, 1994), pp. 178–219; Alan Sked, *The Decline and Fall of the Habsburg Empire, 1815–1914* (London, Longman, 1989), pp. 187–234;

C. A. Macartney, *The House of Austria: the Later Phase, 1790–1918* (Edinburgh, Edinburgh University Press, 1978), pp. 147–65.

20 Richard English, *Radicals and the Republic: Socialist Republicanism in the Irish Free State, 1925–37* (Oxford, Clarendon Press, 1994), esp. pp. 1–52.

21 The best study of the *ancien régime* French State remains P. Goubert, *L'Ancien Régime*, ii, *Les Pouvoirs* (Paris, Armand Colin, 1973). See also for its Byzantine but changing character in the eighteenth century the essays in K. M. Baker (ed.), *The French Revolution and the Creation of Modern Political Culture*, i, *The Political Culture of the Old Regime* (Oxford, Pergamon, 1987).

22 P. M. Jones, *Reform and Revolution in France: the Politics of Transition, 1774–1791* (Cambridge, Cambridge University Press, 1995); I. Woloch, *The New Régime: Transformation of the French Civic Order, 1789–1820s* (New York and London, Morton, 1994); J. McManners, *The French Revolution and the Church* (Westport, Conn., Greenwood Press, 1982 edn).

23 The French State employed 135,000 civil servants both centrally and locally in 1845 and 500,000 in 1890: see R. Tombs, *France, 1814–1914* (London, Longman, 1996), p. 101. For an exhaustive account of the growth of the French State see F. Burdeau, *Histoire de L'administration française du 18e au 20e siècle* (Paris, Montchrestien, 1989).

24 F. Olivier-Martin, *Histoire du droit français de ses origines à la Révolution* (Paris, Domat-Montchrestien, 1948).

25 P. Sahlins, *Boundaries: the Making of France and Spain in the Pyrenees* (Berkeley, University of California Press, 1989).

26 These were corporate institutions unknown in eighteenth-century Great Britain: see D. Roche, *Le Siècle des lumières en province: Académies et académiciens provinciaux, 1680–1789*, 2 vols (Paris, Mouton, 1978), esp. ch. 4.

27 The only nationwide account of a corporate profession is Laurence Brockliss and Colin Jones, *The Medical World of Early Modern France* (Oxford, Clarendon Press, 1997), esp. chs 3 and 8. But there are several local studies, notably M. P. Fitzsimmons, *The Parisian Order of Barristers and the French Revolution* (Cambridge, Mass., Harvard University Press, 1987), and L. Berlanstein, *The Barristers of Toulouse in the Eighteenth Century, 1740–93* (Baltimore, Md, Johns Hopkins University Press, 1976).

28 R. Chartier, M. M. Compère and D. Julia, *L'Education en France du XVIe au XVIIIe siècle* (Paris, SEDES, 1976), esp. chs 5–7; D. Julia and P. Presley, 'La Population scolaire en 1789', *Annales, économies, sociétés, civilisations*, 30 (1975), 1516–61; P. Marchand, 'Un modèle éducatif original à la veille de la révolution', *Revue d'histoire moderne et comtemporaine*, 22 (1975), 549–67.

29 A. Aulard, *Napoléon 1er et le monopole universitaire* (Paris, Colin, 1911), pp. 62–116; R. Anderson, *Education in France, 1848–70* (Oxford, Clarendon Press, 1975), esp, chs 4 and 9; R. Gildea, *Education in Provincial France, 1800–1914: a Study of Three Departments* (Oxford, Clarendon Press, 1983), ch. 5.

30 Private, especially Catholic, schools continued to exist and were patronised especially after 1830 by the old nobility, but their educational level was generally not high before the Second Empire.

31 Aulard, *Napoléon*, pp. 343–9; V. Karady, 'De Napoléon à Duruy: les orgines et la naissance de l'université contemporaine', in J. Verger (ed.), *Histoire des universités en France* (Toulouse, Privat, 1986), pp. 276–81, 317–22.

32 T. Shinn, *Savoir scientifique et pouvior social: l'Ecole Polytechnique, 1794–1914* (Paris, Presses de la Fondation Nationale des Sciences Politiques, 1994).

33 Anderson, *Education*, pp. 42–3. It should be said that the beginnings of formal education for State careers antedate the revolution.

34 Surprisingly little has been done on their social and geographical recruitment, but see T. Shinn, 'Scientists and class structure: social recruitment of students at the Parisian Ecole Normale Supérieure in the nineteenth century', *History of Education*, 8 (1978), 99–108; A. Daumard, 'Les élèves de l'Ecole Polytechnique de 1815 à 1848', *Revue d'histoire moderne et contemporaine*, 5 (1958), 226–34.

35 Theology faculties were introduced but they were boycotted by the Catholic Church, which trained its priests in its own seminaries.

36 Aulard, *Napoléon*, pp. 119–23; Karady, 'De Napoléon à Duruy', pp. 263–9.
37 Chartier *et al.*, *L'Education en France*, p. 274; E. H. Ackerknecht, *Medicine at the Paris Hospital, 1794–1848* (Baltimore, Md, Johns Hopkins University Press, 1967), p. 36
38 Aulard, *Napoléon*, chs 3–8.
39 The best study of a French profession in the nineteenth century is M. Ramsey, *Professional and Popular Medicine in France, 1770–1830: the Social World of Medical Practice* (Cambridge, Cambridge University Press, 1988), esp. Part 1. See also a number of the essays in G. Geison (ed.), *Professions and the French State, 1700–1900* (Philadelphia, University of Pennsylvania Press, 1984); and R. Fox and G. Weiz (eds), *The Organization of Science and Technology in France, 1800–1914* (Cambridge, Cambridge University Press, 1980).
40 Woloch, *New Régime*, ch. 13.
41 R. Price, *A Social History of Nineteenth Century France* (London, Hutchinson, 1987), ch. 8 (esp. pp. 331–8, on literacy).
42 Especially E. Weber, *Peasants into Frenchmen: the Modernization of Rural France, 1870–1914* (London, Chatto and Windus, 1977), part ii. Also, for information about more recent research, see Tombs, *France*, part iii, 'Identities'.
43 Admittedly Bretons seem to have retained a deeper sense of regional identity than other Frenchmen, thanks to the development within the province of a Christian democrat tradition which promoted both Catholic Breton culture and republican values: see C. Ford, *Creating the Nation in Provincial France: Religion and Political Identity in Brittany* (Princeton, Princeton University Press, 1993).
44 All modern studies stress this last connection, which appears most strikingly in the fact that the Prussian States simultaneously reformed its poor relief system and introduced its first systematic legislation on citizenship on the same day in December 1842; see e.g. R. Brubaker, *Citizenship and Nationhood in France and Germany* (Cambridge, Mass., Harvard University Press, 1992), pp. 61–3; R. Grawert, *Staat und Staatsangehörigkeit. Verfassungsgeschichtliche Untersuchung zur Entstehung der Staatsangehörigkeit* (Berlin, Duncker und Humblot, 1973), pp. 140–3; and in general on the orgins of these laws H. Beck, *The Orgins of the Authoritarian Welfare State in Prussia: Conservatives, Bureaucracy and the Social Question, 1815–70* (Ann Arbor, University of Michigan Press, 1995), pp. 152–66.
45 See above all M. Hanisch, *Für Fürst und Vaterland* (Munich, Oldenbourg, 1990).
46 W. Schwentker, *Konservative Vereine in Preussen 1848–49* (Düsseldorf, Droste, 1990).
47 See especially G. Zang (ed.), *Provinzialisierung einer Region. Zur Entstehung der bürgerlichen Gesellschaft in der Provinz* (Frankfurt am Main, Syndikat, 1978).
48 H. Best, *Die Männer von Bildung und Besitz. Struktur und Handeln parlamentarischer Führungsgruppen in Deutschland und Frankreich 1848/49* (Düsseldorf, Droste, 1990), *passim*.
49 I. Veit-Brause, 'Partikularismus', in O. Brunner *et al.* (eds), *Geschichtliche Grundbegriffe*, iv (Stuttgart, 1978), 735–8, 744.
50 See P. Laband, *Das Staatsrecht des Deutschen Reiches*, i, 5th edn (Tübingen, Mohr, 1911), 96–7; Grawert, *Staat und Stattsangehörigkeit*, p. 210.
51 The key work here is T. Schieder, *Das Deutche Kaiserreich von 1871 als Nationalstaat*, 2nd edn (Göttingen, Vandenhoeck und Ruprecht, 1992), esp, ch. 5.
52 See D. Düding, *Organisierter gesellschaftlicher Nationalismus in Deutschland 1808–1847. Bedeutung und Funktion der Turner- und Sängervereine für die deutsche Nationalbewegung* (Munich, Oldenbourg, 1984), pp. 145, 180, 233–4.
53 See the many examples of tensions in the National Association between 'Greater Prussian' and federalist visions of the future German State in S. Na'aman, *Der Deutsche Nationalverein. Die politische Konstituierung des deutschen Bürgertums 1859–1867* (Düsseldorf, Droste, 1987), e.g. at pp. 23, 198–203.
54 See, for example, M. Hughes, *Nationalism and Society: Germany, 1800–1945* (Edward Arnold, London, 1988), esp. ch. 5.
55 The key work here is M. Dreyer, *Föderalismus als ordnungspolitisches und normatives Prinzip. Das föderative Denken der Deutschen im 19. Jahrhundert* (Frankfurt, etc, Saur, 1987).
56 See the stimulating comments on these matters in J. Breuilly, 'Sovereignty and boundaries: modern

State formation and national identity in Germany', in M. Fulbrook (ed.), *Natioanl Histories and European History* (London, UCL Press, 1993), pp. 121–9; cf. Schieder, *Das Deutsche Kaiserreich*, ch. 2.

57 Quoted in M. Busch, *Das Uebergangsjahr in Hannover* (Leipzig, 1867), p. 148.

58 See Na'aman, *Nationalverein*, p. 100, on the growing anti-Polish sentiment among East Elbian members of the National Association in the early 1860s.

59 These two contrasting ethics form a major part of Weber's analysis in his 'The profesion and vocation of politics (1919)', in P. Lassman and R. Speirs (eds) *Weber: Political Writings* (Cambridge, Cambridge University Press, 1994), pp. 309–69.

60 [Anon], 'Das Schillerfest nach seiner nationalen Bedeutung', *Deutsche Vierteljahrs-Schrift*, 23: 1 (1860), 350.

61 John Lynch, *Bourbon Spain, 1700–1808* (Oxford, Blackwell, 1989); Raymond Carr, *Spain, 1808–1975* (Oxford, Oxford University Press, 1982); Sked, *Habsburg Empire*.

# Further reading

## Britain and Britishness

Anderson, P., *The Printed Image and the Transformation of Popular Culture, 1790–1860* (Oxford, Clarendon Press, 1991)

Bann, S., *The Clothing of Clio: a Study of the Representation of History in Nineteenth Century Britain and France* (Cambridge, Cambridge University Press, 1984)

Bayley, C. A., *Imperial Meridian: the British Empire and the World, 1780–1830* (London, Longman, 1989)

Black, J., *The British Abroad: the Grand Tour in the Eighteenth Century* (Stroud, Alan Sutton, 1992)

Colley, L., *Britons: Forging the Nation, 1707–1837* (New Haven and London, Yale University Press, 1992)

Colley, L., 'Britishness and otherness: an argument', *Journal British Studies*, 31 (1992), 309–29

Daniels, S., *Fields of Vision: Landscape, Imagery and National Identity in England and the United States* (Cambridge, Cambridge University Press, 1991)

Ellis, S. G. and Barber, S. (eds), *Conquest and Union: Fashioning a British State, 1485–1725* (London, Longman, 1995)

Grant, A., and Stringer, K. J. (eds), *Uniting the Kingdom? The Making of British History* (London, Routledge, 1995)

Hemingway, A., *Landscape, Imagery and Urban Culture in Early Nineteenth Century Britain* (Cambridge, Cambridge University Press, 1992)

Hempton, D., *Religion and Political Culture in Britain and Ireland* (Cambridge, Cambridge University Press, 1996)

Hobsbawm, E., and Ranger, T. (eds), *The Invention of Tradition* (Cambridge, Cambridge University Press, 1983)

Jewell, H. M., *The North–South Divide: the Origins of Northern Consciousness in England* (Manchester, Manchester University Press, 1994)

Kearney, H., *The British Isles: a History of Four Nations* (Cambridge, Cambridge University Press, 1989)

Mandler, P., *The Fall and Rise of the Stately Home* (New Haven and London, Yale University Press, 1997)

O'Dea, M., and Whelan, K. (eds), *Nations and Nationalism: France, Britain, Ireland and the Eighteenth-Century Context*, Studies on Voltaire and the Eighteenth Century, 335 (Oxford, Voltaire Foundation, 1995)

Philp, M. (ed.), *The French Revolution and British Popular Politics* (Cambridge, Cambridge University Press, 1991)

Porter, M., and Teich, M. (eds), *Romanticism in National Context* (Cambridge, Cambridge University Press, 1988)

Robbins, K., *Nineteenth Century Britain: England Scotland, and Wales: the Making of a Nation* (Oxford, Oxford University Press, 1988)

Rose, R., *Understanding the United Kingdom: the Territorial Dimension in Government* (London, Longman, 1982)

Rubinstein, W. D., *Capitalism, Culture and Decline in Britain, 1750–1990* (London, Routledge, 1993)

Samuel, R. (ed.), *Patriotism: The Making and Unmaking of British National Identity*, 3 vols (London, Routledge, 1989)

Smith, A. D., *National Identity* (Harmondsworth, Penguin, 1992)

Speck, W. A., *The Birth of Britain: a New Nation, 1700–10* (Oxford, Blackwell, 1994)


## England

Altick, R. D., *The English Common Reader: a Social History of the Mass Reading Public, 1800–1900* (Chicago, University of Chicago Press, 1957)

Corrigan, P., and Sayer, D., *The Great Arch: English State Formation as Cultural Revolution*, new edn (Oxford, Blackwell, 1991)

Dinwiddy, J. R., 'England', in J. R. Dinwiddy and O. Dann (eds), *Nationalism in the Age of the French Revolution* (London, Hambledon Press, 1988)

Duffy, M., *The Englishman and the Foreigner* (Cambridge, Chadwyck-Healey, 1986)

Eastwood, D., 'Robert Southey and the meanings of patriotism', *Journal of British Studies*, 31 (1992)

Gash, N., *Sir Robert Peel: the Life of Sir Robert Peel after 1830* new edn (London, Longman, 1986)

Newman, G., *The Rise of English Nationalism: a Cultural History, 1740–1830* (London, Longman, 1987)

Ousby, I., *The Englishman's England: Taste, Travel and the Rise of Tourism* (Cambridge, Cambridge University Press, 1990)

Perkin, H., *The Origins of Modern English Society, 1780–1880* (London, Routledge, 1969)

Read, D., *Peel and the Victorians* (Oxford, Blackwell, 1987)

Taylor, M., 'John Bull and the iconography of public opinion in England, c. 1712–1929', *Past and Present*, 134 (1992), 93–128.

Wiener, M. J., *English Culture and the Decline of the Industrial Spirit, 1850–1980* (Harmondsworth, Penguin, 1981)


## France

Anderson, R., *Education in France, 1848–70* (Oxford, Clarendon Press, 1975)

Ford, C., *Creating the Nation in Provincial France: Religion and Political Identity in Brittany* (Princeton, Princeton University Press, 1973)

Geison, G. (ed.), *Professions and the French State* (Philadephia, University of Pennsylvania Press, 1984)

Gerbod, P., *Voyagers au Pays des mangeurs de Grenouilles: la France vue par les Britanniques du XVIIIe siècle à nos jours* (Paris, 1991)

Sahlins, P., *Boundaries: the Making of France and Spain in the Pyrenees* (Berkeley, University of California Press, 1989)

Tombs, R., *France, 1814–1914* (London, Longman, 1996)

Weber, E., *Peasants into Frenchmen: the Modernization of Rural France, 1870–1914* (London, Chatto and Windus, 1977)


## Germany

Applegate, C., *A Nation of Provincials: the German Idea of Heimat* (Berkeley, University of California Press, 1990)

Breuilly, J. (ed.), *The State of Germany* (London and New York, Longman, 1992)

Breuilly, J., *The Formation of the First Germany Nation-State, 1800–71* (Basingstoke and London, Macmillan, 1996)

Brubaker, R., *Citizenship and Nationhood in France and Germany* (Cambridge, Mass., Harvard University Press, 1992)

Hughes, M., *Nationalism and Society: Germany, 1800–1945* (London, Edward Arnold, 1988)

Schulze, H. (ed.), *Nation-building in Central Europe* (Leamington Spa, Hamburg and New York, Berg, 1987)

Schulze, H., *The Course of German Nationalism from Frederick the Great to Bismarck, 1763–1867* (Cambridge, Cambridge University Press, 1991)

Sheehan, J., *Germany History, 1770–1866* (Oxford, Oxford University Press, 1989)

## Ireland

Connolly, S. J., *Priests and People in pre-Famine Ireland, 1760–1845* (Dublin, Gill and Macmillan, 1982)

Cook, S. B., *Imperial Affinities: Nineteenth Century Analogies and Exchanges between India and Ireland* (New Delhi, Sage, 1993)

Fitzpatrick, D., 'The geography of Irish nationalism, 1910–20', *Past and Present*, 78 (1978)

Hoppen, K. T., *Elections, Politics, and Society in Ireland, 1832–85* (Oxford, Oxford University Press, 1984)

Hoppen, K. T., *Ireland since 1800: Conflict and Conformity* (London, Longman, 1989)

Kerr, D., *Peel, Priests and Politics: Sir Robert Peel's Administration of the Roman Catholic Church in Ireland, 1841–46* (Oxford, Clarendon Press, 1982)

Latkin, E., 'The devotional revolution in Ireland, 1850–75', *American Historical Review*, 77 (1972), 625–52.

MacDonagh, O., *States of Mind: a Study of Anglo-Irish Conflict, 1780–1980* (London: Allen and Unwin, 1983)

MacDonagh, O., *O'Connell: the Life of Daniel O'Connell, 1775–1847* (London, Weidenfeld and Nicolson, 1991)

Macintyre, A., *The Liberator: Daniel O'Connell and the Irish Party, 1830–47* (London, Hamish Hamilton, 1965)

Pringle, D. G., *One Island, Two Nations? A Political Geographical Analysis of the National Conflict in Ireland* (Letchworth, Research Studies Press, 1985)

Vaughan, W. E. (ed.), *A New History of Ireland*, v, *Ireland under the Union*, i, *1801–70* (Oxford, Oxford University Press, 1989)

Wusten, H. H. van der, *Iers verzet tagen de staatkundige eenheid der Britse Eilanden 1800–1921* (Amsterdam, Sociaal-geografisch Instituut, University of Amsterdam, 1977)

## The Professions in Britain

Bamford, T. W., *The Rise of the Public Schools* (London, Nelson, 1967)

Buchanan, R. A., *The Engineers: a History of the Engineering Profession in Britain, 1750–1914* (London, Jessica Kingley, 1989)

Cock, R., *Foundations of the Modern Bar* (London, Sweet and Maxwell, 1983)

Corfield, P., *Power and the Professions in Britain, 1700–1850* (London, Routledge, 1995)

Haig, A., *The Victorian Clergy* (Beckenham, Croom Helm, 1984)

Kirk, H., *Portrait of a Profession: a History of the Solicitors' Profession, 1100 to the Present Day* (London, Oyez Publishing, 1976)

Lawrence, C., *Medicine and the Making of Modern Britain 1780–1920* (London, Routledge, 1994)

Loudun, I., *Medical Care and the General Practitioner, 1750–1850* (Oxford, Oxford University Press, 1986)

Perkin, H., *The Rise of Professional Society: England since 1880* (London, Routledge, 1989)

Roche, J., *A History of Secondary Education in England, 1800–70* (London, Longman, 1986)

Rosner, L., *Medical Education in the Age of Improvement: Edinburgh Students and Apprentices, 1760–1826* (Edinburgh, Edinburgh University Press, 1991)

## Scotland

Brown, S. J., *Thomas Chalmers and the Godly Commonwealth* (Oxford, Oxford University Press, 1982)

Ferguson, W., *Scotland 1689 to the Present*, new edn (Edinburgh, Edinburgh University Press, 1987)

Hanham, H., 'Midcentury Scottish nationalism, romantic and radical', in R. Robson (ed.), *Ideas and Institutions of Victorian Britain: Essays in Honour of George Kitson Clark* (London, Bell, 1967)

Hutchison, I. G. C., *A Political History of Scotland, 1832–1924* (Edinburgh, John Donald, 1986)

Kidd, C., *Subverting Scotland's Past* (Cambridge, Cambridge University Press, 1993)

Mechie, S., *The Church and Scottish Social Development, 1780–1870* (Oxford, Oxford University Press, 1960)

Morton, G., 'Unionist nationalism: the historical construction of Scottish national identity, Edinburgh 1830–60', Ph.D. thesis (Edinburgh University, 1994)

Paterson, L., *The Autonomy of Modern Scotland* (Edinburgh, Edinburgh University Press, 1994)

Phillipson, N., 'Nationalism and ideology', in J. N. Wolfe (ed.), *Government and Nationalism in Scotland* (Edinburgh, Edinburgh University Press, 1969)

## Wales

Davies, J., *A History of Wales* (Harmondsworth, Penguin, 1994)

Edwards, H. T., *The Eisteddfod* (Cardiff, University of Wales Press, 1990)

Herbert, T., and Jones, G. E. (eds), *The Remaking of Wales in the Eighteenth Century* (Cardiff, University of Wales Press, 1988)

Herbert, T., and Jones, G. E. (eds), *People and Protest: Wales, 1815–80* (Cardiff, University of Wales Press, 1988)

Jenkins, P., *A History of Modern Wales, 1536–1990* (London, Longman, 1992)

Jones, I. G., *Mid-Victorian Wales: the Observers and the Observed* (Cardiff, University of Wales Press, 1992)

Simles, S., *The Image of Antiquity: Ancient Britain and the Romantic Imagination* (London, Yale University Press, 1993)

Williams, G. A., *When was Wales? A History of the Welsh* (Harmondsworth, Penguin, 1985)

# Index